PAKISTAN
IN SEARCH OF MODERNIZATION

PAKISTAN
In Search of Modernization

ATTAR CHAND

ANMOL PUBLICATIONS

ANMOL PUBLICATIONS
4378/4B, Ansari Road,
Darya Ganj, New Delhi-110002.

Pakistan : In Search of Modernization
ISBN 81-7041-559-7

PRINTED IN INDIA

Published by J. L. Kumar for Anmol Publications New Delhi, and Printed at Sangita Printers, Maujpur Delhi-53.

Foreword

Government will continue the endeavour to reduce tensions with Pakistan. Agreements have been reached on several confidence building measures, including on providing advance notification of military exercise and prevention of airspace violation by military aircraft. We believe that all differences with Pakistan should be resolved bilaterally and peacefully on the basis of the Simla Agreement. However, Pakistan's support to terrorism in Punjab and Jammu and Kashmir is a matter of serious concern and stands in the way of a genuine and sustained improvement in our relationship.

July 11, 1991
New Delhi

R. Venkataraman
President of India

Acknowledgements

The writers are generally acknowledged masters in human intelligence. In India, may I request the Civil Liberty people who were very vocal for Kashmir and Punjab terrorists, take up the case of a writer (of Indian origin Britisher Salman Rushdie—the author of *Satanic Verses*) who is fighting for his life in this 20th Century for his 'sin' of writing a book?

We live in times when nobody can afford to wait for anybody. The pace of change is breath taking in every field, in technology, in management, in R & D. and unless a writer quick on the uptake he loses out. Like a Chief Executive, a writer, too must think fast and act fast and get his writings published and marketed whatever be the constraints. And of course the biggest constraint a Freelance writer faces is that he cannot get finances from the public sector financial institutions. The question of any encouragement from the government does not arise at all—thanks there is no need of a license for writing a book.

Sales turnover is the only indication of book business growth, as I see it. Other parameters like return on investment and profits flow automatically as long as one can ensure a consistent increase in turnover. Developing people, establishing stable management structure and a proper systems orientation are what I call the 'qualitative' indices of publishing business growth.

The present study could not have reached fruition without the encouragement of my well-wishers, who suggested sundry improvements and provided nourishing guidance and inspiration. I am much obliged to my fellow writers, journalists, academicians and professors whose writings I have consulted and taken notes, in parts or in full, in writing this book of global interest.

Preface

Environmental protection is a popular phraseology today. Developed countries are in the grip of environmental movements and it has become a forceful denominator shaping national policies and determining modernisation process. It is not an uncommon word in Pakistan either. One hears it in news media and national and provincial environmental safeguard agencies have been instituted to promote green efforts.

Already, changes at the global level are visible. Let us look at air pollution, increasing carbon dioxide contents in the air, effect on ozone layer, deforestation, desertification, salinisation, erosion, pollution of water bodies. Man's activites are all encompassing and his lethal industrial tools have equipped him with fatal arsenal capable of damaging nature at an accelerated pace.

Natural environment will be protected from the hazards of the rapid industrialisation while policy will be made for the planned development of urban centres. This was stated by the Federal Minister for Environment and Urban Affairs, Sardar Yaqub Khan Nasir in his first interview in Islamabad, on November, 11, 1990.

He said that environment was not a national but a global issue today and Pakistan with other members of the world community will play its role in protection and preservation of the environment.

Sardar Yaqub Khan Nasir said that his ministry will help provide policy guidelines to the provinces for planned urban development so that the people could get healthy environment and basic amenities.

The government of Prime Minister Nawaz Sharif has assumed office at a time when Pakistan's economy faced a near collapse with the loss of US economic aid and the Saudi Arabia refusing to accord Islamabad any significant role in the Gulf.

Pakistan has not been included in the list of countries most affected by the Gulf crisis and after the US congressional aid embargo because of Islamabab's nuclear programme, there is no sign of anyone coming up with $ 2 billion the new government needs immediately to avert the collapse.

Pakistan hopes that the Gulf crisis could become a bonanza, like the Soviet intervention in Afghanistan proved to be a decade ago now appears unlikely to be fulfilled.

The recent talks between Pakistan and Saudi Arabia on sending Pakistani armoured division to the Gulf have broken down following the Saudi's refusal to provide the tanks needed for the force.

The news comes as a heavy blow to Pakistan's military establishment, which hoped to gain greater regional clout and financial benefits from the Gulf crisis.

Pakistan, which has all its armoured tied up because of tension within the country, had offered to provide all the manpower for an armoured division to defend Saudi Arabia as long as the Saudis were prepared to supply the tanks. Hopes that Pakistan could also provide extra maintenance for western units already in Saudi Arabia have also been dashed.

Pakistan has so far sent just 2,000 of a promised 5,000 infantry troops to Saudi Arabia. These soldiers were sent without any heavy equipment, and the Saudis have said they are not interested in the remaining 3,000.

Pakistan's powerful military has been banking on the Gulf crisis to stave off a looming economic crisis due to the huge rise in the cost of oil and recent cut-off of US aid because of Islamabad's nuclear weapons programme.

In recent times Arab leaders have made it clear that they will not welcome non-Arab Muslim states playing any leading role.

Foreign aid flows have grown through the years. Though these have helped sustain the pace of growth in the economy, the rising external debt has put mounting pressures on the economy. Debt service payments have risen from $ 959 million in 1984-85 to $ 1,237 million in 1988-89. A major chunk of the aid disbursed goes in servicing the debt obligations. For instance, in 1986-87 of $ 1,398 million disbursed, net inflow was only $ 175.1 million or 13 per cent of the total. Net transfers had, however, risen to nearly 53 per cent in 1988-89. Total external debt as on June 30, 1989 was put at $ 14 billion or nearly 33 per cent of the GNP. Foreign assistance is now available with a shortened maturity period and at higher interest charges.

Despite the standard of living having been continually dragged down by years of economic mismanagement, Pakistan's new government of Nawaz Sharif is now promising a robust future for the country's aid-addicted economy.

"Where is the collapse?" finance minister Sartaj Azia shot back when questioned about the dark comments abroad that suspension of U.S. assistance and fallout of the Gulf crisis spelled disaster for the Muslim country's economy groaning under a foreign-debt burden of $ 16.5 billions.

Debt burden of $ 16.5 billions. "Our industry is doing better than last year. Agriculture is in fine shape. The inflation is settling down to 11. We have not defaulted even a cent in on-time repayment of foreign loans. So where is the collapse," he said in Islamabad on December 31, 1990.

Aziz confirmed that the country's foreign exchange reserves went below 100 million dollars in the two months following Iraqi occupation of Kuwait, and that inflation rose to 12.5 per cent.

A 25 per cent increase in exports and 7 per cent rise in remittances by Pakistanis elsewhere have boosted the reserves to around 200 million dollars.

Islamabad hopes the International Monetary Fund and the World Bank will come to the rescue by March, 1991 in the meantime it has arranged about 150 million dollars in short-term commercial loans from two gulf-based Islamic banks and two western banks.

There is however littte prospect of Washington resuming its much-needed aid to Pakistan as the Muslim country has rejected the condition of opening its secret nuclear facilities for inspection.

"We are effectively borrowing to pay back past debts," Aziz said, relecting the popular argument that Pakistan does not need foreign aid.

But Benazir Bhutto, who was dismissed as prime minister last August and who now leads the Parliamentary opposition, thinks differently.

"I believe very third world country needs aid. And Pakistan needs it more than any other, because we have such terrible problems with the budget," she said.

Pakistan's new trade policy, announced on June 25, 1990 contains "structural changes" aimed at ensuring greater exports and better import framework for the promotion of overall trade.

The policy for the new year (1990-91) has fixed an export target of 5,494 million dollars on FOB basis, higher by 15 per cent over the preceding year.

The imports are estimated at 6.9 billion dollars, almost equal to the estimated import bill of the preceding year.

Ninety items have been made freely importable and the number of items on the restricted list has been reduced from 52 to 11 to ensure cheaper availability of imported raw materials.

The new policy is aimed at liberalising imports and creating a climate of competition between the industry and foreign suppliers.

The government wants to gear up import policy in a direction where the agricultural and industrial needs for raw material and machinery are fully met and items required by the common man are made easily available.

A separate corporation for the administration of export credit guarantee scheme will also be set up with an initial capital of 25 crore rupees.

At present exports worth 120 crore rupees were covered by the scheme, but with the new corporation this coverage will increase to exports valuing 500 crore rupees.

Seventy per cent of the income derived from the export of services will be exempted from income tax and the existing 100 per cent exemption in case of export of consultancy services will continue.

Leading insurance companies have been allowed to issue

insurance policies in foreigh currencies for the protection of bid bond and performance bond.

Travel agents and tour operation operators have been allowed to utilise five per cent of their foreign exchange earnings for opening offices abroad for marketing purposes.

A new scheme has been evolved to increase investments in the export-oriented industries will be eligible for exemption from duty and surcharges on the import of their machinery, and with regard to duty and surcharges such units will be treated at par with those in the Export Processing Zone.

Pakistan intends to abolish exchange controls and slash tariffs on imports as part of a radical economic reform programme, finance minister Sartaj Aziz said.

Within three to four months there will be a major liberalisation of exchange controls provided the nations' foreign exchange reserves are at an adequate level, said he in Islamabad, on December 26, 1990.

"We are going to reduce gradually and ultimately abolish exchange controls", said Aziz. He described the plan as a "calculated risk".

The uncertainty created by the Gulf crisis could eventually benefit Pakistan as Middle East capital looked for a more secure home, the minister said. "Don't forget that after problems in Lebanon there were people looking for a place to put their money," added Aziz.

Currently Pakistan has tough restrictions on transfer of funds in and out of the country. Pakistan's highly protective tariff system would be dismantled over the next two years with the average tariff rate cut to 30 per cent from 75 per cent currently. The plans are part of an ambitious drive to reform the economy. The new conservative government of Prime Minister Nawaz Sharif, which was elected at the end of

October, 1990 has announced a major privatisation programme and a package of tax and duty incentives to promote industry. If Pakistan could make its economy more outward looking then annual economic growth rates of 9 to 10 per cent would not be beyond it. The Pakistani government is desperately trying to promote exports through incentives and is seeking emergency economic aid to increase its foreign exchange reserves and replace lost revenue. The revenue gap had been partially closed by a 25 per cent rise in export earnings in the first five months of the fiscal year ending June 30, 1991 from the year-earlier period. He did not disclose the precise figures. In June the government of former prime minister Benazir Bhutto set an export target of $ 5.5 billion for 1990-91 against $ 4.8 billion in 1989-90.

Meanwhile, in Karachi the staff at most of Pakistan's major banks went on strike for two hours on Wednesday to protest against the privatisation of the state-owned Muslim Commercial Bank (MCB), union leaders said.

The stoppage stretched beyond two hours in some cities and effectively closed many banks, which are open to the public for four hours daily.

The strike was in defiance of an injunction from Pakistan's top labour court declaring it illegal, Pakistan's six biggest commercial banks are state-owned and recent industrial action affected five of them. The banking unions have long opposed privatisation and prevented the government of former prime minister Benazir Bhutto from selling shares in MCB early 1990.

It has been reported the owners of three different co-operative corporations functioning in Shorkot town and also in the cantonment area have embezzled money collectively to the tune of Rs. 30 lakh of various account-holders and disappeared from there.

According to details owners of the said corporations

opened their offices and started collecting money from different unemployed young men on the pretext they would be accommodated in the organisations. But after sometime, the owners of the said corporations closed down their branches and fled away with their money.

Local people and the affectees have appealed to Punjab Government to take stern action against the cheaters and also arrange refund of their money.

Pakistan plans to set up three steel mills based on indigenous iron ore in remote parts of the country. The country's biggest Karachi-based steel mills is adopting measures to carry out techno-ecónomic feasibility studies for setting up a mini-steel mills with the capacity of 250,000 to 350,000 tonnes per year of billets in Balochistan based on Nokkundi iron ore and a steels mills of half a million tonnes expandable to one million per year of billets based on Kala Bagh and Chichali iron ore in the Punjab province.

The Government of Pakistan has approved a major power-generation plan costing 23 billion rupees. Already, the government has given a go-ahead to a big plant of 1,292 mws based on oil to be located in Balochistan province near Hub. The project is to be completed in 42 months. This will be the maiden private venture in energy sector, and the biggest investment ever made by the private enterprise in a power project. Many more projects in the private sector are now in the final stages of negotiations and the government is confident that at least 2,000 mws of power would be available soon.

A new oil and gas field has been discovered in Pakistan. Located at Bhal Syedan, about 52 kilometres southwest of Islamabad, the new well would produce 1,000 barrels per day after coming into production. The country is already producing 58,000 barrles per day. The new discovery has entirely been done by the Oil and Gas Development Corporation (OGDC), a state-owned undertaking.

One fertiliser plant for the Sindh province of Pakistan has been approved. The plant, to be set up in the interior of the province will have the production capacity of 57,000 tons of urea fertiliser. Estimated to cost 6.500 million rupees, the new plant will make the country self-sufficient in urea fertiliser.

Pakistan's Minister of State for Finance has reiterated the government's determination that "there will be no nationalisation" in the country.

Addressing a gathering of leading industrialists and businessmen in Karachi on March 21, 1990 he said the government firmly believed that "industrialisation should primarily be undertaken by the private sector."

He said the government attached great importance to the role of the private sector and it had accordingly undertaken policies and programmes conducive to the growth and expanded role of the private sector in the development of the country. Measures taken for privatisation, disinvestment and liberalisation were key elements of this policy.

Despite many hurdles, the country's economy was growing and the atmosphere for production and investment was becoming more conducive and congenial.

In his first address to the nation on November 7, 1990 the Prime Minister promised a tax holiday and speedy denationalisation. A week later he told industrialists that the procedure for sanctioning new units was being liberalised further and that projects costing more than 100 million rupees (no upper limit was mentioned) would not require sanction.

References have been made to further reducing the list of specified sectors from seven to two. Steps to boost exports have also been announced.

These statements do not indicate any substantial change over the Bhutto government's policies.

There may, however, become differences on the level of priority to be given to various sectors. The crucial question is whether Nawaz Sharif will be able to overcome the constraint that prevented governments over the past decade from achieving policy goals.

The economy cannot be made sound unless the administration expenditure is drastically reduced and the country learns to live within its means. Significantly, nobody is talking about the defence burden. While economists agree that a sizeable reduction in defence spending is a essential for Pakistan's economic revival, no parliamentary party dares talk about it.

The Bhutto government not only failed to reduce the defence budget, but could not also check unbudgeted expenditure shown under defence but which did not qualify as such. It is extremely unlikely that Nawaz Sharif will be able to achieve a break through in this direction.

Taxation is an equally difficult field since Sharif does not believe in taxing industry and trade.

The last two years (1989-90) witnessed marked increase in industrial activity in Pakistan, with the highest ever industrial sanctions and activity at the Karachi Stock Exchange at its peak. During 1987-88, the sanction of industrial investment amounted to 23.9 billion rupees. Annual average for the Sixth Plan (1983-88) was 22.3 billion rupees. Against this, during the 11 months period (December 1988 to October 1989) the government had sanctioned 62 projects worth 33.5 billion rupees including a foreign exchange component of 18 billion rupees. The foreign investment during the same period increased four-fold from 4.2 billion rupees to 19 billion rupees. Preliminary estimates for sanctions of the industrial investment for the 12 months period (December 1988 to November 1989) comes to 43 billion rupees.

In sharp contrast to India's reservations on the creation

of a SAARC regional fund with external resources, Pakistan has expressed "full agreement" with the proposal. The differing perspectives of the two-member nations of SAARC came into focus in their countries statements delivered by their Foreign Secretaries at the opening of the two-day meeting of the SAARC standing committee in Male, on July 2, 1991.

While India stressed the need for raising funds within the region, saying there was no dearth of resources, Pakistan welcomed the move to attract foreign resources. It wanted details such as the sources of funding, quantum of the fund, criteria for selection of activities and modalities of its administration to be carefully worked out.

Maldives Acting Foreign Secretary Salah Shihab admitted that there were differences among the member nations on various issues, but noted that this was understandable as the seven countries had varied socio-economic and political systems.

He, however, said the differences were not "major" and he had no doubt that these would be ironed out by the end of the meeting.

Later he said that Maldives had an "open mind" on the question of external funding for SAARC and said it would go along for with the consensus.

Shihab said one issue on which the member nations agreed was their keenness to make the organisation more "cost effective than it is at the moment".

"There is a lot of criticism at the way some SAARC activities are conducted and there is a feeling that SAARC needs a good look at the way in which its programmes are conducted."

Unlike the Indian statement, which expressed its reservations on the foreign funding for SAARC projects, the

Pakistani statement, while expressing "full agreement" with the creation of a regional fund made only a passing reference to the issue.

The Sri Lankan statement also supported mobilisation of extra-regional resources but "under certain conditions".

"There is no cause to fear that extra regional funding would be against our collective interest," it said.

Nawaz Sharif government has, no doubt, decided to take some steps aimed at giving relief to the consumer, nonetheless the surging rate of inflation can hardly be checked by piecemeal measures. The next logical development in a situation like the one emerging in the country would be an all-round clamour for wage raise and the industrial sector will be most vulnerable an unrest. At a time when the government is contemplating large-scale denationalisation to ensure higher growth rate, a measure which in the short-term is likely to increase unemployment, mass discontent will thwart the chances of economic rejuvenation. Unfortunately, things have been happening too fast for the new government and it hardly had time to think of long-term policies. Nevertheless, sensing the gravity of the situation and the magnitude of the task ahead, the people at the helm of affairs have been talking about self-reliance. Rhetoric apart, if safeguarding national honour has any place in our scheme of things, the nation will sooner than later have to learn to cut its coat according to the cloth. The path of self-reliance, however, entails colossal sacrifices and the tightening of belts will have to be shared by all and sundry, including the ones who have traditionally been considered more equal than others.

Meanwhile, the abrupt cancellation of the Pakistan Prime Minister, Nawaz Sharif's visit to Japan from July 1, 1991 the summoning of a high-power meeting and the decision to convene the National Assembly at the earliest are all pointers to the alarming law and order situation in the country and the desperate need for new measures to stem the downslide. Adding to the disturbing situation in Sindh are a series of gruesome murders in Punjab. In a region inured to violence the cold-blooded slaughter of two whole families in Lahore Sheikupura in Punjab has nevertheless come as a deep shock. A group of killers stuck in one of the most crowded localities of Lahore in daytime, killing 12 members of one family and their driver. All the victims were stabbed or had their throats slit. What is even more frightening about the whole episode is that the killers did not spare even little children and had apparently no motive since they neither took away any valuables nor were the victims known to have any enemies. This happened on June 27, 1991.

It was followed by a similar atrocity in Sheikupura town on June 20 in which six members of a family including two minors and three women were stabbed to death. This incident took place at 3 p.m. and once again no motive could be readily pinpointed.

On June 30, 1991 two men shot and robbed a person in Lahore in the busiest part of the city and, right in front of a police outpost, just as the victim came out of a bank after withdrawing Rs. 6 lakhs. Police did nothing and an infuriated crowd threw stones on policemen and passing vehicles. A Lahore-based daily On June 30 reported that a gang had been spotted in the same Kishen Nagar colony of old Lahore where the first incident took place. Someone, however, spotted a gang member before they entered the targeted house and upon an alarm being raised neighbours rushed to the spot with all available weapons and were able to foil the attempt.

In all these instances, the victims belonged to families involved in trade. From the manner and time of the killings, the avoidance of loot and the background of the victims it has been deduced that political motives are involved. The business community which stands much to gain from Nawaz

Sharif's new economic programme is among his staunchest supporters and the specific targeting of it, so goes the theory, is to sow disenchantment with a Government which cannot ensure their personal security. Of course, the opportunity to point the finger at the favourite whipping boy – India – has also not been missed.

During his now-cancelled trip to Japan, Nawaz Sharif was to have concentrated on the economic issues. In Japan and Hongkong, which he was to visit on return Nawaz Sharif was to have met business leaders to persuade them to invest in Pakistan. A major impediment to increased investment has been the deteriorating situation. So far, alarms on the crime front have been occasioned by the situation in Sindh where besides widespread dacoity in the interior, armed clashes have broken out among factions of the Mohajir Quami Movement. Now Punjab has turned almost as bad. (see *The Hindu*, 3 July 1991).

The Chief Ministers of all the provinces are to participate in the special Cabinet meeting called to deal with this situation. Other issues have also to be sorted out with them. A conflict has been brewing between Sindh and Baluchistan ever since the Sindh Chief Minister, Jam Sadiq Ali arrested a Baluchistan Minister. In Punjab too the Chief Minister has come in for some flak for having stood by legislators against policemen when the former were arrested for breaking traffic rules. The Cabinet meeting which started on July 2 to would provide the occasion to review all these issues.

Meanwhile, the Pakistan Government on July 2 set a 15-day deadline for the surrender of illegal weapons, warning that the failure to turn them in would result in the confiscation of property and life imprisonment.

"Last chance to surrender illicit weapons," said a front-page report adding that the government was determined to root out criminals.

Nawaz Sharif's government has decided to publicly hand dacoits, robbers, kidnappers and other anti-people criminals.

The government has also decided to rearrest members of the Al-Zulfikar organisation, who had been released by Benazir Bhutto's Government before they completed their jail terms.

These decisions were taken at a five-hour cabinet meeting in Islamabad on July 1, 1991. Nawaz Sharif, who cancelled his visit to Japan because of the deteriorating law and order situation presided over the meeting.

Sharif's Adviser on Information Sheikh Rashid Ahmed said after the meeting that those who possessed illegal arms had been given 15 days to surrender to the nearby police stations.

Nawaz Sharif, feared there was a "hidden hand" trying to destabilise his government. "This hidden hand did not want a strong, stable, democratic and Islamic government in Pakistan", Pakistan Prime Minister declared.

Contents

1

Environmental Protection

"Some say the world will end in fire

Some say in ice from what I've tasted of desire I hold with those who favour fire but if it had to perish twice. I think I know enough of hate to say that for destruction ice is also great and would suffice" —*Robert Frost*

The world is in a deep environmental crisis. This crisis is rooted in global patterns of human behaviour that are ecologically unsustainable, socially alienating and economically unjust. We need a transformation of human purpose that unites material and spiritual realities and creates a common conscience. A conscience which restores and nurtures a world of balance and harmony, peace and justice; caring through community trusteeship, stewarship and accountability for now and future generations.

Recognizing that unity is essential if diverse people are to work towards a common future, we the citizens of this earth, hereby proclaim this Universal Environmental Code of conduct.

All peoples and their governments should strive:

— To recognize that we cannot segregate the human heart from the environment; humanity is organic with the world: its inner life moulds the environment and is itself also deeply affected by it;

— To advocate economic and social justice for the inarticulate masses who bear a disproportionate burden of the consequences of environmental degradation;

— To support the individual's right of access to access to information from all sources relating to the environment;

— To value the intrinsic worth and diversity of nature; protect, promote and support lifestyles that enrich both cultural diversity and moderation of wants based on ecologically sustainable principles, growth and development;

— To recognize that bio-regions, their organic rhythms, cycles and species, transcend political boundaries and therefore endeavour to enhance inspired global and regional action;

— To protect the natural heritage of future generations by adopting an all-embracing perception and the vision of non-exploitative technology in industrial, agricultural and aquatic practices;

— To maintain the integrity and sanctity of nature by exercising extreme caution in the disposal of wastes and the use and propagation of man-made substances and organisms;

— To develop rural infrastructure that sustains life and avoids the crowding and alienation from nature characterized by urban society today;

— To encourage and urge social and environmental accountability by governments, powerful global enterprises and organizations;

— To nurture the spirit of this Code in ourselves and in all people and plant the seeds of responsibility to protect and conserve the environment;

— To initiate a process of consultation with governmental, inter-governmental and non-governmental bodies which would lead to the establishment of a Global convention on Environmental Right and Duties.

Environmental conservation (EC) is a popular phraseology today. Developed countries are in the grip of EC movements and it has become a forceful denominator shaping national policies and determining development directions. It is not an uncommon word in Pakistan either. One hears it is news media and national and provincial EC agencies have been instituted to promote EC efforts. However, in under-developed countries it has neither the force nor pervasiveness of the developed world. Widespread hunger, malnutrition, poor clothing and shelter among millions make it another basic need fails to aquate it with their life and it has motive and meaning ulterior to their wants. How EC is related to their well-being is not clear to them; even the literate section of society has only limited understanding of EC. The relation of EC with human well-being becomes clear too soon too quick. Human civilisation have flourished on the globe and will depend on it in future. Vast as it may seen, it is nonetheless, limited. Its limited nature has become increasingly obvious with population increase. Many parts of the world with dence population are suffering from food, fuel and potable water scarcity. Although we have not reached the limits of world resources, their endowment varies from region to region, causing abundance at places and scarcity at others. This has brought home the fact that earth resources cannot be stretched beyond limit, therefore, the only alternative is to abide by and respect its delimitation. Air, water, soil, plant and animal wealth are our resources, albeit, limited in quantity. Therefore, their loss, in quantity or quality, is our direct loss and is already at the base of hunger, malnutrition and sickness in several parts of the world.[1]

What is environmental conservation? Does it encompass the efforts which these two words literally mean — saving soil, water and air? If this is what EC means, it would be a narrow perception of the terminology. It has deeper and wider connotation and means preservation of balance of nature. Recent advances in human understanding of the working of nature clearly demonstrate that efforts directed at mere saving of soil, water and air will fall short of expectation, and the goal of maintaining self-sustainability and self-perpetuability of the globe will remain elusive. Preservation of the balance of nature would entail judicious use of world resources — soil, water, air, animal and plant life — through management which minimizes human interference.

Our globe is a piece of marvelin this universe. Its undulating plains, rising mountains, flowing rivers, dense forests provide abode to a variety of animals and plants which are connected with each other in a complex relationship. Diverse as it is, everything merges into the other to form a dynamic and self-sustaining system. Plants, animals and the physical world around us from the components of this system. Physical endowments of the globe, however, set the limits in which the system operates. In other words, nature has created a world which, within limits, can perpetuate itself indefinitely. If the limits are exceeded or violent external forces distrupt one or the other component, the whole system may bog down and its amazing self-healing capacity may suffer. In the recent past, we have witnessed development of both these disrupting elements. Population increase is stretching the system to its limits. It has had more disrupting effect than anything else before. Vast areas of forest and range lands have been cleared to grow-crops to provide man his increasing food needs and erosion thus caused, fertilizer and pesticide pollution and loss of natural habitat of wind life have endangered many plants and animal species. Added to this is man's industrial activity with no less unfortunate effects. Pollution stemming mainly from human industrial activity is today a forceful external agency threatening our life support system. How is nature preserving itself on the earth and how does human interference affect nature's working is illustrated in simple situations or in wild natural preserves, where both predators and preys exist together. The preys have not been eliminated in milleniums because of nature's checks and balances. In fact, what appears to man a cruel act of predation is only a cleaning process in which mostly sick and old are eliminated, leaving the healthy to thrive. Food supply is one of nature's major check. If plants are abundant, grazing animals would increase and, in turn, predators would converge upon the ample preys. Over-grazing would reduce food availability, setting in starvation of migration, thus, stemming off over-population. The animal and plant population has fluctuations, but over the long run stick to an average. This is balance of nature which nature has preserved all along but which is endangered by human activities. Already, changes at the global level are visible. Look at air pollution, increasing carbondioxide contents in the air, effect on ozone layer, deforestation, desertification, salinisation, erosion, pollution of water bodies. Man's activities are all encompassing and his lethal industrial tools have equipped him with fatal arsenal capable of damaging nature at an accelerated pace. The adverse effects are now rebounding and biting man hard. Consciousness, often under compulsion, to these deleterious effects is increasing and efforts are now afoot to contain and reverse these trends. But, unfortunately, consciousness is lacking where it is most needed. Majority of the Third World countries lack both resources and knowledge to cope with the situation. What is more, these are the areas where population increase is building pressure on land, forests and water and poverty has forced man to exploitative approaches rather than judicious management. How delicate is balance of nature is not obvious to common man and scientists have started understanding it only recently, through sketchy information here and there. What is more, we are apt to see it at macro-level, ignoring its micro-dimension. One should, however, remember that macrodimension stems from micro-level activities and one such activity illustrating the delicacy of balance of nature was reported recently in an international magazine. A guided tour through the wildlife sanctuary in a South American beach spotted a predator bird attacking a sea turtle hatchling as it was emergency from the underground laid eggs at duck. The hatchling was sticking to the ground with only its head above the ground and the bird was picking at it trying to pull it. A tourist, unable to tolerate this crueltly, scared the bird away. The bird would, however, return to its prey and others lay lurking around for the feast they knew was there underground. In view of the imminent danger to the young hatchling and in his infinite love for preservation of wildlife, the tourist finally decided to deliver the hatchling away from danger to the saftey of the sea. He pulled out the hatchling to carry it to water. The moment the hatchling was pulled out, several others who were in safety below in the ground started emerging and heading towards the sea. The emergence of the first acted as a signal and assured others of safety outside, but once they were out, due to misplaced sympathy of the tourist, most of the hatchlings were picked by the hovering birds in the air. Few could escape this massacre and reached the sea. Obviously, the tourist turned out a foolish friend, ignorant of nature's working. This is one case of human interference in nature. Though benevolent it was an act of interference and led to a catastrophic result. Had he left the nature to itself, only one hatchling would have died. It would have died sticking to its place there, but ensuring safety of the others. This is nature's working and it has proved its soundness over milleniums. Has it not saved every living species through these years? Man cannot interfere in nature with impunity.[2]

Natural environment will be protected from the hazards of the rapid industrialisation while policy will be made for the planned development of urban centres. This was stated by the Federal Minister for Environment and Urban Affairs, Sardar Yaqub Khan Nasir in his first interview in Islamabad, on November 11, 1990.

He said that environment was not a national but a global issue today and Pakistan with other members of the world community will play its role in the protection and preservation of the environment.

Sardar Yaqub Khan Nasir said that his ministry will help to provide policy guidelines to the provinces for planned urban development so that the people could get healthy environment and basic amenities.

For the poor nations the word development has carried the cannotation of something necessarily good of "progress", of a break with traditional, "backward" ways and adoption of the ways of the technologically advanced countries. To build a dam for controlled irrigation or to convert a rain forest into farmland would seem to be obviously a useful and dramatic measure towards modernisation. But scientists and conservationists are now becoming alarmed about the environmental hazards of headlong development. The price of development has included pullution problems, loss of farmlands and habitat (for people as well as for wildlife) and even the spread of diseases. Some environmental disruption is an un-avoidable but, as ecologists and other environmental scientists insist, harmful effects can often be anticipated and minimised if development is preceded by ecological studies and careful planning. These "horror stories" as they were called, involved a variety of activities, such as colonisation of new lands, dam building and irrigation, pest control, and extraction of minerals and timber from oceanic islands. A sampling of these case histories follows.[3]

In Branzil's Amazon basin an agriculural colony was established in the late 40's at the confluence of the Maderia and Madre de Dios rivers. Raid forests were cut away and the land was tilled with disastrous consequences. For the soils of the region, rich in iron oxide and alumia, are highly subject to a process called laterisation which can quickly turn cleared lands into rocky, brushy barrens. The colonist cultivated their fields among blocks of laterite and found the soils they were working compacting to rock in five year's time.

Kariba Dam, constructed in the 50's on the Zambezi River between Zambia and Zimbabwe, has formed a huge, seventeen hundred-square-mile reservoir rivaled in size only by the reservoirs created by the Volta Dam in Ghana and the Aswan Dam in Egypt. Planned largely for generating hydro-electric power, the Kariba project is said to have led to a variety of unanticipated problems. According to a confe-rence paper by Theodore Scudder professor of anthropology at California Institute o Technology, serious soil erosion is occuring because farmers who were flooded off their former lands have refused their traditional farming habits to suit conditions in relocation areas. Also vegetation along the shores of Kariba Lake has created habitat suitable to the tsetse fly, aggrevating the pest control problem in this Central African region, where the population is heavily dependent on animal protein.

Other problems beset the project. Acquatic plants invaded Kariba Lake, and, within four years of dam's com-pletion, coversed more than one-tenth of the lake's surface, interfering with commercial fishing and creating other diffi-culties. Egypt's Aswan High Dam with its hydropower, irrigation, navigation, and flood-control potential, has been considered one of the most promising developments. Yet, in conference paper, Henry van der Schalie of the University of Michigan's Museum of Zoology, viewed this project pessi-mistically. He said that it is virtually certain to lead to a disastrous spread of schistosomiasis along the upper Nile, a region where heretofore the incidence of this debilitating, often fatal parastic disease has been comparatively low. This is predictable van der Schhalie explained, because the project to bring year-round irrigation has long been practiced, the incidence of schistosomiasis is high, nearly all the inhabitants of some villages being infected. Moreover, attempts to combat schistosomiasis by snail eradication and sanitation measures, or by the treatment of infected persons, are said to have had only limited success. Heavy use of synthetic organic pesticides for the control of cotton pests in Peru's Canete Valley during an 8-year period that in 1956 had ruinous results. A former director of the Canete farmer's agricultural experiment station, Theodore B. Barducci, said he had recommended against reliance on these pesticides but found that farmers of the valley had been lured by the promotional claims of the pesticide manufacturers. Target insects gradually develop immunity to the insecticides while useful insects that had helped to keep the pests in check were destroyed. However, biological methods were once again applied, useful insects were reintroduced and farmers were told to prepare their soils dry. The new programme proved to be a success, the pest population declined and cotton yields returned to satisfactory levels.

Oceanic islands: F. Raymond Fosberg, of the Smithsonian's Museum of Natural History, described oceanic islands as being especially vulnerable to mismanagement. This is so, he said, because such islands are small and are often characterised by unique, irreplacable flora and fauna having a history of more or less local evolution. The islands of Banaba in the Central Pacific, he reported, was recently abandoned by its inhabitats following phosphate mining operations. Most of the vegetation had been eliminated and most of the topsoil removed. Supplies of fresh water, always marginal, had become undependable. Hosphate islands of the eastern Indian Ocean also have been mined, Fosberg says, and, are now scarcely capable of supporting life. For many of their more ambitious public projects, developing nations depend on assistance from the industrialised nations and from international institution such as World Bank. These donor nations and institutions would seem, therefore, to be in a strong position to insist, as a condition for grants and loans, that ecological factors be considered in all project selection and pre-investment survey and in the carrying out of the project itself. While aid-grant agencies of nations have not been indifferent to the environmental effects of projects which they sponsor, it seems clear that they have not exercised their potential influence as forcefully as they could. The long term solution to the problem of reconciling development planning with ecological factors was seen to lie in research and education, a conviction which would seem to find support in the increasing in, and influence of ecology in the United States. The question in whether it may be possible to infuse public throughout the world with a simple valid concept such as "spaceship earth". Ultimately, science-meaning verifiable knowledge of ecological processes should prove decisive. "In the long run", Professor Caldwell observed, "science is a very powerful influence. We do not burn witches any longer. We don't treat the insance as though they were invaded by devils. Science does change human behaviour, but to change it massively takes time and time is rapidly running out".[4]

As someone who has been associated with Kalabagh Dam Project since 1976, I have been a serious student of the progress (or lack of it) that this dam has made. The mistrust between two of the provinces and the exaggerated apprehensions in the minds of a third province—mostly based on imaginary fears—were inlarged by our politicians and their "political engineers". This confusion provided an opportunity to the Government of Pakistan and foreign donors to consign the project to the cold storage. The time has come for us to explain to the people of the provinces the facts about this project and remove their apprehensions and fears. A series of programmes on the Television and Radio to take the explanation to the masses, as opposed to seminars where some people play to the galleries, is required urgently. As a first step the Justice Alim report should be debated at the provincial levels and waters of the Indus Basin justly distributed. The fears of the third province can be allayed if they are assured that handsome compensation for the land submerged by the reservoir would be paid and that whenever the "once in a hundred years flood" is experienced, then it is the constriction caused by the Attock gorge and not the presence of a dam at Kalabagh which will cause submergence of parts of the Nowshera Valleys[5]. I don't wish to cover nuclear energy — its cost, disposal of waste, dealing with disasters, and politics, etc., sufice it to say that however, much nuclear energy we may be able to develop in the future, it will be not substitute for Hydel energy generation because of its costs and other factors attached to it. The sooner we start with Kalabagh Dam—which is the only large project where we are ready to go to tender within three months time—the better. It should be followed by other Hydel projects as their feasibilities become available. Meanwhile our efforts to develop nuclear energy must continue as our needs for energy in the first decade of the 21st century are going to be collosal.

Another minor benefit of Kalabagh Dam project would be the generation of thousands of jobs, where we can absorb our manpower returning from the Middle East.

Once again Pakistan has been plunged into an extremely dangerous crisis. The crisis engulfs the political, constitutional and economic spheres of our national life. Additionally, the situation in the Gulf region has further compounded the severity of the internal crisis. Such a grave situation undoubtedly demands that issues of national importance are seriously debated and understood before we venture into prescribing solutions. The political leadership, more than any one else, bears the responsibility of rising above immediate or personal gains while considering such issues. Unfortunately, however, it is our politicians who, bent upon not learning any lessons from our highly non-serious and fatally amateurish approach towards issues of extreme national importance in the past, continue with the deplorably casual attitude even at this juncture. They, in their pursuit of catching votes of the simple, honest and straightforward citizens of Pakistan, resort to sloganeering that is fraught with grave implications. One such slogans pertains to the construction of the now famous and controversial Kalabagh Dam on the River Indus. Some politicians, especially from the Punjab, have found it fit to use this issue to create an emotional atmosphere in order to manipulate voters of rural Punjab into voting for them. It is a rude shock to read the statements of highly-placed leaders, like Madam Abida Hussain, the former caretaker. Information Minister, Ghulam Haider Wyne, the Chief Minister of the Punjab, Syed Fakhr Imam, former Speaker. National Assembly, Nawabzada Nasrullah Khan, Chief of PDP and the former caretaker Finance Minister of Punjab making commitments regarding the construction of Kalabagh Dam on "priority basis", in their respective election rallies and statements. I am surprised rather than amused that all these IJI leaders in one chorus have sung the song that Kalabagh Dam has been politicised and politicians have exploited it for the sake of their evil designs. How would one describe the IJPs raising of the slogan for the construction of Kalabagh Dam in its election campaign. If this is not politicising, then what is it? There is simply no storable water available for construction of any high dam such as Kalabagh Dam on Indus Basin System. It will not be incorrect to say that no indepth study has been done by WAPDA to analyse the basic question of water availability in its proper perspective for the proposed dam.[6]

It would be pertinent to point out that the Minister for Water and Power, in reply to my question No. 169 in the Senate sitting on 19th May 1990, had stated that no scientific study has been carried out to ascertain how much discharge will have to be allowed to maintain ecological balance including requirements of Mangrove inland forest, irrigated areas, fauna and flora, fisheries and sea intrusion downstream of Kotri. This is one of the pivotal issues in the determination of storable water availability for dams, as the fate of over one million people residing in 600 square miles downstream of Kotri is linked with this issues, besides other environmental problems, President Ghulam Ishaq

Khan expressed concern in his speach at the National Institute of Oceanography that reduced flow from River Indus into the Arabian Sea has created serious environmental problems in the region. One could well imagine what would happen to the already serious problem of environmental degradation in the region as the flow from river into the sea would significantly be reduced without any doubt if Kalabagh Dam is constructed. It may be pertinent to point out that the Chairman Port Qasim Authority, Admiral Akbar Hussain Khan in the article captioned Protection of Mangrove dated 6th October 1990, is reported to have stated that "industrial pollution will be carefully monitored within his jurisdiction and that healthy mangrove forests are vital to the area".

Further, Port Qasim Authority, National Institute of Oceanography and a team of American scientists have joined together in an effort to understand and protect the mangrove forests, east of Karachi. The Indus delta Mangrove is the sixth largest in the world. It cannot be denied that further reduction in the flow of water downstream Kotri will adversely affect the Mangrove Forest.

There are many more wrong assumption in WAPDS's estimation of water availability which have been dealt with in great details in my earlier articles. Even the period of filling for proposed Kalabagh Dam indicated by WAPDA viz. 21st July to 30th September is apparently incorrect in the light of the reply given in the Senate sitting on 19th May, 1990 by the Minister of Water and Power to my question No. 167 wherein it has been established that Tarbela Dam right from its inception until 1989 was never completely filled earlier than 20th August and was even depleted as early on 5th September.

I would, in the light of the above mentioned facts, say that the construction or otherwise of the Kalabagh Dam is a technical issue and needs to be treated as such. It has never been a political issue and should not be politicised. The construction of Kalabagh Dam could not get a green signal even during the all-powerful government of the late General Zia-ul-Haq. Thereafter decision on Kalabagh Dam in the Council of Common Interest (C.C.I.) meeting of 26.1.1988 during Muhammad Khan Junejo's government was defered as the consensus between the provincial governments could not be arrived. In fact Arbat Jehangir, the then C.M. NWFP, and Ghous Ali Shah, the then Chief Minister, Sindh, gave stiff resistance. Arbab Saheb was reported to have gone to Islamabad in his private car as he had decided to resign in case as decision was taken in favour of constructing the Kalabagh Dam. The two past provincial Assemblies of NWFP and Sindh are on record to have passed resolutions unanimously opposing the construction of Kalabagh Dam. The same situation exists today as there is no consensus of the provinces on this issue. The Chief Minister, Sindh, is opposed to the construction of the dam, and so is Wali Khan whose statements have appeared recently. The PPP government was of the view that prior to a decision on the construction of Kalabagh Dam, than other issues of the apportionment of water between the provinces and the determination of storable water to justify construction of the dam had to be resolved.[7]

It may be pointed out that the former Federal care-taker Minister for Finance on behalf of the ex-caretaker Minister for Water and Power in reply to question No. 71, raised by Aijaz Ali Khan Jatoi in the Senate sitting on 22nd August, 1990 during the debate, had stated that basically the subject of Kalabagh Dam was linked with the issue of water distribution and water apportionment among provinces. In fact that issue had to be decided first before a decision on the Kalabagh Dam on technical or feasibility or power requirement could be done. He further stressed that the Kalabagh Dam would come into existence when there is consensus of the provinces.

The Senate was further informed that the total expenditure so far incurred on the Kalabagh Dam was Rs. 1031 million against the estimated cost of Rs. 100 billion of the project which forms 1 per cent of the total proposed investment on the basis of 1987 costs. This meagre part of the total expenditure shall not become the determining factor for our decision regarding the construction of this dam. That the water availability to justify construction of a high dam, such as Kalabagh, has not yet been established is evidently clear from the National Commission on Agriculture's report dated 15th March, 1988. According to the report, "there is divergence of opinion on the additional quantities of water that would be available for future development." It is also a matter of regret that the Governments of the Punjab and N.W.F.P have asked for high-level outlets with capacity of 15,000 cusecs each on the left and right banks for withdraws of water from Kalabagh Dam for irrigation purposes. This is despite the fact that the ex-caretaker Minister for Water and Power is on record to have stated, in reply to my question No. 129 in the Senate sitting on 26.7.1989, that technical feasibility of the Right Bank and Left Bank Kalabagh Canals has not yet been established. And furthermore that the consultants of Kalabagh project in their early studies had indicated that the construction of the above high-level canals will be extremely uneconomical. The WAPDA itself has been on record to have stated, on 24.5.1989, that it will therefore be premature to make projections of water requirements of these canals.

Under these circumstances, it is imprudent to raise the hopes of the mases of Punjab that the Cholistan desert will turn green. This is nothing short of playing with the sentiments of the simple and straight forward masses of Punjab. As regards the power generation issue, may be stated that there is a potential of generation of 17,000 megawatts on the run of the River of Indus and Jehlum. It is high time that we, instead of pursuing the controversial Kalabagh Dam project, should concentrate on the undisputed hydropower projects on the run of river of the Indus and Jehlum. It is also regrettable to pointing that the cost of generation of hydel power is ten times lesser the other form of power generation. In view of the above, I feel, it will be appropriate to appoint a judicial commission with the Chairman nominated by the Federal Government and one judge of the status of not less than Supreme Court by each province. This commission will need to be assisted by an impartial, neutral, international expert of repute with adequate experience of having dealt with such issues of water apportionments. Each province in turn will be asked to present its case. Parties will be heard in joint sitting of the provincial teams for questions and counter-questions before judgement is passed and recommendation sent for the approval of the competent authority.[8]

While most factory managements recognise environment, health and safety (EHS) issues attendant to their own operations, little if anything is done beyond limited and basic industrial safety measures. The full extent of EHS conditions is not generally known. Standards are either non-existent or not enforced. The impact of industrial emissions upon health and the environment is not often recognised because existing concentration of industry are generally not large enough to seriously over-whelm the assimilative capacity of the surrounding environment. At the tanneries at Kasur or outside Karachi, adverse environmental impacts have beeen severe enough for the local populace to react and for resentment to be voiced. However, even in those cases, government agencies have not seen fit to react in a meaningful way. In most situations, the political system does not engender responsible environmental management nor does it allow for the effective implementation of remedial measures once problems are spotted, responding to local pressures, industrialists at the number of locations. However, these were strictly palliative rather than emeliorative. For example, funding was being sought to build drainage ditches "... to take the pollution far away", in the words of one industry association president. When asked where the pollution would go the answers were no more precise than to indicate that their was a river somewhere in the distance which would dilute the offending effluent. These persons admitted the knowledge of existing technology that could avoid generation of the waste or prevent pollution through recycling or recovery. Even when the payback of such investments was two years or less, there was reluctance to implement them because of uncertainty regarding future regulatory requirements or enforcement practices. Almost complete reliance is placed on the assimilative capacity of the environment to absorb emmissions, effluents and wastes. There is little attention to long range considerations, potential liabilities and responsibility to the community.[9]

In contrast to this, some multinationals operating in Pakistan are utilising sound environmental practices as a matter of company policy. These, however, are not always up to the same standards as at the home or other developed countries. Aside from legal and stockholder pressures, they recognise the economic benefits, improvements in quality control and efficiency, and protection of assets which are available through modern waste minimisation techniques and good management practices. The study team found a small number of Pakistani firms that also try to operate in a similarly enlightened fashion.

For the most part, industry views the installation of pollution abatement equipment as too costly, it does not understand that sound environmental management can also bring substantial economic returns. The PIE programme, therefore, has an opportunity here to bring educatioal and training activities to all levels of the private and public sectors.

There is no effort to measure the effectiveness of the very limited health and safety effort in factories. Some regulatory inspections do occur. However, based on observed conditions, these have minimal impact. There is some effort on the part of unions to provide safety training to workers.

This appears to be limited to occupations which have high injury rates such as electrical workers.

Industrial accident rates are many times those of industrially developed countries. Even in large companies with well trained safety staffs, the accident rates are sufficiently high that statistics are kept only on lost-time accidents.

Regarding emergency preparedness and accident prevention programmes, none was evident beyond that enforced by multinational companies.

Industrial health, safety and pollution control laws and regulations exist but are virtually not enforced. Statutory fines are insignificant. The only realistic penalty available is the power to refuse a renewal of a company's operating permit or imprisonment. These extreme measure are rarely, if ever, used.

As a result of ineffective enforcement, both industrial and municipal (provincial) pollution controls are frequently planned or installed only to the minimum extent required to receive an operating permit. After permits are granted, pollution control equipment is often not operated, or is operated in a perfunctory manner with limited effectiveness. Such equipment is not maintained in good operating order. Furthermore, new investments have been encouraged to locate at industrial estates and locales which have greatly simplified permitting and administrative other procedures.

The draft Pakistan National Conservation Strategy (PNCS), published in early July 1990, provides a programme for sustainable development as one strategy for increasing the efficiency of industrialisation. The team applauds the PNCS initiative but feels that some additional measures, outside the conventional institutional strengthening steps, are required.[10]

The recommendations are summarised below :

1. This report proposes that an existing non-governmental organisation (NGO) in Pakistan be strengthened by the support of a WEC staff project manager who would coordinate and carry out the goals of the environmental component of Private Investment Expansion Programme." The NGO to be selected would be a neutral information gathering and support unit whose role is to assist other private sector organisation in Pakistan. It will be a bridging institution which promotes and carries out the exchange of technical expertise and information on environmental management issues. Through its offices, institutional and factory assessments, technology transfer, training workshops, study tours, and on-the-job training will be available. The project manager from the WEC, with an office in the selected NGO would act as liaison with participating US Organisation mentioned later in this report (i.e. those that provide experts to go to Pakistan or receive Pakistanis for training programmes).

2. If additional core funding under WEC's existing cooperative agreement can be allocated to Pakistani activities, the IEDS can respond to the immediate needs by the study team during its visits to various industrial facilities and sites.

3. Through IEDS, Pakistanis can be trained in a variety of programmes including waste minimization, recycling and recovery, pollution prevention, emergency response planning, and industrial health and safety.

4. An advisory panel of labour, management, academic, and the public should be formed. This panel would provide advice and technical assistance, as well as disseminate information.

5. Each manufacturing facility should conduct an environmental assessment (environmental audit) of its operations. The results of the work should be integrated into an environmental management programme which ties together environmental regulations, specifically discharge and emmission limitations, with timetables for meeting those limitations.

6. A programme for determining the extent of groundwater contamination should be initiated.

7. PIE is encouraged to continue the programme of exchange of ideas with the US private sector. This would include technical assistance for training in environmental safety and health, environmental management and public education programme.

8. Environmental education at all levels of society is lacking. Currently, workers do not understand why safety requirement exist or that their actions can affect the environment either at work or at home. "If I don't see it or if it doesn't affect me then it doesn't exist" is representative of the general attitude that the study team encountered. The lay public is not aware of the full effect of pollution and is certainly not aware of anything that they can do to improve their circumstances. People cannot be expected to accept and act upon good industrial environment, health and safety practices until they understand and accept their value.

9. Current regulations are ineffective. Regulations need to be reviewed to improve their effectiveness. Quantitative objective should be established, as well as goals for the workplace and the community. Industry can be responsible for meeting these goals.

10. Environmental training programmes do not exist at most facilities. Programmes should be established to train people in the elements of EHS management, community and workplace monitoring, facility assessment and waste imnimisation.

11. There is no review procedure for new facilities to be constructed that will assure sound environmental management practices will be adhered to designs and operating procedures for new facilities need to be reviewed to identify methods, for pollution prevention, safety controls, and opportunities for conservation of resources and waste minimisation. If waste minimisation were given greater consideration, waste treatment planning would be less burdensome technically and economically.

12. Integrating concepts of environmental protection into the workplace and local community is needed. A programme for the assessment of EHS practices should be conducted by existing facilities. As part of the assessment, action plans that include timetables for compliance with facility specific objectives should be developed. These objectives should include workplace, as well as community goals.

As part of a demonstration programme technical experts should be provided to review plans and procedures to determine what improvements can be made utilising current technology and good practices. Pakistani professionals, agencies, academia and industry should be sent to the US to observe and be trained in current practices and to act as trainers for others when they return to Pakistan.

The Pakistan Council for Scientific and Industrial Research (PCSIR) is an appropriate organisation to involve in future studies and to report to on existing conditions. Although the study team met one industrialist that did not agree, the team feels this groups may play eventually a useful role in the environmental component of the PIE programme.[11] PCSIR is an example of the team's perception of Pakistani institutions generally. Its members tend toward a rigid interpretation of PCSIR's mandate. Based upon a combination of hearsay and the team's visit to the All Pakistan Federation of Trade Unions, organised labour is relatively inactive in the field of EHS. A Cooperative Programme in EHS issues between the Pakistani and US private sectors with ad hoc GOP and US Government participation should be established.

The Federation of Chambers of Commerce and Industry located in Karachi formed an environment committee at the team's suggestion. That intiative should be encouraged by prompt follow up action. A working-level advisory panel of labour, management, academia and public representatives should be established. The function of the panel should be to provide advice, technical assistance and information on environmental, health and safety matters, as well as to work on the drafting of regulations and enforcement procedures.

References

1. M. Aqil Khan, Environmental Conservation, *Nation*, 16 November, 1990.
2. *Ibid.*
3. Bilal Farouq, Environmental Hazards of Development, *Nation*, 22 November, 1990
4. *Ibid.*
5. Fazli Raziq, Kalabagh Dam, *The Nation*, 18 November, 1990.

6. Abdul Majid Kazi, Kalabagh Dam, *The Nation*, 17 November, 1990.
7. *Ibid.*
8. *Ibid.*
9. Environment, Health and Safety, *Pakistan Times*, 20 November, 1990.
10. *Ibid.*
11. *Ibid.*

2

Nuclear Strategy

Pakistan would carry on an ambitious peaceful atomic plan for the prosperity of its people.

This was announced by Prime Minister Nawaz Sharif in his first address to the nation over radio and TV on November 7, 1990.

The Prime Minister said rapid peaceful atomic development has become imperative in view of the recent increase in the oil prices. In this connection, he added, his government was determined to fulfil its responsibility in accordance with aspirations and wishes of the nation.

He said the fulfilment of his dream for the industrial development would be impossible without atomic energy.

Nawaz Sharif made it clear that Pakistan atomic plan would be for peaceful purpose "we are against disastrous use of the atomic power" he added.

The Prime Minister said the country was facing the major test in the field of power energy.

Pakistan Prime Minister Nawaz Sharif on December 7, 1990 said his country would not abandon its "peaceful nuclear programme" for foreign aid.

"We will eat dry bread rather than beg for aid" he said in Lahore as US Deputy Assistant Secretary of State Teresita Schaffer met with Pakistani officials, in Islamabad.

In an interview the Dubai-based *Gulf News*, Nawaz Sharif said on November 3, 1990, that "India is a nuclear power......we would be happy to sign the Nuclear Non-Proliferation Treaty (NPT) provided India did the same. It would be rather unethical to pressurise Pakistan to sign it if India were not to do the same."

Pakistani Premier Nawaz Sharif says, "He will not open the country secreat nuclear plants to inspection or sign a nuclear non-proliferation treaty without India."

Speaking at a rally in Karachi on December 11, 1990, he said, "He would not succemb to US pressure on Pakistan's nuclear programme for the sake of getting back American military and economic aid suspended in October, 1990.

Denying that foreign teams would be allowed to inspect Pakistan's main Kahuta nuclear plant outside Islamabad Nawaz Sharif said, "The country would not compromise its principles."

"The time has come that we stand on our own feet and the nation should be prepared to offer sacrifices for the same."

Pakistan has offered to sign the non-proliferation treaty but only if India agrees to sign too.

All $ 564 million US military and economic aid earmarked for this was automatically suspended on October 1, 1990 when President George Bush failed to certify to the US

Congress that Pakistan was not trying to make nuclear weapons.

Sharif's speech was the latest in a series of tough statements on the nuclear issue. President Ghulam Ishaq Khan and army Chief General Mirza Aslam Beg have also rejected international pressure and demanded that Pakistan becomes self-reliant.

The suspension of American aid to Pakistan, on the ground that U.S. suspected Pakistan of trying to build nuclear weapons, would confirm India's suspicion that Pakistan had already built them. To that I added the assumption that this would only further fuel the demand in India that "if India does not have a nuclear weapons programme yet, it must begin one now, and if India has a covert one it must be made public so that the right kind of message goes to Pakistan before that country launches some adventure in the expectation that it will catch India at a nuclear disadvantage."[1]

This demand is gathering force, but no example I gave is as weighty as the Gen-Sundarji's (Retd.) own; in disproving my assumption he says "Nuclear catastrophe can be avoided in the sub-continent only by India and Pakistan sending each other clear and unambiguous deterrent signals. This cannot be achieved by prolonged practice of strategies of uncertainty. Hence going on to an overt declaratory posture should not be seen as a disaster."[2]

I too do not consider it to be disaster, and did not say I did. In fact I pointed out that as the conviction grew in India that Pakistan had built or acquired nuclear weapons, a chain reaction would follow in which the first step would be that India would also build and acquire them, and the second would be that both countries would go overt with them. But my position also is—and remains despite the General—that before pushing each other up this escalatory path, both Indian and Pakistan should examine, jointly and with such other third party help as they might find useful, whether there are technically sound ways of inspection and verification by which each side can convince the other that it is in fact abstaining from this path. General Sundarji dismisses this possibility of escalation as one of my "wrong assumptions". But he himself gives two proofs of its inevitability. He points out, first that deterrence is needed "both at the strategic and tactical levels." If this is a plea that India should build tactical nuclear weapons as well, the General needs only a brief reminder of what he obviously must know, that even the superpowers could invent sactical nuclear weapons long after they had perfected and amassed strategic nuclear weapons, and only after spending further large sums of money on developing the more refined technologies required for making tactical nuclear weapons, which have to be more compact and more accurate. And I also think that, considering the great proximity of Indo-Pakistani war threat to each other and to large concentrations of population, the demand for precise and compact tactical weapons in addition to large strategic ones, which have a vast destruction spread, will come up very powerfully in both countries as soon as either declares that it has entered the nuclear arena. The second proof of inevitability given by General Sundarji relates to China. He describes "mutual deterrence" between India and China as a condition for "genuine mutual respect" and "genuine give and take" between the two countries. That means India must not only acquire enough capability to deter Pakistan whose capability is as yet in its infancy, but also enough to deter China which has an arsenal described by all accounts as large and varied.[3]

China has also positioned a part of its arsenal in Tibet, from where all the key industrial and logistical Indian targets which are in the Gangetic basin are only a few minutes flying time away for a missile. On the other hand all the key Chinese targets are several times that distance away from Indian launching pads. To point this out is not to confess—that one is among the persons dismissed by the General as "our nervous intellectuals" but ouly to say that before we take the first step let us also foresee the tenth to which it lead. Therefore when one thinks of the nuclear equation with China, all kinds of other factors come in as well, such as a capability to detect and destory the intruder. In this task India is at a geographical disadvantage apart from being late at the start. Ever escalating search for such capabilities was the path followed by the U.S. and the Soviet Union in the midsummer of their madness, and I have seen no argument which would convince me that our region would convince me that our region would display greater restraint or wisdom, once we make a start down that road. Perhaps because he counts me among such inferior people as intellectuals, General Sundarji appears to attribute to me an assumption which I did not make. I am not a moralist or a fundamentalist in the matter of the bomb. If it is indispensable for the country's defence let us have it by all means even if in Bhutto's colourful phrase, we have to "eat grass for a thousand years." After all, half of our people are doing just about that anyhow, and if the rest also have to do it, so be it. I make only one assumption in this nuclear matter, that before we opt for such a drastic change in our dietary habits, we must find satisfactory answers to four questions. The first relates to China. General Sundarji has quoted a very relevant observation from Kennath Waltz who asks, "What issue between (India and China) could justify Chinese leadership risking a city or two?" I presume Waltz is referring to Chinese cities, and to reinforee his observation that "India needs little to deter China." But what answer do we get if we reverse the question? What issue between India and China could justify Indian leadership risking a city or two anywhere from Amritsar to Guwahati? Would the Aksai Chin plateau do so, which is the only matter really in dispute between the two countries, or a race with China for "a respected position in the comity of nations", which the General says China achieved because of its nuclear status? (China had acquired its highly prized position of a permanent seat in the United Nations Security Council long before it acquired the bomb, a fact which we sometimes over-looked because of the syllogism that because all the five permanent members of the Security Council are also nuclear weapon countries, therefore the latter is a compulsory qualification for the former "respected position"). The second question relates to General Sundarji's sage observation that a nuclear war is neither" 'fightable' nor 'winrable'. In that case, should we not first see whether it is also avoidable by means more affordable than the costly status of mutual deterrence? Apart from being costly, this status is also inflammable. It generates the high heat of mutual resentment in which the slightest miscalculation or misunderstanding can bring down the unthinkable upon our heads. Or do we find the glamour of deterrence irresistible in it own right? The third question relates to the mundane matter of costs, which people out of uniform worry about a littele more than those in them. How much will it cost India to ahieve a reliable level of mutual nuclear deterrence in relations with China, considering where India is today and where China is? How much did it cost China to reach that level with the Soviet Union? How much will it cost India to reach such a nuclear level in relations with China that India may, as he prescribes, inflict on China unberable damages in a second strike, that is after absorbing a nuclear strike by China? Is that cost bearable for the Indian economy? One never gets a clear answer to this question, neither from the uniformed nor from the un-uniformed advocates of the Indian bomb. Nor to the inevitable supplementary question, whether the costs of the nuclear arm of our defence will be in addition to the present and projected costs of conventional arms? And will the nuclear arms also keep costing us ever more and more as conventional arms have always done? This is a war which civilians have found unwinnable in their arguments with soldiers, and not only in India but in all countries.[4]

The souring of relations between the US and Pakistan over Washington's efforts to stall what it views as Islamabad's efforts to develop a nuclear weapons capability by halting all military supplies and economic and pledged for the fiscal year

July 1990-June 1991, has drawn angry and defiant response from Pakistani leaders. Self-reliance and freedom from foreign aid are now being loudly proclaimed as the corner-stone of the new Pakistan Government's policy, which diplomatie observers see as an attempt to turn a lack of options into a virtue. In addition to Washington's move to strangle Islamabad's nuclear weapons programme, the current friction in Pakistan-US relations is also characterised by a widening divergence of views on other issues of mutual interest. These centre primarily on the US presence in the Gulf, the role of Iraq's armed forces, Afghanistan and the strife in Indian-controlled Kashmir. Pakistan has made it clear if favours the replacement of US forces in Saudi Arabia with a pan-Islamic force — a suggestion the US has ignored, according to local officials. Army commander Gen. Mirza Aslam Beg has described Iraq's armed forces as a source of strength which could help save the international Islamic community from destruction. The US is displeased with Pakistan's support for the Kashmiri militants and there is growing divergence between Islamabad and Washington on how to settle the Afghan civil war. The fallour from the deepening rift between the two countries has led to mounting concern that US decision to halt new aid will influence the consortium of countries and banks which jointly contribute around US $ 3.2 billion a year in economic assistance to Pakistan. They are due to next meet in 1991, probably in April, and Islamabad fears the US action could result in no pledges for fiscal 1991-92. For a country currently spending over 42 per cent of its available fiscal resources servicing old debts and over 39 per cent on defence, the loss of these funds would be a disaster. The effects of the aid cut-off on the military are less clear, though while the Pakistan Air Force has denied reports its US — supplied F 16 fighters have been grounded by a lack of spares, Prime Minister Nawaz Sharif has argued the country must try to end foreign control over a vital area of its defence. Beg has suggested the armed forces can make do with modifications to locally produced weapons considered obsolete. Washington's publicly stated case against Islamabad's nuclear programme rests on its assertion that Pakistan has been enriching uranium far beyond the 3-3.5% needed to make fuel for its nuclear power station at Karachi, which is monitored by the International Atomic Energy Agency (IAEA). According to US officials, Pakistan has underestimated the sophistication of the equipment which secretly monitors activity at the country's enrichment facility at Kahuta, near Islamabad.[5]

Pakistan's response is that it is faced with a widening energy gap, which will grow into a power deficit of some 4,000 MW over the next decade. The country is estimated to be loosing around US $ 1 billion a year in GNP due to the energy shortfall. The Chairman of Pakistan's Atomic Energy Commission, Munir Ahmad Khan, has said the country ultimately must meet 85% of its energy needs from nuclear power generation. Pakitan officials argue that the peaceful thrust of their nuclear programme is emphasised by their efforts in international forums to reach bilateral, regional of international agreement's to bring all nuclear facilities — including Pakistan — under the full scope of safeguards. Their sole condition is that India must be a signatory to any of these agreements. India has said it would not sign any agreement that would apply to all without a single exception, and would not accept any discriminatory non-proliferation regime. Pakistan also argues that US objections are set against tumbling world prices of both natural and enriched uranium. Current spot price of uranium at US $ 25 per unit is the same as in 1972, making it in real terms 25% of the 1972 price. The enrichment price, which was US $ 160 per unit some years ago, is now US $ 50 and with recently introduced laser technology, this could halve in a few years. This being the case, the Pakistan argument continues, buying atomic fuel on the international market is far cheaper than investing in the high cost of uranium mining and enrichment equipment, facilities and teehnology. Following the suspension of US aid, some hawks in Pakistan have said the country should test an automic bomb to send a "hands off Pakistan" signal. They argue that whatever sanctions the US might seek to impose would have to be quickly withdrawn, for fear Pakistan would transfer nuclear weapons and technology to Middle East and North African countries. The US, they maintain, would have no option but no normalise ties with Pakistan, which by than would have gained tremendous prestige and created a long-term deterrence against potential aggression. Others claim the US objection to Pakistan's nuclear programme is rooted in the industrialised countries' reluctance to share advanced technology with the Third World. As an example, they cite the US policy reversal that followed an agreement signed between Pakistan and France for the supply of nuclear reprocessing technology and equipment in the early 1970s. The US then secretly transfered nuclear weapons technology to France that enabled it to develop a multi-warhead system. Paris reneged on its agreement with Islamabad shortly afterwards, these sources maintain.[6]

Since 1979, Pakistan has made great efforts to obtain materials and technology for its uranium-enrichment and other nuclear-weapon activities. Leonard Spector, who closely monitors these Pakistani efforts, discovered that it has involved the use of "dummy corporations and trans-shipments through third countries (which) has by now been well-documented in the press and officially recognized by West Germany, Canada, Britain, the Netherlands, and the United States either in the course of prosecutions or in published government reports. Perhaps the most egregious case involved the smuggling from West Germany between 1977 and 1980 of an entire plant for converting uranium powder into uranium hexaflouride, the easily gasified material that is the feed-stock for the Kahuta enrichment facility. The plant, located in the town of Dera Ghazi Khan, is continuing to operate, producing material that is essential for the Pakistani nuclear-weapons effort. Another well-publicized example of the smuggling of nuclear components to Pakistan is the Vaid case. In October 1983, Nazir Ahmed Vaid, a Pakistani from

Lahore, visited the American firm EG & G is the Salem, Massachusetts, EG & G is the only company in the western world that commercially manufactures krytons — very high-speed, extremely reliable electrical switches that deliver an extremely precise pulse of electrical current in a very short time (about a millionth of a second). Krytons are used for a number of highly specialized purposes – in high-energy lasers, for example. But their most important function is as part of the triggering mechanisms for nuclear weapons. They are easy to buy if one is in the United States; they cost about $ 90 each. But, because of their use in nuclear weapons, overseas sales are strictly licensed and monitored by the US Government.[7]

Vaid bought 50 krytons. He told EG & G that he was commissioned to buy them by the University of Islamabad. But, as the EG & G employees knew, there is no conceivable reason why the university would want 50 krytons. They would be required, however, for a unclear-weapon programme. The EG & G employees promptly informed the FBI which asked them to sell Vaid the krytons. When Vaid obtained them he tried to air frieght them to Pakistan, and it was when he tried to get them through US customs described as office supplies including 50' bulbs/switches' that he broke the law. He was arrested, tried, served three months in jail, and was discreetly deported. The judge thought that he was an ordinary businessman who had been rather careless about US export regulations—hence the light sentence. But Seymour Hersh, a *New York Times* journalist, discovered cables showing that Vaid, far from being an ordinary businessman, was a Pakistani agent in direct contact with senior officials of the Pakistan Atomic Energy Commission about the purchase of the krytons. It turned out that the krytons were actually ordered by a director of supply and procurement for the Commission. A second case of nulear smuggling from the USA by a Pakistani agent was that of Ashad Pervez a Pakistani-born Canadian—who was arrested in Philadelphia on 10 July 1987, charged with attempting to purchase and ship to Pakistan 25 tons of Maraging steel. The Pakistan Government has claimed it had nothing to do with the Pervez case. In August 1985, according to *Der Stern*, a shipment af Maraging steel had been sent to Pakistan from West Germany. People with Pakistani connections arranged for 880 kilograms of the material to be sent to an address in Karachi. The steel went in the form of cylindrical rods whose diameter was exactly right to fit a type of centrifuge of a design known to Dr. Khan. Yet another nuclear smuggling case involving Pakistan came to light in the same week as the Pervez affair. Three individuals—two Americans and one from Hong Kong—were charged with smuggling sophisticated electronic equipment to Pakistan in 1982 and 1983, which could be used in Pakistan's nuclear-weapon programme.[8]

Pakistan's clear stand on the nuclear issue did not in the end, find a place in the 5th SAARC Summit. Male declaration that was issued at the conclusion of the meeting as a collective document of consensus. The reason is not far to seek and India's objections are too well known to require a detailed recital here. Briefly stated, New Delhi has in fact, taken a consistent stand, publicised over the past several years, that the question of nuclear non proliferation must be clinched at the global level. in a manner that would not discriminate between the nuclear club and the potential nulear powers. India also feels that, unlike Islamabad, New Delhi will always have to see its security environment in a larger international political ambience even within a regional framwork. Shorn of diplomatic niceties, this simply means that India cannot ignore the fact that China, already a nuclear power of considerable standing, had fought a border war with India in the past. Pakistan's foreign policy-makers on the other hand, do not have to see China in the same light as their Indian counterparts. It should be recognised in this context that Sino-Indian relations have certainly improved since the border conflict of 1962, and visibly so, after the former Indian Prime Minister, Rajiv Gandhi's visit to Beijing nearly two years ago. Yet, China as a factor in India's foreign policy cannot be equated with Pakistan's perception of China in the "new international ambience of detente and peace." In fact, the Pakistani leader's proposal for a South Asian pact on nucler celibacy is consistent with Islamabad's being view to Beijing.

Nawaz Sharif did not discuss the question of South Asian nuclear non-proliferation with his Indian counterpart, Chandra Shekhar, when the two leaders met for a bilateral exchange of views on the second day of the three-day Male summit, which was reserved for informal consultations among the summit leaders. Apparently, the Pakistani Prime Minister, still new to his job, had not yet evolved a strategy to discuss the volatile nuclear issue with India, especially in the dominant context of the U.S. administration's latest, and also unusually eagle-eyed, evaluation of Islamabad's nuclear intentions. This does not, however, mean that the Pakistani leader was not interested in pressing his proposal as a diplomatic gambit to deflect South Asian opinion from the reports of Pakistan's current preparations to join the nuclear club. In the end as it turned out, Nawaz Sharif and Chandra Shekhar focussed their attention primarily on Kashmir and Punjab, the two ground-level problems which, in fact, lent a sense of unspoken urgency to the nuclear question as well.[9]

There is another subtle dimension to Nawaz Sharif's shadow-bosing with India on the nuclear question. According to authentic inside information, Indian diplomats at the Male meeting were unusualy pleased with the presummit atmospherics, because, as Indian diplomats said Pakistan did not pursue, with single-minded divotion, it pet theme of a South Asian pact on nuclear abstinence. As India saw it, the summit-eve atmosphere at the previous SAARC conferences was, in contrast, vitiated by the burz of the mythical Indian nuclear bee in Pakistan's diplomatic bonnet. Pakistan had invariably pressed the issue of a regional nuclear pact at behind-the-scene discussions during the previous SAARC summits. To be sure, the Pakistani Foreign Minister, Shahabzada Yakub Khan, did make the customary references to a South Asian pact on nuclear non-proliferation during the pre-summit deliberations at Male too. But India did not find him obstructive or even obsessive, as he did not make a big issue of this question before the start of the summit. Apparently, Yakub Khan was also hamstrung by the reports of Pakistan's own preparation to enter the nuclear club.[10]

It is interesting to note that at a time when Pakistan's Foreign Minister, Gen. Yakub Khan, was claiming at the SAARC meeting that his country was "committed to disarmament and nuclear non-proliferation", the U.S. Ambassador in Islamabad in a letter to the Editor of the daily. *The Nation* on November 19, 1990 was emphasising that the United States no longer found it possible to certify the non-nuclear status of Pakistan Ambassador Rober Oakley, formerly on the staff of U.S. National Security Council, clarified that even the possession of components of a nuclear device contravenes the U.S. law and therefore, disqualifies Pakistan from receiving economic and military assistance. It may be recalled that it was generally believed that the definition used previously by the U.S. was applicable only to an "assembled" device. In reality any distinction between the two was purely academic. All the same, the clarification, supported by U.S. Congressional records and the fact that the U.S. was forced to suspend aid after October 1 after an obortive attempt to seek Congressional approval for a delay in applying the otherwise automatic suspension, and in spite of the visible need for support in the West Asian crisis, only reconfirms that Pakistan now possesses nuclear weapons(s). Evidence of Pakistani nuclear weapon programme has been accumulating since the late 1970s. For nearly ten years now Pakistan has been making numerous commitments to the U.S. and opportunistically circumventing/violating them in the single-minded pursuit of the bomb. Despite explicit pledges given to Washington. Pakistan crossed the "red line" limit of uranium enrichment set by President Reagan in September 1984. By late 1986 a Special National Intelligence Estimate of the U.S. had concluded that Pakistan had produced weapon-grade material; and it had tested the nuclear trigger devices. By the time Ms. Bhutto took office, Pakistan was believed to have material for five to ten weapons. On May 18, 1989, CIA Director William

Webster testified to Congress that "clearly, Pakistan is engaged in developing a nuclear capability." In direct contradiction of Ms. Bhutto's statement to U.S. Congress a month earlier, Gen. K.M. Arif, the former Vice Chief of Army Staff and the man is charge of building the Kahuta plant, declared in July that Pakistan's "effort in this field already enjoys bipartisan and popular support and is above political controversy. Her national interests demand that her nuclear capability be taken to its logical conclusion."[11]

It is in this context that in 1989 the U.S. Administration had given clear indications that it was already finding great difficulty in providing the certification necessary before Congress would approve aid. When the certification was given on October 5; an involved justification was constructed largely based on Prime Minister Bhutto's June 1989 commitment to U.S. Congress that "we do not possess nor do we intend to make a nuclear device". But by September Prime Minister Bhutto had shifted her stand to say that "we do have knowledge, if confronted with a threat, to use." Significantly the Army Chief, Gen. Aslam Beg, declared in October that "Both the nuclear option and the missiles (that Pakistan has developed) act as a deterrence and these in turn contribute to the total fighting ability of the army." At the same time he has been exhorting his officers to follow the Quranic concept of war (expounded by Brig. Malik under Gen. Zia's patronage) of instilling "terror into the heart of the enemy", before and during a war. Pakistan has been in possession of credible nuclear weapon delivery systems for some time now in the shape of Mirage and F-16 aircraft. It signed a Memorandum of Understanding with China for a ten-year co operation in the field of defence procurement, R & D, technology transfer and co-production; and has been developing surface to surface missiles with Chinese assistance (Besides having received help in design of the bomb). Its nuclear weapon delivery capability would be significantly enhanced if the originally planned supply of 60 additional F-16 aircraft is implemented by the U.S and/or with expanding missile capability with Chinese assistance. The additional aircraft are modified version of the F-16 A and Pakistan's Air Chief has been reported to confirm that existing F-19s in Pakistan Air Force would also be retromodified. The significant modification involves the fitment of LANTIRN (Low Altitude Navigation and Targeting Infra-Red by Night) poods for all weather day night "blind" bombing, and an improved airborne radar. Supply of these aircraft (and retro-modification 6 existing F-16s) strictly speaking cannot take place as long as aid remains suspended. But if and when aid is resumed, the U.S. will need to seriously reconsider the question of clearance of enhanced capability F-16s which would serve nuclear strike role more effectively.[12]

The cold war is over. The US and the USSR have officially pronounced that nuclear was between them would have no winners and would jeopardise the planet's survival. Thus nuclear war or anything which has a high probability of leading to it cannot be used for the achievement of national foreign policy objectives by the big two. However, circumstances which threaten their very survival may lead to one of them resorting to a nuclear first strike in desperation. Hence they are unlikely to give up a deterrent nuclear second strike retaliatory capability for now. Nuclear weapon stockpiles which are estimated to be about 300 times the requirement will reduce as confidence builds up. A ban on nuclear weapons may also ensure. In this heady ambience many analysts in our country somewhat equphorically extrapolated it to a likely sub-continental detente and, till a few months ago, recommended largely reduced defence spending hoping that by example we could hasten a regional 'entente cordiale'. Then with Pakistan's highly increased moral and material support to Indian insurgents, the pendulum swung the other way with much talk of war. Both reactions indicate too much 'heart' and too little 'head' in the analytical mix. When the cold war was on, the hold of the superpowers was pretty strong on their client states, and on states dependent on them for military economic and political support. In the even of any brinkmanship by such states, they could be ruined in by their superpower mentor. If third World countries not in their orbits started a local war, the superpowers generally took up for the opposing sides almost by knee-jerk reaction. Fears of this leading to a big power nuclear exchange led both the big boys, jointly in many cases and with UN assistance in some, to bring the war to a quick end. Of course, there was the odd exception like the Iran-Iraq war which was permitted to drag on. But then, that was a series of blitzkriegs interspersed by long 'sitzkriggs'; war which was neither likely to be decisive, nor leading to a change in the regional balance of power. The big two generally kept off what was tactily accepted as the other's turf, moved very cautiously for gaining advantage in areas of the globe where neither side's interest was so marked, and competed freely for influency elsewhere. Now, with the end of the cold war, and the big two abjuring war as a policy option, much of their leverage with erstwhile dependent states has been eroded. The almost automatic linkage between warring Third World nations and the superpowers has gone. Any nuclear conflict in the Third World no longer has a high probability of escalation into a nuclear exchange between the bigh two. So, any hard-headed analysis would indicate that, paradoxically, big power detente has indeed increased the freedom of beligence of the lesser fry. Conventional hostilities between countries that have, or assumed to have, nuclear weapon capability can also easily turn nuclear. This is because, though the damage in absolute terms will be considerable to both the belligerents, at the expected level of nuclear weapon use, there would be no danger to the world as a whole. Thus the logic of nuclear war being neither fightable nor winnable in the case of the superpowers, regretfully does not translate into a similar conclusion in the case of small nuclear powers. This fact normally escapes the average Indian security analyst, who average Indian security analyst, who depends on predigested western wisdom for his punditry. Nevertheless, these two facts have to be cranked into the equation by countries like India, when they do their national security homework. What are the implications for us? The restraint that the US could exercise over Pakistan's brinkmanship vis-a-vis India, say in Kashmir, which might lead to war, would be less than before. Assuming that Pakistan has a nuclear weapon capability (any practical strategic planner in India has to make such an assumption), the threat of use of nukes before a conventional war breaks out, or during such hostilities cannot be ruled out.[13]

The current American focus on Pakistan will inevitably broaden to include India. The India-Pakistan military relationship is hostile enough to ensure that. Besides, Pakistan's nuclear diplomacy has been centered on this relationship and has created the image of an inextricable linkage between the nuclear status of the two countries. Like Pakistan, India is vulnerable. There is no Soviet card left. America is India's largest single trading partner and source of foreign investment and technology, which means economic pressures can have adverse effects. At the very least, India may have to consider major economic concessions in order to offset its weak bargaining position on nuclear proliferation. Alternatively, the cost of resistance to both non-proliferation and economic pressure will be very high. It is important to be clear about Indian interests in the context of nuclear policy. Current policy is based on the understanding that unilateral nuclearisation will not enhance security, and that closing the nuclear option will also reduce secutity by precluding a nuclear response in case someone else poses a nuclear threat. In a sense, India's nuclear strategy is essentially no different from that of Pakistan. Both know that a near-nuclear status achieves more than conventional deterrence at minimum possible cost (a nuclear arms race is too expensive for India as well as for Pakistan). It is therefore in India's interest that Pakistan should remain a near-nuclear state. Anything less is unrealistic. Even if Pakistan were to sign the NPT unilaterally (which is highly unlikely), it might still 'cheat' Advanced computers and miniaturised laboratory explosions for testing can circumvent the best of controls. Nor are international safeguards foolproof. Even an NPT signatory can go nuclear at short notice. It is also in India's interest that Pakistan should not succumb to tremendous pressure from the non-proliferation regime, or that pressure would almost certainly turn against India next. What can India do in this context? It may already be too late. The best way to counter non-proliferation pressures in the short run is to reduce the potential for conflict, which in turn alleviates fears of a conflagration breaching the nuclear threshold. It is not at all clear, given the history of mutual hostility and the intensity of the Kashmir crisis and its cross-border effects, whether there is much scope for reducing Indo-Pakistan tensions. Still, in the pursuit of long-term interests, it ought to be tried. Confidence-building measures such as development of forces away from the border, and serious negotiations on extending the ceasefire line in the Siachen region could help. On the nuclear relationship itself, a small start has been made with the 1989 agreement on not attacking each other's nuclear facilities. An important further step might be taken by informally agreeing to slow down, perhaps even temporarily stop, the acquisition of advanced materials (such as Pakistan's recent procurement of tritium processing equipment, which helps build more powerful bombs). This might keep the non-proliferationists at bay, the central point is that it is about time the two countries recognised their common interests—even amidst prolonged tensions—and moved positively to stabilise their relationship and stave off external pressures. This is no time for smug satisfaction Pakistan's nuclear problem is inescapably ours too.[13a]

By 1985, Pakistan had obtained the design of a tested bomb from China and started preparing to enrich uranium to weapons grade. It was putting itself in a position to build a bomb without violating a surviving US prohibition on testing that could have cut off the aid. Congress responded by requiring the President to certify each year that "Pakistan does not possess a nuclear explosive device." This was, what has come to be called Pressler amendment, the device invented by the US authorities to allow the aid flow to continue despite the full knowledge that Pakistan was proceeding relentlessly with its programme of acquiring nuclear bombs in direct violation of US law. Gen. Zia reneged with impunity on his promise to President Ronald Reagan to stop producing bomb-grade uranium. The country persisted in its illegal buying sprees for weapons components in the United States. It built plutonium and tritium production plants with equipment acquired illegally in Europe. It is known to have been designing accodynamic bomb castings for nuclear warheads and outfitting its US supplied F-16s planes to deliver them. Americans went on turning a blind eye to all this and the US President went on ritualistically certifying every year to Congress that Pakistan does not "possess a nuclear explosive device." He is no more prepared to do so now as with the end of the Afghan war, Pakistan has ceased to be strategically that important to the defence interests of the US. The sudden cessation of US aid at a time when the country was already under heavy economic strain has come as a big blow to Pakistan. Prime Minister Nawaz Sharief is going to negotiate with the US on the resumption of the aid which his country needs for sheer survival as a solvent nation. For that, however, he will have to accept the nationally humiliating conditions of throwing open the Kahuta facility to US experts for their inspection and dismantle the weapon grade uranium production and aerodynamic bomb carrying facilities that it has so sedulously built up over the past ten years. This may be too high a price for Pakistan to pay to get US aid resumed but there is no escape for the country from it. President Bush and US Congress would not settle for anything less than that. But that will not be the end of the matter. Pakistan's economic crisis is too deep and too pervasive to be resolved by the single act of resumption of US aid. Due to sharp fall in remittances from Kuwait and Iraq in the first quarter of fiscal 1990-91 (July to June) and repayments of some military debt, Pakistan's foreign exchange reserves dropp d from US $ 500 million to US $ 150 million and had at one time plunged to US $ 40 million.[14]

It is not enough if a country has nuclear technology materials and components to assemble a weapon. To deter a nuclear adversary, specific steps towards weaponsiation, operational procedures, command and control and doctrine of use if necessary need to be developed. At present most of the knowledgeable observers outside India has not taken these steps and remains a non-nuclear country and that is not their perception about Pakistan. This asymmetric perception poses a very grave threat and may tempt Pakistan on a path of adventurism. The gravity of the security environment calls for comprehensive planning to counter the threats. Such a plan has to aim at keeping our defence and para-military forces at the maximum effciency and state of readiness and sealing our borders as effectively as possible using not only conventional measures but also high technology available within our country. Such signals to Pakistan that it does not have an asymmetric advantage in the respect of nuclear weapons, should be followed up with appropriate steps within our government and armed forces, and above all diplomatic measures to contain Pakistan. Fortunately, there is evidence to conclude that the US is getting concerned with Pak nuclear capability and its implications for the stability of the region and the fundamentalist threat in South West and West Asia.[15]

In a major shift in US policy, if his home government confirms that it does reflect US policy now American Ambassador to Pakistan Robert Oakley is quoted by Islamabad Radio as saying in effect that it is all right for Pakistan to have nuclear weapons if India has them.

According to the version given by Islamabad Radio in its domestic service in Urdu at 200 GMT on December 24, 1990, Ambassador Oakley said, "If India had acquired nuclear capability then Pakistan also had the right to do so for its own defence."

What the Ambassador did or did not say become highly relevant, analysts in Washington point out, because the Bush administration is known to be keen on resuming military and economic aid to Pakistan which are barred under American law because of the nuclear issue. There is another issue of drugs.

Any change in existing policy on the nuclear issue, covered by the Pressler Amendment, will require active administration lobbying to change the law as it stands. This is how Islamabad radio put it.

"According to the Associated Press of Pakistan, US Ambassador Rober Oakley has said Pakistan's nuclear programme should not be made an issue of controversy between Pakistan and the United States. It should be solved at a regional level."

Talking to Qazi Hussain Ahmad, Amir of Jamaat-i-Islami, in Islamabad on January 4, 1991, Ambassador Oakley said, "If India had acquired nuclear capability, then Pakistan also had the right to do so far its own defence. He stressed the need, however, to reduce tension in the region and said both Pakistan and India should take effective steps to mitigate the hostile situation."[16]

Apparently prevaricating remarks of the US Ambassador in Pakistan Rober Oakley, have once again activated concern in India about the neighbouring country's nuclear programme and its security implications for this country. His reported remarks criticising the tendency in Pakistan to view its nuclear programme as a controversial issue with the USA and asserting that it was essentially one that required to be resolved at the regional level appear to have touch off a debate : this could end up in arguing unwittingly for an Indo-Pak nucler non-proliferation arrangement the USA has had at heart for a long time. Oakley, according to the government owned daily Pakistan Times, also said that "if India had acquired the nuclear capability, then Pakistan, too, had a right to do so for its defence." One could interpret these remarks as implying a recognition of India's right to develop nuclear weapon but does the USA really accept this logic? Will it, for example, accept the same argument for West Asia and concede that the Arab states have an equal right to possess nuclear weapons because Israel already have this capability? Or, will it allow Latin American countries, including Cuba, to go nuclear since the USA already possesses large stockpiles of nuclear weapons? No, because, as on other issues so in matters nuclear, the USA has a different stick to beat each party with. Which only means that there could be catch in Oakley's remarks as there could be in President Bush's inability to give Pakistan the certificate it requires under the Pressler amendment to qualify for continued US assistance. The catch could be to alarm India into over-reacting to Pakistan's nuclear prowess and jettisoning its traditional position on the nuclear non-proliferation treaty (NPT) to fall for a regional NPT arrangement.[17]

Deter India and pressurise America these appear to be among the most important twin objectives of Pakistan's military bureaucratic-political establishment. Being fed on sinister 'leaks' as well as overt expressions of belligerence by none other than Mirza Aslam Beg, Chief of the Army Staff, Pakistani analysts have already started painting scenarios of the years to come. Writing in *The Dawn* recently columnist Shaheen Sehbai quoted 'top' political contacts as saying that Pakistan should lose no time in exploding the bomb and announcing to the world that it has joined the nuclear club. Whether anybody likes it or not.

"Pakistan would be able to achieve in one go what it has not been able to do in the last 43 years—secure itself from a foreign threat". In the process Sehbai wrote, the country would also be able to undertake revolutionary domestic reforms that have been kept pending for decades in such fields as agriculture, taxation and defence. The thinking in the establishing apparently is that in spite of the worldwide 'hysteria' particularly in India and the United States. New Delhi would be effectively deterred while "Washington Congressmen would come running to Islamabad pleading that the nuclear capability should be confined to only Pakistan's own needs of security and it should not be exported. As a quid pro quo the Americans would express their willingness to do business as usual with Pakistan, like they are "already doing with many other nuclear countries like India, Israel and South Africa" Sehbai quoted top sources as lamenting that the stage had reached when Pakistan was "reaping the disadvantages of being a nuclear power, but it had yet to take the advantage of being one." It appears from reports in the Pakistani media that it is Gen Beg himself who has been encouraging thinking along these lines in recent weeks. He set the balerolling in early December when he outlined the country's new defence policy (normally a prerogative of the civilians) in an extempore speech at a seminar on defence technology organised by the Pakistan Ordnance Factories. Despite his injunction that his remarks be "confined to this forum, "they were widely reported in the Pakistani press. They gave rich fodder to columinsts who laced what the General said with their own 'inside' informatioe. Gen. Beg made bold to comment on the likely scenario that could emerge in West Asia after the Iraqi annexation of Kuwait and what he called Baghdad's "strategic defiance" of the United States the only superpower left in the world.[18]

Pakistan would not compromise on its nuclear programme under pressure from the U.S. or any other quarters, the country's Foreign Minister, Sahabzada Yaqub Khan, said in the National Assembly on January 1, 1991.

The Bush administration had in October 1990 suspended military and economic aid of about $560 millions to Pakistan on a suspicion that it had developed a nuclear bomb. George Bush had failed to certify to the Congress nuclear weapons as mandated by the Pressler Amendment. Winding up the debate on the President's address to the joint session of Parliament he said "Our Government is determined that on no occasion will we compromise our principles or our independence of actions or national interests. This is a hard road, but we have decided to follow it."

Khan said, "We are determined to safeguard national interests as a proud and sovereign nation and will not bow under any pressure."

Conceding that relations between Pakistan and the U.S. were passing through a difficult phase, he however, said efforts were on to resolve differences on the nuclear issue.

In what is being viewed as a velled warning to the U.S. he said if the Pressler Amendment was pressed on Pakistan, it would just bring the opposite results.

The Foreign Minister said legislations such as the Symington of the Pressler Amendments could not stop proliferation of nuclear weapons.

Nuclear device not made Khan said Pakistan had not produced a nuclear device, nor had it exploded one like, India "We have not even shared our technological advances with a third country and, therefore, Pakistan does not believe it can come under the purview of the Pressler Amendment." He described the amendment as an "outmoded, discriminatory and inviduous piece of legislation."

There should be a clear understanding of what would be the core vital interests of such a threat to which would very probably escalate into a nuclear exchange. This can only be achieved by discussions and debate within each country. followed by mutual discussions between experts from both sides. Given a tacit understanding of the basic ground rules, one can expect many confidence building measures to follow, both in the nuclear and conventional arms. Agreed limitations in nuclear systems can also follow after India's requirement for deterrence vis-a-vis China is taken into account. An era of cooperation in various realms of military activity can also be envisaged. This bilateral exercise can also be enlarged to embrance South Asian Association for Regional Cooperation. In the mid "70s when I was commanding an armoured division, I told my colleagues informally, that we ought to take Pakistan into our confidence and carry out future nuclear development jointly. This was received with incredulous looks and eloquent silence. In hindsight, I am absolutely certain that such a supreme confidence building measure might have changed the entire subcontinental history. Similarly, dealing with the insecurity of India's smaller neighbours, and credibly allaying their 'Kuwait Syndrome' could perhaps also be done by India fighting them a few short to medium range nuclear weapon systems without strings.[19]

A lot of debate is going on in India on Pakistani nuclear threat. Although opinion differs, one strong lobby has emerged in favour of India taking some immediate steps to go nuclear. Even military experts are veering round to this view. The debate has assumed importance in view of Pakistan's determination to go ahead with the bomb manufacturing programme. Some reports in the West say that Pakistan is having about half a dozen nuclear bombs. Perhaps it is because of this that Washington is going slow on providing military and monetary aid to Pakistan. But the Pak rulers had defied the world opinion and had declared their intention not to succumb to any pressures. Prime Minister Chandra Sekhar has been repeatedly saying that India had the capability to face any challenge from Pakistan if that country dared to go in for nuclear misadventure. He was not against India entering into a non-aggression treaty, prohibiting both countries from attacking each other's nuclear installations. But India would not discuss her nuclear programme with Pakistan or anybody else, he clarified. The Prime Minister referred to his talks with Nawaz Sharif in Pakistan at the SAARC summit in Male and hoped that there would be some positive developments for improving bilateral relations. He had told Nawaz Sharif that India was willing to enter into any agreement for improving relations. The tension at the border should ease. During the last meeting of the Foreign Secretaries of the two countries, this issue was taken up. It was pointed out of Pakistan that she should stop aiding the ultras in Punjab and Kashmir. But later, the tension at the border should ease. During the last meeting of the Foreign Secretaries of the two countries, this issue was taken up. It was pointed out to Pakistan that she should stop aiding the ultras in Punjab and Kashmir. But later, the Pakistani leaders reiterated their determination to help the extremists. The goings on in

Pakistan, particularly on the nuclear front, had to be viewed with concern.[20]

Pakistan's nuclear weapons development programme had reportedly gone ahead to a stage where the United States thought it had to be helted in pursuit of its non-proliferation objective. The US has yet to issue the certification clearing the Pakistani nuclear programme for continuing its economic and military aid to Islamabad. It was natural for members of our Parliamentary Consultative Committee on Defence to express concern over the issue and caution the government to be alive to the security risks involved. The Prime Minister Chandra Shekhar, who holds the Defence portfolio, saw no reason for apprehension in the minds of the people and hoped Pakistan would not risk the terrible consequences of a nuclear misadventure. Part of the hope, perhaps arises from the positive attitude which Chandra Shekhar found on the part of his Pakistani counterpart Nawaz Sharif during their meeting in the course of the fifth SAARC summit at Male. It would be a double-edged weapon for Pakistan to go ahead with the manufacture of an atom bomb, for that would increase pressures on the government of India to deviate from the path of peaceful nuclear development which it has scrupulously followed. It is in the interest of both countries to abjure nuclear weapons development and concentrate on utilising the latest technology, including in the nuclear field, for promoting the basic objectives of economic development and poverty alleviation. There is a vast potential for mutual cooperation in this field, once the major irritants in Indo-Pakistan relations are removed. The temptation to exploit the anti-bomb sentiments to tall stall peaceful nuclear development should be resisted. Chandra Shekhar assured the Members of Parliament attending the Consultative Committee meeting that tension of the type which existed some months ago, with armed forces of the two countries being on the alert along the Indo-Pakistan border, had disappeared. Yet the problem caused by extremist elements remains. The efforts being put in by our Security Forces both on the Eastern and Western sectors would be effective if Pakistan cooperates by withholding aid and assistance to the militants. The issue no doubt has figured prominently at the current Foreign Secretary-level talks at Islamabad. Our Foreign Secretary, Muchkund Dube, who had a meeting with the Pakistani President Ghulam Ishaq Khan emphasised that the core issue of Pakistani assistance to subversion and terrorism in Punjab and Kashmir had to be tackled urgently. Such assistance he pointed out, is a clear violation of the Shimla Agreement. The Pakistan President while expressing his country's desire to establish good neighbourly relations with India also said that it required a constructive response from the Indian side. Does this mean India recognising the political compulsions of their leaders to take an unreasonable stand on issues like Kashmir and making uncharitable references to the recent disturbances in India? Dube pointed out to the President that the communal situation in India is an internal affair of this country and its projection in an exaggerated and wrong manner in the Pakistani media is unhelpful. According to a Pakistani official release, President Ishaq Khan expressed deep anguish over the situation in Kashmir. It would be unrealistic to hope for an early change in Pakistan's stand on Kashmir or a toning down of its rhetoric, but actions on the ground should be watched to gauge its sincerity in improving bilateral relations, which would be of mutual benefit to the two countries.[21]

Prime Minister Chandra Shekhar on January 7, 1991 warned Pakistan that India was fully capable to meet the challenge if the former strayed into nuclear "misadventure."

The Prime Minister assured the members in the Rajya Sabha that India was not scared or worried about the reports that Pakistan had developed nuclear capability, "I am sure Pakistan will not enter into any misadventure in this regard. If they do India is quite capable to meet the challenge", he added.

Chandra Shekhar was responding to the clarifications sought by the members in the Rajya Sabha on his suo motu statement, on the recent SAARC summit in Male, made earlier in both houses of Parliament. The members expressed grave concern at the reports that Pakistan had developed nuclear weapons. They wanted to know what was the basis of the Prime Ministers's optimism that the Indo-Pak relations would take a turn for the better.

Chandra Shekhar said in course of his talks on bilateral issue with Pakistan Prime Minister Nawaz Sharif in Male, he received some "positive indications" which might lead to positive results. "But when the bilateral relations of the two countries have not been very friendly for the last four decades, we cannot expect miracles," he added.

The Prime Minister said when the foreign secretaries of the two countries met recently, for the first time after 1989 they discussed the Sir Creek boundary dispute in a positive manner. The Surveyors-General of both the countries would meet very shortly in order to come to some agreement.

He also told the members that he had recently a talk on telephone with Nawaz Sharif and a meeting of the sub-commission on India and Pakistan would be convened shortly.

The Director-General of Military Operations had agreed to get in touch every week on the hotline.

This would lead to lot of easing of tension because "Whenever an army action is there all sorts of rumours are spread in this country and also in Pakistan," he added.

Reiterating his country's keenness to normalise relations with Pakistan Chandra Shekhar accepted in principle a suggestion made by some members about sending an Indian Parliamentary delegation to Pakistan. He also told the

House that the foreign secretaries of the two countries would again meet some time next month.

The Prime Minister reacted sharply to the remarks made by the Congress-I member, Bhuvanesh Chaturvedi, that certain Press reports had suggested that India's offer for normalisation of relations with Pakistan was at the prompting of the United States. Refuting the insinuation, he said "I am not influenced by Press reports nor have I time to contradict all such reports."

Chandra Shekhar said he did not see the United States interfering in Indo-Pak affairs. The US on their own had decided not to support Pakistan's inssistence on plebiscite in Kashmir, he said.

The Prime Minister said there was a difference in preceptions on Kashmir problem between the two countries. As far as India was concerned it was not only the question of some territory but also of upholding the principle of secularism.

Sharing the members concern at Pakistan's assistance to terrorists in Punjab, the Prime Minister said that if Islamabad continued to interfere in Punjab, India would treat it was an unfriendly act. However, his impression was that "there is slight change" in the attitude of Pakistan with regard to Punjab.

Referring to the members suggestion that visa restrictions should be liberalised among the SAARC countries, the Prime Minister said it was decided at the Male summit that the Members of Parliament, Judges of the Supreme Court and all heads of national academic institutions would not require any visa for visiting SAARC countries.

"In my bilateral talks with Prime Minister Nawaz Sharif I was impressed by his positive approach. He showed an awareness of the cost of both the countries of continuing an adversarial relationship as well as of the benefits inherent in a cooperative relationship. I fully reciprocated his sentiments and sought his cooperation in restoring trust and confidence between our two countries. I expressed our concern at continuing support from across the border to terrorism in the States of Punjab and Jammu and Kashmir. I emphasised that this a serious irritant in our relations. We agreed that all diffences between India and Pakistan should be resolved peacefully and through dialogue and that the proress of reconvening discussions on the various pending issues should be resumed. Consequent upon our meeting, the Foreign Secretaries of India and Pakistan have met and made progress towards reaching agreement on several confidence building measures to reduce tension in our relations. They have also determined the time table for the resumption of discussions on issues such as the demarcation of the land boundary at Sir Creek; the Tulbul Navigation Project and the meeting of the Sub-commissions, he said.

Chandra Shekhar reiterated India's commitment to South Asian Cooperation under SAARC. This is essential for accelerating our economic development, for building individual and collective self-reliance and for enhancing our bargaining strength in multilateral negotiations. Such cooperation has become all the more necessary in the context of the present trend towards economic integration in the world.

Chandra Shekhar said at India's suggestion, regional cooperation under SAARC had been extended to the field of biotechnology also, India's proposal to create a fund for identification and development of regional projects, to be financed by national development banks of members countries, was accepted. India will host a meeting of representatives of these banks to work out modalities for funds's operation.

Herein lies the clue to the development of the nuclear controversy. By March 1990, tensions betwen India and Pakistan had reached the boiling point and two or three scenarios emerged. First, Pakistan exceeded the enrichment limits with the US getting definite knowledge. It was unlikely that this alone could have led to such sharp US action because it had earlier concluded that Pakistan had after all crossed the 5 per cent limit in 1987 itself. Secondly, some plans for preparing for a detonation or the refitment of the F-16s done to carry the bomb were discovered or thirdly, the US got irrefutable evidence that the bomb was in place and was meant to be used. The Gates mission clearly indicated that Pakistan had crossed the rubicon and significantly Rober Gates met only the two men who really matter—General Beg and Ghulam Ishaq, while ignoring the be eagured Benazir. For the US, the crossing of the March levels represent an abject failure of its non-proliferation policies in South Asia and that the guns for nuclear restraint policy has come a cropper. More importantly, the dangerous implications of the unilateral Pakistani action that would unleash a nuclear arms race in the region has produced the present hardline attitude in US policy. For Pakistan, with the ambiguity cover all but blown off, it signifies a new and unknown situation, to contend with and for India, the worst coming true.[22]

The innocents talk of a nuclear arms race and the enormous expenditure involved. Most of these arguments are imported ones, manufactured abroad and not thought through in the context of realities on the subcontinent. Until the end of Eisenhower era, the US President reduced the defence budget and there was talk of a 'bigger bang for the defence back'. In those days, some 25-100 weapons on either side were considered adequate deterrents. It was the subsequent development of tactical nuclear weapons and the wild ideas of nuclear war-fighting that led to the proliferation of arsenals, concepts of first and second strikes, sophisticated delivery vehicles and extremely costly and complicated command control, communication and intelligence systems. The arsenals became so numerous, so complicated and so sophisticated that a nuclear war become an impossibility both to wage and win, given the very large arsenals. But countries with a dozen or two of simple air-droppable weapons, dispersed widely in a relatively large country, can exercise effective deterrence without enormous costs, provided they do not contemplate actual war. In any case, war in the subcontinental context is totally unthinkable. While command, control communication and intelligence systems have to be adequately provided for, they are not going to cost too much in our situation. A dozen well-concealed air-droppable weapons cannot be eliminated and therefore, constitute a credible and survivable deterrent. The Chinese, the Pakistanis, the Iraqis, the Israelis and the Indians all understand this. That is the reason why China, Israel and Pakistan have neither gone nor will they go bankrupt on account of their nuclear weapon programme. Western strategists today admit that nulear war-fighting is not feasible and that effective deterrent can be sustained by five per cent of the present arsenals. Therefore, it is not necessary for countries going nuclear to copy the totally invalidated and mindless strategies of the US and the USSR. It is possible to have a credible minimum deterrent at affordable cost. This is what the Pakistanis are aiming at. Even a couple of dozen air-deliverable bombs and a few squardrons of F-16 and Mirage IIIs said Vs. aircraft presumably already in Pakistan's possession, are adequate to deter India and totally neutralise all rural or imagined (more the latter) Indian superiority in conventional forces. With that assurance Pakistan can make use of its asymmetric advantage (the Khalistani and Kashmiri extremism) and wage a sustained low-intensity war on Indian soil without fear of retaliation of the 1965 kind. They may also be watching for an appropriate opportunity to realise the aim they voiced to Professor Stephen Cohen, the Pakistani military men pointed out that nuclear capability would provide Pakistan an umbrella under which it could reopen the Kashmir issue. A Pakistani nuclear capability would paralyse not only the Indian nuclear decision, but also Indian conventional forces. A hold Pakistani strike to liberate Kashmiri might go unchallenged if the Indian leadership was weak or indecisive. Given this background it is futile for India to focus on the issue of preventing Pakistan going nuclear. The latter has already done so and, therefore, the sensible step for India is to accept this harsh fact and take appropriate measures to deter the enhancement of Pakistani nuclear capability. Those measures are not costly. The rest of the world, especially the US, is likely to understand the compulsions on India. Simultaneously, India should also initiate a dialogue with the US to develop the mutualty of interests with that country on preventing the use and the threat to use nuclear weapons in the subcontinent.[23]

The Prime Minister Chandra Shekhar warning to Pakistan during the meeting of the consultative committee for the ministry of defence, was clearly an attempt to deter that country from embarking on a nuclear misadventure. It was also a signal to the people of India and the rest of the world that the situation in the sub-continent has moved beyond the pre-weaponisation stage with Pakistan now having the bomb. India tried to set a unique example by not weaponising its demonstrated nuclear capability for the last 17 years since the Pokhran nuclear test. Unfortunately, nuclear abstinence by this country neither evoked appreciation from an international community conditioned by western nuclear theology nor deflected Pakistan from its quest for the Islamic Bomb, so christened by the father of the programme, the later Zulfikar Ali Bhutto. The United States subordinated its nonprolifera- tion goals to its cold War ubjective of pushing the Soviet Union out of Afghanistan. Consequently, in order to obtain Pakistani cooperation to reach weapons to Afghan tribal insurgents, a totally permissive attitude was adopted by the US administration towards the Pakistani nuclear weapons programme. Today the US has no leverage on Pakistan and the latter, having gone beyond the stage of weaponisation, cannot be disarmed. Even as the US and the west are attempt- ing to prevent Iraq going nuclear, they have to reckon with a nuclear Pakistan with all its implications for the region vital to western interests because of its oil reserves. Nothing can be gained by crying over spilt milk. India, and the world have to reconcile themselves to a nuclear Pakistan and start exploring ways and means for not halting nuclear prolifera- tion, which has already occured, but to prevent the use and threat of use of nuclear weapons in the subcontinent. That this can be successfully achieved is demostrated by the deve- lopments in Europe, on Sino-Soviet border and between US and China. The case of Pakistan calls for special attention because it is sole instance where the command and control over nuclear weapons is exclusively in the hands of the military and not the elected civilian government. In these circumstances India's efforts should be focussed on confidence building and risk reduction measures in regard to use and threat of use of nuclear weapons in the subcontinental situation. India took the first step in this direction by proposing and concluding with Pakistan an agreement on no-attack on nuclear facilities in 1988.[24]

Meanwhile, the High Commissioner of India in Pakistan J.N. Dixit on January 27, 1991 deposited the instruments of ratification of the agreement on prohibition of astack on nuclear installations and facilities, with Pakistan's Acting Foreign Secretary, Afzal Qader.

Article two of the agreement specifies that the two countries would inform each other the latitudes and longitudes of the nuclear installations and facilities in their respective countries at the beginning of each year, and would inform each other of any changes in locations.

Though India was prepared to submit the detailed list rightway, Pakistan has referred to stick to the letter of the agreement and the lists would hence be exchanged on January 1, 1992. This does not preclude an exchange of lists before this date.

It was also explained that Article one which prohibits a direct or indirect attack on nuclear facilities is comprehensive and effectively precludes any breach of agreement by either side acting under the pretext of being insufficiently informed.

References

1. Pran Chopra, The Year of the Bomb? *The Hindu*, 28 December, 1990.
2 *Ibid.*
3. *Ibid.*

4. *Ibid.*

5. *Far Eastern Economic Review*, 20 December, 1990.

6. *Ibid.*

7. Rajiv K. Bajaj. Pakistan's Nuclear Programme. *Surya India*, October 1990.

8. *Ibid.*

9. P S. Suryanarayana. SAARC and the Nuclear Issue. *Indian Express*, 19 December, 1990.

10. *Ibid*

11. Jasjit Singh. Pakistan's Nuclear Weapon. *Indian Express*, 20 November, 1990.

12. *Ibid.*

13. K. Sundarji, Dangers of Detente. *India Today*, 31 October, 1990.

13a. Rajesh M. Basrur. The Fall Out of Pakistan's Nuclear Policy. *The Independent*, 22 October, 1990.

14. B.M. Bhatia. Pakistan. *The Hindustan Times*, 26 December, 1990.

15. K. Subrahmanyam. Defence Policy for the Nineties. *The Business and Political Observer*, 17 December, 1990.

16. *The Hindustan Times*, 6 January, 1991.

18. Joginder Butalia. Pak Bomb. *National Herald*, 15 December, 1990.

19. K. Sunderji. Declare Nuclear Status. *India Today*, 31 December, 1990; p. 163

20. *Democratic World*, 27 January, 1991.

21. *National Herald*, 20 December, 1990.

22. Asha Dixit Pakistan and the Bomb. *The Bisiness and Political Observer*, 9 January, 1991.

23. K. Subrahmanyam. Nuclear Proliferation of the Sub-continent. *The Sunday Observer*, 23, December, 1990.

24. *The Business and Political Observer*, 20 December, 1990.

3

Agriculture, Land Reforms, Rural Upliftment and Poverty Removal

The Prime Minister Nawaz Sharif said in Islamabad, on November 7, 1990, that "those raising slogans for the peasants and labour had practically done nothing for their uplift cause, the world over. The facts were before the nation. I do not have slogans. Instead, I possess certain projects for the welfare of peasants and labour class. Instances of which could be cited from my period as administrative head of the province. Details about my future planning for both these brackets of the society shall soon be known."

The new government and Nawaz Sharif in particular have had the best possible mandate under the peculiar circumstances existing in the country and therefore, an opportunity is lying at the feet of the Prime Minister. Late Z.A. Bhutto had a similar one and he cashed on it by carrying out land reforms a more still paying dividends. However, the mistake committed in this particular field by the late Bhutto was that he did not see it properly done in Sindh and Balochistan and even in the Punjab, there were lapses. Nevertheless it has been proved beyond doubt from the Bhutto family stance that the poor people of Pakistan solidly stand by anyone they consider to be their benefactor and friend. Whether they got a fair deal or not is a debatable point, but if the ones at the receiving end are happy all objections become futile. Nawaz Sharif has an advantage over his predecessors, as he has an overwhelming support among the powerful business community and thus has an invincible urban base. With almost all the provinces in his hold and a solid unsplitable majority in the Parliament he should have no difficulty in freeing the rural masses especially in the Sindh and Balochistan from the age old clutches of feudalism. If he can manage this, it will go a long way in bringing peace and order in the strife ridden province of Sindh and he will earn an everlasting place in the hearts of the hapless poor.[1]

In his address to the joint session of Parliament on November 9, 1990 President Ghulam Ishaque Khan said that the Gulf crisis had placed an unprecedented burden on the country's economy and asked the new government to restructure the existing economic edifice by adopting a revolutionary approach. The President said that incredible oil price rise has inflated our import bill and trade and have remittances have also been severely hit. On the top of it there are threats of aid cut off and an uncertain border situation. Such pressures demand sacrifice from us and bringing about substantial changes in our economic policies, he said. Prime Minister Nawaz Sharif has also stated that the new government would look into different ways to generate revenue and reduce unemployment by adopting policies aimed at "privatisation, denationalisation of big state enterprises and incentives for banking". This is a long term approach and if implemented honestly would improve national economy but what about the promise of examining different ways of generating revenue. Revenue base can be broadened only by bringing structural changes in the taxation system. Our current taxation system is based on the premise that he who can not escape from its payment must pay the tax. This must be altered and replaced with the premise that he who has the ability must pay the tax. It is with this end in view that a case can be built for levying farm tax. Farm tax has been the subject of an intense debate for a long time but each time a government considered implementing it the feudal lobby wielding enormous economic and political power succeeded in opposing it. The issue was first raised in United Pakistan by members of the National Assembly belonging to the then East Pakistan who mostly came from the middle class families but the move was opposed by the West Pakistan feudals in the Assembly. The first PPP government levied tax on agricultural income though an ordinance on January 5, 1977. The ordinance was passed by the National Assembly in its next session and collection of tax was to start from the following Rabi crop. However, when martial law was imposed in July that year, General Zia repealed the ordinance through an executive order to appease the landed aristocracy whose power and influence he knew well and needed most. That was the closest the country ever came to bringing agricultural income within the purview of tax. A number of arguments are usually advanced by the landed aristocracy against imposition of agricultural tax. It is said that farmers are already paying taxes in the shape of ushr. development tax, malia and aabiana. But to say that an agriculturiest should be exempted from the tax because he pays land revenue is like saying that an urban property holder should not pay income tax on rentals because he pays property tax water tax and other service charges. It is also said that a farmeabiding by the statute cannot increase his acreage and thus raise agricultural production while others can possess scores of industries, dozens of businesses and a multitude of plazas. But those possessing industries, businesses and plazas are not exempt from tax. Nor does possession of industries and businesses by some prevent big landlords from diversifying their activities too. A farmer no doubt should be encouraged by the government to increase output per acre by helping him to improve production techniques, introduction of new high yielding varieties of crops and providing credit and building of the rural infrastructure. But after such measures have been taken to help increase income from agriculture there seems little justification not to tax it. After all taxation is always on the income: it is not occupation oriented. It is also sometimes said that there are millions of poor farmers who barely manage a living from their land and taxing their incomes would drive them out of their jobs and meagre means of livelihood. This is merely to seek refuge behind the plight of small farmers who are as hard hit as an ordinary industrial worker and who must be protected. It may be true that 90 per cent of the farmers comprising over 3 million farming units are unable to bear the taxation burden.[2] No body will ask for taxing their incomes which in any case would fall below the taxable income. But this does not mean that exemption should also be extended to most of the remaining 10 per cent of farmers who collectively own more than 40 per cent of the farmlands having land holdings of over 25 acres and incomes (after defraying expenses) well over Rs. 2500 per month, roughly the current taxable income. It is also argued that the average earning from agricultural sector is very low and taxing the income would be too heavy a burden. But the average earning is low because of very poor incomes of the bulk of farmers (almost 90 per cent) which brings down the average of the remaining rather well to do 10 per cent farmers. To say that farmers with higher incomes should not be asked to pay income tax because the average earning in agricultural sector is low is like saying that the industrialist should not be taxed because the ordinary industrial workers is too poor to bear the tax burden. And extending this argument still further one can say that since the average per capita income of the country is below Rs. 30,000/ per year, therefore no body should be taxed, the average income being below taxable limit. Pakistan is one of those countries where revenue collection through indirect taxes is one of the highest being almost 83 per cent. Placing heavier reliance on sales tax as it does, indirect taxation pushes up commodity prices, reduces the purchasing power, and further squeezes the middle and lower middle income groups indirect taxation is believed to be a regressive form of taxation as its incidence is more on the poorer classes than on those who can afford to pay. The share of direct taxes in revenue collection can be increased only through farm tax. It should also be remembered that exemption of farm income from tax has also been used as cover by a variety of criminals including smugglers and drug peddlars. They are known to have converted huge amounts of black money by showing it as income derived from agriculture and that too without paying any-tax. The taxation commission appointed sometime back has in its report also pinpointed wideranging financial malpractices usually resorted to behind the cover of farm incomes. It is time that these loopholes are plugged. A few days before elections the former caretaker prime minister Ghulam Mustafa Jatoi said that he favoured the imposition of farm tax and that a parliamentary bill to this effect would be introduced by the new government. It would also be interesting to recall the 1977 manifesto commitment of PNA, the forerunner of present IJI, on this issue. With a view to countering Bhutto's ordinance levying tax on agricultural income, the PNA had declared that it will abolish absentee landlordism being unislamic and hand over the land to its actual tillers. It was on this account that the PNA then adopted plough as its election symbol.

The second PPP government also constituted a committee to study the feasibility of leving tax on income derived from agricultural activity. It is not known what happened to its report. Setting up of committees is usually a notorious design for deferring hard decisions. The PPP government, however, could not have decided the issue because of lack of parliamentary majority. Under the Constitution levying of agricultural tax is in the provincial domain and transferring the subject to the centre would require amendment in the Constitution which the previous PPP government was not able to do.

The new IJI government can easily muster the necessary majority in the Parliament to amend the Constitution, if considered necessary. The ANP and MQM which together have 22 MNAs have already voiced their support for taxing farm income. With the election to Parliament of many industrialists and other members belonging to middle and lower middle income group, the hold of the feudals is no longer unassailable. Perhaps a great chance has presented itself to attack the country's economic problems with, as the President said, a revolutionary approach.[3]

Agriculture in Pakistan remains in many ways the most dominant economic activity although it has made uneven progress. It provides a way of life to almost three quarters of the country's population. Over 55 per cent of the total labour force was engaged in this sector in 1975.[4]

The share of agriculture in the Gross Domestic Product (G.D.P) is 29 per cent. Its share in the GDP has declined over the years, representing high growth in industry and infrastructure. However, agriculture itself has maintained a steady pace of growth of over 4 per cent per annum throughout the period since the advent of the sixties. This places Pakistan in a select group of developing countries which have succeeded in inducing and sustaining high agricultural growth. During the period 1948-55 the agricultural sector went through a period of acute stagnation arising out of a number of factors. The stagnation was halted by the end of the fifties by a sure of private tubewell installation. The growth rate of the agricultural sector, which was less than 1 per cent in the first half of the 1950's rose to 27 per cent in the second half. The period 1950-60 as a whole recorded a 1.7 per cent growth rate in agriculture. The decade of 1960-70 recorded a 5.0 per cent compound rate of growth for agriculture, but the growth rate was higher during the second half of the decade as the effects by the new agricultural strategy became more wide spread.[5]

During the 1970's the growth rate in agriculture had again fallen to the level in the 1950's i.e. below 2 per cent, although the year to year fluctuation were much larger than in the preceeding decades. The slowdown of agriculture in the seventies has had deep adverse effects on the economy in many ways especially since the population grew at an apparently accellerated rate, increasing from around 2.5 per cent per year in the early sixties to 3.0 per cent or more in the mid-seventies. Pakistan had to import 2.6 million metric tons of wheat during 1978-79, which was over 25 per cent of its domestic production of 10.10 million metric tons.

Among the probable causes of the evidently slow growth in agriculture, the most generally stated is that Pakistan has suffered a number of setbacks in the seventies, including the war with India (1971), an abrupt and high increase in the cost of imported oil (since 1973-74) and a series of natural disasters in the form of floods (1973-77) and droughts with consequent destruction of crops. Pest attacks has also been identified as a major source of loss in output of wheat and cotton in same years. The other important point of view is that the slow down in economic activity in the country could be attributed to the various reforms carried out by the Pakistan People's Party during its rule between 1972-77.[6] These reforms are said to have created a climate of uncertainty and fear among the dominant interests on land. The same argument has been used to discredit the pricing and marketing facilities of the PPP. These arguments quite naturally surfaced following the imposition of Martial Law, which removed PPP from power in July 1977. The performance of Pakistani agriculture should be examined in the context of emerging power equation prevailing over a period of time.

Much of the debate on the performance of the agricultural sector in Pakistan has centred around and has been conditioned by the somewhat phenomenal performance in the 1960's. It is however, only proper to view the performance in this period in its historical perspective.[7] The major question about this performance in the extent to which the growth impulses generated in this period were shared by different groups in rural Pakistan and whether institutional mechanisms existed both to sustain this growth process and to mitigate the harmful distributional effects. Before examining the employment and income distribution and also agrarian structure effects of agricultural growth particularly during the Green Revolution phase we must briefly examine the production profile, achievement and important steps taken to develop the agricultural sector.[8]

Between 1960 and 1972 there seems to be a net decline of about 0.9 million households who depend on farming. The gross decline, however, is much more, i.e. of 1.42 million households mostly with holdings below 5.0 acres. The changes in farming areas of different size and tenurial groups have also been significant, though the over all changes in total farming area during last two decades has been small. Both the size group and tenurial changes in number of households and area show that the weight of the higher size groups and of owner-cum-tenants is increasing in the distribution of operational holdings. The weight of small size groups (in all tenurial categories) and of tenants (in all size categories except 7.5-12.5 acres) has sharply declined.

There is also evidence that share-cropping, though still the dominant mode of tenancy, is declining in importance. Thus the area under share cropping (as a percentage of total tenanted area) declined from 88.7 to 83.4 between 1960-1982. The decline is sharper among very small and very large size groups, where absentee landlordism is, perhaps more prevalent. The plausible answer for these significant changes in the agrarian structure may be slow rate of growth of non-agricultural employment to absorb surplus labour on land.[9]

The 1960's was the period during which significant changes took place in Government policy to stimulate agricultural production and to take advantage of Green Revolution technology. There was also some attempt to introduce land reforms, whose efficiency in making more land accessible to small farmers, tenants and landless was marginal. It is, therefore, not unreasonable to surmise that the changes in agrarian structure were associationed with, if not directly caused by these policies.

It would not be out of context to point out here the debate between Alavi[10] and Burki[11] who have presented sharply diverging thesis as to who were the pioneering and benaficiary classes in the Green Revolution that took place in Pakistan during Ayub Khan's regime. New Para Burki's contention is that it was the 'rural middle class' whom Burki defines as farmers who own between 50 and 100 acres. Prof. Alavi does not dispute the contention that the middle farmers utilized their inputs much more efficiently than the large farmers. He argues that the political aims of the two are not at variance with each other. But Alavi disputes Burki's contention that the Ayub Khan's land reforms have significantly shifted the power balance away from the big landlords. Burki's analysis, thus suffers from what he himself accuses other analysists to be guilty of, viz, "too much aggregation".

Pakistan has been substantially affected by new crop varieties over the last 15-20 years; it also benefitted from a boom in the use of tubewell beginning in the late 1950's and permiting a significant expansion of irrigation facilities.

Estimates of relative productivity and employment generation in Pakistani farms of different size as based mainly on estimates from data provided in the 1959-60 agricultural census on micro data from the Punjab Farm Accounts and Family Budget Survey (hereafter referred to as (FAFBS) on a recent survey and analysis by M.H. Khan[12] and on the 1972 agricultural census. Both the 1959-60 agricultural census and micro evidence available from the Punjab FAFBS indicate a negative relationship between size of the farm and value of output per acre. A substantial part of the negative relationship between farm size and land productivity emerging from these data is due to aggregation process but there is no strong suggestion that it can be wholly explained in this way. Both the Census data and FAFBS data point to the same correlates of the lower productivity of large farms lower cultivated area relative to total area, lower cropping intensity (cropped area/net sown area), lower share of output from livestock, and lower ratio of labour to land.[13]

In Pakistan there is evidence that mechanisation has led to the growth in farm size using tractors. A survey jointly conducted by the World Bank and Agricultural Development Bank of Pakistan (ADBP) of farmers who received loans to purchase tractors, showed that there was a 142 per cent increase in the average size of such farms, from 45 to 109 acres. Only 10 per cent of the farms did not increase their average. The sources of additional land were :

Previously uncultivated land	:	22 per cent
Previously rented out land	:	42 per cent
Newly rented in land	:	24 per cent
Newly purchased land	:	12 per cent

The big farmer bias of the tractor mechanisation programme in Pakistan has also been noted by Professor Hamza Alvai.[14] He points out that those districts of Punjab which have above average size holdings were also the districts where tractors were concentrated.

Although the government's policy has been to encourage the use of tractors, principally by providing credit on easy terms, the number of tractors is not very large. Although the present rate of growth of tractors and the consequent displacement effects on employment are not very high as compared to the total labour force in the rural economy, the trend towards greater use of mechanical power and the rural development strategy implies the causes of great concern. As pointed out by Prof. Johstan and Carnie, it will lead to a dualistic pattern within agriculture in which increases in productivity and output will be concentrated to a large extent in a sub-sector of large-scale, capital-intensive farm enterprises, instead of being equitably shared by the majority of farmers.[15]

As is well-known, the major problem in developing agriculture, like Pakistan, is under-employment rather than unemployment. In spite of the fact the agricultural production in the last three decades has grown at a compound rate of 2.8 per cent and since 1960 at the rate of 2.6 per cent per annum, the degree of under-employment have increased over time. Professor J.J. Stern estimated under-employment in agriculture to be 23.3 per cent in 1960-61. He assumed that a fully employed man in agriculture works for 2,600 hours each year.[16] He also assumed that the average hours required per cropped acre is 395. Thus the amount of land required to keep a person fully employed is a little over 6 acres. According to different calculations, under-employment in the agricultural sector in Parkistan has increased overtime, rising upto 28.33 per cent in 1970, with increase in population. As a result of an increase in yield per acre, due to Green Revolution, there has been an increase in labour requirements per unit of land. Dr. Dilawar A. Khan has in a study for Punjab,[17] the heart of Green Revolution estimated that as a result of increase in crop activity caused by the Green Revolution during the 1960's there was an addition of 1.22 million man years of employment per year. Even this was only half the increase in agricultural labour force during this period.

A more recent estimate of under-employment has been attempted by the I.L.O. Employment Strategy Mission Report based over the 1972 Agricultural Census Data. The Report finds that 26.7 per cent of those operating small farms were under employed in 1972 a total of over 2 million or some 27 per cent of the family workers.[18]

In the First Five Year Plan the development of agriculture was the most important task. Production growth was to be ensured through expansion of the sown areas and also through use of mineral fertilizers, improved seed varieties, etc. Under the Second Five Year Plan about 15 per cent of all expenditures of the private and public sector were allocated for the development of agriculture, a greater part of these funds being invested in fertilizer production, the purchase of improved seed varieties and agricultural implements and equipment for tube wells.[19]

In the first half of the 1960's more attention was devoted to irrigation. During this period high yielding grain varieties adapted to local conditions were evolved on the basis of Philoppine and Mexican wheat. The prerequisite of Green Revolution were provided in the first half of the 1960's when more fertilizers began to be used, new farming teehniques were introduced and irrigation was developed. The development of the Green Revolution marked a qualitative leap in the development of the agricultural productive forces. The introduction of high-yielding varieties of cereals required considerably greater application of chemical fertilizers. During the Third Five Year Plan (1965-70) this became one of the basic factors in expanding agricultural production. Non plan period (1970-78) was marked by many institutional changes to increase the productivity of food grains and also efforts were made to diversify the crops, multiple cropping was encouraged.

In the Fifth Plan (1978-83) agricultural growth rate was roughly 4.4 per cent per annum against the plan target of 6 per cent. There was an impressive growth recorded in the four major crops viz. wheat, rice, sugarcane and cotton.[20] Roughly 80 per cent of the major crop target for incremental production envisaged in the Fifth Plan were actually raised according to published data. Difficulty was however, experienced in extending the dynamics of agricultural change to what are regarded as minor crops, notably pulses and traditional oil seeds crops. Shortfalls were also experienced in the live stock (other than poultry) and fishery sector.[21]

Twenty months were a nightmare for the farmers of Pakistan under Benazir Bhutto. They were victims of the politicians who were not only averse to agricultural progress but also excelled in nepotism, the parallel of which cannot be traced in the history of Pakistan just 44 years.[22]

They were not only inefficient and incompetent but were also lacking vision. They could not plan, could not stand up against foreign influences and foreign dominations, could not resist monetary temptations, could not keep their relatives and friends at bay from decision makings, but worse than that they plundered the sector to the extent that once again we are short of food and the farmers are in a state of distress. Most of them are in debt and many are out of business. This, in brief, is the balance-sheet of the performance and conduct of federal agricultural ministry which the new government has inherited. Agriculture sector has been the worst to suffer.

As a field farmer, I take the liberty to think which could assist, to some extent, the planners of the Nawar Sharif government.

1. Small farmers and landless farmers must become the local point of all policies, short and longterm planning and all decisions of federal agriculture ministry.

2. De-urbanisation and employment of the rural youth being corrupted and degenerated in cities must immediately be undertaken or it will be too late to save cities from rural population pressures and robust young villagers from becoming city vagabonds.

3. Agro-based industries must be installed in rural areas specially to process farm waste products like sugar-cane bagasse, rice straw, wheat straw, cotton sticks, paddy husk and many other such wastes. These should be evenly spread over the country specially the rainfed regions and the backward tracts. This will not only improve the economy but also such back the rural population from cities where they are misfits and alien to urban environments.

4. Cost of production of crops must immediately be brought down drastically so that small farmers could afford inputs and implement recommendations of farm specialists without any hesitance. Instead of raising periodically support prices of crops which is not well reckoned both in home and foreign markets, resolve should be made to bring down prices of inputs thus enabling the small and the landless farmers to raise the yields. A bold policy for lowering inputs prices will

enable the government to slash down support prices resulting in plenty and cheap farm products both for our city consumers and for foreign markets, thus saving previous foreign exchange earnings.

5. Inputs warehouses on premises of all rural bank branches for giving loans in kind to small farmers to set up loans have to be closely linked with inputs. Bank loans to small farmers and landless should be forthcoming without reluctance and any reservations, and should not be linked with recoveries. All farm loans for productions should not be encumbered with mark ups'.

6. RECP and CTC should be made more aggressive for buying paddy and seed cotton from farmers fields. Their monopoly should be completely broken and they must in competition with private sector function in fields for purchases. Every grain, cereal, fibres and seed that farmers produce must immediately be bought through field purchasing centres set up in heart-lands of production areas. Payment should be made through banks. PASSCO and food departments should also be involved to buy paddy and not rice. Farm marketing, the weakest link, must be revalutionised to benefit small farmers.

7. A branch of the International Basmati Rice Research Institute in the rice bowl of Pakistan should be established for linking research with production marketing and exports will once again help to recapture our lost basmati markets abroad because of quality control.

8. Agricultural attaches should be accredited to countries which excel in crops like wheat, rice, cotton, oilseeds, dairy products, livestocks, tropical forests, etc. They must serve as agricultural intelligence abroad.

9. Crops-cattle insurances must be launched in fields. There has been too much of waiting for it benefiting poor

farmers. A system to compensate farmers immediately be evolved who suffer heavy losses caused by natural calamities.

10. Cotton and rice tracts must also develop on the pattern of sugarcane growing areas. In fact research and development share in term of cess must come out of earnings made by major crops exports. Research must be taken to fields and should shun "show window" concept.

11. Agriculture and livestock graduates must under an incentive scheme be encouraged to become field workers and assist to raise yields-per acre specially of small farmers. Agricultural scientists like other scientists should be given status and recognitions to form the elite of our society. Pri vate field consultances by our retired scientists should be encouraged and financed.

12. Quality and price control of chemical fertilizers and pesticides must be exercised strictly. Cypsum, the cheapest mode to reclaiming salined tracts – fields, should be heavily subsidised. Small farmers deserve this concession and it cannot be denied to them any longer.

13. Foodgrains, edible oils, dairy products and other farm praducts in deficit must received immediate attention as we cannot afford to waste our meagre foreign exchange on their imports. Crash programme projects linked up with incentive schemes will help to overcome shortfalls.

14. 'Barani' tracts deserve special attention special status and plenth of funds, population explosion can only be looked after and met by rain-fed regions. Long-term planning must concentrate on these tracts.

15. Deserts must be converted into forests and not be utilised for crops. Plantation of rich commercial forests and de-desertification will to a great extent employ the unemployed rural manpower. Poor kind plantations of America done in early thirties is an example to follow.

By all means industrialise Pakistan intensively and extensively but do not concentrate wealth and manpower in cities. Industries, manpower, wealth and talent must be widely and fairly spread all over the country. Dynamic youthful leadership can definitely change the face of the countryside and make agriculture attractive, paying and the country a 'food basket' for the Third World countries, if only agricultural planning is more indigenous and rural oriented. Agricultural industry is our 'mainstay' therefore please no more politicisation to hamper its progress. Revolutionary and unconventional approach is the solution to pick up and reactivate the sluggish sector.[23]

Even though it is beset with several formidable economic problems that merit urgent attention, the Banazir Government will have to address itself without delay to the task of resolving problems facing Pakistan's agriculture. Though Pakistan has done reasonably will in this field, stable self-sufficiency in foodgrans has yet to be achieved and hence the need for occasional food imports. The policies followed over the past several years have led to lop-sided development of agriculture. Population pressure on land has been rising unabated, aggravating the problem of unemployment. The gaping deficit of edible oils is gradually widening. So is indeed the case of some other essential items like pulses, sugar and milk. The urgency of rejuvenating agriculture can be gauged from a succinct observation made by Pakistan's National Commission on Agriculture in its final report that even if the current average annual growth rate of 3.8 per cent on the farm front is sustained, this would not permit much improvement in the standard of living of a growing population. The commission was headed by an internationally respected agricultural economist Mr. Sartaz Aziz. The commission adds that the present population growth rate of 3 per cent a year would make it extremely difficult to provide a balanced diet and still produce surpluses for exports without a considerable acceleration in the pace of agricultural production. The commission does not mince words in pointing out some significant policy lapses of the past. Though the importance of agriculture was recognised, it had "never been regarded as a leading sector". Even within the farm sector, the policies guiding research, as also pricing and other commercial aspects, have been directed towards the staple, wheat, and traditional foreign exchange earners like cotton and rice but little attention has been paid to the wide range of high value crops that could be adapted to Pakistan's agro-climate conditions.[24]

"Oilseeds represent the most notable agricultural policy failure of the past," says the commission. From a position of self-sufficiency, the country has now turned into a major importer of edible oils with imports currently accounting for as mush as 65 per cent of domestic consumption. In a striking similarity with the Indian experience, the edible oil crunch in Pakistan is the result of faulty pricing policy. Due to an excessive concern for the consumer's pocket, the prices of vegetable oils have been deliberately kept low, encouraging a rapid increase in domestic consumption and a loss of interest among growers in raising oilseeds production. As in India, the green revolution in Pakistan has been confined only to a few crops. The major difference perhaps is that while India realised this anomaly years ago and started taking measures to rectify it, awareness of the shortcoming in Pakistan is only recent. The success of the green revolution, triggered off in the late 1960s thanks chiefly to the availability of widely adapted high-yielding and fertiliser-responsive crop varieties, was made possible in both countries by three factors in particular, effective price support for major crops; subsidies to popularise new inputs; and enhanced credit facilities enabling farmers to adopt modern inputs and technology. While India has managed to develop an agricultural research network counted among the largest in the world, Pakistan's research infrastructure, notwithstanding its rapid expansion over the decades, has kept its priorities limited to a narrow range. The neglect of crops such as oilseeds, maize, sugarcane, pulses, fruits and vegetables, besides subsidiary agricultural occupations like animal husbandry, has cost the country heavily. Though the prices of meat have been kept under check to some extent, thanks to the development of a poultry industry, the shortages of other commodities and their prices have been on the rise. Even in areas where research in agriculture has been undertaken on a significant scale, the transfer of technology to the farmers has been inadequate due to a stereotyped approach to extension. The training and visit system of extension, tried out in several developing countries with a fair degree of success, has posed several insurmountable problems in Pakistan. To top it all, direct public investment in agriculture has declined over the years from 9.5 per cent of the total public investment expenditure in the country's first plan to a mere 4 per cent in the fifth plan. It indeed went down further to 3 per cent in the just concluded sixth plan. Farmers have time and again suffered from price controls designed to keep down the urban cost of living. Notwithstanding subsidies, about 40 to 60 per cent of value added in agriculture in estimated to have been transferred out of this sector in the past 25 years, the beneficiaries being the manufacturing sector, urban consumers and the government. It will be an uphill task for the government to reverse this trend, especially at a stage when the overall economy is facing a severe resource constraint, But the commission feels that this has to be done. The capacity of agriculture to meet domestic demand and generate an expert surplus can be restored only if the agricultural growth rate is stepped up from 3.8 per cent to about 5 per cent in the remaining years of the current century and the rate of population growth brought down from the present 3 per cent to about 2.5 per cent. The three-pronged goal set by Pakistan's National Commission on Agriculture before the nation aims at raising the status of small farmers, expanding employment in rural areas and boosting farm exports. Both private and public investment in agriculture must be stepped up greatly to bring about technological changes necessary for increasing agricultural production at 5 per cent. "Without such an increase, 'the country's requirements of food, raw materials and exports would not be met."[25]

Among the sources of agricultural growth in Pakistan, water resource development and, since 1976, fertilizer and new seeds have a prominent role. In addition, the Government has been active in providing incentives for higher production through increase in support prices for major crops, subsidies to yield augmenting inputs like fertilizers, seeds and insecticides and, through the provision of subsidized credit, for capital inputs such as tubewells and tractors. It was the Government's policy to reverse the unfavourable term of trade against agriculture and this policy has been largely successful. The effect on employment and income distribution of the various technological innovations in Pakistan agriculture have varied with their diffusion among different classes of farmers. The inputs of tube wells, fertilizer and new seeds require a considerable amount of investment on the part of farmers. The ability to reap benefits of technological break through thus depends on the ability to mobilise enough resources, either through saving or borrowing, for undertaking such investment. Although technology itself is not biased towards big farmers, institutional arrangements such as access to credit and scare inputs to give large farmers an advantage. The high incidence of tenancy may also have reduced the incentives to invest in these inputs.[26]

Land ownership being highly concentrated and bureaucratic controls being widespread in Pakistan, access to the key inputs is directly proportional to the size of one's land holding.[27] Even the cooperatives and other Government Department tend to discriminate against the small farmers. Many studies of the Green Revolution in Pakistan have claimed, however, that despite the bias of the administrative setting there has been broad-based participation of small farmers in at least the initial stages of seed, fertilizer revolution.[28] There is some evidence which exhibite that small and marginal farmers have lagged a year or so behind the big farmers in adopting the new techniques and that their application of fertilizer per acre has been lower than that of large farmers.

Regarding tubewells, the diffusion of technology has been less uniform. Subsidised credit available for the purchase of tubewells has gone mainly to large farmers, because of standard of credit worthiness imposed by the lending agencies, the greater familiarity of large farmers with the procedure of obtaining credit and because of their ability to obtain from the Government, electricity to run the pumps. According to Farm Mechanization Survey of 1986, 70 per cent of the tubewells in Pakistan were installed by farmers having more than 25 acres. Only 4 per cent were installed by the size group ranging from 0 to 13 acres — the group that includes more than two third of Pakistan cultivators.[29]

The development of agricultural sector in Pakistan has been satisfactory to a great extent. But at the same time agrarian structure has marginally changed in favour of poor and marginal farmers. The New Technology, Mechanization of farm and private Tube Wells have led to capitalistic mode of production relation in the agricultural sector of Pakistan. Though much of the literature on the so-called Green Revolution suggests that this new Technology is scale neutral, however, this may be so at a purely technological level. The actual effect which the New Technology has on the size distribution of farm in any particular society depends upon the prevailing pattern of land ownership and the social organization of agricultural production. In Pakistan, the agrarian structure is characterized. In Pakistan, the agrarian structure is characterized by a highly skewed distribution of landownership and a pattern of extensive renting out of land to tenants. 0.5 per cent of land owners own 30 per cent of total cultivated area. In such a situation where the High Yielding Varieties Technology (H.Y.V.) became available and made owner-cultivation highly profitable, there emerged a tendency for structural changes in favour of large farmers. The availability of the H.Y.V. Technology along with subsidized tractors, induced large owners to resume their formerly rented out land for owner cultivation on large tractorized farms. The resultant changes in the size of distribution of farms and changes in the production relations generated a powerful process growing affluence of the big farmers simultaneously with the pauperization of the poor peasantry.[30]

When the 1960 Agriculture Census (adjusted for biases inherent in its methodology) is compared with the 1972 Agriculture Census, a picture of polarization in the size distribution of farm emerges, i.e. the percentage share of small farm in total farms area and that of large farms has increased while the percentage share of medium sized farms has declined.[31] The fact that many small farms were disintegrating under the impact of tenant eviction is indicated by the rapid increase in landlessness over the period. While attempt at land reforms have been made on three previous occasions, the resultant land re-distribution has not been regarded, as effective by observers who are of the view that agricultural growth have been accelerated through effective implementation of a judicious package of land reforms. Another unhealthy feature is the inability to fix an economically viable minimum size of holdings.

According to Economic Survey 86-87 agricultural production increased by 6.5 per cent in 1985-86. During the first four years of the Sixth Plan, an average growth rate of 4.4 per cent has been raised against plan target of 4.9 per cent. This is attributed to excellent performance in the crop sector particularly wheat, cotton, maize and gram. Table-I indicates growth rate in the production of the these crops from 1982-83 to 1986-87.[32]

The total cropped area in Pakistan is around 19.81 million hectares and average cropping intensity is 97 per cent. Only 21.3 per cent of the cultivated area is double cropped while 25 per cent is fallow. Some 15.62 million hectares of the cultivated area (or 75.8%) is irrigated of which 11.34 hecrares if irrigated from the indus valley canal command and 4.28 million hectares from other sources.

According to 1980 Agriculture Census there are 4.07 million farms in the country of which half (50.9%) are smaller than 3.0 hectares, accounting for 15.5 per cent of all farm land. Owners operate 2.2 million farms (55 per cent of private farms) and 52 per cent of the farm area (9.9 million hectares) owners cum tenants operate 0.8 million farms and 26 per cent of the farm area (5 million hectares). The remaining 1.1 million farms are operated by tenents who operate 22 per cent of the farm area (4.1 million hectares) and 26.8

per cent of these are less than 5 hectares in area. Thus, 45 per cent of the farmers in Pakistan rent all or part of the farmland which they cultivate.[33] Table-3 shows number, area and average size of private farms classified by tenure 1980.

Table 3.1

Number, Area and Average Size of Private Farms Classified by Tenure 1980

	Farms		*Farm Area*		*Average Size*
Unit of tenus	*Number Million*	*Share %*	*Hectores Million*	*Share %*	*Hectores*
Owner cultivator	2.23	55	9.93	52	4.5
Owner cum Tenants	0.79	19	5 02	26	6 4
Tenants	1.05	26	4 11	22	3.9
Total	4.07	100	19.06	100	4.68

Source: Agriculture Census, 1980, *Government of Pakistan, Islamabad.*

Population explosion, Pakistanis eating habits, turbulent Gulf situation, cooling-off of relations with old friends and our resolve to become exporters of food and self-sufficient in all crops that our rich vast tracts can grow are such issues that need urgent attention. The new government must give a serious thought to raising of low yields marring agricultural progress generally. National crop averages are very low because over 70 per cent small landless farmers cannot afford or cannot get on time 'input package' as recommended by agricultural specialists. Average difference between affluent and small farmers is very much on the high side. This desparity will continue unless some one in the government immediately had looked into the entire crops production strategy and radically changed it in favour of the small farmers. They are the ones who matter and deserve fair treatment. The issue is whether cheap inputs package will help small farmers to raise their yields or high support prices. The answer is that slashing, down of inputs prices will definitely not only increase acreage under crops but also produce required results of at least doubling national averages. The political approach of appeasing the farmers community by raising support prices having no relation with costs of production, periodically should be suspended. It will not help, on the contrary it will cause undue hardships to urban consumers at home and decrease quantum of exports abroad reducing drastically foreign exchange earnings. Our foreign friends will not desire that we should be surplus in farm products, specially food, because they have to dump their huge extras in Third World countries because of the economic interests — political pressures of their farmers and also the International politics.[34]

In any country in the Third World can compete against agriculturally advanced countries, specially America, it is no other country but Pakistan. The World Bank, IMF, the Asian Development Bank and such other international financial empires are there to look after the interests of their sponsors, financiers and their own people. Therefore we are always under their surveillance and sway. We in subordination to their interests, plans, policies and decisions must continue to suffer deficit in most crops. This is best achieved by making chemical fertilisers including expensive gypsum, seeds exorbitantly priced, electricity beyond small farmers reach, irrigation water scantly and dear, pesticides criminally retailed, agricultural machinery obsolete and the most expensive in the world, diesel adulterated and over-valued: production loans not forthcoming and high service charges imposed definitely a disincentive in their utilisation; farm technology foreign and expensive and for the rich West. This is no prescription to raise national yields closely linked to average yields of small farmers. Decisions are ours and not of those who on their loans charge us interests which have definitely not only ruined our farm economics but have completely subordinated our agricultural sector to their interests. We have our local problems, and those have to be solved by us in consultation with our own people with a purely indigenous approach. Therefore a practical farmer recommends. "Bring down support prices, provide complete low-priced inputs package on time as a loan in kind, in pure form close to his fields and get it back from him in kind at harvest time." It will definitely result in foreign exchange reserves rising: We exporting food; small farm economies getting a boost and more rural population getting involved in farming and thuse de-urbanisation. To allay fears of the concerned cynic economists; what we lose on bringing down prices of inputs drastically. We will save our precious foreign exchange manifold on not importing, and many times make more in foreign exchange on exports.[35]

Dr. Ghulam Rasool Chaudhry Secretary Agriculture Punjab has exhorted the agriculturists to redouble their efforts, to meet the challenges of population explosion in Pakistan. Presiding over a National Wheat Seminar in Ayub Agriculture Research Institute (AARI) Faisalabad on November 6, 1990 he said that China and India had surpringly increased their agriculture production upto six times only during the preceding year by exploiting hi-tech.

He said that these results are an open challenge which could be faced only through collective and concerted efforts. He told that East Punjab shares common socio-economic and environmental climates hence we could also achieve increase in our per acre yield as obtained in the neighbouring country.

Secretary, Agriculture, further told that Punjab Govt. is committed to provide every possible facility to agriculturists and it is our moral and national duty to work for the self-sufficiency in wheat production. He disclosed that AARI and University of Agriculture would be converted into centres of excellence, and strengthened to play their pivotal role for attaining self-sufficiency in agriclture production.

He told that under this programme both of these institutions would be provided with ample funds to carry out their research activities for evolving new wheat varieties and modern technology to increase our per acre yield.

Earlier, inaugurating the one-day Seminar on Wheat Research and Production the Vice-Chancellor, University of Agriculture, Dr. Abdur Rehman said that the demand for wheat in this country was going to increase manifold in the years to come with increase in population which is likely to double early by the end of 20th century.

Dr. Rehman further said that in the year 2000 we would need over 18 million tonnes of wheat for our own consumption. Since possibilities for increasing wheat acreage are limited the increase in production will have to come from higher acre yields which is a function of genetic, agronomic and economic manipulations, he added. We have all the necessary resources, human institutional, physical and material. There is nothing wrong with them but what is at fault seems to be their inadequate mobilisation and ineffective application, he explained. In spite of our struggle to make them click, perhaps, we are taking it easy, by default and by design. Nevertheless, our wheat breeders have made splendid contributions in the form of evolution of a series of new wheat varieties adapted to different production situations in the country, he said.

Dr. Rehman stressed upon the scientists to manage properly the varieties which have the potential to raise yields significantly to make all the difference.

The Peasant Commission on November 20, 1990 recommended to the Punjab Government to revive the panchayat system though in a greatly modified and effective form to provide quick and cheap justice to the rural people living in over 25,000 villages in the province and to lesson the workload on the police and the judiciary by about 90 per cent.

The Peasant Commission has also drafted a bill to introduce this system of justice and presented it to the Punjab Chief Minister. The draft law is now under consideration of the Provincial Government.

To run the system, the Commission has proposed the appointment of "*Panchs*" and "*Munsifs*", the later with powers of a senior civil judge as well as a first class magistrate. The "Munsif" will work under the district judge. The Commission has also outlined a comprehensive blueprint of the procedure of appeals against their decisions.

The following are the salient features of the proposed judicial system :

The Procedure of Panchayats: first information. All cases, both civil and criminal, will be reported to the village Panchayat and entered in a register maintained for the purpose. The Sarpanch or any member of the Panchayat will be informed.

The Sarpanch or, in his absence, any member, who gets the information about a criminal offence, will immediately call a meeting of the Panchayat. The meeting will be open to all.

The preliminary meeting will try to find out what actually happened and how. The victims, the witnesses and all others who have any knowledge about any aspect of the incident will give details. The offenders, if known, in case of fights or disputes will also be asked to be present in the meeting.

Then the Panchayat members will come to a conclusion and will announce their judgement. If the Panchayat has final powers in a matter, no appeal will be against its judgement.

In all criminal cases, the Panchayat will send its report to the Munsif and the SHO of the relevant Thana and ask both of them to visit the village as soon as possible, but not later than seven days. On the day indicated by the Munsif, an open meeting will be held in the village.

The *Munsif* will record all statements and examine the entire evidence.

The *Munsif* will announce his judgement and prepare his report on the spot and give one copy each to the Panchayat and the SHO right there. If the accused is/are found guilty, the munsif will order their arrest and the police will take them into custody on the spot.

In a criminal case (such as murder), the SHO will take the initial Panchayat and Munsif report (with its preliminary findings) as the FIR. He will proceed further on the lines of the two reports. He will not deviate from the two reports unless some substantial evidence to the contrary becomes available to him. Even then, he will have to consult both the Panchayat and the Munsif before taking the new evidence into proper consideration.

The Munsif's will be a new office, dealing with all criminal and civil cases that occur in the villages and are beyond the final jurisdiction of the Panchayats. He will have power of a senior civil judge and a first class magistrate and will have powers of both. He will hear evidence, record statements and give judgement on the spot. An appeal could be filed with the district judge against his judgement.

There will be a district judge dealing with both civil and criminal cases in a district. There will be additional judges under him if the number of cases justify it. They will have same powers as the district judge. Appeals against the judgements of the district judge and the additional judges will be only with the High Court.

Addressing the NGO workshop organised by the Rural Development Foundation, Malik Miraj Khalid has called for a village development movement to end the rural urban disparities. To his credit, the former Speaker of the National Assembly could not have chosen a more appropriate word for the kind of effort required to close the rural-urban gap in development opportunities. Nothing short of a movement to resuscitate the national will can take up the inequality in development approach we have endorsed in past years Mobilising a total change in outlook requires a vertical reform in all the policy fixtures, starting from education and resource development to industrialisation and employment opportunity and the whole gamut of issues that fall in between. The life-giving mass mobilisation formula anticipates no less than a nation-wide network of voluntary help, which is where the NGO function comes in handy. But that also is too limited in scope to provide the mobilisation equated with a 'movement'. There is a view that this mobilisation will come automatically with equal opportunity in education and a long-term investment in rural economy. It is also apparent that without a will for change at the grass roots such development projects can be subverted or modified to insignificance. Verbal mileage can too often substitute for change, unless the rural public is the Prime mover of the change. How the new government formulates its policy to mobilise voluntary help for rural reforms is what will distinguish it from others that paid mere lip-service to the issue.[36]

The Federal Minister for Education, Law, Justice and Parliamentary Affairs, Syed Fakhar Imam, has said that the main thrust of the IjI manifesto is to provide maximum facilities of life to the people. The present IJI government of Nawaz Sharif would make its best efforts to bring about quality in education, eliminate poverty in education, eliminate poverty and unemployment from the society to fulfil all its promises made to the people, he said.

Addressing a reception hosted in his honour by the people of Serai Sandhu, Multan, on November 16, 1990 he said that the people had changed the direction of politics in the couuntry for the first time. The government would now put in its best efforts to solve the problems facing the people and come upto their expectations, he said.

He said that the present government would provide inexpensive and quick justice to the people to resolve this problem.

The Chairman, Municipal Committee, Serai Sadhu, Rao Tariq Iqbal, presented the address of welcome.

At village Fasil Shah, near Kabirwala, the Minister also addressed a big gathering of the people and assured them that he would do his best to get solved all their problems, including provision of PCO at village Fasil Shah under the annual development programme. He also said that a programme of training teachers at the federal level would also be started soon. He said that the literacy rate in India is 38 per cent, and in Bangladesh 37 per cent, but unfortunately it is only 28 per cent in our country. We would spare no efforts in increasing the rate of literacy in Pakistan, he declared.

Dr. Muhammad Shareef presented the problems of the area. The Minister also addressed receptions at Abdul Hakeem and village Bindi Sargana.

Prime Minister Nawaz Sharif expressed the hope that they would make efforts to bring the country to the path of progress and prosperity and work for the welfare of the common man.

References

1. Raashidi Lateef. An opportunity, *The Nation*, 18 November, 1990.
2. F. Babar. Broadening Revenue Base, *Muslim*, 16 November, 1990.
3. *Ibid.*

4. Planning Commission, Pakistan. *The 5th Five-Year Plan*, Islamabad, 1978.
5. Khan, M.H. *The Economic of Green Revolution in Pakistan*, New York, 1975.
6. See *The 5th Five Year Plan.*
7. Abdullah, A. *The Historical Background of Pakistan and its People*, Karachi, 1973.
8. Asmi Raza. Economics of Agricultural Development in Pakistan. *Third Concept*, May 1989.
9. *Land Reforms During Ayub Khan Regime*, Islamabad, 1959.
10. Alavi, H. and P. Bevtocie; *eds*, *Rural Development in Bangladesh and Pakistan*, Hawai, 1976.
11. *Ibid.*
12. M.H. Khan. *The Economics of the Green Revolution in Pakistan*, New York, 1975.
13. Asmi Raza. *Op.cit.*
14. B. Johnson and J. Cawnie, *Op.cit.*
15. Raza, Asmi. *Op.cit.*
16. J J. Stern. *Employment by Regions and Sectors, 1969-75.* (Mimeographed)
17. Slavi, H. *The Rural Elite and Agricultural Development in Pakistan*, Karachi, 1976.
18. *Employment Strategy*: *Pakistan*, Geneva, I.L.O., 1975.
19. *Government and Economic Development*, London, 1971.
20. Planning Commission Pakistan. *The 6th Five-Year Plan*, Islamabad, 1983.
21. *Ibid.*
22. S.M. Hussain. Agricultural Sector. *Pakistan Times*, 15 November, 1990.
23. *Ibid.*
24 Surinder Sud. New Blueprint for Pak Agriculture. *Times of India*, 17 May, 1989.
25. *Ibid.*
26. Raza, Asmi. Economics of Agricultural Development in Pakistan. *Third Concept*, May 1989.
27 Johnson, Band J. Cownie. The Seed Fertilizer Revolution and Labour Absorption AER, September 1969.
28. Naseem, S M. *Rural Poverty in Pakistan*, Geneva, I.L.O., 1977.
29. *The Consequences of Farm Tractors in Pakistan*, Lahore, 1972.
30. Azfar, Jawed. The Distribution of Income in Pakistan, 1966-67. *Pakistan Economic and Social Review*, 14(1), Spring, 1973.

31. A. Hussain. *The Agrarian Structure of Pakistan*, D. Phil. Thesis, Sussex, 1980.

32. Ministry of Finance, Pakistan. *Economic Survey, 1986-87*, Islamabad, 1986.

33. Alavi, M. *The Rural Elite and Agricultural Development in Pakistan*, Karachi, 1976.

34. S.M. Hussain. Farmer Corner. *Pakistan Times*, 19 November, 1990.

35. *Ibid.*

36. *The Nation*, 17 November, 1990.

4

Industrialisation—Structural Changes

A new class of industrialists has come of age. The process was started by President Mohammad Ayub Khan whollaboured hard and launched the first phase of modern industrial economy in the country through a handsome package of incentives viz. liberal licensing, import of machinery, equipment and technical know-how, and prolonged tax holiday. The result was evident. Nawaz Sharif is the second leader who has perceived the need for a full-fledged industrial revolution. It is to be sincerely and fervently hoped that industrialist bureaucrats and others will extend him full co-operation in the uplift of the impoverished Pakistan.

The election of Nawaz Sharif, Chief of the IJI, as the Prime Minister of Pakistan, on November 7, 1990 was widely welcomed by the trade and industry circles.

Majyd Aziz Balagamwala, Chairman of Pakistan's largest industrial sector, the SITE Association of Industry while felicitating Mian Nawaz Sharif said that this is the occasion for which the industrialists and the businessmen were waiting since long.

The SITE Chairman said that Nawaz Sharif originally an industrialist, who has already gone through the cumbresome procedures of taxation faced by the industrialists and other bureaucratic bottlenecks, will defintely come out with the radical and structural changes to put our economy on the right track.

He expressed the hope that the dynamic leadership of Nawaz Sharif will not only solve the economic problems but also help bringing national integrity by uniting the various segments of the society.

He expressed the hope that Pakistan will emerge as a strong nations under the able leadership of Mian Nawaz Sharif.

Manzar Alam Shaikh, Chairman Pak-Bahrain Trade Committee of the Federation of Pakistan Chambers and Industry and the member of the Managing Committee KCCI while felicitating Nawaz Sharif on his historic role in Pakistan's politics said that Almighty Allah has not only saved the country as a result of the recent elections but has given national leader in the shape of Mian Nawaz Sharif. He said that as a matter of fact there was a total vaccum in the national politics in the absense of a leadership acceptable to all the four provinces of the country.

Shaikh, while expressing his full confidence in the leadership of Mian Nawaz Sharif, said that he will not only emerge as a strong man of the country but would also be binding force of the Muslim world.

He said that the trade and business community feels proud that for the first time in the history of Pakistan the Prime Minister has emerged from their country.

Shaukat Ahmed, Chairman Pakistan Plastic Manufacturers Association and the Chairman of Lasbella Association of Trade and Industry has also congratulated Mian Nawaz Sharif and said that the day has arrived when the nation can hope for the betterment of the common men.

He said that the efforts and struggle demonstrated by Nawaz Sharif for the socio-economic uplift to Punjab during his tenure of chief ministership of Punjab, will now reflect from all over the country.

Liaquat Jangda, Chairman Pakistan Readymade Garments Manufacturers and Exporters Association while felicitating Mian Nawaz Sharif on assumption of office as the Prime Minister of Pakistan has said that the well known zeal of Nawaz Sharif and his dedication for industry production and exports, the trade and industry community looking forward to speedy allround industrialisation in the country for ameliorating the economic condition of our people.

He said that the nation after passing through a nightmare is now hoping for a bright future of the country.

Prime Minister, Nawaz Sharif has announced that tax holiday would be enforced throughout the country, to create congenial atmosphere for free industrialisation.

Addressing the nation, over radio and television, on November 7, 1990 Prime Minister Nawaz Sharif said that his government would also transfer nationalised sick industrial units to the private sector, which were not only an impediment in the way of free industrialisation in the country but also a burden on the national exchequer. It was ironical, he said, that these sick units were eating away billions of rupees of public money. He said that he wished that even the defence equipment should also be produced by the private sector, leaving aside only sensitive material. Pakistan industrialists, he said, were capable of producing everything within the country. If private companies of other countries could produce defence material for Pakistan, why this could not be done by the Pakistani industrialise themselves.

Prime Minister Nawaz Sharif also announced that the domestic and foreign entrepreneurs, setting up new industrial units in the country, would be given complete tax holiday, with the condition that they would take responsibility of the health and education of the workers and their children.

Prime Minister Nawaz Sharif said that the present oppressive economic system would be changed under which millions of people in the country were groaning.

He said that this cruel system would be replaced by the economic system of Islam based on justice which could bring happiness on the face of the common man.

He said it was his faith that so long as happiness and prosperity was not reflected from the face of a common man, the face of Pakistan could never glow with happiness.

Nawaz Sharif made it clear that the enforcement of Islamic principles would no longer be a slogan and these would practically be implemented.

He said that Zakat and Ushr would be utilised in fulfilling the needs of the deserving persons and for the education of the children.

He said that the Government was bound by Constitution as well to enforce Islamic laws. He said he was mentioning those bright and golden principles of Islamic Shariat which could bring equality and create equal opportunities for the society and the principles which would eleminate the poverty and ignorance.

Nawaz Sharif announced that residents of all recognised katchi abadies throughout the country, would be given proprietary rights.

He said that he had also decided that the hutments would not be allowed to remain in shabby and sub-human conditions. It would be his effort to enable the residents of these Katchi abadies to live in conditions with necessary civic facilities.

He has, therefore, decided to set up development authorities, for katchi abadies, on the pattern of KDA CDA and LDA. These authorities, he said, would be responsible for providing wholesome water to these abadies, besides making arrangements for the disposal of sewer water.

He said that these authorities would also provide Sui-gas, transport and pucca roads, in these abadies wherever possible.

Prime Minister Nawaz Sharif also announced that his government would provide residential plots to the people, who did not have own houses, on cheap rates and on easy instalments. The poor and widows would be given reference in such schemes, he added.

Nawaz Sharif said that he was conscious that the housing problem was an extremely difficult aspect of human life, especially for the have nots. He had many proposals and plans to solve this problem on a large-scale basis, throughout the country.

Nawaz Sharif said in Karachi, on November 11, 1990 that he will embark upon a crash programme of industrialisation. In order to encourage it, he announced that from now on no permission will be needed to set up an industry no matter what its size. He said that the government will endeavour to provide all facilities and help in this respect.

In order further to facilitate industrialisation he announced a blanket tax holiday for all investors, foreign or domestic.

The crash plan, announced by Nawaz Sharif, appears to envisaged the reintoduction or retenion of subsides on essential consumer items. The premiers also indicated that the government would soon raised the prices of petroleum products, gas and electricity amidst anticipated spurt in most prices.

Prime Minister Nawaz Sharif has called for an industrial revolution and pursuit of that goal on a war footing. He has followed up his call with an early meeting of the industrialists of the country. Once again he made it clear during the five hour meeting that he wants to get the best out of the existing industries and banks as well as set up new industries quickly without the usual official bottle-necks. He proposes to disinvest the five nationalised banks, privatise the development finance institutions and sell public sector industries through open auction, giving preference to the original owners. He has abolished the Board of Investment headed by the prime minister, reduced the list of specified industries to two from seven and announced that unlike in the past industries with an investment of over Rs. one billion too do not need government permission. Banks are expected to fund this industrial revolution and they have been freed from the control of the prime minister and the finance ministry for sanctioning loans on merit. Clearly key details of these far reaching decisions would be worked out by the six committees set up under various ministers with the private sector representatives as their members. Among the issues to be addressed are taxation, de-regulation, export promotion etc. Reports are to be submitted by the end of November and in case of consensus their implementation can begin in December as the prime minister wants. While the workers of the industries and financial institutions to be denationalised and privatised will oppose the move for fear of losing their privileges and protected jobs, funds for the industrial revolution will also be a major deterrent. Banks are now free to fund the new industries on the basis of their viability but their financial position is very weak and they cannot do much of funding unless the large loans taken by the private sector are repaid. Meanwhile, the banks need heavy recapitalisation as the World Bank has been urging. Hence the banks need money as much as real autonomy to fuel the industrial revolution. Of course, if the public sector industries are sold the banks can recover some of the large amounts lent to them. But will the profit-making public sector industries also be sold off along with the heavily losing companies? In the past when sales of such units were moved prospective buyers wanted large bank loans instead of using their own funds. The banks will not be able to provide loans to such buyers now at all, unless they constitute a small part of the sale price. But the buyers of these units and new investors can certainly seek collaboration with foreign investors and Pakistani nationals abroad with investable funds. Major deterrents to rapid industrialisation have been shortage of power and paucity of indigenous raw materials. Untill recently 50 per cent of our imports were industrial raw materials which have now come down to 41 per cent. Also forming a substantial quantum of imports has been machinery. Hence import substitution will have to be attempted in a determined manner by producing more of the raw materials we need and far larger funds will have to be made available for import of machinery, while the indigenous capital goods industry is developed resolutely.[1]

Leave aside appointments at the lower level, over 235 officers were appointed in the Pakistan Steel Mills through the placement bureaus between the period December 1988 to July 1990 by the Benazir Bhutto's government.

These appointments were made against "no vacancies" and those appointed did not fulfil the desired qualifications. Proper recruitment producedure was also not followed by the then management of Pakistan Steel.

According to Pakistan Steel although these appointments were made on purely political considerations, after a 2/3 month long review, termination notices have been issued to only 65 officers.

This has been done in accordance with the decision of October 23, 1990 irrespective of any other consideration. These officers neither have necessary experience nor educational qualifications commensurate with their posts and could not be even accommodated inspite of 2 to 5 years relaxation in their age and experience respectively.

However, a high powered committee has been constituted by Pakistan Steel and effectees dave been asked to submit full particulars of their educational qualifications and experience which they could not submit earlier.

The committee will review their cases and will put-up necessary proposals to be considered by the government.

In case their educational qualifications, experience etc. do not correspond with their present jobs, they will be recommended for consideration against other posts commensurate to their qualifications and experience.

This appears to be a very apologetic attitude of Pakistan Steel. Such a decision makes no sense and sound rediculous in view of Prime Minister Nawaz Sharif's recent directives banning all direct recruitments in all government and autonomous bodies below Grade 16 and all appointments in Grade 16 and above will be purely on merit basis through the Public Service Commission.

Can Pakistan Steel afford to ignore Prime Minister's clear cut directives? Is the question being asked by those qualified people who had become victims of placement bureaus of PPP?

The Pakistan Industrial Credit and Investment Corporation Limited (PICIC) has sanctioned loans totalling 312.23 million rupees for three industrial projects in the country. The projects include establishment of new units for manufacturing of cement and vegetable ghee and expansion of a spinning unit.

Habibullah, President of Rawalpindi Chamber of Commerce and Industry (RCCI) Rawalpindi has highly applauded the efforts initiated by Mohammad Nawaz Sharif Prime Minister of Pakistan for rapid industrialisation in the country in order to uplift the economy and to provide job opportunities.

In a statement issued on Number 14, 1990 he said that is quite heartening that in the first week of his taking over as Prime Minister, Sharif has convened a high level meeting of the businessmen and industrialists to discuss the bottle-necks hampering industrial expansion and to solve the problems of the businessmen and industrialists."

This categorical announcement of the Prime Minister to accellerate the process of privatisation and to take immediate measures to remove the bottle-necks in the expansion of trading and industrial activities, has infused confidence in the private sector, he added.

The Chamber's President also hailed the announcement of the Prime Minister of Pakistan that the banks and the sick industrial units working in the public sector would be denationalised very shortly.

He hoped that the actions initiated by Sharif, would bring industrial revolution in the country in a short span of time which would go a long way in achieving economic stability self-reliance and prosperity of the people as well as to eliminate problem of un-employment.

Habibullah, assured the Prime Minister that the Rawalpindi Chamber of Commerce and Industry as well as rest of the business and industrial community would extend fullest co-operation to the Government in all efforts aimed at expansion of national economy, bringing industrial revolution and attaining self-sufficiency.

The Executive Committee of the Pakistan Vanaspati

Manufacturers Association in its specially convened meeting which held in Lahore, on November 14, 1990 under the chairmanship of Mahmood Ali B. Hatti, passed resolution of sincere felicitations for the new leader of the Federal Government Nawaz Sharif, who assumed the office of Prime Minister.

The meeting of the industrialists observed that it was for the first time in the history of the country that leadership has gone to a man, who represents the class which toiled for the new industrial Pakistan, which possessed the potential to leave behind the backward feudal heritage and usher in a new era of industrial progress.

The meeting was confident that Sharif was fully aware of the problems being faced by the country and the major and more pressing among them were the economic disparity among the regions which would have to be undone and to build a firm economic bridge between the regions to forge one Pakistani nation.

The Industrialists realised that the with Sharif at the helm their responsibilities have increased manifold because at this juncture to leave Mian Sahib alone would be unpatriotic. They unanimously assured their advises and the uninstinted support to the new leader.

The resolve of the new Prime Minister Nawaz Sharif to work on "war footing", for industrialisation in the country is heartenning. The first step towards this direction cou'd be the denationalisation of industries which were taken over in 1972, by the then PPP Government through an ill-conceived decision. It is unfortunate that the progress made in setting up of industries in the country in the sixties was reversed in the seventies mainly on account of nationalisation The highly non-professional management of the taken over units led to the closure of may of them. The others are running into losses or making much less profits than they are capable of earning. Such circumstances have prevailed generally in all the nationalised industries and specially in the light and heavy engineering group. The State controlled capital intensive chemical and fertiliser plants have performed slightly better mainly due to the automatic technology used in the construction of these plants. I believe that they are capable of producing much more and giving far better quality of products if run by efficient, competent and professional management teams. This fact can be established by drawing a comparison of output of these plants with similar ones and of the same capacity in the private sector. Hence the only way to achieve optimization of available resources is through privatisation of all nationalised industries. If the present government is able to usher in an era of industrialisation in the country through sensible and realistic industrial policies, it will also provide job opportunities to the high calibre workforce which has returned to the country from Kuwait and other Middle East countries. Before treading on the path of industrialisation, the government must frame a law for environmental protection. The factories Act 1934, does not contain any provisions laying down the limits on emission and flow of toxic gases, liquids and other waste material from the factories. It is also silent about the permissible noise levels in the factories. In this respect we should not lag behind the developed countries as we are entering into the 21st Century in less than a decade's time.[2]

References

1. *The Muslim*, 15 November, 1990.
2. Parvez Rahim. Industrialisation. *Dawn*, 16 November, 1990.

5

Restructuring the Economy

As an entrepreneur, Nawas Sharif's rise to National pre-eminence marks a historic transition in the political culture of Pakistan—power moving from the traditional feudal aristocracy to an emerging class of entrepreneurs. With this change, modern, progressive forces, more in tune with the times and forward-looking, start taking over from the status quo and tradition-bound forces. It completes the first cycle of transformation that has been taking place gradually in Pakistan, from a feudal to an industrial society, as a result of economic and industrial development of the last more than four decades.

Nawas Sharif in his inaugural address as Prime Minister of the country, declared that his government would give more attention to the health of the economy. He perceived that without a strong economy, based on the principle of self-reliance, one could not think of a stable political system. His declared strategy is to infuse into the economy massive doses of industrial investment all over the country. This would supposedly accelerate the process of restructuring the economy, so as to attain a rational sectoral balance. The process is also expected to generate large job opportunities and foreign exchange earning by export of value added goods. The main vehicle in this exercise is expected to be private sector. Within a week of this announcement, he initiated moves to implement his programme. He invite all the industrialists and businessmen of the country to a meeting on November 13. This large gathering, at a very short notice, was an evidence of the confidence of the traders and industrialists in the new administration. The Prime Minister alongwith the ministers incharge of industry, finance, commerce, food and communication addressed the meeting. He was very precise and to the point. He said that he wanted to rely more on domestic resources, physical and human, in the process of economic uplift. He warned that the path he had chosen was not easy and called for sacrifices by all concerned He advised the nation to stop thinking of what this country has given but to concentrate more on what we have done and what we should do for this country. This country has given them everything in the form of a homeland in which they live with honour and dignity, according to our own social and cultural values. He announced that the special cell in the Prime Minister Secretariat to monitor lending activities of nationalised commercial banks and development financial institutions, had been disbanded. Now the banks have been asked to govern their own affairs, according to the merit of the cases. Any deviation from this rule will not be tolerated. Steps will also be taken to increase the participation of private sector in the ownership of the existing financial institutions. There will be no bar on the opening of the new commercial banks in private sector. The new healthy competition, he said, would raise the efficiency in this sector. He said that there existed no ambigui y between the roles of private and public sectors. Their roles are complementary rather than competitive. Public sector is requireu to provide a conducive milieu, in which private sector can play its role of cementing the foundations of the economy. Public sector should use its energies in the establishment of law and order and infrastructural facilities. This specialisation of economic function of public and private sectors is expected to give optimal results.[1]

Taking about taxation, the Prime Minister said that the prevailing system was such as it provided opportunity for concealment and corruption. On the one hand this tendency is adversely affecting the moral fibre of society and on the other it does not provide enough financial resources to government exchequer. The government is forced to either borrow from within or without the country or print more currency notes. This situation has brought us to a stage where debt servicing has become No. 1 item in our revenue budget pushing defence to a secondary position. This is a negation of the principle of self-reliance and all efforts will be made to curb it. The first step in this direction will be to reframe the taxation system in such a way that in future the tax assessees could pay according to their real ability to pay and these payments should reach the government teasury without any leakage. Furthermore the taxation proposals would not only aim at revenue generation but these would also be designed to give maximum boost to the economic activity.[2]

He was very clear about the directions of the new industrial strategy. He was of the view that there should be no curbs no industrial investment. No sanction be required for the establishment of industries, of any size and type anywhere in the country. The source of funds will not be questioned. He reiterated that constitutional guarantee with respect to takeover would be strictly adhered to. The whole system of sanction and its follow up will be deregularised. Labour policy will be formulated to meet the demands of justice and equity. In order to rationalise the geographical distribution of industrial investment, rural areas and agro-based industries will be provided more lucrative incentives. Every effort will be made to induce foreign investment. The government role will be restricted only to providing assistance to the entrepreneurs, irrespective of their political affiliation. He announced that committees would be set up to work on tax reforms, self-reliance measures, deregulation and disinvestment, exchange and payment reform, export promotion and the working of commercial banks. The Prime Minister asked the representatives to volunteer themselves to work on such committees. These committees were supposed to give their opinion by the end of the current month, after which the action plan was expected to become operative. In the meeting, everyone was relaxed and allowed to say whatever he wanted at any length. The Prime Minister was taking down notes from the suggestions of the participants. It is difficult to believe how a chief executive of the country used to call the honest businessmen thieves and thus the businessmen were insulted and sometimes forcibly deprived of what they had earned by hard work over years. This attitude of government discouraged the entrepreneurs to the point of despair with the result that sluggishness occurred in industrial investment. No incentive was considered sufficient inducement to overcome the shattered confidence. The new Prime Minister was able to reconstruct that broken link, which is so vital. Every one coming out of the meeting was full of confidence, as he believed in every word spoken by the Prime Minister.[3]

The trade and industry circles are pinning high hopes to the meeting between Prime Minister Nawaz Sharif and the representatives of the industry in Islamabad to chalk out a master plan for broadening the industrial base in the country.

The Karachi Chamber of Commerce and Industry (KCCI) has prepared a package of suggestions for rapid industrialisation emphasising the need of restoration confidence of the entrepreneurs by denationalisation of the take-over industries as the first step towards the industrial revolution.

The KCCI suggested that the process of privatisation be initiated by providing 70 per cent management share to the private sector.

Provincial location policy for industries, which the miserably has failed to attain the objectives for which it was initially designed needs to be immediately done away with so that the areas like Karachi should not be deprived of further industrialisation.

There must be clear cut definition of small cottage and vendor industries which should be promoted through incentives and facilities.

There should also be a chain of down stream industries of automobile sector on the lines of down stream industries of Pakistan Steel.

There should be no restriction or bar in raising the textile spindles upto 50,000 which would also be required in produce 50 per cent cloth. This would provide much needed fillip to garment industry and export of textile value added. Meanwhile dyeing and finishing industry should also be encouraged.

The market forces be allowed to operate in case of sugar and edible oil, industries both in respect of their raw materials as well as prices of their products.

The private sector be associated with the defence production in a big way and items for production under private sector be clearly identified.

The Karachi share market opened on an easy note on November 16, 1990 but later staged a rally on account of some positive developments. The volatile performance in the beginning reflected the extension of the reactionary trend of the preceding week. This was attributed to lack of buying support, country-wide transporter's strike and worsening Gulf situation. The sceptre of war kept demand at bay.

Reports that a massive increase in oil price was in the offing also scared away buyers and trading interest remained confined to selective buying. However, later the market got a psychological boost following a meeting between the Prime

Minister, Nawaz Sharif and leaders of trade and industry. In the parleys, the newely-elected Prime Minister revealed his economic plans envisaging disinvestment of all the five nationalised banks, privatisation of the DFIs and sale of public sector units through open auction. The Prime Minister announced the abolition of Board of Investment and lifted all restrictions on setting up industries costing over rupees one billion. Specified list has also been cut down from seven to two or three with all commercial projects including automobiles being opened for private sector without any prior sanction. The private sector never had it so good and, therefore, the decisions evolked a positive response in the share market. Prices staged a smart rally amid brisk trading. However, some of the analysts also attributed the rally technical grounds. Now it remains to be seen what would be the market's reaction to 42 per cent increase in petroleum prices, announced at the weekened. The economic analysis opine that the decision could embarrass the Nawaz Sharif government. However, even this sweeping increase in oil price, the second this year under IMF conditionalities — would not be enough to wipe out the daily loss of Rs. 70 million being suffered by the Government. Meanwhile, its cost-push effect will have a disastrous effect on national production and exports. It is, therefore, feared that the market trend will be reversed next week on the resumption of trading and values will be sharply croded.[4]

The market opened on a mixed note amid selective trading. Some of the leading operators withdrew to the sidelines despite the announcement of major concessions to the industry by the new Prime Minister. The cold response was attributed to the perception that the economy needed short-term rather than long-term measures to offset the ill-effect of US aid cut-off and the Gulf crisis. In normal circumstances, the lifting of restrictions on setting up industries, tax concessions for the industrialists and acceleration of the pace of privatisation would have generated considerable buying interest in the market but it did not because of the looming danger of world conflagration and serious financial squeeze in the wake of the suspension of US aid and Gulf crisis.

The immediate source of concern was the apprehension of serious resource constraints and sharp increase in the production cost and low productivity. The investors looked forward to the proposed increase in oil prices with an air of apprehension. Opinions were also sharply divided on the Sindh situation. While a section believed that peace would soon be restored, another said that only time would tell what course the law and order situation takes. However, while majority believed that the situation was still somewhat fluid, some analysts maintained that the market could stage a rally on technical grounds alone.

With its highly oversold position, the market's turnaround could not be ruled out. Afterall, the new government has generated optimism among the investtors. Its pro-private sector stance and receptiveness to the problems and demands of the business community are definitely encouraging portents. This was expected to add a new dimension to the trading pattern.

The increasing fear of outbreak of war in the Gulf forced some of the leading operators to liquidate their long positions. Others un-nerved by the development stayed away from the market. Even active buying by institutional traders could not evoke sympathetic buying at the falling prices and this accounted for the intensification of the bearish feeling in the earlier half of the week. However, a happy change was brought about in the mood of the market by the new settlement period. With all the plus points in its favour, the market staged a moderate recovery owing to brisk short covering.

The rally was initially slow due to transporters' strike which badly affected the supply of raw materials and distribution of finished goods leading to heavy losses to national industry. The strike was also expected to create law and order problem and thus the rally was restrained.

But later businessmen's meeting with the Prime Minister and Sindh Chief Minister's firm assurance to restore peace in the province generated considerable enthusiasm which resulted in a smart rally. The trading was although dominated by technical support. Genuine buying also helped the sentiment. Reports of higher earnings attracted buyers on selective counters where some of leading issues recorded handsome gains.

Against this backdrop, Sapphire Fibre made its debut in the ready section slightly below the provisional rates but remained in strong demand.

Despite strong rally, the base of new buying remained narrow and the buyers did not want to move out of safe havens. Low priced shares came in for brisk buying following reports of good earnings and expectations of higher dividend. While general investors were still in two minds, the institutional buyers provided the lead.

A good deal of bargain-hunting and speculative support was also witnessed. Though the weekened rally reflected the positive response of the investors to the economic and industrial priorities outlined by the Prime Minister, the market was still haunted by some of the immediate problems. It could not reconcile with the idea of attaining self-reliance in the short-term. It is long draw-out plan.

The Institution of Engineers, Pakistan (IEP) has come up with an ingenious scheme for laying out a rapid rail mass transport network in Lahore costing Rs. 9.8 billion. The IEP study envisages a two-phase implementation of the plan. Phase A will cover construction of under-ground, depressed-on-surface or elevated metros of rail track while Phase B will include an outer circular railway system, an inner circular railway and a suburban canal railway network. When fully operational, the rail transport network in expected to provide transport facility to 20,000 city commuters daily during peak hours. The IEP study also suggests the formation of a "metropolitan transport authority". Further, in order to press home the urgency of implementation of the proposed plan, the study details some of the main difficulties faced daily by an average commuter which include extreme vehicular congestion on major traffic arteries, especially during peak hours, a growing parking problem in the city, frequent road accidents, inadequate traffic control, as also the twin problem of environmental and noise pollution.

The need for long-range planning in such vital sectors of national import as transport cannot be denied. Taking a long term view of the poblem, the IEP study has made some very useful suggestions. The speed with which the number of vehicles in the city is increasing is simply mind-boggling. With the existing level of communication infrastructure in the city (or for that matter in the country), it is difficult to conceive of any mobility on choked roads ten years hence. The IEP study in the light of the existing appalling state of affairs is a good scheme which should give our planners food for thought. The proposed plan can, of course, be carried out over a longer period of time in stages because of the massive expenditure involved. The transport authorities should give it the attention it deserves. The time is fast running out. Thev should sit together to ponder over the transport mess and devise ways and means to handle the crisis before it gets out of control.[5]

Pakistan has signed an agreement with a Danish Firm for the supply of a cement plant, to be set up with the assistance of the World Bank at the Associated Cement, in Wah. The plant would have a production capacity of 3000 tonnes of cement per day. The plant is the biggest cement production unit on single line basis in Pakistan and is expected to commence production within three years. The total cost of the project has been estimated at Rs. 2,144 million. The World Bank has provided a loan of US $ 96 million, to finance the foreign exchange requirements of this project. On the other hand, US $ 0.5 million contract has also been signed between the State Cement Corporation of Pakistan and the China Building Material and Industrial Corporation for supply of equipments for balancing, modernisation and replacement (BMR) of Gharibwal and Mustehkam cement factories. After installation of these equipments, the major bottlenecks in the production processes of these two cement factories will be overcome. The supply of equipment will be completed by the end of November, 1991. It is expected that the equipment will be completely installed by February 1992. Another three units for BMR including Zeal Pak, Hyderabad, Maple Leaf, Wah, and Javedan Cement, Karachi, have been approved by the Government, which will not only increase the life of these plants for another 20 years, but will also reduce the existing cost of production by five to 10 per cent. In the Budget 1990-91, plant and machinery imported for manufacture of Portland Cement has been exempted from customs duty. This concession has also been extended to machinery for manufacture of any type of cement. Cement is an important building material. Its use increases, with improvement in real income, urbanisation and education. More and more buildings, flats, new factories, schools, colleges, universities, hospitals, houses and office accommodation have to be built, and irrigation facilities have to be extended. All these generate demand for cement as an important construction material.[6]

At present there are 25 cement factories, working in the country with an installed capacity of 8.1 million tonnes per annum. Of these factories 6.0 million tonnes capacity, are in public sector and remaining 2.1 million tonnes capacity, in the private sector. Local production of cement, increased from 5.8 million tonnes in 1985-86 to 7.5 million tonnes in 1989-90, thus reflecting an annual average increase of 6 per cent. On the other hand, cement producing units also increased from 17 in 1984-85 to 25 by the end of June, 1990, as given in table below:

Local Production of Cement

Year	Number of reporting mills	Production (000 Tonnes)
1985-86	17	5,773
1986-87	18	6,508
1997-88	19	7,072
1988-89	19	7,125
1989-90	25	7,488

Source: Federal Bureau of Statistics.

Province-wise production of cement shows that Sindh produces 38 per cent of the total production and Punjab 36 per cent, NWFP 18 per cent and Balochistan 8 per cent.

In the budget 1990-91, the rate of excise duty on local production of cement, has been increased at the following rates:

— Ordinary grey portland cement from Rs. 332 to Rs. 400 per tonne.

— Slag cemet from Rs. 300 to Rs. 362 per tonne.

— All other sorts of cement from Rs. 350 to Rs. 422 per tonne.

Portland, white cement, and other industrial cements are being imported from Dubai, France, Thailand, Italy, Netherlands and Germany. Import of cement increased from 123,000 tonnes worth Rs. 59.38 million, in 1977-78, to 4,493,000 tonnes, worth Rs. 1.125 million, in 1981-82, due to the construction boom. However, there has been a significant decrease in the import of cement during the last five years.

Import of cement decreased from 707,000 tonnes, worth Rs. 388 million in 1984-85, to 40,000 tonnes, worth Rs. 79 million in 1988-89, thus showing a decline of 80 per cent, in terms of value. The reduction in imports has been due to the commissioning of new plants in the private sector and expansion in the capacity of the existing plants in the public sector. The demand for cement is directly related to the growth in construction activities and demand is likely to go from 7.6 million tonnes in 1989-90, to 9.0 million tonnes by the end of 1983.

Prime Minister Nawaz Sharif wants an industrial revolution in Pakistan, and he wants to achieve that on a war footing. And he is ready, he says, to do what it takes to make that revolution a success. The Industries Minister he has chosen, Shujjat Hussain, too wants to work on a war footing to achieve the industrial revolution. And he is very familiar with the problems of industry, and the vast prerequisites for achieving an industrial revolution. He is an industrialist himself, and he was Federal Industries Minister in the past as well. But the scope and pace of the present task will be far different from the modest scope and slow pace of his earlier assignments. Nawaz Sharif wants to take Pakistan into the 21st century with firm steps. As industrial revolution is imperative for that, along with several other revolutions in the political, social and cultural spheres. He has to make the maximum use of the men, materials and skill and talents available from among our population of 110 millions, which may be over 150 million by the year 2000. And he has to turn a nation of smug consumers which depends on a excess of foreign aid into a nation of active producers and exporters, and do that quick enough. He has to begin all that by focusing on rapid development of the human resources as that is usually at the root of all major economic transformations. In this age of technological revolution and information explosion we have to strive relentlessly for full literacy instead of the nominal literacy of 32 per cent and effective literacy rate of 12 per cent we have achieved after 43 years of Pakistan. We have to strive for full employment instead of the unemployment rate of 15 per cent and a larger percentage of under-employment in a country in which most women do not have opportunities to work. And that employment has to be according to merit and qualifications and not the misemployment that is common in our midst. Nawaz Sharif has promised all that and more.[7]

References

1. Sajjad Haider, The Building of a Bridge, *Pakistan Times*, 18 November, 1990.
2. *Ibid.*
3. *Ibid.*
4. *The Nation*, 17 November, 1990.
5. *Pakistan Times*, 17 November, 1990.
6. N.A. Memon, Cement Industry, *Dawn*, 17 November, 1990.
7. Sultan Ahmed, Industrial Revolution, *Dawn*, 17 November, 1990.

6

Self-Reliance—A Slogan or A Goal ?

After the cut-off of $560 million worth of US economic and military aid to Pakistan in October 1990 because of Islamabad's nuclear weapons programme, Nawaz Sharif has made "self-reliance" the slogan for his new government. Although Pakistan is still a long way from that, the move towards privatisation will encourage timit industrialists to bring out money and invest it in industry.

It will also strengthen the hands of the new self-made industrialists such as Mansha. After inheriting his father's textile mill in 1970 at the age of 22, Mansha's Nishat group owns eight mills and exports 1.4 bn rupees (£ 31 m) worth of textiles to 40 countries including Britain. His cotton sheets can be brought in Selfridges.

Nawaz Sharif likes to mention that in the 1950s South Korean officials came to Pakistan to study its industrial growth. Since then Pakistan's economy has stagnated while South Fores's surged ahead Nawaz Sharif's main task now will be to ensure sufficient political stability so that Pakistan can catch up.

The Prime Minister Nawaz Sharif said in Islamabad on November 7, 1990, that the target of self-sufficiency was no doubt difficult but not impossible. A number of nations have during our lifetime speedily advanced and prospered. Such nations had not only overcome ravages of atomic disasters but had simultaneously attained remarkable industrial growth records, South Korea was one amongst these nations. "Who benefitted out of our expertise in planning". On the other hand, we ourselves had drifted into pathlessness, "for our pointers to advancement have over the past themselves lost track of progress. I shall not be able to regain those lost precious years, but can certainly search out the lost track."

To Nawaz Sharif the recipe for Pakistan's economic ills is to go in for rapid, massive industrialisation, by mobilising private sector. He is in favour of Pakistan making determined efforts to reduce dependence on foreign aid and achieve self-reliance as quickly as possible.

Pakistan, having become an addict of foreign assistance which flowed in great abundance during the last decade as a result of the Afghanistan crisis, faces an abrupt aid cut-off from the most important source of aid—the United States. That country has been providing about 20 per cent of the total economic aid and the entire quantum of military assistance to Pakistan. If Washington choses to be vindictive and decides to punish Pakistan for its so-called defiant posture on the nuclear issue—the principal bone of contention—it can adversely affect the decisions of other donors as well—indirectly through the IMF and the World Bank and directly through pressure on other donors. That stage may not, however, come because we have now raised the POL prices and undertaken to implement other conditionalities of the IMF and also because, by all indications the initiative for aid suspension has not come from the US government. It has come from a number of Senators, who seem to have forced the hands of the US President by taking advantage of certain aid-related legislations. Our own indiscretion in publicising the progress of our nuclear technology in recent years, too, might have made some contribution to the application of the aid freeze.[1]

Whatever the reason, the crisis for Pakistan is real and has come at a time when the Gulf events are taking a toll of Pakistan's economy : oil price hike, reduction in remittances and the decline in export earnings. The aid suspension coincided with our elections when national emotions were running high and contestants were prone to make political capital out of every development regardless of its merit or relevance positions. The persistence of that even after the elections is indeed unfortunate. While every Pakistani would like the President and the Prime Minister to stand firm on issue of national self-respect and fundamental national interests and goals, he is equally aware of the strategic importance of foreign assistance to our economy and our special relationship with the US. The government has already made it clear that it was keen not only to maintain the warmth of these ties but to improve them. The US should logically be expected to reciprocate this spirit and not strengthen the impression that its friendship and commitments are no more durable than its transient interests and shifting priorities.

Having said this, we need to remind ourselves that foreign aid today constitutes about 80 per cent of our Annual Development Programme; that about 25 per cent of government revenues originate from it and about the same proportion is contributed to the balance of payments. We, as a nation and individual citizens, have been living beyond our means for a long time. Our elite classes, controlling the State power, are not prepared to share the sacrifices which they routinely pass on, year after year, to the common man. Given this context, our dependence on foreign aid would seem irreversible. That context must change. The determination and political will expressed by the President in recent days and by the new Prime Minister not to obtain aid at any cost should not be made contigent on whether the donor countries are adequately mindful of our national honour and dignity or not. Protection of these must be our supreme concern and giving these a secure basis in the realities of life our cherished long-term national objective. To achieve self-reliance, however, abjuring consumerism by all classes and adoption of austerity on national and individual levels are imperative. Comprehensive effort will have to be mounted to raise domestic savings —currently a paltry 6 per cent of GDP and the lower even among the developing countries. Living within means has to be practised, not preached. Waste in government expenditure and individual living has to be ruthlessly eliminated. Equity in taxation system is indispensable. All incomes need to be treated equally and all exemptions withdrawn. Evasion of taxes has to be declared and treated as a serious social crime, severely punishable under the law which must be enforced effectively and without discrimination. All obstacles to full utilisation of the existing productive capacities of land, manpower and industry have to be removed and the productivity of all the three sectors fostered. A comprehensive strategy such as this alone can restore budgetary balance, respond to citizens' needs for education, health and welfare, improve the external payments position and provide fillip to industrialisation. These measures require, first and foremost, a social revolution aimed at changing the outlook and consumption habits of the people and the false values of contemporary life and drastic economic reforms. Time is past when tinkering would do. Are the managers of the national affairs ready for it? Without firm determination, and a clear policy of tax reforms, self-reliance may remain just a slogan and an elusive goal.[2]

The federal cabinet, in its first meeting, chaired by Prime Minister Newas Sharif on November 12, 1990 decided that accountability, merit and output will be the pillars of the present government's policy.

Specifically, the areas it will focus on will be self-reliance, de-regulation and denationalisation, taxation reforms, foreign exchange and payments reforms, agricultural productivity, increase in exports, administrative reforms and law reforms.

Briefiing mediamen about the meeting, Petroleum Minister Nisar Ali said the Prime Minister had directed all the ministries to set their targets within this overall framework. They would also submit policy guidelines suggesting measures for fulfilment of people's expectations which were the basis of their massive mandate to the goverment.

After detailed discussion, the Prime Minister remarked that while an increase in oil prices was unavoidable, it should be low enough not to further worsen the condition of the poor people. At the same time, the government would provide some relief to people to minimise the additional burden on the people. He rejected the price hike proposed in the Finance Ministry's summary, Nisar disclosed.

He drew the mediamen's attention to the situation in the Persian Gulf which has exacerbated the difficulties of the Third World, in particular. It had been particularly hard on Pakistan because remittances from Pakistanis abroad had come down substantially since the return of Pakistani workers from Kuwait.

The Minister pointed out that several countries in Pakistan's neighbourhood had affected drastic increase in oil prices—India by 41 per cent and Turkey by 66 per cent, for example.

He, however, dispelled the fear expressed by journalists that the dealers might start hoarding petroleum fuels in view of the cabinet's decision to revise the price upward. The matter would be discussed in detail by the Economic Coordination Committee in its forthcoming meeting, but a final decision would be taken by the cabinet in its meeting which may not take place before a fortnight. He, therefore, ruled out the possibility of hoarding.

The cabinet set up a sub-committee headed by Maulana Abdus Sattar Niazi, Minister for Local Government and Rural Development to review the Zakat-Ushr Ordinance with a view to ensuring equitable distribution of the Zakat Ushr funds. Ch. Nisar noted that the present system had bred many scandals. Other members of the sub-committee are Minister of Finance, Minister of Law, Minister of Production and Minister of Railways.

Prime Minister Nawaz Sharif ordered that in future all recruitments will be made through the Federal Public Service Commission. Merit alone would be the criterion and the commission would make selections disregarding recommendation of any person in the government.

As regards the posts below the EPSC's jurisdiction, the Prime Minister ordered total ban on fresh recuitment till such time new recruitment policy is formulated by the government. Competence and merit would be the only criteria in the new policy.

The decision would apply to all the ministries, attached departments and autonomous bodies, he stated.

The cabinet abolished all discretionary quotas for allotment of plots without any examption. It discretionary quota of the Prime Minister, Mian Nawaz Sharif declared.

The decision would apply to the provincial governments too, it was also decided.

Apart from the plots which will be sold by open auction, the remaining allotments would be reserved for the deserving people, widows and orphans in accordance with a policy to be announced soon.

No government servant would be given extension after retirement, the Prime Minister also announced in the cabinet meeting. However, an exception would be made as provided in the rules.

Replying to a question, Ch. Nisar said it would be the governments' endeavour to create a climate of confidence for industrialisation so that the local investor as well as the entrepreneur from abroad might feel encouraged to set up industries in Pakistan.

At the juncture, he disclosed that the cabinet would discuss the foreign policy in its next meeting.

"The I.M.F. does not govern Pakistan, Nisar told a foreign journalist who wanted to know the government's policy in regard to the IMF's conditionalities. The government had to take into account the problems of the people of Pakistan. "What IMF says is not necessarily the government's policy," he added.

The minister also accounced that in future all the branches of National Commercial Banks would receive payments of electricity bills in the usual afternoon hours.

Nisar Ali Khan told mediamen that a more easy and simple procedure would be adopted for depositing of utility bills.

To a question, he said that the decision would be effective soon.

Austerity and Officialdom

In a feudal and tribal society in which the poor and the middle classes imitate the rich in their wasteful ways, and become even more impoverished, austerity ways, and become even more impoverished, austerity and simplicity have to begin at the top to become effective nationwide. That is all the more necessary in a country in which domestic savings are very low and rural indebtedness is excessive. The rural poor are indebted to merciless usurers with their high compound rate of interest. A major reason for such indebtedness is heavy borrowing by the poor for the marriages of their children, which begin with a lavish Jehez (dowry).

In such a context, Prime Minister Nawaz Sharif, in his first address to the nation had appealed for austerity and simplicity and said he, his colleagues and officials would not attend wedding parties in which more than one dish was served. Clearly he neither wants legislation to check the wastage at wedding parties of the rich nor seeks to check the number of guests invited to such parties. Instead he has proposed a voluntary restraint on the ministers and officials. Obviously those who do not seek VVIP presence at their wedding parties are free to perpetuate their lavishness. The public will be skeptical even while welcoming the move as such restrictions officially proposed in the past many times did not work. Not only did the people not take such restrictions on wedding parties seriously but also they soon saw the officials who made the laws led by Gen. Zia attending lavish wedding parties, disregarding those limitations and also violating them merrily when it came to playing hot at their own children's wedding parties. It is hence to be hoped that the Prime Minister, Chief Ministers, and officials would not only abide by the limitation which Mr. Nawaz Sharif has set when attending wedding parties but also be equally austere when they play host at their own relations' wedding parties. When we talk stridently of doing away with aid and becoming self-reliant and self-respecting, wanton waste not only at weddings but also in every other sector of life and cussed obstentation have to be given up punctiliously. The rulers and officials hence must stay by what they have decided, and not make a mockery of that, as their various predecessors had done in the past.[3]

Self-reliance, industrialisation and economic development are the passwords of the new government thrown up by the recently-concluded electoral process. These words are not new to the Pakistani people. Over the last 44 years, every government through whatever method it has assumed power has invariably employed these very words to push itself ahead. Consequently cliches, and backneyed expressions, which despite being high-sounding, have lost their meaning. Coming into power after such a bitter, hard and controversial elections, there arc reasons to believe in sincerity of the new government's promises. It would be hard for any government to survive if it fails to keep its promises and live up to the expectations of the masses notwithstanding the overt and covert support of the establishment extended to the IJI Government. Rapid industrialisation on scientific and modern lines presupposes creation of conducive social and political conditions in the country. Leaving behind the bitter stuff of his electoral speeches against the PPP leadership, the new Prime Minister, Nawaz Sharif is now soft pedalling and transmitting peace-signals towards the opposition. It is for the first time that the opposition led by Ms. Benazir Bhutto has accepted the results of the elections though under protest over the alleged massive rigging. Additionally, there is another positive statement from Nawaz Sharif as reported by the Arabia daily. Al-Ittihad saying that "My government is not intending to continue with the special tribunals as we do not believe in the politics of revenge. I think the special tribunals should wind up their functions. But I cannot comment on what these special tribunals have done as I do not want to interfere in the functions of the judiciary". This offering of the olive branch to the opposition augurs well for the development of the political institutions of the country. By translating these words into concrete reality, the new government would really be doing a great service for the consolidation of the fledgling democracy in the country.[4]

Another factor needed for creation of conducive conditions in the country is settling the issue of provincial autonomy. There is no denying the fact that there is a need for greater quantum of provincial autonomy. The provinces have been at logger-heads with one another mainly because of the acute sense of deprivation. Once the issue is settled amicably by strictly adhering to the existing quantum of provincial autonomy as guaranteed under the existing Constitution, the permanent clash between the Federation and the provinces would of the feudal ruling class to promote education or for that matter industrialisation. It is the import-based economy that is in their interest. A close look at the history of this country is enough to convince you of the truth of the assertion that the elite ruling classes are not interested in the promotion of education and basic industries. In all the elections, the backward areas have always thrown up the most conservative leadership. The problems of Balochistan, for example, are the product of the conservative tribal chiefs and Sardari system. The Sardars of Balochistan are the least interested in the development of their province. If education is promoted, the Sardars have everything to lose. In the Tribal areas of NWFP, the tribal chiefs have stood in the way of allowing universal suffrage because it is not in their interest to let every adult have the right to exercise his or her vote. In utter disregard of the Constitution, the tribal chiefs are allowed to have their way. Those whose job it is to take notice of the violation of the Constitution, are keeping their fingers crossed though they take pride in their constitutionalism and self-righteousness. Hence it is all the more important that the new government in Pakistan should undertake sound plans for the spread of education and creating of awareness in the public about their political rights. For strengthening of political institutions, the imparting of the primary and basic education to the citizens is necessary. This is the sure way to end the long night of the elitist and feudal rulers.

For national cohesion which is a must for economic development, cultural renaissance is as much necessary be averted. If the letter and spirit of the Constitution on this issue is followed by all, the mutual antagonisms would disappear for good. May be the cries of greater quantum of provincial autonomy would no longer be raised then. The problem in the case for the demand for provincial autonomy is in essence that of implementing it. By allowing the provinces the right to administer their affairs in accordance with their wishes under the limits placed by the Constitution, the

Federation would be acting in accordance with the spirit of the Constitution. Anti-Federalist force in the provinces have come to the fore due to the overzealously centralist role played by the successive governments and regimes in the affairs of the provinces. One Unit idea did the greatest damage to the country as a whole. Though in physical terms, the One Unit was dismantled, its ghost dominated the thinking of every feberal set-up. What we directly need now is to get rid of this ghost and exercise it from our political thinking. The Federation would become stronger once the provincial autonomy guaranteed under the Constitution is allowed to have full play in the political culture. This would in turn help create peaceful conditions in the country which are a must for industrial development. Another condition for the industrialisation of the country is development of human resources to which the governments in Pakistan have paid no heed. Our spending on education has been the lowest in the world. Lack of education has stood in the way of both, industrialisation and democracy. The country has been ruled by the classes who find the educated public a stumbling block in their designs to keep this country firmly under their thumb. The greater the ratio of education, the greater the degree of public awareness. Hence it is not in the interest Culture-has always been an anathema to the governments in Pakistan and they have neglected it sorely. We have stifled the aspirations of the people by denying them opportunites of developing their cultural entities. Traditional culture, literature, language and art and living style of the provinces have become the victim of the negligence of the elitist rulers in this country. This attitude has fostered tensions among the people of different regions and resultantly breeded prejudices and hatred among them. By letting the provinces develop their own languages, literature and traditional crafts, we would in fact be promoting national cohesion. If an individual from one particular province loves his culture and literature, he would likewise be more accommodating to the culture and literature of the other province. There is a dire need of institutions for the promotion of languages of all the provinces at the Federal level. The Academy of Letters which should have done this job, has miserably failed to do this very task. Over and above this institution, the Federal government should set up separate institutes to develop the languages of Pakistan. By according direct patronage of the Federation to the languages spoken in Pakistan, we would be conveying the message to the people in all the provinces that the Federation represents all the provinces and is equally interested in the promotion of their languages. National cohesion and a liberal atmosphere devoid of fundamentalism are pre-requisite conditions for boosting economic activity.[5]

Two features of Pakistan's national urgeney were underlined by Prime Minister Nawas Sharif during his meeting with the country's leading industrialists and entrepreneurs on November 13, 1990 and both were aimed at achieving the same result, that of self-reliance. The urgencies were payment in entirely taxes that were due to the Government and increase of exports through rapid industrialisation.

The five-hour discussions touched almost every aspect of the problems relating to the country's development, and according to business circles, the Prime Minister agreed to do all that the industrialists wanted him to do to ease the situation.

The task, however, is not as easy as the Prime Minister or the industrialist community thought, nor as simple. The havoc that has been wrought to the concept of development during the last over two decades—from 1969 when Field Marshal Ayub Khan departed from the scene—has been awful. It has brought everything at a standstill and at the same time has morally debased major section of the country's industrialists, businessmen and bureaucracy. A mere freedom to the entrepreneurs would not yield the results which Nawaz Sharif expects and which the participants in the Tuesday meeting promised. One thing which may not be fully comprehensible to the industrialists even if they honestly want to do the job, nor perhaps also to the Prime Minister, is the close relationship between the manufactured goods and the scientific know-how of the manufacturers. As a leading Western scientist-cum-economist, Steven Dedijir, said some years ago. "The scientific base of all products and processes is becoming stronger. The more science a new product or process has the more it is liable to be competitive."[6]

It was in this context that he lamented the fate of Third World countries which he said, "have hardly any science." His estimate was that "ninety per cent of world research potential is concentrated in about 35 countries with about 25 per cent of the world population. Hence the imperative necessity for a Third World country to find the most effective policy to bring about rapidly a macro science transfer on which to base its development."

His verdict was clear and an eye-opener for every Thrid World leader. He said, "Without such a science transfer a Third World country will continue to be technologically and hence economically and politically, one sidedly dependent, more simply said exploited in its international exchanges."

It is in this context that the recent meeting has to be assessed as to the possible results, we have to evaluat what science we have and what we intend to produce, what research in the field of production and competitive technology is being undertaken by the country's major industries.

"Pakistan has never had a coherent science policy", once grumbled Prof, Abdus Salam. If at all we did try to evolve one it was eliminated after Field Marshal Ayub's exit. What is, therefore, needed is not merely removal of red-tape hurdles in the way of industrialists, or elimination of bureaucratic control but also and probably as a much greater urgency, is needed development of science through universities, institutes of technologies and partici ation direct or indirect of our industrialists. Of course, they have to provide for the needs of their workers and workers children, but they must also provide for research in production technologies to be able to complete in the foreign markets. We are living in a strange age, an age which is competent as well as corrupt, an age of manipulated currencies. The slogan of self-reliance is alluring, but if it is to be more than a mere slogan; we must precure and produce science, we must have the small absolute size of science commensurate with our economy's technological needs as well as our cultural sophisticative. However, we have new and a fresh leadership, more confident and more courageous than any before, because it is an elected leadership, because its backing is massive and because it is unencumbered by all that the previous leaders thought, said and did. The vigour that has already been reflected in Nawaz Sharif's firelessness, the combination of youth and experience embodied in his cabinet, and the restlessness that he has exhibited in setting things right soon after taking over as Prime Minister augur well for the country's future.[7]

It is difficult to say who has been a great menace for honesty, integrity and morality, the bureaucrats or the politicians, but the senario at the present moment is senario of full power in the hands of politicians, more so in the hands of those who belong to the ruling party. If these politicians are determined to enforce the will and moral conceptions of merit and lawfulness that the Prime Minister has been articulating, we will soon have a clean life and clear view of our destiny. The slur on politicians will also be removed once for all.

Action, and not slogans, is what Nawaz Sharif wants. Perhaps nobody knows more than him that more production is the need of the 'hour, and also more equitable distribution of wealth. Therefore, the action he must be meaning actual results in these two sectors-production and distribution. Equitable distribution is not thinkable without production and distribution. Equitable distribution is not thinkable without production which in turn cannot be conceived without science and technology. What, therefore, is needed is the evolution of comprehensive programme of development of piety science and national power to be enforced as a religious compulsion.

The evolution of such a programme is basically the responsibility of the Prime Minister and the thinking, creative section of his Cabinet. A country has no self-reliant economy if it lacks in self-reliant science and technology. A crash programme must and can be prepared for this purpose in consultation with the country's scientific elite as he has done in respect of industrial and business sector.

Senator, Prof. Khurshid Ahmed on November 21, 1990 identified enforcement of strict financial discipline increase in domestic production and revision of import policy as short-term measures towards realising the goal of self-reliance.

Prof. Khurshid, who is Chairman of the Committee on Self-reliance announced by Prime Minister Nawaz Sharif recently, said that a new multi-pronged strategy will be introduced to rid the country of severe burden of foreign as well as internal debt.

He said that the Prime Minister was very sincere and eager to pursue a fresh approach for rapid economic development of the country and give due weight to recommendations of his committee.

Answering a question, he said he cannot re-empt the recommendations at this stage, which are to be formulated after detailed meetings and consultations with the experts.

He was of the view that the development strategy so far adopted, merely resulted in enhancing dependence on foreign loans which have exceeded $ 16 billion besides domestic debt of Rs 38 billion.

He said that the foreign loans sought for political reasons could always have catastrophic impact on the country's economy. Such a strategy was unacceptable in view of national interests and country's sovereignty.

The task of the committee is very vast as it has to suggest a new strategy with alternate ways and means to achieve self-reliance both in short and long terms, the committee will examine various aspects of new economic approach including the shape of industrialisation priorities for transfer of technology and setting of basic industries to ensure strong indigenous industrial base, he said.

"We have to examine defence, enery and infrastructural requirements to gradually minimise the reliance on foreign aid. We will also examine the wastage and leakages responsible for budget deficit", he said. The whole psychology of imports which neglected development of domestic capabilities, will have to be changed, he said.

The committee, he said will propose as how the resources could be mobilised domestically and internationally outside the aid-framework created during the last three years. The committee, he observed, will give concrete suggestions to complete task assigned to it, that was why, he added it needed more time for the purpose.

He observed that one month period was enough for giving initial recommendations however, the committee will require three months for the presentation of complete report.

Whatever resistance from the elements of vested interests towards, self-reliance must be crushed, he said. In response to a question about black money, he said, that this is fact there is a black economy however, different people have different views about the extent of the economy. "We can bring it into the country's economic framework and resources can be mobilised for national development," he added.

He pointed out that the basic need for self-reliance was de-regulation of the economy in true spirit however, he added, "I do not believe in wholesale de-nationalisation."

The professionals, he said, should have the control of public sector with accountability and efficiency criteria. The sick and inefficient units, he said should be given in private sector by carefully prepared plans which could ensure improvement in efficiency and profitability of the units and protection to the interests of the workers and labourers.

Replying to a question, he said the revision of import policy should aim at protecting foreign exchange reserves and importing essential items to set in example for austere of life.

References

1. *Dawn*, 16 November, 1990.
2. *Ibid.*
3. *The Muslim*, 17 November, 1990.
4. Mohammad Yasin, Keeping Promises a Must. *Muslim*, 17 November, 1990.
5. *Ibid.*
6. Shabbir Hussain, P.M's Self-Reliance. *Pakistan Times*, 15 November, 1990.
7. *The Nation*, 22 November, 1990.

7

Privatisation

Pakistan Prime Minister Nawaz Sharif, on January 10, 1991, launched his government's programme of disinvesting the public sector by privatising the state-run Muslim Commercial Bank.

"It is our first step towards putting Pakistan on the road to self-reliance and self-sufficiency", Nawaz Sharif said handing over the ownership document to a group of 12 private sector industrialists.

But the premier, himself an industrialist, cautioned that the road to prosperity is not without pitfalls. Difficult days lie ahead.

Under the deal, the new owners will control 51 per cent of the shares of the Muslim Commercial Bank, one of five banks nationalised in 1972. They will pay about $ 40 million dollars for 26 per cent stake and have also underwritten another 25 per cent to be offered to the general public.

"Privatisation will rid the country of corruption, mismanagement and waste and help fight unemployment, our number one problem"; said Nawaz Sharif.

Soon after the Nawaz Sharif government took charge, it announced a poliey decision to hand over the management of public sectors to private industrial groups and entrepreneurs.

The employees of the bank have protested against the government's decision saying the new employers will now be at liberty to hire and fire them.

Finance Minister Sartaz Aziz said privatisation would be undertaken in different phases and under the first phase, loss-making units in the public sector would be given to the private sector.

Sartaz Aziz said that in order to protect the bank employee's interest, it had been laid down that the terms and conditions of service would not be varied to their detriment.

An opening up of Pakistan's banking sector to private investment could fall victim to years of government-directed uneconomic lending, a confused regulatory environment and ingrained corruption and inefficiency. The new government of Prime Minister Nawaz Sharif announced in early December 1990, that it intended to privatise the nation's seven state-owned commercial banks. New private domestic banks will be allawed to open in the near future. Currently there are no private banks operating in Pakistan, though a number of foreign banks have a total of 66 branches in the country. Muslim Commercial Bank selected by the outgoing Benazir Bhutto's government for privatisation ahead of other nationalised banks, is to be sold immediately. A 26 per cent stake will be put up for auction to a single bidder which will manage the bank, and 25 per cent of the remaining shares will be sold to the public. The flotation will raise Rs. 1.03 billion (US $ 47.2 million). Afterwards, Habib Bank, United Bank and Allied Bank are to be offered to the public. The National Bank of Pakistan and the Women's Bank are not mentioned as candidates for a sell-off to the private sector, while Punjab

Bank owned by the state government, has been resisting efforts by Islamabad to sell its shares to private investors. Private companies wishing to set up new banks must have a track record of paying regular dividends to their shareholders and must not have defaulted either in payment of taxes or in meeting debt-servicing liabilities, whether personal or corporate. Further, the chief executive directors and all shareholders owning 5 per cent or more of the share capital must guarantee to keep their shareholdings at the same level for five years to ensure that any new bank does not become a family monopoly with close linkages between owners and their other business undertakings. The regulatory creteria for new banks my prove too onerous for investors. Capital and general reserves must equal at least 7.5 per cent of liabilities or Rs. 300 million (US $ 3.76 million), whichever is the greater. Foreign participation is allowed, but capital and profit cannot be repatriated. And the new bank must be listed on the stock exchange. Business cricles believe investors will be more attracted to setting up new banks than to investing in state-owned banks in the process of being privatised. State banks have been reluctant to reveal the real state of their balance sheets, where rescheduled loans are said to extraordinarily high. Most state-owned banks avoid losses by rescheduling the interest and principal of their bad debts year after year while booking the interest on these non-performing loans as profit. One banker told the Review that earlier this year, prospective private investors asked management at all nationalised banks to disclose the extent of rescheduled loans in each institution's loan portfolios. The request was ignored.[1]

Investors will also want to know how the government pays interest rates of obout 15-18 per cent a year on Rs. 2 billion worth of government led saving schemes, such as socalled Defence Bonds and Khas Deposits, which help the government meet its administrative budget shortfalls. Islamabad counts these deposits as revenue in the nation's annual budget, even though the bulk of these deposits are used for deficit financing. Investing in new private banks also has its dangers, primarily in the form of a host of patently un-economic or foolhardy directives hidden in the government's bank regulations. For example, private bankers could be required to compete with state banks' easy farm credit, which is now dispersed free of interest for the first six months of each loan under specific minimum limits fixed for each bank branch. State-owned banks also are about to introduce an interest-free loan programme for self-emloyed artisans and unemployed youngsters wanting to set up a business. It remains unclear whether private banks will have to follow Finance Ministry directives on the allocation of loans.[2]

It is also necessary to privatise all the commercial banks and development finance institutions. In their case necessary professional controls and proper surveilance by the State Bank, which should be made into the custodian of monetary policy instead of an adjunct of the Finance Ministry, must however, be ensured. Industries should be encouraged to look to the money market and stock exchanges to find finances for their schemes. That would need a drastic change in the present debt-equity ratio of 70 : 30 to 20 : 80 or even 10 : 90 so that bank loans play a small part in the schemes of industrialists. Let no politician, however powerful, twist the hopless bank presidents to pay out large handouts on fictitious financial appraisals in which bank loans also cover the sponsors' equity and some through dubious manipulation. One does not consider local finance to be much of a problem. External investment should be encouraged with removal of restrictions and red tape combined witn a tax free regime. Infrastructure and lack of trained labour may pose problems. These can be tackled with some foresight combined with proper enterprise. Let industrialists also be encouraged to set up industrial estates on which they can charge a proper price for industrial plants and subsequent servicing. Some industrialists would also be encouraged to train their own manpower provided they are freed from uncalled for interference. The labour must allow the entrepreneur the freedom to "hire-and-fire" and the liberty to make recruitment on merit combined with loyalty to the establishment. We can learn much in man management from Japanese practices. One does feel that much economic progress can be made provided the broad outline of possible changes announced by the Prime Minister can be implemented honestly and sincerely. If a change in attitudes and our colonial administrative techniques Is brought about then Nawaz Sharif's vision of putting Pakistan on the fast track of prosperity like Japan and South Korea can be easily realised.[3]

Nawaz Sharif has been sworn in as Prime Minister of Pakistan at a most crucial juncture when the country is beset with problems arising out of Gulf crisis; suspension of US aid, low remittances, exodus of Pakistanis from Iraq, Kuwait and other Arab states, flight of capital from the country, population explosion, lowest rate of literacy, poor health facilities, rampant corruption, nepotism, favouritism, law and order situation and rising prices of essential commodities besides an atmosphere wherein students feel shy of going to schools colleges and universities which remain closed mostly in a year and there is almost nil output of people working in government/semi government/natienalized institutions. The country is on the brink of bankruptcy and the masses are frightened by the oil crisis and its consequences. In the circumstances the people of Pakistan have given a comprehensive mandate in favour of the new regime and pinned high hopes on it. Mian Nawaz Sharif and other economic experts have considered rapid industrialisation as the immediate solution for the major economic problems. I am of the view that the desired objective can be achieved by privatisation in almost all economic fields, motivating investors by giving them the absolute right to hire and fire, and allowing the workers to make unions to safeguard their rights. But there should be no strikes and lock-outs in any case, for industrial disputes high-powered industrial courts be established to visit the spot, hear the parties and give decisions there and then. Arrangements should be made to provide necessary paraphernalia for establishing industries at the door-steps of prospective investors.

Foreign investor be encouraged by providing them with necessary surities in addition. All hurdles be removed on an emergency basis.

Most important is the change in the labour laws according to the changing circumstances and the creation of a positive attitude in the masses towards development/investment and consumption.[4]

In the early seventies the Government of Pakistan adopted the nationalisation policy. Accordingly the industrial institutions, banks, ginning factories, rice husking and flour mills were nationalised. Experience shows that nationalised industries remained overstaffed and produced little while the Government had invested colossal funds in them. Confronted with heavy losses, the government has no choice but to return them to the private sector so as to make them a source of more employment and boosting up exports to earn more foreign exchange for the country. Privatisation is a new idea. It means transfer of public sector activities to the private sector. In private ownership decisions are made by those persons who have an intimate understanding of the problems. Private enterprise managers place more weight upon profit and increase the internal efficiency of the firms. Maximum benefits can be achieved from privatisation which is the means of minimising deficits. It is an experimental activity for developing countries. Many industrialised countries have privatised State enterprises in the recent past and many developing countries are following them. Privatisation mobilises private investment, promotes risk sharing and stimulates foreign investment in the domestic economy. It is therefore important for the developing countries to allow trade liberalisation alongwith privatisation. For making privatisation more successful it is necessary to negotiate with the potential buyers privately the government owned enterprises can put to auction or the shares can be sold through the Stock Exchange Market. It is important to note that in taken over enterprises there is perpetual deficit which creates the need for more bank borrowings. These days many developing countries are shifting to deregulation, privatisation and liberalisation because it will be helpful in increasing productivity and lowering costs. Also competition will force the private sector to become more efficient to survive in future. According to the available information the first privatisation was introduced in Germany after World War II. It was a most successful privatisation progamme which was accomplished through open sales of shares. In United States it emerged as an important economic requirement and various government services were given to private enterprises including health care, garbage collection, map-making, weather forecasting and military air craft maintenance. In the same way several developing coutries of the world have assigned their airlines to private aviation companies. Argentina sold its airline Australia to a private company.[5]

In Britain too more stress is being placed on privatisation. It is stated that State enterprises shares worth billions of dollars had been sold to private buyers between the years 1979 and 1988. They privatised the telephone system, the national rail-road, and air-lines, hotels, British channel ferry service, British Petroleum, British Aerospace, Britoil National Freight Corporation British Gas and British Airport Authority. All this was accomplished through open sale of shares. France plans to transfer about 65 companies to private hands by 1991. Turkey has sold the Bosphorus Bridge and Keban Hydro-plant. The sale of the National Airlines to employees has since started. Since 1970 Chile has a successful privatisation programme to increase private participation in electric utilities and tele-communications, insurance, national air-lines, water supply, oil exploration and the social-security system. But the most extensive privatisation started in Chile from 1973 during which 600 enterprises were privatised. Since 1981 participation of workers in the private system is mandatory as a result the Chilean reforms have been a smashing success because workers are more willing to support policies that enhance economic growth. Mexico has drawn plans for privatisation through mergers. The Mexicana Copper Mining and Airlines were sold to private investors. Malaysia and Singapore have privatised airlines, portfacilities and telecommunication system. Malaysia and Thailand are negotiating with private contractors for providing the basic infrastructure. In Thailand some of the passenger lines on the State owned railroads are operated by private enterprises. Indonesian government has given customs services to the private contractors which has reduced the expenditure, increased the revenue and also reduced corruption. In Tunisia many privatised enterprises went through their stock exchange market. Bangladesh and Jamaica have formed divestment boards to arrange the sale of the government enterprises. China's system of privatisation is stated to be the world's most spectacular example of privatisation. To ensure wider use of farming and freer markets for outputs, farmers are given the right to sell above-quota production at prices prevailing in the markets. For several years it is transferring the public sector enterprises to the private sector through share offerings. As a result of this programme about 6,000 enterprises are now owned by the workers through sale of shares.[6]

Nawaz Sharif wants privatisation of banks. How soon he can achieve that in the face of resistance from bank employees remains to be seen. Meanwhile the number of private sector investment banks in the country can certainly be increased; but their accounts will have to be audited carefully and misuse of funds checked. The new investors will have to be encouraged to rely on more funds from the public as capital than on the banks. They have to offer a substantial number of their shares to the public, give fair dividends to them and have clean corporate practices. Corporate ethics have to improve rapidly and a real share-holders democracy come into being, bridging the large existing gap between the managements of companies and the small share holders. The strong support of a large number of share holders is good for the companies vis a vis the government and the unions as well as consumers. A large part of the seed capital of the industrial revolution has to come from the vast mass of the public — from their small or larger savings. Clearly, any kind of industrial revolution cannot be a one-way street. While the government should do all it can, the entrepreneurs should be ready to play their part in full. They should earnestly strive for indigenisation in the industrial sector to the maximum possible extent. Simultaneously import substitution efforts have to be stepped up, particularly in the area of industrial raw materials which now from 47 per cent of the overall imports. Both increasing indigenisation and import substitution have become urgent in view of the shrinking foreign aid and fall in home remittances, which reduce our capacity to pay for such imports. The industrial producers have to focus on improving the quality of their products not only for exports but also for domestic consummers. When imported raw materials cost a great deal because of the steady devalution of the rupee and inflation abroad and the consumers have to pay a variety of heavy taxes, they certainly deserve for better products than they have been getting. Producing shoddy goods in such an environment is a crime and must be checked. Simultaneously business ethics and efficiency, too, have to improve for them to give their best. They have to come to accept lower profit rates and seek larger profits on the basis of a larger turn-over.

Prime Minister Nawaz Sharif has invited industrialists and entrepreneurs to join hands with his government to usher in a new era of industrialisation in the country. The Prime Minister soon after taking over had said that he would convene a meeting of the industrialists of the country in the near future for preparing a plan to turn Pakistan into an industrialised country like Japan and South Korea. Coming from a successful industrialist, the promise to promote industry on correct lines sounded sincere and credible. Elaborating the strategy for strengthening the industrial frame-work he has said that the new government will enter into a new partnership with the private sector to promote common objectives to replace the present relationship based on lack of confidence and distrust. This would augur a new era in industrial development as it would free the industry from the bureaucratic grip. To tackle the problem of unemployment through industrialisation, the government will give special incentives for rural industrialisation and agro-based industries. This will help bring the rural areas and even industrially neglected regions within the mainstream of industrialisation and generate not only new employment opportunities but would also check the migration of rural population to the cities. Industries based totally on locally available raw materials will not require government sanction irrespective of cost. In the 1970s the nationalisation programme implemented by the then government demoralised the private sector which virtually went on an investment strike. The public sector was expanded at the cost of the national exchequer and ultimately proved a white elephant. The financial institutions, the nationalised commercial banks (NCBs) and development finance institutions (DFIs) were sunsequently made subservient to the political influence which resulted in huge loans advanced in violation of banking principles and practices and even without adequate colateral. The genuine entrepreneurs were not only denied the requisite finance, but the recovery of politically motivated loans became a big problem. The Prime Minister has assured that his government is committed to a policy of deregulation and denationalisation which would be implemented soon with a concrete programme. NCBs and DFIs have been instructed to sanction loans on merit, based on economic considerations and without any political consideration of influence from any quarter. The cell created by the previous PPP government in the Prime Minister's Secretariat to sanction investment and loans has been abolished with immediate effect. This will give the much needed financial independence to NCBs and DFIs. The Prime Minister has established six committees to prepare concrete proposals for new industrial policies and their implementation in different priority areas within the next 6-8 weeks. This is the step in the right direction which should help remove roadblocks in achieving the goal of industrialisation. In Pakistan, which started its life with almost a clean industrial slate, industrial growth may be called impressive, but its impact across the board of the national economy has remained limited, particularly in the field of employment. This is due to the fact that Pakistan lacked an industrial base which could produce the requisite momentum for speedy industrialisation. A proper industrial culture, as is visible in the Asian Industrial tigers, could not be developed to ensure commitment and dedication to improve the quality of products, modernise the plants and ensure financial viability. We encouraged mostly import substitution industries. The degree of protection has always been high and, if international prices are used for analysis the value added in a number of cases may be negative. We must allow the market economy to find its own level. The demand and supply forces it enabled to work without any interference, create their own momentum. Needless to say the private sector has to play a crucial role in creating new industrial prosperity in Pakistan.[8]

Prime Minister Nawaz Sharif called a meeting of the Deregulation and Disinvestment Committee on November 22, 1990 and discussed various aspects of the Government of Pakistan privatisation plans.

Lahore Chamber of Commerce and Industry President Iftikhar Ali Malik, was nominated as a member of the Committee by the Prime Minister, and said that the Committee had been formed to implement the GOP privatisation policy at the earliest.

The Deregulation and Disinvestment Committee (DDC) reviewed the progress made on the privatisation front so far and draft proposals for its speedy implementation to achieve the desired objectives.

References

1. *Far Eastern Economic Review*, 27 December, 1990.
2. *Ibid.*
3. M. Hasan, Economic Miracle, *Dawn*, 17 November, 1990.
4. Muhammad Fahim, Rapid Industrialisation, *Pakistan Times*, 17 November, 1990.
5. Nasir Mujahid, Privatisation, *Pakistan Times*, 20 November, 1990.
6. *Ibid.*
7. *The Pakistan Times*, 15 November, 1990.

8

Liberalisation

The election of Nawaz Sharif as the Prime Minister of Pakistan has aroused hopes of an economic revival in the country. Felicitating him, the Chairman of Karachi's SITE Association of Industry has stated that this is the occasion for which the industrialists and businessmen had been waiting for long. Most of our economic problems are ultimately linked to the slow pace of industial development. Rapid industrialisation is considered by cconomic experts as the sovereign remedy to put the economy back on tracks. A serious roadblocks, is however, the bureaucracy. It makes decisions in the industrial field that require technical knowledge which it hardly possesses. Unless the private sector is taken out of the clutches of the bureauratic control it will not be able to reveal its full potential in raising the tempo of industrialisation. Rapid industrialisation in Pakistan demands certain structural changes. "One-Window Operation" was instituted some time back to meet the needs of the industrialists through one source. But the scheme has yet to take a positive start. It is imperative that this operation is streamlined to produce the required results. We have also not been able to attract foreign investment to the extent some other Asian countries have been able to do. Foreign investors should be attracted by the offer of all possible incentives. We are also faced with serious shortage in the field of energy. Loadshedding causes heavy loss of industrial production. The private sector should be induced to enter this sector. Agro-based industries should be encouraged to bring the rural areas into the mainstream of industrialisation and expand employment opportunities. To convert black money into productive assets the entire country should be declared a tax free zone. No one understands the problems of industry better than the Prime Minister. People will expect him to take the necessary measures to give a new fillip to industry.[1]

Ever since the Nawaz Sharif government came to power, after rigging in a sophisticated manner the elections, it seems, as if, it is under the spell of some curse. It is forced to take steps, which it very well knows, would go against its own interests. But even the steps, which it takes to defuse the situation, instead of coming to its rescue, further aggravate the situation. After the accession to power, the IJI Government immediately increased the prices of fertiliser at a time when the farmers were preparing to sow the Rabi crop. This step at once raised the prices of necessities and sent the fertilisers into the black market which further pushed up its prices. The poor farmers found themselves between the devil and the deep sea. On the one hand, the prices of fertilisers had gone skyhigh and on the other, the price of paddy went below the government fixed prices because the commission agents deliberately refrained from buying it, knowing fully well that the farmers desperately needed money to buy seed and fertilisers for the Rabi crop. As this situation cropped up immediately after the elections, it left the farmers bewildered and demoralised. They had not yet recovered from this shock, when the prices of oil were increased by 41.5 per cent. It broke the backs of the people. The price rose a second time during a span of one month and seriously affected the employees with fixed incomes and the down-trodden workers. In order to ward off the biting effect of this, the President promulgated "Qassas and Diat" Ordinance in order to rope in the clergy. The government claimed that it was another step towards Islamisation. This ordinance provides for compromises in the murder cases on the payment of compensation, as provided by the Islamic injunctions. It also provided that drivers of different types of vehicles shall have to pay Rs. one lakh sixty thousand to the next to kin of the person dying in road accidents. This ordinance, though wrapped in religious phraseology and pious words, however, proved the last straw. Drivers of buses and trucks, trawlers and wagons and even rickshows, spontaneously went on a "wheel jam countrywide strike" and brought all means of communication, except railways, to a standstill. The strike was total and so massive that it paralysed the life in the country. Pakistan has never witnessed such a transport strike in its entire history. It continued for five full days and affected not only the general public, business community and the production process, but also eroded the credibility of the interpreters of Shariat and put them in a quandary.[2]

The strike was only withdrawn when the government gave assurance that the ordinance would be suitably amended, which meant that the Shariat was not something immutable but could be changed to suit the interests of the rulers. The action of the transport workers was not only a victory for them but also laid bare the irrational claims of the clergy. Under the pressure of the IMF and the World Bank, Nawaz Sharif repeatedly announced that the industries in the public sector would be denationalised and be sold to the private entrepreneurs as they have almost gone bankrupt due to the mismanagement of the bureaucracy. It is indeed strange that the very same bureaucracy is continuing to run the country and even today, the Head of the State is an old bureaucrat. Though time and again, voices have been raised against its misdeeds, still it remains at the helm of affairs and no way is found to deal with it.[3]

Privatisation seems to be the new cure prescribed by conventional wisdom for our economic ills. Even the Soviet

Union is supposed to be embarking on a capitalist route under the guise of a transition towards a 'market economy' although the eventual outcome of this course is far from clear. In the absence of a precise definition and a lack of clarity about its scope and objectives, the 'privatisation' process means different things to different people. An objective analysis of the background of this process and its relevance to our economic situation would therefore be helpful.

It is fashionable to quote the British example in support of privatisation. Sweeping generalisations may have given the impression that privatisation is universally acknowledged as a sound instrument of economic policy and has had the unqualified and enthusiastic support of the vast majority of the British electorate. However, the Conservative election victories in the last decade were largely due to the outcome of the Falklands war, the formation of the break-away Social Democratic Party and Labour's soft policies on national defence. The split in the left-wing vote, coupled with the single-member constituency system, resulted in disproportionately large Conservative majorities in the House of Commons although the party polled well below fifty per cent of the votes cast.[4]

The privatisation plank therefore was not the decisive factor in the Tory victories. It was however an ideological objective of the radical wing of the Party headed by Mrs. Thatcher who took full advantage of her Parliamentary majority to achieve her avowed aim of dismantling Socialism. Privatisation, on the scale introduced by Mrs. Thatcher, also had its opponents within the Tory Party, as symbolised by Lord MacMillian who compared this process to the 'selling of the family silver.' Finally the most significant point that is often over-looked is that generally all state run enterprises in Britain, including those with a previous history of losses, were operating profitably at the time of privatisation and sold their stocks to the general public at considerable premiums. Evidently if the British state is required to sell off all its profit making enterprises, then the success of privatisation becomes a self-fulfilling prophecy. It would be erroneous therefore to eulogize the 'success' of privatisation in Britain where this measure was inspired more by an ideological commitment rather than on its 'economic or social' merits. Perhaps more pertinent to us is the example of the mixed economies of Italy and France, with higher per capita incomes than Britain, and a record of several successfully run state enterprises. Privatisation of stocks of state enterprises can generally take one of two forms. In the first the State (that is the Federal, Provincial or Local Government or its agency) retains a majority share-holding. This method of privatisation can in fact be part of a strategy of increasing both state control and ownership of productive assets in the economy. For example if the State sells Rs. 50 out of a Rs. 100 share-holding in company A and invests the sale proceeds to acquire a 50% interest in Company B it will be in a position to control two companies (A & B) instead of one (A). An important consequence of partial privatisation of state owned companies is that such companies are under an economic compulsion to offer a market rate of return on their equity base. For this to happen an adequate level of profitability is required, which if attained, would benefit both the state and the private shareholders. The second form of privatisation generally entails a complete disinvestment of shares held by the state or a relinquishment of control over the company's manegement whilst retaining a minority shareholding. Under this method the State may retain a 'Golden share' having veto rights on certain pre-defined strategic issues, such as sale of stocks beyond a given percentage to foreigners or compliance with specified investment programmes.[5]

The debate on privatisation is linked with the pros and cons of public sector management but it would be misleading to draw any universal conclusions on this subject. A large number of criteria such as, operating efficiencies, professional management. wage levels, job security, taxes paid to the

Government, growth, value added, quality of entrepreneurship and security of loan and equity capital have a bearing on this debate.

Loss making businesses are not in the sole domain of state enterprises as is evidenced by the massive amount of bad and doubtful debts incurred by financial institutions on private sector units. The fact is that both sectors have had their share of good and bad projects and in the case of the latter the contributing factor generally is the quality of management rather than ownership of the project. Ironically, broadening the base of ownership is one of the advantages cited in favour of privatisation. For, on this creteria, the ultimate form of privatisation can best be achieved through Federal ownership which implies a per-capita sharing of the state's assets by the entire population. The cause of egalitarianism can be further promoted under state ownership if the income from such assets is applied progressively to benefit the poorer sections of society. Hence the case for privatisation can essentially be argued on the basis of efficiency rather than altruistic motives. Privatisation is also used as a means of reducing budgatory deficits. In our situation this can be a financially imprudent course if the shares sold are not replaced by equivalent income producing assets. The consequences of selling state assets to meet rising budgetary revenue defcits can be disastrous in the medium and long-term leading to additional taxation on an already improverished nation. The state therefore must establish an appropriate mix between profits and taxes in meeting its budgetary expenditures. It must discharge its various roles as a entrepreneur regulator of economic activity and tax-levying entity in an efficient manner. In our objective conditions both private and state enterprises have an important role to play in the country's development with varying degrees of emphasis in the different economic sectors. We therefore need to concentrate on improving the performance of businesses within these sectors rather than indulge in radical experiments in the hope of solving our economic problems and building and egalitarian society. The key factor for improving profitability in state enterprises is to structure these as profit centres having operational autonomy and continuity of management similar to private sector units. The writer is in good company in propagating a case for the state's entrepreneual role. After all Mr. Galbraith — an eminent citizen of the world's largest capitalist country — himself said during a television interview that it would make no difference if the stocks of General Motors were held by the Federal Government. Our policy makers should tread with caution on the privatisation route and restrict this process to a partial sale of shares with the state retaining majority control. This would be a sensible way of synthesising public good and efficient management of resources.[6]

The compromise hammered out at the ministerial talks on inclusion of the textile trade within GATT dispensation is like the proverbial elephant that is to be described by blind men; no particular country is sure if the decision to maintain the Multi-fibre agreement (MFA) for another ten years is advantageous to it or not whereas the developed countries would have preferred that MFA to continue for 15 years or more, developing countries, in particular India, rooted for a six year period within which the restrictions could be dismantled. Dr. Swamy, India's Commerce Minister, felt that a ten year period was a consensus, but no one is fooled that India views the decade of restrictions as a victory of sorts for the developed countries.

India is not the only country that feels cheated by the compromise. Pakistan's Commerce Minister, Malik Naeem Khan, called the compromise an "illusion of liberalisation", because the agreement lists items for inclusion within GATT which are in any case permitted free entry; some of these items will figure in the statements that EEC will exhibit according to the time-frame agreed for the phased liberalisation. So who has won the current about for concessions? The developed nations, by any measure, will win for two reasons.

The obvious one is that the decade will let them introduce any number of barriers as replacements for the MFA. Quantitative restrictions could gather prominence putting paid to any gains from MFA abolition. Ample evidence exists to substantiate this since newly industrialised countries like Taiwan and South Korea, currently not covered by MFA, are subject to such quantitative restrictions.[7]

The more fundamental reason is the transformation that the European textile industry is undergoing at present. The EC programme for unification in two years has galvanized the textile and clothing industry to strive for greater economies of scale and modernise with the latest technology. Southern member-states like Spain and Portugal too are claimbing on the badeagon to a market which promises, but 1992, to generate an annual growth in demand for textiles by 6 per cent to 8 per cent. Couple this with the potential that reform in Eastern Europe offers the textile industry in EC by way of subcontracting to exploit lower labour costs and the only comparative advantage that Indian textile exports enjoyed over EC or the South East Asian countries, will have vanished into thin air. But all is not; let the MFA abolition should generate a second look at the mainstay of our textile exports—cotton fabrics of the grey variety, catering mainly to the lower segment of the market.

Beyond and above all this, however, Pakistan's establishment has come to realise that political independence is predicated on economic freedom. This is the area (within the plan framework drawn up by Sartaj Aziz) where the industrialist Sharif will be asked to perform. It was appropriate that the first Cabinet meeting was devoted to economic matters, and guidelines have been laid down for rapid denationalisation, privatisation, widespread liberalisation and tax and administrative reform. Before all this gets off, however, Pakistan will have to cope with a new price spiral likely to be set off by the oil price hike. Economic liberalisation is being posited as the panacea for Pakistan's dire condition. And only with a self-reliant economy can it exercise true political independence. A business boom will, however, also mean the tribe of Nawaz Sharif will grow. If it does, he will have a powerful constituency. But will the establishment be happy about it?[8]

References

1. *Pakistan Times*, 8 November 1990.
2. Sardar Shaukat Ali, Troubled Times for Nawaz Sharif, *Patriot*, 31 December, 1990.
3. *Ibid.*
4. Shahab Azfar, The Limits of Privatisation. *Dawn*, 17 November, 1990.
5. *Ibid.*
6. *Ibid.*
7. *The Business and Political Observer*, 8 December, 1990.
8. Kesava Menon, New, Nawaz Sharif, *Frontline*, 24 November, 1990.

only with a self reliant economy can it exercise true political independence. A business community will, however, also be an the tribe of Nawaz Sharif will grow. If it does, he will be a powerful constituency. But will the establishment be happy about it?[8]

References

1. *Pakistan Times*, 9 November, 1990.
2. Sardar Shaukat Ali, 'Troubled Times for Nawaz Sharif', *Patriot*, [illegible] December, 1990.
3. *Ibid.*
4. [illegible] Aziz, 'The Euphoria of Privatisation', *Dawn*, 17 November, 1990.
5. *Ibid.*
6. *Ibid.*
7. *The Business and Political Observer*, 4 December, 1990.
8. [illegible] Menon, 'Now, Nawaz Sharif Triumphs', 28 November, 1990.

9

Tax Holiday

Prime Minister Nawaz Sharif has announced that tax holiday would be enforced throughout the country, to create congenial atmosphere for free industrialisation.

Addressing the nation over radio and television in Islambad on November 8, 1990. Prime Minister Nawaz Sharif said that his government would also transfer nationalised sick industrial units to the private sector, which were not only an impediment in the way of free industrialisation in the country but also a burden on the national exchequer. It wasironcial, he said, that these sick units were eating away billions of rupees of public money.

He said that he wished that even the defence equipment should also be produced by the private sector, leaving aside only sensitive material. Pakistani industrialists, he said, were capable of producing everything within the country. If private companies of other countries could produce defence material for Pakistan, why this could not be done by the Pakistani industrialists themselves, he asked.

Prime Minister Nawaz Sharif also announced that the

domestic and foreign entrepreneurs, setting up new industrial units in the country, would be given complete tax holiday, with the condition that they would take responsibility of the health and education of the workers and their children.

Prime Minister Nawaz Sharif said that the present oppressive economic system would be changed under which millions of people in the country were groaning.

He said that this cruel system would be replaced by the economic system of Islam based on justice which could bring happiness on the face of the common man.

He said it was his faith that so long as happiness and prosperity was not reflected from the face of a common man, the face of Pakistan could never glow with happiness.

Nawaz Sharif made it clear that the enforcement of Islamic principles would no longer be a slogan and these would practically be implemented.

He said that Zakat and Ushr would be utilised in fulfilling the needs of the deserving persons and for the education of the children.

He said that the government was bound by Constitution as well to enforce Islamic laws. He said he was mentioning those bright and golden principles of Islamic Shariah which could bring equality and create equal opportunities for the society and the principles which could eleminate the poverty and ingorance.

Nawaz Sharif announced that residents of all recognised katchi abadies throughout the country, would be given proprietary rights.

He said that he had also decided that the hutments would not be allowed to remain in shabby and sub-human conditions. It would be his effort to enable the residents of these katchi abadies to live in conditions with necessary civic facilities.

He has, therefore, decided to set up development authorities, for katchi abadies, on the pattern of KDA, CDA and LDA. These authorities, he said, would be responsible for providing wholesome water to these abadies, besides making arrangements for the disposal of sewer water.

He said that these authorities would also provide sui gas, transport and pucca roads, in these abadies wherever possible.

Prime Minister Nawaz Sharif also announced that his government would provide residential plots to the people, who did not have own houses, on cheap rates and on easy instalments. The poor and widows would be given reference in such schemes, he added.

Nawaz Sharif said that he was conscious that the housing problem was an extremely difficult aspect of human life, especially for the have nots. He had many proposals and plans to solve this problem on a large-scale basis, throughout the country.

Nawaz Sharif, who says he has a "grand plan for the future," has announced that he has lifted all restrictions on industrialisation, seeks privatisation of the public sector enterprises and declared tax holiday for the whole country. But these brave words have to be couched into specific and clear-cut policies. And he has committed himself to making no adverse changes for the next five years. It will be even better to have a national commitment in this regard for the next ten years so that the momentum of industrial development is not disturbed until the year 2000. Before we go all out for new industries we have to have a crash plan to achieve the best out of the established industries. We have to achieve capacity utilisation in the industries established and scrape the long idle industries which are now being used as begiging or borrowing bowls for larger funds from public banks or development finance institutions.

Some of the industries are producing far below capacity for want of power or frequent disruption of supply. Some industries in Karachi are often hit hard by paucity of water. Of course, law and order problems have been a major deterrent to full production in Karachi and Sindh as a whole. And genuine credit needs of industries in a period of inflation and devaluation have to be met by the banks and DFIs if their tracks record as borrowers has been good enough. Before large scale investment is made in a big way, heavy investment on the infrastructure has to be made in all suitable industrial sites. And the investment on power has to be very heavy. Nawaz Sharif talks of making more nuclear power available, but that may take six to seven years or more as the nuclear reactors we have negotiated with China and France are not expected to start production before that. Hence more power has to be produced through the use of gas coal, or oil. New measures will have to be devised to induct the private sector in a big way. And industrialists have to be encouraged to produce their own power wherever they can; but that will enhance the cost of overall investment a great deal, discourage the investors, and force the banks to give larger investment loans. So unless the infrastructure problems are solved resolutely rapid industrialisation, and even more an industrial revolution, will be a distant dream. Most of the funds for investment will come from the public sector banks and DFIs. But their capacity to lend is limited in view of the poor recovery from industrial investors as well as public sector units to which large loans had been given. In this context, can Nawaz Sharif and his fellow businessmen in office persuade the new investors not to divert 15 to 20 per cent from their investment loans to their accounts here or in foreign banks? If that is accomplished the cost of industrialisation would come down, the companies will be financially healtheir, and they will find it easy to repay the loans instead of being tempted to declare them sick and default on debt servicing. If Nawaz Sharif economic diplomacy can succeed in this vital area that will be a major achievement, and mark the beginning of real industrial revolution.[1]

Pakistan has continued to enjoy strong economic growth, averaging 6.7 per cent in real terms since the late about half that rate, with, the population (estimated at 103 million in mid-1988) increasing by 3.1 per cent a year. This explosive rate of increase threatens prospects of Pakistan climbing out of poverty (per capita income stood at US $ 390 in mid-1988), given the country's ratio of natural resources to population. A very low literacy rate of about 26% is another development handicap (and some economists maintain, a major cause of the population problem).[2] Even in the short—to medium-term, growth is somewhat fragile. Export income is heavily dependent on a single commodity, cotton. The country's role as a front-line state to the Afghanistan conflict has brought it civilian as well as military aid from the west. With an end to the conflict in sight, this strategy imperative will weaken. Remittances from Pakistanis working in the Middle East have continued to run down with the curtailment of projects by all producers. From a peak of nearly US $ 3 billion a year in the early 1980s, remittance inflow was down 13.6 per cent, to US $ 2.006 billion in fiscal 1987-88 (July-June).

Priorities remain to boost domestic savings. National income data puts the savings rate at only 4.5 per cent of GDP, compared with nearly 20 per cent for other countries in the Sub-continent. This may ingore much informal sector savings and investment, but shows a serious weakness. The government sector also suffers from a chronic narrowness of the tax-base, with Islamabad unable to wield the political muscle to tax the important rural industry (accounting for about 25 per cent of GDP). A flourishing "black" economy —widely estimated at about 25 per cent of top of the US $ 38.5 billion official GDP (mid-1988) and weakness in collection robs the treasury of much that is owing to it. The

National Taxation Commission has estimated tax evaded to be 263 per cent more than tax paid.

In 1987-88 defence outlays took 38 per cent of current expenditure of Rs 129.7 billion, while a further 35 per cent went on debt service. The government deficit of Rps 52 billion or 7.9 per cent of GDP was reduced from the previous year's alarming figure of Rps 54 billion (8.9 of GDP), but still esceeded the Rps 48 billion development (capital) side of spending—meaning that the government was still mortagaging the future to pay for current costs.

The narrowing of the gap was due to some success in boosting revenues at a faster rate than spending. The finance minister in the mid-1988 caretaker government, Mahbubul Haq, continued this drive in the budget for 1988-89 encouraged by the withholding of a World Bank loan earlier in the year in protest at government inaction. Certain key tax rates were lowered, and at the same time their application extended. Corporate tax rates came down from 55 per cent to an effective 49.5 per cent while tariffs and indirect taxes were simplified and extended.

Haq announced that farm income would be "clubbed" with non-rural income, so that at least the latter would be taxed at a higher marginal rate even if the former remained exempt. Penalties for evasion were drastically increased. Provincial governments were placed on a tighter rein, while the 183 government corporations will be expected to generate more of their own funding. The deficit was predicted to be slightly higher in absolute terms, but down to 7.6 per cent of GDP. Whether the new government can maintain the impetus of tax reform—in the face of a backlash by business will be an early test of its effectiveness.

On the foreign payments side in 1987-88, Pakistan enjoyed a 23 per cent lift in exports to US $ 4.3 billion, chiefly on the strength of a cotton boom, while spending 12.7

per cent more on imports, and the trade deficit fell 3 per cent to US $ 2.2 billion. However, with lower remittances, the current account deficit rose from US $ 719 million the previous year (2 per cent of GDP) to US $ 1.07 billion (2.75 per cent of GDP). Foreign exchange reserves decline to US $ 500 million, one month's imports, in June 1988 from US $ 865 million a year earlier. Foreign civilian debt rose 18 per cent to US $ 13.9 billion.

Foreign import quotas place ceilings on export volumes, so that Pakistan is highly dependent on world commodity prices. Production of exports is also dependent on natural conditions. Late rains in 1987-88 caused wheat production to fall short of self-sufficiency at 12.6 million tonnes by some 20 per cent, so that Pakistan had to use imports for the gap. Rice was also affected. Cotton production rose 11 per cent to hit a record high of 8.7 million bales. Flooding early in 1988-89, was expected to keep production of major commodities slightly below the previous year's levels.

Manufacturing exports, mostly based on local commodities, showed good results in 1987-88, with exports of cotton cloth up 39 per cent, cotton yarn up 18 per cent and leather up 17 per cent. Overall, manufacturing grew by 7.6 per cent with the small-scale sector slightly more expensive than the large enterprises. Investment in cotton textile plants was feverish, with some reports suggesting that 150 new factories were built or committed. Quotas in key markets caused concern about over-capacity.

The outgoing government took tentative steps to begin privatising the huge state sector, with national carrier Pakistan International Airways and the five state-owned trading banks (nationalised in 1974) likely targets for floating of about 20 per cent of equity to the public. The incoming Bhutto government has vowed not to carry out further nationalisations, but is vague about reducing the existing state presence in industry and services. One approach to privatisation already advanced in discussion is the contracting out of power generation by the Water and Power Development Authority (WAPDA). The state utility was believed to be talking with private groups about their construction of power plants in Baluchistan under guarantee of long-term off take contracts from WAPDA—thus freeing state capital funds for activities where user-charges are harder to levy.

About one-third of domestic oil requirements were met by local production of 47.884 barrels per day in June 1988. Natural gas (402,450 million ft^3 in 1987-88) was another important source of commercial energy. Oil and gas exploration have surged under incentives. Hydro-power supplies about 35 per cent of the 67,00 MW installed electricity capacity. This has been augmented by expansion of the Tarbela Dam scheme, though the future of two new dams, at Kalabagh and Basha, is cluded by interprovincial disputes about water usage on the Indus River system.[3]

Prime Minister Nawaz Sharif assured the nation that his government would strive hard to protect the poor masses from the current worldwide wave of price hide, especially on essential items.

Addressing the nation over ratio and television networks, on November 7, 1990. Prime Minister Nawaz Sharif said that he had started examining various proposals in this regard.

He, however, categorically said that every endeavour would be made not to allow increase in the prices of atta, vanaspati ghee, cereals, pulses and cotton cloth.

Nawaz Sharif said that Pakistan had been plunged into a difficult phase due to the Gulf crisis, as she had to bear an additional burden of two billion dollars (40 billion rupees). Besides, there are problems of rehabilitation of Pakistanis uprooted from there and the worldwide prices of oil had also doubled. Pakistan was also not safe from its impact, he said.

He said that it was the increase in the prices of oil, due to which the nation would be confronted with a new wave of the general price hike.

He asserted that the present government had no hand in this situation. Pakistan had also become victim of this vicious wave which could not be blunted. Efforts, however, could be made to save the poor people from it, he said assuring the people that his government would take all necessary steps to do that.

Prime Minister Nawaz Sharif said that Pakistan had talented experts, whose knowledge and services would now be utilized for the benefit of the poor people. It was unfortunate, he said, that the advantage of their services had henceforth accrued to the well-to-do people.

He said these experts would recommend to the government as to how the poor people could be spared of the current wave of price spiral and how the affluent classes of society could be further burdened to meet the budgetary deficits, so that the poor could be fed and clothed.

The Prime Minister said that these were the immediate measures to obviate the impact of the price hike. The real diagnosis and solution to this problem would have to be done by undertaking the task of national reconstruction and progress.

He said that he proposed to do some emergency planning in this regard.

Prime Minister Nawaz Sharif, however, declared that historically, the hour of decision had struck, and the nation had to decide once for all, whether it desired to live as a self-respecting people, like free and sovereign nation or it wanted to roam about the world with begging bowl.

He said the present government strongly felt that the only course open before the nation was the course of self-respect, he said, adding nations and individuals had to render sacrifices for their self-respect.

He, therefore, demanded the people of Pakistan to inculcate spirit of simplicity, austerity and, hard work, to achieve this cherished goal of self-reliance.

Nawaz Sharif said he would not like to paint rosy pictures before you, as the coming days would be of trials, tribulations and per-severence. He asked the nation to be ready for them.

Prime Minister Nawaz Sharif said that those who led lavish and extravagant lives at the cost of their younger generation's future, were selfish. He had firm faith in and commitment to the future generations and his government would therefore, never resort to anything which would amount to bartering away the future of the younger generations, he said, adding "we will lead an austere life at the present, so that the future of the coming generations may be glorious and prosperous.

He emphasized that the paucity of resources did not mean that the nation should become vagrant. "We will expand our resources, as a self-respecting nation and turn the future of our future generations prosperious and glorious," he said.

Prime Minister Nawaz Sharif pleaded for one dish menu at social gatherings and wedding parties, to curb tendencies of extravagance in the people.

Prime Minister announced that to promote austerity and simplicity, his government had decided that he, his colleagues and officials would not participate in wedding parties, having more than one dish on the menu.

He regretted that extravagence and lavish spending was eating into the vitals of our society, in addition to creating many economic difficulties. It was, therefore, imperative that such tendencies were vigorously avoided.

The Prime Minister said that it was unfortunate that such tendencies were specially resorted to at the wedding parties. Besides multi-dish menu, jehez and other unnecessary traditions were also being adhere to in our society due to which the grey-haired fathers had to pay back debts till their death, he said.

He, therefore appealed to the people to inclucate, promote and strengthen the habit of saving and austerity.

He concluded his remarks on the subject with the appeal ...... "give me austere life and hard work, I will give you prosperity and stability : give me discipline, I will give you peace and tranquillity."

In his maiden address to the nation, Prime Minister, Nawaz Sharif, announced his first measure to stimulate investment, an income tax holiday to be given to industry located anywhere in the country. This incentive has been well received in business circles. It is being referred to as a positive step, in the right direction. What, if any, are the laudatory features of such a concession? What success is it likely to have in achieving the underlying objectives, acceleration in industial investment and production and employment growth? What impact will it have on the government urgent need for additional resources to finance the mounting budgetary deficit? What will be the political implications of such a measure, especially when the government is forced (it is already under severe pressure to do so) to raise revenues from other sectors and other sections of the society? Will the

World Bank and the IMF view kindly yet another concession that, at least potentially, threatens to widen the already huge deficit? Finally, although the Prime Minister, while announcing this incentive, stated that it would only be made available provided claimants take care of the educational and health needs of their labour, can a system based on such a quid pro quo, in fact, be implemented. These are some of the issues that this article will attempt to address. An income tax holiday to all sub-sectors of industry is, of course, both meaningless and inequitable. The Prime Minister cannot surely by arguing that no distinction need be made whether the industry is providing luxury consumer goods ranging from toiletries, cosmetics and confectionery to assembling colour televisions and airconditioners or manufacturing products like fertilisers, light and heavy engineering goods. He certainly cannot be advocating the development of an industrial structure founded on such a base. If not (which I presume is a safe assumption) then is there a need to remind him that the existing tax structure already accords income tax reliefs and holidays to a number of what can be called nationally important sectors of the economy. As regards the applicability of the concession to the entire country it is patently clear that it is addressed to the lobby of Lahore and, to some extent, Karachi-based industrialists. Even today the tax holiday incentive is available in the whole of NWFP, Balochistan and the bulk of interior Sindh and some backward districts of the Punjab. How it will increase the pace of urbanisation, with all the social and other complications it entails, and accentuate the problem of rural urban migration is another matter whose implications will not be lost on many.[4]

Before one proceeds to examine whether the concession will succeed in attracting investment in the productive sectors of the economy it is worthwhile nothing that even if it were to stimulate investment in the central parts of Punjab and Karachi (areas which have the necessary infrastructure, markets and skills) it will largely be at the expense of the more depressed areas of the country. This will enlarge the income differentials between the more developed and relatively backward areas of the country, in particular between central Punjab and Karachi and interior Sindh and Balochistan. Lack of employment opportunities and widening differentials will heighten frustration and discontent among the youth in these areas, thereby damaging prospects for national unity and integration. One of the objectives is the stimulation of industrial growth of employment opportunities. From the discussion above it should be apparent that the outcome in terms of additional employment per unit of investment will depend largely on the type of industry, its regional distributional consequences notwithstanding. Moreover, it is difficult to say to what extent it will lead to actual additional involvement. Entrepreneurs do not invest simply because there is a tax holiday. New investment depends upon rates of return in other economic activities, availability or access to infrastructure and energy and markets for the products of the manufacturing concerns. The domestic market is rather small and not growing fast enough and the purchasing power of many is being squeezed by inflation. As for the international demand for our traditional exports, the signs do not at least in the short-term, and particularly after the Middle East crisis, look encouraging. It is, therefore, difficult to assess whether it will stimulate new investment or result in its shift from one, relatively less developed area of the country to another area, better serviced by physical (roads, telephones, etc.) and social (schools, hospitals, etc.) infrastructure. Furthermore, any perceptive observer of the industrial scene in Pakistan will tell you that the incentive which entrepreneurs find most attractive (partly because it reduces the cost of initial investment) is an exemption/relief from import duties on plant and equipment. A 5 to 6 year tax holiday incentive is not tempting partly because it takes almost 2-3 years for most projects to break even and partly because they have largely succeeded in their tax evasion endeavours. The tax administration machinery in Pakistan has not been terribly successful in collecting income taxes from the domestic private sector; the main income tax-payers are multinationals and some of the profit-making large public sector corporations.[5]

It is difficult to imagine that the IJI will be able to extract more revenues from all segments of the community; if industry were to be exempt from tax. In particular, it will be impossible (if it is not already) to get the landed elite to pay taxation on their incomes derived from agricultural activity. Furthermore, as the government needs to mobilise resources, on an urgent basis, to finance its expenditure obligations, particularly in respect of defence, debit servicing and the higher oil bill, it will have to generate revenues by raising indirect taxes. The distributional repercussions of this route should be obvious. The burden of additional taxation will have to be borne dis-proportionately; those least in a position to do so will have to bear a higher burden. Some might argue that if domestic industry is not contributing large sums of revenue in the form of income tax this relieve will not make a major difference to the government's revenue generating efforts to bridge the budgetary gap. The problem with this argument is that it underplays the role of perceptions in politics. What is more important than reality is the perception of it. If there is a feeling that despite the resources crunch some, relatively better placed, sections of the population are being excused from contributing to national needs, then the government's credibility as an institution, treating all sections of the society fairly will be badly damaged.

Similarly, it does not appear likely than our major donors, in particular the IMF and the World Bank, will applaud the government for expanding its list of exemptions (already large) that they have been urging different governments over the years to whittle down.[6]

The eruption of the Gulf crisis in early August 1990 and the jump in petroleum prices to about 40 US dollars a barrel (threatening to reach the figure of 60 dollars should the war "escalate" has caused a drop in the value of the US dollar, the world's most important currency. While the dollar continued losing its attraction as a "safe port" for investors in times of hardship, gold and the Swiss frank gained in value. The dollar's rate of exchange droped to under 1,600 German marks in August this year while in September it rated only 1.56 marks, less than the bedrock of 1.57 at the end of 1987. So far the Swiss frank has gained most from the dollar's drop (1 $= 1,30 franks). It has become a "magnet for floating capital" in the Middle East, because of its traditionally stable value and relatively high rates of interests. In August the price of gold jumped to over 415 dollars per ounce (31.103 grammes), and was later stabilised at about 400 dollars.

From April to August 1990, the dollar depreciated 6% as against the Japanese Yen and 10% as against the Deutsche Mark. It continued falling also in relationship to less important currencies. All this is taking place in a situation when individual crucial elements point towards a stronger dollar. In the middle eighties, due to the formidable deficit in the balance of payments the US dollar's rate of exchange decreased, but it strengthened again towards the end of the same decade as the deficit in the payments balance and the budget decreased. Although this year the results in America's trade balance are unexpectedly good (lower deficit) the value of the dollar continues wanting. The savings of the American population have increased while domestic demand is a below expectations, largely due to reduced demand for imported goods in the United States.[7]

If one considers the "parities in purchasing power", a comparison of prices for similar commodities in different countries, the dollar was considerably depreciated as against the most important world currencies. According to the London "Economist", the dollar has depreciated 30% as against the yen and the German mark. However the parity of purchasing power is not the most reliable indicator of trends in the rate of exchange as some of the listed costs may vary from country to country for a number of reasons. Therefore some English economists have used an alternative comparison. They computed the average real rate of exchange i.e. the average of nominal rates of exchange between various currencies, adjusted to inflation rates. They considered the strongest world currencies covering a period from 1960 to 1990. According to their calculations if one considers the long-term average real rates of exchange between thesecurrencies, one dollar should be worth 1.99 marks or 217 yen. This means that now the dollar's depreciation as against the mark is 20% and as against the yen 30%.

The question arises : why should the dollar be so weak now? Several reasons are stated. One is that depositors are avoiding currencies whose rates of interests are waning, in so far as a reduced rate of inflation is expected in a given country. If one considers rates of interest, the dollar is now less attractive than it was in 1989. With Iraq's invasion of Kuwait the returns on three months deposits in marks were about 4/10 percentage points higher than on dollar deposits, while in March 1989 dollar deposits brought in four percentage points more than mark deposits. The same applies to yen deposits. Although this year short-term American rates of interests were lower, the dividends on long-term government bonds in the USA increased by 3% percentage points, which might indicate that higher inflation could be expected in America. The higher petroleum prices are expected to escalate these trends in rates of interests and create more difficulties for the dollar.

According to new model of world economic growth (recently elaborated by W. McKibbin from Brookings Institution and J. Sachs of Harvard) a 25% increase in the price of petroleum would increase inflation rates in the USA by about one percentage point, in Germany by less than half, and in Japan halfway between the two. It would also effect a drop in economic growth rate in all three economies, the strongest in the world, amounting to one half percentage point. For this year the growth rate in American economy has been forecast at not more than 1%, while the Americans themselves are more and more concerned over the shock effects of oil prices on production than over growing inflation. On the other hand it is expected that this year the growth rate in the economy of Germany and Japan will be up to four or more per cent. Both countries have pledged themselves to fiscal expansion. Germany will have to allocate at least 2-3% of its gross national product in order to compensate for the switch of East German economy to market economy. Japan has promised to spend as an average of 1% of its GNP on public works every year during the following decade. If both countries are keep inflation under control, they will most probably have to increase short-term rates of interest. It is expected that the petroleum shock will affect the trade of each of these countries, however it is considered it will be least painful for USA. The increasing oil prices will have a stronger negative effect on the current balance of payments in Japan than in the USA, as Japanese imports of petroleum are larger in relationship to the volume of their economies. According to the mentioned growth model, after a 25% increase in oil prices, the current American payments deficit will increase by 0.01% of the GNP, while Germany's surplus will drop by 1.3% of the GNP, and Japan is by 0.4%. The long-term forecast of this model drown up by will known American economic experts, is that the American deficit will actually be reduced as a result of increasing oil prices, as the greately reduced domestic demand in the USA, viewed on a long-term basis, will improve. Finally, if each of the three countries under consideration were to react to the petroleum shock in the same way, it is considered that the US dollar would increase by 0.8% as against the yen and 0.25% as against the Deutsche Mark.[8]

According to initial reactions in many industrialised countries, it might be expected that the effects of the latest jump in petroleum prices will be less than on the two earlier occasions in the seventies (1973 and 1979). The jump in the price of petroleum, the basic strategic raw meterials, has jeopardised current strategy in resolving the serious problem of world debts. Before the crisis erupted in the Gulf it appeared that some progress, albeit minor, had been made in dealing with the foreign debts of the developing countries. Now however the situation is far from having been resolved. The increase in the price of petroleum from 16 dollars per barrel in July this year to about 40 dollars in October will conduce inflation. However, assuming that the crisis does not seriously escalate, some estimates say that many countries will not be involved in recession and "stagflation", as was the case during the other two petroleum crises. Just before the latest crisis, petroleum was comparatively cheap : economic calculations indicate that between 1980 and the summer of 1990 the price of oil was halved in relationship to the purchasing power of industrial products, and many countries had managed to reduce their dependence on imported petroleum as compared to the late seventies. What is more there are now ample oil reserves. The OECD countries have sufficient petroleum stocks to satisfy demand for a period of three months. According to estimates of the International Monetary Fund (IMF) if the price of petroleum is stabilised at 25 dollars per barrel, the industrialised countries, as a grouping, may look forward to a drop in economic growth rate amounting to 1/4 percentage point, this and next year. If this forecast of the IMF is translated into reality, it would mean a slowing down of the economic growth rate of the OECD countries this and next year, to the tune of 2.5%, and a growth in inflation amounting to approximately 5%. The estimates for the developing countries are far worse. Although as a group the developing countries are petroleum exporters, their share in the world consumption of petroleum is 28% (18% in 1973).

The petroleum crisis, caused by Iraq's invasion of Kuwait, changed the agenda of the annual assembly of the IMF and the World Bank in Washington this September. Instead of concentrating on the problems of Eastern Europe and the world's poverty-stricken nations, priority was given to how to help the affected countries to cope with the critical situation created by sky-rocketing petroleum prices. It became amply clear that the world cannot count on commercial banks recycling the surplus capital of OPEC for petroleum importing countries, as was the case in the seventies. There are few countries which will be profited from the soaring petroleum prices. Among the highly indebted countries, the World Bank identified only Venezuela, Mexico, Ecuador, Algeria and Nigeria. In the case of Mexico, the situation is uncertain for recession in the USA, the main export market, may have a negative effect on the Mexican economy.

At this years session of the Bretton Woods Institutions, Finance ministers and world bankers agreed there were two ways to help the economies most hard hit by the sanctions imposed on Iraq. This aid will consist of urgent relief for the so-called countries of the immediate "front line" (Jordan, Egypt, Turkey) and IMF and World Bank assistance to other countries. Addressing the gathering of world financiers, US President Bush sponsored the forming of a "financial coordinating group for the Gulf crisis" under the leadership of American Secretary of Finance N. Brady. This group will consist of the seven richest countries in the world, the European Commission, Saudi Arabia, Kuwait, the United Arab Emirates, Qatar and South Korea. It will coordinate the allocation of 16 billion dollars worth of aid to the three above mentioned countries, which have sustained extensive losses not only in trade with Iraq but also by the drastic drop, in remittances from migrant workers and these countries share in the transport of petroleum and Suez Canal taxes.

After the first petroleum shock in 1973, in 1974 the IMF granted special "oil facilities" as aid to the developing countries importing costly petroleum. Today the IMF is having problems in expanding credits about the permitted ceilings, and if it were to apportion such funds this would impair "conditions" for granting other loans. Therefore the

IMF is striving to use its existing facilities more flexibly. For example compensatory and contingency financing facilities can be used to alleviate the losses in remittances from migrant workers in certain countries. The IMF also consider the suggestion of its General Manager, M. Comdessus, namely that the petroleum producers might use part of their exceptionally high profits from higher oil prices to subsidise the poorer oil-importing countries.[10]

The Government of Nawaz Sharif has finally announced an increase in oil prices under 6 counts ranging from 10 to 40 per cent rise of individual oil products ending speculations about the imminent rise. The economic costs of this decision on the poor man are expected to be massive through the effect on the transportation sector (which the government is attempting to insulate through lowering the capital costs of transport equipment by reducing import duties and raising the conveyance allowance of public and private sector employees); via its effect on the costs of production of prices of other domestic goods. But then what other option was available? In the light of the Gulf crisis which has not only raised the international price of oil our principal import item but has also lowered Pakistan's ability to earn foreign exchange to the tune of 151.77 million dollars annually. It is also pertinent to note that despite the substantial increase in the prices of oil the government has not raised the price by as much as our neighbouring countries India and Sri Lanka have done. While this is laudable in the sense that the interests of the consumer have been kept in mind and the government has not succumbed to the temptation to raise the oil prices by as much as was required from a long term economic point of view so that subsidisation would not lead to a higher budget deficit—a policy which some estimate is more inflationary than a direct increase in the price of oil. And raising the conveyance allowance, though a policy designed to minimise the political costs associated with an increase in the oil price, may eventually lead to galloping inflation through the irreversibility of such a policy even when the Gulf crisis is resolved. It must be borne in mind by the government that in the present crisis only those policies be adopted that can eventually be reversed —a policy which would render inflation a temorary phenomenon.[11]

References

1. Sultan Ahmad, Industrial Revolution, *Dawn*, 17 November, 1990.
2. *Asia 1989 Yearbook*, Honkong, 1989.
3. *Ibid.*
4. Shahid Kardar, Buying Prosperity, *The Nation*, 16 November, 1990.
5. *Ibid.*
6. *Ibid.*
7. Dejan Jovovic, Petroleum Shock, *Review of International Affairs*, 5 November, 1990.
8. *Ibid.*
9. *Ibid.*
10. *Ibid.*
11. *The Nation*, 16 November, 1990.

10

Energy Crisis—Oil Prices and Nuclear Reactors

The Federation of Pakistan Chambers of Commerce and Industry has assured full support to Prime Minister Nawaz Sharif and decided to submit a special report on the problems being faced by the business community.

Support was assured to the new Prime Minister at a largely attended meeting of businessmen and industrialists and office-bearers of Lahore, Karachi, Rawalpindi and Gujaranwala Chambers of Commerce and Industry held at Islamabad on November 7, 1990 with the EPCC & I President, Raja Abdul Rahman in the chair.

Speaking at the meeting Raja Abdur Rehman said that the report would include recommendations for solving the economic problems in an amicable manner. He said that the new government should pay special attention to the law and order situation in Sindh and take adequate measures to normalise it.

Presidents and representatives of other chambers of commerce and industry were of the view that the goal of economic prosperity should be achieved by creating more job opportunities in the country through industrialisation. They hoped that the new government would attend to the energy crisis on top priority basis and give incentives to promote investment. They also hoped that the new government would expedite the process of privatisation in banking and other sectors. They suggested that for industrialisation more industrial estates like Gadoon should be developed in the other provinces of the country.

History of oil exploration in the sub-continent is as old as the oil industry itself. The first oil well was drilled at Kundal (Mianwali district) just seven years after Colonel Drake and drilled the first well in Pennsylvania, USA in 1859. Soon after Pakistan, creation in August 1947. Oil exploration got a boost when a giant gas field was discovered at Sui, Balochistan in 1952. This attracted a number of exploration companies and the fifties saw an increased interest and activity is search of hydrocarbon resources. But there was no significant discovery after Sui, and the foreign oil companies left Pakistan on masse at the end of the decade considering it non-prospective. There was virtually no exploration activity in the country in 1960. A need was felt to create an indigenous exploration capability and the oil and Gas Development Corporation (OGDC) was railed in 1961. It was created through an active cooperation of the Soviet Union and for the first few years, used Soviet technology and experts to start the search for oil. Making its first discovery of gas in 1965 at Sari and oil in 1968 at Toot, OGDC maintained a level of exploration activity till mid-seventies. The emerging geological information base and discoveries of oil and gas fields brought Pakistan back to the category of oil prospective countries. A number of petroleum concessions were granted to foreign companies in seventies. As a national corporation OGDC had thus succeeded in re-attracting the interest of foreign exploration companies in Pakistan. Discovery of oil by Union Taxas of Pakistan (UTP) in 1981 at Khaskeli (District Badin) in Lower Indus Basin opened a new geological province of liquid hydrocarbons. Another important discovery of oil in the previously known prospective window of Potwar Basin at Dhurnal in 1984 by Occidental of Pakistan (OXY) gave the search for oil a major boost. The eighties saw an increasing exploration activity leading to a number of oil and gas discoveries and a substantial increase in indigenous production of crude oil. A number of new exploration agreements were concluded, and at the start of the decade of the nineties, the outlook regarding search for oil and gas seems quite optimistic OGDC is wholy a public sector entity. It has throughout been dependent on government budget for all its funding needs. Although the revenues generated by OGDC covered only a fraction of its budget, a far-reaching decision was taken to make it self-financing with effect from first of July 1989. This was a landmark development in the life of OGDC. It posed a challenge OGDC could make an economic take-off if successful or otherwise go bankrupt and vanish. The first fiscal year of OGDC's self-financing ended on June 30, 1990. It would be interesting to analyse its first years' performance and make some projections. For the fiscal year 1990, OGDC had a debt repayment liability of over Rs. 750 million. Coming off the national budget, and with very meagre revenues, OGDC faced the following three options:

— seek a white-off by the government for Rs. 750 million to give the OGDC an initial start in self-financing, or

— seek a carry forward of Rs. 750 million debt, or

— borrow money from commercial banks at high rate of interest to pay the bebt liability.[1]

Considering that any one of these obvious courses could only extract the OGDC temporarily from its present difficulty but would not lead to its financial autarky, OGDC took a hard choice. It rejected the obvious courses and undertook to improve its revenues by increasing the production of oil and gas, a simple calculation revealed, that if OGDC could double its production of oil and gas during the financial year, it could pay back the Rs. 750 million and maintain its exploration programmes. The challenge was started by fixing a mission that defined a three-pronged strategy as follows: "While maintaining a balanced economic direction the OGDC will achieve short term cash flow by concentrating in the southern district, maintain medium term production stability by exploring in the northern district and undertake an innovative search in new areas for a large reservoir of oil or gas, to give a boost to the economy of Pakistan.[2]

Working simultaneously on all the three pronge of short term cash flow improvement, medium term production stability and long term innovative search for larger reservoirs of oil and gass, OGDC achieved four oil discoveries (Fimkassar, Pasahki north and Bhai Syedan) during the year. Two of these discoveries were in the southern oil window (Badin and Sanghar districts) and the other two in the northern oil window (Chakwal and Attock districts). By rapid development of three of the newly discovered oil fields and optimization of production from the old fields, and optimization of production from the old fields, the OGDC successfully achieved the near doubling of the production of both oil and gas during the year and thus the revenues. Efforts to reduce operating costs by checking losses, improving efficiency, and controlling inventories proved effective, which further improved the cash flow position. The OGDC was able to pay back not only the Rs. 750 million but an additional Rs. 250 million of the arrears out of its own revenue generation in addition, it paid about Rs. 432 million in royalty and about a couple of hundred million in excise duty. It may be noted that before OGDC was taken off the budget on July 1, 1989, it used to get funding from the government and return part of it for debt repayment. The fiscal year 1990 became the first year, when OGDC did not get money from the national budget and instead contributed about Rs. 1500 million in cash to the national exchequer. The increase in production of all, since the start of the new fiscal year on July 1, 1990, has been even more substantial. Since the beginning of the oil crisis resulting from the Iraqi invasion of Kuwait, the OGDC has increased its oil production by over 6000 barrels a day. It may be seen from this figure that OGDC's average daily nroduction of oil in November 1988 was only 7764 barrels. It increased to 14653 barrels in November 1989. The projection for November 1990 is about 28000 barrels daily. The average production during the month of October 1990 was 27363 barrels per day. The OGDC has become the principal oil producer in the country since June 1990. A table of comparative average daily production by various oil producers is as follows: Although OGDC has greatly improved its immediate cash flow position and made a good start towards self-funding, it has many other degree of professional autonomy to the OGDC. There are only two stable configurations of the OGDC. In the first configuration, the OGDC is financed by the government and maintains a government culture and structure in its management OGDC had stayed in this configuration from its raising in 1961 to June 30, 1989 it could survive in this form for as long as the government wanted and there would be no threat to its existence. In the second stable configuration, the OGDC operates under a commercial objective of self-financing and develops a commercial culture and structure is the form, OGDC will not only survive but is expected to make the all too important economic take-off leading the country to self-reliance in oil. There is another permutation of the above configurations that is unstable, in this form, OGDC operates under the commercial objective of self-financing but retains the government culture and structure in management and control. In this state, the OGDC may face a challenge to survive. In reality, during the present phase of transition, OGDC is placed in the third and unstable configuration. It has been rightly made be self-finance but does not yet have the autonomy and flexibility to self manage. It is important that in the extreme national interest it is allowed the professional autonomy to develop a commercial culture of cost effectiveness and profitability. A dynamic structure of OGDC on modern lines of industry holds a great promise of boosting the economy of our country. It needs all the focus and the impetus. Giving the OGDC a degree of professional autonomy is one of the most far-reaching decisions that can give a new meaning to gour search for oil. Self-reliance in oil is an important but difficult objective. Even though our indigenous production of oil has been increasing at about 20 per cent for the last 2 years, our consumption of oil has been growing as well. Although the consumption has been increasing 8.9% per year, the gap between our consumption and indigenous production is continuing to grow. In net effect, we have to import more oil in future unless a determined effort is made to close the gap and move towards self-reliance. This will need a dynamic national policy and direction in oil and gas sector. We need to take a number of far reaching strategic decisions and an integrated effort in their implementation. Some of the points requiring strategic decisions are identified as: Facilitating exploration for oil and gas in Balochistan. A number of foreign and native companies holding exploration licenses for Balochistan blocks have declared force-majeure and have not been able to start the work for almost two years.[3]

Accelerating the processing and finalisation of pending and new applications for grant of exploration licenses. Increasing the indigenous refining capacity by expansion of the existing refineries and adding new refineries on line. Provision of pipelines for crude oil from old fields of Badin and Sanghar for stable, reliable and economical transportation. Application of Enhanced Oil Recovery (EOR) to old and depleted fields in the Potwar area. Removing restrictions from utilisation of newly discovered gas fields for power generation to provide incentives for gass exploration. Revising gas pricing policies for gas from deeper and expensive fields to give a reasonable rate of return on investment. Giving OGDC a degree of professional freedom, flexibility and autonomy enabling it to compete more effectively with the native and foreign oil compancies. Self-reliance in oil may not be possible in the desired timeframe if we concentrate only on increasing indigenous production of oil. It would be prudent to follow a two-pronged approach. Firstly, we need to increase our diversification on to natural gas and reduce the demand for oil. Secondly, we need to increase our indigenous production of oil. Natural gas is already providing an important 36 per cent of our total energy needs. Oil provides about 41 per cent, hydel about 18 per cent and the coal about 5 per cent. About three-fourth of the oil that we consume is imported. Although our indigenous oil production has shown a substantial increase and has touched 70,000 barrels per day in October 1990, the consumption and demand, as mentioned earlier, are also increasing due to our developing economy. The increase in demand is an expected and positive indicator of our growth and development. We need to improve the supply position. Pakistan has an efficient and country-wide infrastructure for transmission and utilisation of natural gas. This may be evident from a simple comparison with other natural gas producing countries. For example, Indonesia produces ten times more natural gas than Pakistan but consumes one-tenth of gas consumed in Pakistan. Most of it is exported by them. Considering our situation, we have already diversified considerably on natural gas as a source of energy. It is important to build on this base and further increase the utilisation of gas to decrease the demand for oil. It is a well known observation of our subsurface geology that we do have good prospects for large reserves of natural gas. There are areas of our prospective basins that have been geologically exposed to higher temperatures and oil, if present, would have been converted into gas. But there is a lack of incentive in exploring for gas. The development of a gas field and utilisation of the produced gas takes 5 to 10 years. Delayed and uncertain returns make the exploration of gas less attractive. One of the reasons for delayed returns is the slow growth in demand of gas since it is linked with the infra-structural development that requires long time and heavy investment. It may be prudent to encourage the gas exploration companies to discover new fields and in case normal demand of the discovered gas is limited, allow them to utilise the newly discovered gas for power generation. Natural gas is a much preferred fuel for power generation. Modern gas turbines are least expensive, most efficient and least damaging to environment as compared to oil or coal based power stations. The prevaling oil crisis is affecting our economy very seriously. We now need to give the oil and gas sector a sharp national focus to reduce our dependence on imported wide oil and the refined products. But most of the measures that we need of take would be long term in nature producing results after a few years. It is important that we take the decisions soon and generate a parallel activity at various levels to move to self-reliance in oil. Envisioning self-reliance in oil as its goal, OGDC is endeavouring to give the national economy a major boost in about 5 years. It will need a degree of freedom, flexibility and initiative of a highly specialised professional corporation to play a vital role in changing the destiny of our people. Given the right environment, the OGDC is ready to delivery in this capital intensive, technologically selective and highly competitive search for oil and gas in the country.[4]

It has been brought to light that the caretaker government of Jatoi, by refusing to increase the oil prices in the domestic market, put a burden on the exchequer amounting to 7 crore rupees a day. In total terms the figure comes to approximately 630 crore rupees which has increased the budgetary deficit to 18,159.2 million rupees from the envisaged figure of 11.854.8 million rupees—a rise not only responsible for an increase in the inflation rate but also the urgent need on the part of the elected government to increase reliance on aid in order to bridge the gap. It is apparent, therefore, that the country has paid dearly for the caretakers election campaign. The responsibility for postponing the oil price rise falls squarely on their shoulders. And if they could consider amendments to floor crossing surely the Gulf crisis required more urgent emergency measures.

And other countries increased their domestic oil prices in order to insulate their economies from its effects as far as their budgetary gaps were concerned. India, the oft quoted country by the Ministry of Petroleum, also decided to increase oil prices by 25 per cent as per *Business India* (Bombay) magazine after a suitable period had elapsed after the Gulf crisis when it was patently obvious that the crisis was not likely to be shortlived. Thus measures were promptly adopted to ensure that the negative fall-out of the Gulf crisis be minimised on the domestic economic scene. It is unfair that the carktakers left this crucial and yet politically unpopular decision to the elected government—a decision that should have been taken during their period of rule; and more importantly to leave the exchequer so depleted for the new government as a consequence.[5]

The Federal Government has taken the unavoidable decision to increase the price of petroleum products. In the wake of Gulf crisis, the international price of oil shot up in the neighbourhood of 35 dollars per barrel while our 1990-91 budget was prepared on the basis of 17 dollars per barrel. Revision of oil prices had become inevitable to meet the enhanced oil import bill, reduced remittances and decline in exports to the Middle East. The increase announced by the Federal government is reported to be the outcome of a great deal of deliberations and is the minimum essential to meet the inflated import bill. The increase in prices of super, regular, kerosene, high speed diesel and furnace oil is 42.90, 43.11, 50.0, 26.68 and 43.04 per cent respectively. This will add to the cost of transport, farm and industrial production. Our economy is already burdened with the ill effects of the economic mismanagement of the previous regime and the generality of the people are finding it difficult to make both ends meet. They need to be cushioned against the new price spiral. The consumers with low income will be hit hard by 50 per cent increase in the price of kerosene which is one of their major items of daily use. But the argument given in support of this increase is that it will bring down the difference between the prices of HSD and kerosene to 70 paisas only which will effectively check the adulteration of the former with the latter.[6]

The chain effect of oil price increase will have to be checked firmly. The Sensitive Price Indicator (SPI) and the Consumer Price Index (CPI) do not always reflect the actual price situation in the market. The main reason is that the prices in Pakistan are not a result of the free play of market forces but are manipulated by the wholesalers and retailers. The government should, therefore, take strong and positive measures to check arbitrary rises in prices.

It was, indeed, a painful decision for the popularly elected government to raise prices of petroleum and petroleum products, but it had to be taken. There could be no getting away from a situation resulting from the Iraqi annexation of Kuwait, the principal source of supply to Pakistan. The crisis caused in the world oil markets due to President Saddam Hussain's adventure in neighbouring Kuwait has seen prices skyrocketing on a global scale. Pakistan could not remain unaffected under any circumstance. In fact, this country has been the hardest hit among those affected by the serious dislocation in the world oil economy. For years together, Pakistan had been benefiting from the special concessionary rates at which the bulk of its oil needs were met by a special arrangement with Kuwait. In view of this, we should have been among those countries who hastened, in the aftermath of the Gulf crisis, to raise the prices of the whole range of petrol and petroleum products. Had we done so, we might have had to go in for a series of increases at short intervals with the fast changing situation in the world oil market. Moreover, it was a caretaker government that was in power when the crisis struck. Its life being too short, it could not take hasty measures that might have added to the problems and complicated issues for the elected government that was expected to take charge of its constitutional responsibilities after the October 24-27, 1990 general election. The caretakers did, however, initiate a search for alternative sources of supply and to do whatever they could to ensure against severe repercussions of the general price hike for Pakistan. Reference may be made here also of the strategy adopted for the conservation of energy in the country as some sort of a cushion against the overall impact of the oil price on the nation's energy needs. The exercise did not succeed in offsetting all the adverse influences of as serious an inter-national development as the multi-dimensional problems created in the wake of the Gulf crisis. But it did succeed, at least, in bringing home to the people the need of exercising utmost austerity in the consumption of energy.[7]

The increase of 35 to 42 per cent in the prices of petroleum and petroleum products, as reluctantly announced by the Federal Government on Wednesday, should have caused no surprise. The step was simply inevitable. In fact, the increase was overdue. The extent of increase might have caused surprise in some quarters where the rise was expected to be in the range of 20 to 30 per cent. The steep rise may, as such, cause resentments here and there. But the government has convincingly explained the reasons for the drastic increases. And these reasons can hardly be disputed, except for the sake of argument. While the rise in oil prices will certainly have a chain effect and increase the inflationary pressure further, it will also add to the misery of the teeming millions who already stand condemned to a life of poverty, hunger and deprivation. As will be seen from the concern to keep the common man's kerosene oil within reasonable limits, the government is quite aware of their problems. This is evident from the pledge of Nawaz Sharif Government to ameliorate the plight of the poor masses by taking a number of revolutionary measures soon. While the increases will make life a little more difficult for the low-income groups, they will also add to the cost of development efforts for their progress and welfare which the new government is committed to bring about. Already plagued by paucity of resources for development, Pakistan will have to go for austerity in a big way. As it is, the government has already announced its policy of strict adherence to the philosophy of self-reliance for the implementation of its revolutionary industrialisation programme. That philosophy will now need to be carried into all spheres of life. The nation will have to bid goodbye to ostentation, in all its forms and shapes, and learn to live within its limited means like all self-respecting people who have succeeded in working miracles through self-reliance. We hope the government would soon announce and strictly enforce a number of well-conceived austerity measures that will not only augment resources for development but also exercise an effective check on inflation.

Petrol prices have been increased by 41.5 per cent, kerosine by 50 per cent and furnace oil by 43 per cent following the 16 per cent increase in POL prices made in March, 1990. As a result, the increase in prices of petrol alone is by 67 per cent within eight months. Ordinary petrol price has jumped from Rs. 7.15 per litre in March to Rs. 11.85. The latest increase in POL pcices will raise transportation costs by 10 per cent, say the officials. But official estimates over the decades in this regard have been gross understatements. It will not be any different this time. What matters for more now, apart from the rise in transportation costs, is the increase in power rates to come following their rise by 8.33 per cent plus five paisa more as fuel adjustment charge effected in June. And as the government has agreed with the World Bank to treat gas prices at par with POL prices, a 40 per cent increase in gas prices can be expected following the 49 per cent increase made in 1988. The cumulative impact of all these higher input and transportation costs on manufacturing and the sales sectors will indeed be very heavy. The initial increase in conveyance allowance for the private sector employees announced by the government, which will be followed by the demand for far higher wages to make up for the heightened inflation, will push up manufaturing, transportation and sales costs further and add to the hardslips of the people.[8]

Unlike in India where the POL price rise is only 25 per cent and it is clearly described as a "temporary Gulf surcharge" to be withdrawn as world oil prices come down, there is no such commitment on the part of the Pakistan government. Sri Lanka, too, has come up with a similar commitment. But in Pakistan the increase may become a permanent feature even if world oil prices crash as the officials will then plead that in the meanwhile the rupee had been devalued. The 41.5 to 50 per cent rise in POL prices here should result in an additional inflation of not less than 5 to 6 per cent, regardless of what the ridiculous official inflation index may say.

The relief in import duties on buses, trucks and other public transport vehicles promised will not reach the people as their operators would have a score of reasons to deny it, including rise in their own cost of living. Despite the enormous rise in the price line to come now. Finance Minister Sartaj Aziz says that he would recoup only Rs. 45 million out of the daily loss of Rs. 70 million because of the delay in raising POL prices and the new price increase would bring in only Rs. 14 billion more until June 30. But he has not told us how much in revenue the government would now collect through the petroleum surcharge, customs duties and excise duties on oil this year, which the budget had earlier estimated at Rs. 11.5 billion. But having announced the stiff increases in POL all along the line, as dictated by the IMF, the government should now ensure that at least the further rise in power, gas and other prices is not too stinging for the already hard hit middle and low income groups.[9]

The long feared raise in the prices of oil products has finally come. The inevitability of the increase following the Gulf crisis had been realised by the people at large but the extent of the raise that has been announced has exceeded all apprehensions. Reports had it that the IMF was insisting on a 40 per cent increase, and, according to the PPP co-chairperson, the caretaker government had accepted it. But this was denied by the government. Indications were that the increase would remain within the range of 25 per cent. The government's resistance to 40 per cent was reportedly based on the argument that, oil being the life blood of almost all branches of economic activity, increase in its price would directly affect the prices of all goods and services, and of a few in direct proportion to the increase. The fixation of new prices may now have come about not purely on the basis of international prices but with the idea of using it to cover the budget deficit to the maximum extent.[10]

The IMF's main focus in framing conditionalities has been on how to reduce the budget deficit which was running out of control. Keeping in view the limitation of Pakistani rulers (who do not accept any suggestion that involves sacrifices on their part) and the components of taxes, the IMF had suggested elimination of subsidies and the raising of the prices of utilities and services. The burden of these conditionalities was to fall mainly, as has been the case year after year, on the common man. The IMF would have no objection indeed if the deficit were reduced through elimination of tax evasion, improvement in the efficiency of tax collection machinery and reduction in as many as 180 tax exemptions. However, the previous governments never attended to an agenda of that sort and a similar start appears to have been made by the new government. An additional compulsion has been the bankruptcy of the Punjab and Sindh governments and the heavy overspending during the elections. For these reasons the budget deficit is projected to have risen severely These economic ralities may have persuaded the government to fix prices at a level even higher than reportedly demanded by the IMF.

On economic considerations such a raise is not justified. The old prices of POL products were fixed in 1984 when the international prices of crude were around 30-3! dollars a barrel. They were revised upward by 16 per cent only in March this year. When the prices fell to 16 dollars a barrel they were not reduced. The excess revenue was supposed to be invested in new explorations. In recent years the OGDC has been excluded from the budget and asked to raise money in the market. Thus no public investment is being made in exploration now. Pakistan is still obtaining crude at less than 32 dollars a barrel and in the meantime our own production of oil has risen to about 60,000 barrels a day which comes to about one-third of the total requirement. It is unaffected by international factors. The only difference between 1984 and today is the depreciation of the rupee which is around 25 per cent. Keeping in view the share of domestic production and the circumstances under which old prices were fixed, the legitimate raise should not have been more than 20-25 per cent.

The old price increase will directly and proportionately affect the tariff of electricity, railways and road transport and indirectly, through cost-push, the prices of all goods and services. Apprehensions seem to be legitimate that the oil price-induced inflation may assume serious proportions which may widen the governments' revenue-expenditure gap, cripple the country's export capability, accelerate depreciation of the rupees and increase debt obligations. The problem of the budget deficit, which is the main consideration of the IMF, should have been tackled with a package comprising oil price increase (not exceeding 25 per cent), tightening the tax collection machinery which is prone to immense leakages, and bringing within the tax net those who can and should pay particularly the earners of higher agricultural incomes. Indirect taxation has reached its limits and the common man now needs a breathing pause. To avert economic disaster, the government must abandon ad hocism and bring about fundamental changes in the economic structure.

The old price hike, as an inevitable fall-out of the Gulf crisis, should create some ripple in the thinking of our "planners" at the Federal level, as the cost of energy is going to touch thc ceiling, beyond which the sky is the limit. Pakistan has never been placed happily, energy-wise, being primarily an oil importing country, producing a small quantity of oil locally, with no high grade steam coal under the crust and only one undependable, low capacity nuclear power plant to boast. It has had to lean heavily on fuel oil to maintain a constant and reliable flow of electricity though the country's grid system in view of the inadequate and seasonal generation of hydel power. Unfortunately, during the second half of the Ayubian decade when firm foundations of medium and long range planning perspectives were being laid, the American nit-wits, masquerading as "wise guys" of Harvard Group, almost besieged our Planning Commission at Rawalpindi, with the blessings of the World Bank; and foisted on this poor country the same perceptions and yard stick which had proved valid in a vastly different country, the USA, which is characterised by affluence, cheap and abundant energy and plentiful availability of all conceivable inputs for phenomenal economic growth. Confining the present analysis to the Transport Sector, attention is drawn to the basic principle accepted by our planners, on American dictation, while framing the Third Five-Year Plan (1960-65) that the future back-bone of passenger and goods transport in this country would not be the railway ramification but a network of highways and super-highways, as in the United States.[11]

As a result of this shift in policy, the actual outlay (as distinct from allocation) for the Railway, out of the total Transport Sector outlay, during the Third Plan shrank to 55.8 per cent from 75.6 per cent in the preceding plan; and it finally faded into 17.8% actual and 21.5% allocated outlay in the Fifth and Sixth Plans respectively.

Now is the time for the Pakistan Railway to play the 'energy card' and made the planners realise how adversely their short-sighted approach has been affecting the long-run interests of this country. The Railway is the most economical user of energy compared to its rival transport modes, both for movement of passengers and goods :

— A fast express train consumes only one-fifth of fuel per passenger, compared to air, and one-third compared to road service.

— A slower train consumes about 30% less fuel.

— Fuel consumption per tonne of freight carried by rail is one-fourth of what it is by a diesel truck.

The Railway, consuming well above a quarter million tonnes of POL products (HSD. Furnance oil and lubricants) is one of the largest users of fuel, cost whereof accounts for as much as 25% of its operating expenses. Its role in the national economy is very vital, and failure to get the maximum output from such a large energy-consu ing apparatus amounts to a criminal lapse on the part of the planners who have, instead, let loose a cut-throat competition between the state-owned Railway and private road hauliers at the expense of the tax payers who subsidies the latter by providing them with the road facility at a cost much higher than what is defrayed by the road users through road tax or tax on POL.

In Pakistan, the Railway carries only about 16% of passenger traffic and 27% of goods, the major part being carried by road, thanks to the liberal policy of the government which follows America, regardless of the fact that it has to pay to the Railway an amount of Rs. 2.35 billion annually to enable it to bridge its resource gap. Leaving aside small countries like Belgium or Holland, in larger European countries as Germany, France and Italy, whose area and population are comparable with those of Pakistan, 40 to 45% of the total freight traffic moves by rail. In the USSR, the average road haul is 20 kms suggesting that almost the entire long-lead traffic move by rail. The Russian planners have remarked that if they were to follow the US and allow the same proportion of goods to move by road then they would have consumed much of the indigenous oil leaving little for export.

The economic geography of Pakistan is particularly suited for railway monopoly in transport, as long-distance passenger and goods traffic preponderates due to the fact that on way to up country from the megalopolis of Karachi, where the two sea ports of KPT and PQA are situated, there is no large city or trading centre for a stretch of 150 kms till one reaches Hyderabad and the distance intervening Karachi and Lahore, the next largest city and commercial centre on the country's map, is 1200 kms, and the expanse between Karachi and Peshawar, the farthest city in the north west extremity, is 1600 kms. Air transport can never carry a big chunk of passenger traffic between the main cities; and buses cannot make a serious inroad in the Railway's preserve of long-distance passenger traffic. Therefor, it is high time that the planners, who have so far starved PR of funds for introduction of as many express services on Karachi-Lahore-Peshawar route as the quantum of traffic demands, should wake up and re-think whether diversion of resources for construction of highways and import of buses has been justificable policy.[12]

The World Bank has made the Planning Commission believe that passenger traffic, even for long distances, does not legitimately belong to the railway (because that was the American experience) and that the Railway should concentrate only on freight traffic. On the contrary Pakistan's railways recent experience has proved that inter-city express trains, for long and medium distances, are no longer a financial burden and that these services are not only meeting their total cost but also contributing substantially towards recovering the over heads.[13]

The wind of change is blowing even in North America, where purely passenger railways are being supported by the Federal Government, e.g. Amtrack in USA and Via in Canada. The former is now covering 60% of its budget and the latter about 45%. In Japan, the Shinkansen, a model railway for passenger traffic, carried 25% of the total passenger-kms JNR and yielding 40% of its revenue prior in the dismemberment of the Japanese National Railway (JNR) into various parts and their recent privatisatian.

The Table below would depict how well the PR has been faring in its passenger business.

	No. of Passengers (million kms) (yearly average)	*Av. length of haul (km)*	*Passenger-kms (billion)*	*Coaching Earning (% of Total Eearning*
1950-55	78.9	85.9	6.8	44.6
1955-60	102.7	78.5	8.1	45.2
1960-75	130.3	77.6	10.3	40.1
1975-89	118.1	150.1	16.3	33.6

It is apparent from the constant increase in passenger-kms. and average length of journey that the patronage extended by long-distance passengers to Pakistan railways despite its faults and failures, is a pointer to the fact that if railways' express trains are improved and made reliable, reasonably comfortable and less cowded, it can carry all the potential long-distance passengers. The fall in passenger-coaching revenue since 1975 is attributable to :

(a) Non-rationalisation of passenger fare structure so as to increase the rate for charge for distances above 300 kms when the bulk of passenger traffic started moving in higher distance slabs ;

(b) Decline in parcels and luggage traffic (which is carried in luggage vans of express trains). In contrast, the railways goods traffic has almost stagnated since 1979 and it carrying about 8 million tonne kms annually despite due attention having been given to this traffic, it being considered as the mainstay. The statistics reveal that :

* The road has yet to dislodge the railway from its long-distance passenger business.

* The road has an indisputable edge over the railway even in long-haul freight business and even in transporting containers from the port area to up country destinations, because of the government²s policy to enable the road hauliers to snatch the railway's goods traffic.

Planning is a function quite different from maintenance of assets or general administration. The former function has, lately not been the strong point of Pakistan railway and its planning department, both in the Railway Headquarters and in the Railway Ministry, has been manned by un-willing personnel or by stop-gap postings. The need for drawing an action plan for (a) running more supper-fast express services for long-distance passengers, (b) improving passenger terminals in preference to building more mechanised marshalling yards of Pipri type or remodelling some of the existing ones, (c) increasing the permisible speed on Karachi-Lahore main line to 150 km/hr on the lines of French Tgv which have attained a speed of 250 km/hr, (d) doubling the frequency of fast passenger services on the main line over a period of 10 years, (e) routing of goods traffic via the alternate route of Kotri-Dadu-Jacobabad-Kashmore-Deraghazi Khan-Multan by developing it adequately. (This is necessary in order to find extra path for additional express services on the main line. The last stek would be advantageous, 'tactically', as the present main line is too vulnerable, being close to the Indian border.[14]

The Pakistan President Ghulam Ishaq Khan, said in Islamabad, on January 20, 1991 that the government has initiated work on a number of "infrastructure projects" which would give the coun'ry the capacity to design and build its own nuclear reactors by the end of the decade.

Ishaq Khan was speaking at the inauguration of the national power control centre set up by the state-owned Water and Power Development Authority in Islamabad with Norwegian and French assistance.

He said nuclear power represented the only long-term viable energy source for Pakistan.

References

1. Gulfaraz Ahmed, OGDC's Self-Financing, *Muslim*, 16 November, 1990.
2. *Ibid.*
3. *Ibid.*
4. *Ibid.*
5. *The Nation*, 18 November, 1990.
6. *The Pakistan Times* (Lahore), 16 November, 1990.
7. *Morning News* (Karachi), 16 November, 1990.
8. *The Muslim*, 16 November, 1990.
9. *Ibid.*
10. *Dawn*, 18 November, 1990.
11. Jafar Wafa, Pakistan Railways, *Dawn*, 17 November, 1990.
12. *Ibid.*
13. *Ibid.*
14. *Ibid.*

11

Population Growth

Pakistan has overtaken Bangladesh as the second most populous nation in the Indian sub-continent due to a higher birth rate.

The Pakistan population in mid-1989 was estimated at 108,68 million against Bangladesh's 106,51 million. The Indian population in mid-1989 was 811.82 against China's 1,119.7 million. The Pakistani population has been growing fastest in the Indian sub-continent. The increase from 1980 to 1989 was 31.6% for Pakistan, 20.3% for India and 20.1% for Bangladesh. The Chinese population growth during the same period was only 12.4%.

The world's total population in mid-1989 was estimated at 5.201 million. The forecast for the year 2000 is world population 6.250.4 million, China 1,285.89 million, India 1,042.53 million Pakistan 162.47 million and Bangladesh 150.59.

The majority of the population is living in the rural areas but there were significant differences existed between the two parts of the country. The eastern wing had been very

very strongly rural since the earlier modern urban developments were in the western delta region. The politically motivated urbanisation was quite strong particularly in administrative industrial and economic terms. As far as the growth of population was concerned it was quite steady but not spectacular. East Pakistan contained the larger share of Pakistan's total population, was closer to evological saturation points and was expected to face the problem of emigration if the urban-industrial development was not in a position to absorb rural surplus in the near future,[1]

In the West Pakistan, the rough hill country is highly populated, although the north-west frontier portions have some high local densities in good areas. The lowland zone has always shown the contraste of heavy population in areas of irrigable land available for agriculture. The population mainly concentrated in trade towns and adminis rative capitals. The urban pattern of West Pakistan is both older and stronger and it has created serious problems of housing, urban planning and the creation of the whole range of urban utilities. It is expected that the rapid growth of industrialisation, however, would give impetus to the urban trend, as many old trade centres would be eonverted into industrial cities and as old villages are turned into industrial towns.[2]

The policy planners of Pakistan are worried about the rapid growth of population because it threatens national development and family welfare. The rate of population growth needs to be reduced at the same time that the rate of economic development is accelerated. However, the problems in reducing rates of population increase, are for greater than those is simulating economic development. The factors which are very common influencing population growth are religious, ethical, social and traditional as well as economic, for the rate of population growth is mainly the difference between the birth rate and the death rate. In theory, rate of the increase could be reduced either by increasing the death rate or by reducing the birth rate. In fact, the limitation of growth though planned, is not conceivable ethically, socially and politically. It has always been the characteristic of Pakistan social set up that the Muslims maintain large families. But slowly and gradually there is a sea change in the outlook of the Muslim population in Pakistan.[3]

The analysis of the origin, formation and growth of the population of Pakistan present complex problems of concept, definition and execution. The population of the sub-continent did not evoke without barriers to movements but those barriers did not coincide with the present boundaries of Pakistan. Over long periods, the growth and development of the population of the subcontinent were unitary processes, or at least processes in which changes in local and wide regions were interrelated. Pakistan's population today is unmanageably large, and is exerting heavy pressure on resources. The country lacks the resources to feed the already increasing number of people to maintain health and welfare services, and also to ensure a maximum rate of growth for the economy. The economist cost of the period of high birth rates and low death rates include the high costs of supporting children, high dependency in families, prevalent ill health and malnutrition, concentration of food crops for sustenance scarcity of capital and chronic unemployment and under-employment. The severity of the population pressure and the danger that population growth will halt economic development alike dictate that positive population policy should be an essential part of longterm planning.[4]

The concern of economists and politicians with population and population growth has come full circle since the day of Malthus and Ricardo. The population is an important variable and occupying a most respectful place in the vulnerable classical inquiry into the cause of growth and stagnation. "A closer approach to the real world of rising capital output rate or, foreign exchange uncertainties, impatient consumers, and imprudent investors would demonstrate yet more clearly that the differential effect of damping growth of numbers may well constitute the difference between self-sustaining growth and a return to stagnation at higher level of national income.[5]

For the proper analysis of the population growth and its impact on the economic development an understanding of the past demographic trends in their long-term setting are must. But in the case of Pakistan past demographic trends (of the pre-independence period) available are of poor quality because the system of birth and death registration is not at all dependable. Her people are having long history but since its emergence as an independent country, tremendous changes have occurred in size (Pakistan was dismembered in 1971) and composition of the population in the Pakistan territory, not only on the basis of religious faiths, but also in regional distribution and to some extent in martial status, age structure and occupational pattern.[6]

From the purely demographic point of view it was felt that the level of fertility in Pakistan would largely determine the potential supply of labour,[7] which is considered to be the backbone on industry especially in the underdeveloped countries. The industrial and economic growth are interlined and are closely related with a country's capability.

The population projections are an essential part of development planning. The Planning Commission of Pakistan from time to time prepares population estimates which serve as the basis of Five Year Plans. The evolution of various growth patterns demonstrated by a variety of estimates provides useful information to policy-makers since they are then in a position to evaluate a sense of alternatives.[8]

The Planning Commission of Pakistan and other related agencies are insisting that at any cost the rapid growth of population in Pakistan must be checked. Pakistan is already under heavy debt and the economic development is going at a slow pace. The dependence on foreign economic aid has been increased manyfold since 1947 and sometimes a country is compelled to sacrifice its national interest and foreign policy assumptions in order to qualify for financial benefits which are essential in the modern world of science and technology for a developing country like Pakistan.[9]

SAARC countries inhabit nearly one billion people (or one-fifth) of world population. India, after China, is the second most populated country in the world (816 million), Bangladesh the eighth (109 million), and Pakistan the tenth (106 million). Generally speaking, members of the group suffer from over-population which shows no signs of abating. The high birth-rates coupled with declining death-rates in these countries provide typical examples of the 'second stage' (also called the stage of 'population explosion') of demographic transition theory. The unbridled growth of population, in most cases, has thrown to winds the gains of developmental plans and the policy-makers are baffled at the prospects of further increases in the numbers. Sharp decreases in the death-rates (per thousand) are and summarized here for individual countries for 1965 and 1988, respectively : India (20,11), Bangladesh (21, 15), Pakistan (21, 13), Nepal (24, 15), Sri Lanka (8, 6), Bhutan (23, 17) and Maldives (...9). Contrarily, the birth-rates (per thousand) continue to remain at high levels in spite of notable decline in some countries, particularly India, and Sri Lanka. The birth-rates in different countries for 1965 and 1988, respectively, are as follows : India (45, 32), Bangladesh (47, 40), Pakistan (48, 46), Nepal (46, 42), Sri Lanka (33, 22), Bhutan (42, 39) and Maldives ..., 46). As direct consequence of high birth-rates and low death-rates, the countries of the SAARC region, with the exception of Sri Lanka, continue to register more than two per cent annual growth rate of population. Pakis.an is the only country in the region registering more than 3 per cent population growth. Infant mortality rate is correlated with birth-rate. It is more than 100 (per 1,000 live births) in 1988 for Bangladesh, Pakistan and Nepal where birth-rate is 40 or above. In India and Sri Lanka where the birth-rate is less than 40, the infant mortality rate is also less than 100. This general pattern does not hold good for Bhutan and Maldives. Sri Lanka stands out distinctly in terms of demographic improvements. Both birth-rate (22) and death-rate (6) are lowest in the SAARC region. It is also the only country in the region where annual growth rate of population is less than two per cent i.e. 1.5 per cent. The infant mortality rate in Sri Lanka (21) is much below as compared to other countries of the group. The high growth-rate of population has led to high population density in SAARC region, leading to pressure on natural resources, particularly land. One main reason for the continuing worsening of land—man ratio in these countries is the ever-increasing pressure of population on land in the face of limited employment opportunities in non-agricultural sector. The land-man ratio in India declined from 0.92 hectare in 1951 to 0.48 hectare in 1981 and is projected to decline further to 0.33 hectare by the year 2000 (Government of India, Seventh Five Year Plan, Vol. I, para 2.20).[10]

The Defence for Children International, Pakistan has appealed to the Nawaz Sharif Government to bring the Children back from Arab countries who had been exported for camel race.

The Defence for Children International Pakistan on November 21, 1990 appealed to the Government to stop the barbaric business of smuggling children to the Arab countries. Some NGOs were working in this context but they were not resourceful enough to meet the alarming situation.

References

1. J.E. Spencer and W.L. Thomas, *Asia-East of South*, New York, 1971, p. 357.
2. *Ibid*, pp. 337-38.
3. S.S. Bindra, *Determinants of Pakistan's Foreign Policy*, New Delhi, 1988, p. 79.
4. *Ibid*.

5. G. Rams, Population Growth and Economic in Pakistan, In M.L. Qureshi (ed.), *Population Growth and Economic Development*, Karachi, 1960, pp. 85-105.
6. H. Rehman, *Some Aspects of the Problem of Population Growth & Economic Development in Pakistan*, Karachi, 1970, p. 106.
7. See *A Report of the Seminar on the Population Problem of Economic Development of Pakistan*, held in June 1967, Karachi, 1967.
8. L L. Beam, *Population Projection in Pakistan*, 1960-2000, Karachi, 1968.
9. S.S. Bindra, *op. cit.*, p. 81.
10 M.M. Sury, SAARC : A Socio-Economic Survey, *Financial Expess*, 18 November, 1990.

12

The Drug Abuse

The drug abuse and trafficking during the year 1990 grew in parts of the Third World including Pakistan. The International Narcotics Control Board, Vienna, reported on January 10, 1991, that the drug abuse in crack cocaine has risen in major Third World cities. Heroin and cocaine seizures have incraased manifold.

The Premier Nawaz Sharif has referred to the evil of drug addiction which had snatched many a bread-earners from its dependents. "We cannot let our valuable national wealth the youth destroy itself, due to the rampant social evil of drug abuse, he asserted.

In this regard, he declared, his government was committed to eliminating narcotics and take steps to rehabilitate the drug addicts.

He said, a positive leap forward, in this context, would be to revive the shattered self-confidence of the drug addicts.

In a society where the gun brings the sense of security to the individual, any effort made would have to be universal in application and non-discriminatory in character. More than the actual measures, the failure of the socio-political structure to withstand ethnic and sectarian stress and reassure the people has been the biggest culprit. In all this strife that engulfs Pakistan, the ethnic, sectarian, communal and anti-social demands of society get enmeshed in producing the perception of an unbeatable and larger than life monster, which no government can demolish. It is here that the greatest danger of the Nawaz Sharif government lies. While, the IJI, with the covert and overt backing of the Establishment may have come together and along with the other anti-PPP parties swept the recent polls, the violent urges of the society can alter the tenuous balance that has existed between Punjab and other provinces. In Sind, the IJI alignment with the MQ Mhas left a broad segment of the population—the ethnic Sindhis, with the feeling of a sense of alienation from the power structure. In Punjab, with the power keg shifting to the northern and eastern districts, the lower Punjab, where the Seraiki supporters have their base is beset with a feeling of being ignored. Soon after the recent elections, the Seraiki movement has received a big boost in its popularity. In the NWFP, the sharp divide between the Afghan refugees and the Pathans over sharing of the scarce resources has come out into the open. Overlaying it is the sectarian problem as several districts of the NWFP have Shia majorities. Baluchistan presents a far more complicated picture. Increased affluence due to government spending over a decade and the pressures of monetary gain through the lucrative trade of smuggling, drug dealing and illegal arms trade has produced two opposite movements. On the one hand, there is an inexorable movement towards a divided and unstable political system, which will be coloured by an ethnic divide and a rapid dissolution of the Sardari system because of internal contradictions, lack of discipline and ambitions. On the other, the sentiment that Punjab is on trial for its capacity to accommodate the aspirations of the smaller provinces will inevitably see a resurgence of Baluch nationalism that will be enmeshed with the increasing strength of the drug dealer-armstrafficker combination.[1]

The United States Congress is demanding that Pakistan demostrate by March Ist, 1991 that it is acting to curtail the cultivation of opium and the production of heroin in about one hundred laboratories near fronties with Afghanistan. Inability to provide convincing evidence against narcotics production and trafficking would create another bar against US aid. The US aid to Pakistan was suspended in October 1990 pending certification by the US President that Pakistan does not possess nuclear weapon.

Pakistan Premier Nawaz Sharif is certain to face criticism in the United States because two indicted heroin traffickers from tribal areas bordering Afghanistan were elected to the National Assembly and sworn despite the cases against them.

It is first time drug lords have openly entered the National Parliament and they see in it a disturbing trend. Both were elected from the Khyber and Bajour districts and support Sharif's Islamic Democratic Alliance. Members from tribal areas are chosen by Loya Jirgas, traditional councils. The production had come down from 800 tons to 40 to 50 tonns during Zia-Ul-Haq's time. But is has now risen to 160 tonns. Recent rise in production may reflect better crops rather than increase in acreage. Pakistan has had the 'tacit willingness' of the United States to let its nuclear weapons programme proceed over the past necade, an American columnist wrote in the *New York Times* on December 5, 1990.

As the U.S. aid suspension stands for the moment and as this affects civil development, military preparedness and narcotics control, certain other suggestions have been made. They sound bizarre but the source which has made them A retired Brigadier, reportedly a high-official in one of the intelligence agencies, has suggested that Pakistan make use of its opium crop to offset the economic consequences of aid suspension. He said the crop could be processed and its medicinal dervatives exported, earning about $ 12 billion. This could help the country acquire a substantial measure of self-reliance, he said.[2]

In a vigorous anti-narcotics drive the Border Security Force personnel of India have seized contraband worth about Rs. 160 crores in the international black market from Kashmir region since January 1990. The contraband seized in encounters on the border and elsewhere in the State, included heroin valued at Rs. 130 crores, the rest being hashish, opium and brown sugar.[3]

The drive against narcotics is apparently related to measures for combating the ongoing anti-India militancy in Kashmir.

Heroin and other narcotics being smuggled into Kashmir from Pakistan and Pakistan-occupied Kashmir were intended to obtain money for purchase of sophisticated weapons for insurgents. Among the 43 persons found smuggling the narcotics from Pakistan into Jammu and Kashmir six had been killed and the rest arrested.

Yet another cause of US-Pak discord has to do with the conviction among Western drug enforcement specialists that elements of Pakistan's Government are involved in the country's booming heroin trade. The traffickers import poppies from Mujaheddin guerillas in Afghanistan, manufacture heroin in Pakistan, and ship the product out clandestinely to Europe and the US. It has been a long-standing complaint of drug enforcement officials here that the Pakistan Government has not done anything to counter the power of the drug barons. The recent, fortutous seizure in Baluchistan of two tonns of heroin, with a market value of over 500 million dollars, is believed here to be the tip of the iceberg. Such multi-ton activity, officials here assert, could not go on without active political and institutional cooperation.

The US Drug Enforcement Administration (DEA) has other frustrations. Two alleged heroin traffickers, being tracked for years by DEA agents, were elected to the Pak National Assembly earlier this year. Dost Jan, the principal accused in the two-tonns Baluchistan heroin case, is closely connected with several prominent politicians and has not been—and is unlikely to be—arrested. Meanwhile, US law requires that the Bush Administration certify early next year that aid to Pakistan will help reduce drug production and smuggling. According to officials here, such certification would be difficult if not impossible in the face of apparent disinterestedness in Pakistan to move against the drug lords.[4]

"We see a pattern in Pakistan much like the Colombian drug cartels," an official said. "They might have been old and teusted friends at one time, but when a friend goes bad and becomes a positive danger, it is time to cut him off."

How should India proceed? First and foremost, with dignity with the realisation that India is a democracy that is too large and too intrinsically stable to be pushed around by anyone. There is, therefore, no need to kowtow to anyone even to the only Super Power left.

At the same time, it would be foolish to go to the other extreme and display a touch of truculence at every imagined instance of big power interference and to pretend as some are wont to do that America needs India more than the other way found.

"Narco-power" is spreading out of control in Pakistan—and Islamabad needs to take a lesson from Colombia before the drug barons take over the country. Islamabad has so far failed to prevent the country from becoming "a mini-Colombia", in the words of one narcotics expert. The American Newsweekly "Newsweek",[5] cited how a few weeks ago, without warning three dozen Baluchi tribesmen opened fire on a routine Pakistan army patrol in the Baluchistan desert with assault rifles, mortars and rocket launchers. After the four-hour fire fight a search in the area yielded what drug experts are calling the world's biggest heroin seizure—1,741 k. of heroin, 255 of raw opium, four tonnes of hashish and an arsenal of combat weapons. When the Pakistan Narcotics Control Board (PNCB) assigned its quetta office to investigate further, all eight local agents reportedly applied for four-month vacations. The suspected traffichers belonged to Baluchistan's powerful Notezai clan, which is linked to some of the country's top politicians and major supporters of Prime Minister Nawaz Sharif. No one has accused the Prime Minister himself of any involvement in narcotics. An exploding trade in heroin and hashish has brought enormous wealth to the country's drug barons in recent years—and their political influence has grown to match it. In some ways Pakistan's traffickers seem to have surpassed leaders of Colombia's cocaine cartels : in October one prominent alleged drug trafficker, Haji Ayub Afridi, was elected to the National Assembly. Ayub has denied any connection with drugs, insisting that he's in the crockery business. Nevertheless, a warrant was issued against him in 1983 in connection with 17 tonnes of hashish that was discovered in a Baluchistan warehouse. The businessman was sentenced to one year in jail for failing to appear in court to answer the charges. Three years ago another warrant was issued against Ayub after a drug courier in Belgium named him as a supplier. The warrant was reissued last year, but Ayub is yet to be arrested. This venture into national politics worries western analysis. As one western displomat in Islamabad put it, Ayub's election "is also a signal to traffickers—that official politics is not beyond the psle". According to narcotics experts, Ayub began his career as a truck driver, but these days he leaves IA vishly in a massive walled compound protected by anti-aircraft guns in the Khyber Pass. When the General Government threatened to arrest him last year Ayub gathered 5,000 armed tribesmen on his estate and dared authorities to come and get him. They declined. The Pakistani policy and the military have no legal jurisdiction in the tribal areas where most of the drug barons are based although in practice Islamabad occasionally intervenes in non-drug related disputes.

Even outside the tribal areas it is dangerous to challenge the traffickers. They think nothing of hiring hit squads to eliminate their enemies. With the kingpins safe in their strongholds the brunt of Pakistan's anti-drug efforts falls on the small-time couriers known as "Mules", who earn as little as 25 dollars a trip for hauling heroin from Peshawar to Karachi. One of them was arrested in March 1990 with 17 of heroin strapped to the bicycle he was pedaling down the Grand Truck Road. In Karachi the shipments are often handed on to foreigners to be smuggled to Europe, Australia and the United Slates.

A year ago, in the space of a few weeks, more than 100 Nigerians were arrested in Karachi for attempting to smuggle out heroin by wrapping it in balloons or condoms and swallowing them.

Pakistani drug agents now routinely stop departing Nigerian Airline passengers.

Lacking sophisticated detection equipment, the officers instruct the passengers to lie down on the conveyor belts that carry luggage through X-ray machines.

Not all the heroin leaves the country Pakistan currently has an estimated 1.5 million addicts—more than one per cent of the country's total population. The supply that created such a high demands shows no sign of slackening.

Domestic production of opium from which heroin is refined, crew from 135 tonnes last year to 160 tonnes in 1990, and western drug experts say the figure could soar to 600 tonnes next year.

The United States Congress has set a deadline of March 1, 1991 for Pakistan to provide proof that it is making headway against narcotics trafficking.

Recently, Prime Minister Nawaz Sharif made some gestures towards stepping up the war on drugs most notably by elevating the Narcotics Minister to full cabinet status.

But the Drugs Minister, a Hindu minority, is unlikely to find many allies in the fiercely Muslim tribal areas. The lessons to be learned from Colombia's experience should be enough for Islamabad.

Unless the Pakistani Government moves quickly to confront the drug barons, the country may find itself increasingly helpless to stop them.

The transfer of a Pakistan Army official who seized $ 500 million worth of heroin in Baluchistan and failure of the Pakistani Government to announce the seizure reflects "a pattern of involvement by elements of Pakistan's Government in the country's booming heroin trade," according to the Washington Post. In a report from Quetta on December 24, 1990. The Post said despite occasional promises of tough action by government officials, independent drug barons politicians army and intelligence service officers "all continue to profit from heroin manufacturing and smuggling in this sparsely populated desert province and in the tribal belt of the country's north west frontier province." Quoting western drug enforcement specialists the report said : "They have not done anything at all to counter the power of these guys", referring to heroin traffickers who import poppies from Mujaheddin guerrillas in Afghanistan, manufacture heroin in Pakistan and then ship the product by land and sea to Europe and the United States. The despatch said two alleged heroin traffickers whose activities have been tracked for years by the US Drug Enforcement Administration but who have not been charged with any crime, have been elected to the National

Assembly earlier this year. Dost Jan. the principal accused in the two-tonnes Baluchistan heroin case, ' is closely connected to several prominent politicians and has not been arrested in the case," according to Pakistani law enforcement officials.

The despatch said the drug issue "threatens to exacerbate already strained relations between the United States and Pakistan. The US law requires the Bush administration to certify early next year that aid to Pakistan—budgeted at about $ 560 million annually—will help reduce drug production and smuggling. However, US officials said such certification would be very difficult now, since law enforcement officials in Pakistan seem disinterested in moving against drug barons, and favourable weather conditions have produced a bumper opium crop, flooding the country's export channels with heroin.

India's preoccupation with our political instability and burning issues like the Ram Janambhoomi and the Mandal Commission as well as the increasing violence in Punjab, Kashmir and Assam has pushed what should have been a major concern our external security—to the background. There appears to be more debate on Pakistan's nuclear status in the United States than in India, Nor has the doubling of Pakistan's major naval surface combatants in the last two years evoked widespread comment Pakistan Prime Minister Nawaz Sharif's meeting with the Indian Prime Minister in Male in November 1990 and his ritualistic statement about Pakistan's interest in having good relations with India despite his continued commitment to extend political and moral support to the Kashmiri secessionists appears to be taken at its face value notwithstanding the seven years of low-intensity conflict (LIC) Pakistan has been waging on the Indian soil using Indian secessionist elements. Though the secessionisms of Khalistanis and JKLF and Hizebe Islami insurgents are of indigenous origin, their kalashnikov rifles did not originate in India. Even the American officials and academic strategists today take note of the linkage between the narcoitics traffic from Pakistan and its support to terroristic and insurgent activities in Punjab and Kashmir.[6]

Pakistan's Islamic fundamentalists didn't object to New Year's eve (December 31, 1990) parties—as long as the celebrants did not dance, drink or mingle with the opposite sex. A group calling itself the tigers of Allah strung banners throughout the city of Karachi denouncing new year's eve celebrations as a product of the decadent West.

Skull-and-crossbone insignias emblazoned the banners, which included the warning "beware". Leading the drive against festivities to welcome in 1991 was the small but powerful Jamaat-I-Islami (party of God), a key member of Pakistan's rightwing coalition government. "We have warned people that we could not allow these types of celebrations in country where Muslims are in government, "said Khalid Rehman, a Jamaat leader. Threats cancelled parties at all hotels, none of which serve alcohol because it is banned in this pre-dominantly Muslim nation of 120 million people.

In spite of a fall inpoppy production in Pakistan, the number of people taking drugs has shown no appreciable decline. According to statistics, opium production stood at 800 metric tonnes in 1979; it had come down to 130 metric tonnes in 1989 Yet there are an estimated 2 24 million drug addicts in Pakistan a million of them hooked to heroin alone. Against these harsh realities, it is good to know that a meeting presided over by the NWFP Governor took stock of the situation and made a number of decisions to strengthen the crop substitution policy and step up development projects. Although adequate incentives could wean the growers away from poppy cultivation, the temptation for the drug barons—an estimated annual turn over of some 300,000 million dollars—makes them take the risk of violating anti-drug laws. By incentives of their own, they influence the growers, give them credit, intervene in legal disputes and operate private militias. This perhaps is the gut issue. Pakistan's borders are porous. In the context of drug smuggling, it is the north-western border that counts. Until the Soviet invasion of Afghanistan, heroin was an unknown commodity in this country. In its wake come not only genuine refugees but also manufacturers and smugglers of heroin. Here during the heyday of the CIA's covert operations against the Soviet-backed Kabul regime, the heroin smugglers seemed to have found and developed the right connections. Their financial and political clout is enormous. The last government despite public pledges to wipe out the menace of heroin, failed to achieve any results. In fact, not a single known drug baron was convicted. The new government, too faces the same challenge. It has begun with a lot of good will, and it has to prove that it can capitalise on it by waging a conserted war on the drug barons.[7]

Its strength in the five assemblies should help it prosecute the war on drugs relentlessly. The IJI governments should also be able to deal effectively with any sections of the bureaucracy which may not want to cooperate because of a vested interest in heroin trade. Such vested interests can be dealt with effectively under the new dispensation, so well-placed it is politically and socially. Without breaking the back of Pakistan's socially well-entrenched drug mafia, success on the anti-drug front will always elude the government. Crop substitution policies, rehabilitation of the addicts and a publicity campaign designed to elicit the people's cooperation in the war on drugs are welcome but their success will stand nullified to a great extent if the powerful mafia that manufactures, distributes and smuggles heroin remains unpunished. Iran, which once faced a similar problem, had made headway in recent years by coming down heavily on smuggling. It is time we followed our neighbour's example. Trafficking through third world countries also needs to be given due attention in view of the truly international scale of the problem. Pakistan must step up the level of cooperation with other countries so as to be able to grapple with smuggling.

With Pakistan acquiring nuclear weapons the option

earlier available to India of escalating the externally supported lowintensity conflicts into hot pursuits across the border no longer exists. Even if India were to acquire nuclear weapons and deter Pakistan there has to be careful calculation about escalation from low-intensity conflict to higher levels lest it should lead to use of the weapons of last resort. On the other hand, serious consideration should be given to containing Pakistan with a view to making it counter-productive to that country to support the low-intensity conflict in our territory and simultaneously tackle the insurgent or terrorist elements on our soil.

Pakistan's capability to sustain the low-level conflict is based on two factors, the narcotics trade which generates the finances to support such conflict and is associated with the vested interests on the Indian side involved in the narcotics traffic and the porous border. Unfortunately, the narcotic linkage with the extremist activity and organised crime on our side of the border and the military, narcotic barons and political establishment in Pakistan have not received adequate attention. Since there is significant vested interest in getting narcotics across on our side of the border, there have not been adequate efforts for reducing the porosity of the border. These days, new techniques in terms of laser beams, optical cables and night vision devices are available which can reduce the border-crossing to negligible dimensions. It is a question of political will.[8]

In concrete terms the Male Summit saw the signing of a Convention to Combat Drug Trafficking in the region, while there was agreement on a wide range of subjects like exploring the modalities of setting up a regional fund for financing joint venture projects (as in cottage industries and handicrafts). It was decided to set up a nucleus human resource development centre in Islamabad, a regional tuberculosis centre in Kathmandu and a regional documentation centre in New Delhi. It was at India's initiative that the idea of preparing the SAARC for a post-Uruguary Round of North-South economic and political dialogue gained currency. The Summit was unanimous in urging Iraq to vacate its occupation of Kuwait. It also agreed to extend the visa exemption facility for travel within the region to heads of national academic institutions (besides the Supreme Court Judges and MPs who already enjoy this as per the 1988 Islamabad Declaration). The Summit paved the way for increasing exchanges among South Asian journalists with the same objective of promoting people-to people contacts. As at the previous SAARC Summits, the Male Summit too helped to provide a favourable setting for bilateral talks so essential at a time when tensions and misgivings in the region are once more on the rise. The Chandra Shekhar-Nawaz Sharif meeting assumed expected significance in this context and though one cannot possibly share our Prime Minister's excessive optimism over the fate of Indo-Pak ties following his discussions with his Pakistani counterpart (one must necessarily be wary of Pak designs in the light of Nawaz Sharif's press statements on the Simla Pact not being binding on his government, on Kashmir being an "international issue, and an Islamabad's uninterrupted aid to the Kashmiri militants) to minimise the importance of the decision to resume the dialogue at the level of the two countries' Foreign Secretaries this month would be myopic, to say the least.[9]

Chandra Shekhar's talks with the other summiteers were also of substantial value. The bilateral cooperation agreements signed later in New Delhi with Bhutan and Nepal in the presence of the Bhutanese King and the Napalese Prime Minister are welcome offshoots of the Male meet. In the overall framework the Fifth SAARC Summit's modest outcome of trying to unfold new avenues of regional interaction is doubtless a small step towards arresting, if not reducing, regional tensions keeping pace with the spirit of our times.

References

1. Aabha Dixit, Pakistan's Kalashnikov Culture, *The Independent*, 4 January, 1991.
2. *The Hindu*, 12 December, 1990.
3. *The Hindu*, 7 December, 1990.
4. N.C. Menon, Affinity with America, *The Hindustan Times*, 28 December, 1990.
5. Quoted in *National Herald*, 11 December, 1990.
6. K. Subrahmanyam, Defence Policy for the Nineties, *The Business and Political Observer*, 17 December, 1990.
7. *Dawn*, 19 November, 1990.
8. K. Subrahmanyam, Para-Military to the Force, *The Business and Political Observer*, 3 December, 1990.
9. *Mainstream*, 1, December, 1990.

13

Drugs Addiction and Social Chaos

According to a survey conducted by a private agency there are about 15 lakh drug addicts in Pakistan. What steps had Gen. Zia government taken to overcome this menace?

The figures you're seeing are exaggerated, but there are a larg number addicts. We place the figure at three lakhs. As a society we are likely to be badly mauled by this manace, if we don't take measures in time. But we're taking proper steps. I think both India and Pakistan should get together to confront this menace. Whereas previously whatever came into Pakistan, went out from Karachi : for the last few years, it is being smuggled out through the Indian borber from where it goes to Bombay and then goes out. I talked to Prime Minister Rajiv Gandhi personally on this subject.[1]

The Indo-Pak committee to combat drug trafficking and smuggling helds its third meeting in New Delhi, on May 10, 1989 to review its activities and suggest steps to further strengthen bilateral cooperation.

The two-day meeting discussed how the two countries step up exchange of information between their customs officials to facilitate movement of passengers and cargo at the Attari-wagah border.

The Narcotics Control Bureau (NCB), whose representative headed the Indian delegation to the joint boby, said the committee would also consider convening periodic meetings between officials of the two countries to widen the cooperation.

Kalim Dail Khan, officer on special duty for narcotics matters in the Prime Minister's Secretariat, headed.

The Indian delegation was led by the NCB Director General, M.B. Bhatnagar, other members include the Director general of revenue intelligence, P.K. Kapoor, the NCB Deputy Director General, Dalbir Singh, Collectors of Customs and Central excise of Chandigarh and Jaipur and senior officers of Border Security Force, Finance Ministry and External Affairs Ministry.

The two countries had constituted the joint committee to combat drug trafficking and smuggling across the border after a secretary level meeting in December 1986.

The Federal and Provincial Governments on November 21, 1990 are considering a proposal to provide drug detection system to various government and non-government drug addicts' treatment centres on subsidised rates.

The machines could detect urine based drugs like cannabis, cocaine, alcohol, barbiturates, benzodiazepines, heroin, and methedrine.

DRUG ABUSE is one of the major social problems of present generation and, characteristically, starts amongst teenagers. Initially it probably represents a process of curiosity and experimentation, a desire not to be excluded from the group, a rebellion. In the majority it is a temporary breakdown in the normal pattern because they only experiment with the soft drugs. The danger lies when they come in contact with hard drugs, specially because narcotics health hazard is enormous as a stready deterioration in the personalitp occurs and the sole driving force becomes restricted to the need to acquire more drug.

It is well know that drugs have been used by men for thousands of years in nearly every part of the world. Man has discovered plants whose juices and powders, on being properly prepared and consumed, have caused desirable alteration of consciousness. In ancient times these substances were used in religious ceremonies, but they have also been used for recreational purposes. As the science of chemistry progrersed and medicine advanced, the variety of drugs increased. The analgesic drugs derived from the poppy plant have been particularly susceptible to abuse since they produce euphoria, as well as analgesia. Substances which produce an altered state of consciousness, euphoria and special feeling of relief from anguish and anxiety have been in use from prehistoric times. The use of alcohol was wide before recorded histosy. Opium was used thousands of years ago in Egypt Mesopotamia (Iraq) and was common in China until the last century till the time of the opium wars, Cannabis has been used for centuries and is still widely used in Asia, Africa and America. Hallusigenic drugs and stimulants derived from coca plant were well known in primitive Siberia and to the Indians of South America. Brewing of alcohol from dates, grapes and honey was generally popular among pre-Islamic communities livingin Arabia.[2]

At the beginning of the Islamic era, the drinking of wine was clearly identified as a disruptive social evil and was effectively dealt with. Even after 14 centuries, the successful Islamic model of alcohol extinction stands out as exceptional, indeed almost unique, in human history, whereas in the recent era prohibitions and bans in the West as well as in the East without appropriate strategies have had no or little success. Indeed in crrtain cases it led to the spread of drug abuse in various countries.

Drug abuse had no boundaries. No country is immune. Men, women and even children are victims and experience serious health problems as a result of their physical and psychological addiction. The prevalent use and abuse of drugs, both medical and non-medical, has aroused serious concern, around the world and Pakistan is no exception. Medical men, law-enforcing agencies and social welfare organisations are all trying to fight the growing problem of drug abuse. There are certain drugs whose use is against the law and yet these are used and abused by a section of population. Again, there are certain drugs which are mainly used for therapeutic purposes and are freely available across the counter at any chemist shop. For a vast majority of people, the use of these drugs starts with a doctor's prescription but later may go on to self-medication, drug abuse and drug dependence, a pattern all too familiar to psychiatrists. The use of various substances to modify mood or behaviour is generally regarded as normal and acceptable in our society despite wide cultural differences. Many people drink coffee or tea for the stimulant effects of caffeine or engage in the social drinking of alcohol. Certain drugs may be used medically to relieve tension and anxiety, e.g. sedatives, hypnotics and tranquillisers. The young are not alone in turning to the drugs. If we stop a while and think, we are all potential drug takers, if not heroin, then tranquillisers, sedatives, alcohol, stimulants, sleeping pills, nicotine, etc. In fact, we have pills to sedate us when we are anxious or nervous, excite us when we are dull and depressed, slim us when we are fat, fatten us when are thin, wake us up when we are asleep, and put us to sleep when we are awake. The abuse of alcohol, cigarettes and both illegal and legal drugs is by far the most important cause of premature and preventable illness, and death in our society.[3]

THE PROBLEM of drug abuse has been with us for some time now. Prior to the promulgation of the Prohibition Order, 1979. (Enforcement of Hadd), the traditional use of opium to a very large extent and the use of alcohol to some extent was tolerated and generally ignored. It will not be wrong to say that the Prohibition Order demanded not less than a radical change in the attitude of the users as well as the general public towards the abuse of narcotics. Unfortunately, attitude change does not necessarily follow the changes in law and require adoption of appropriate strategies for its modification.

The epidemic spread of the use of heroin has given rise to an unprecedented situation variously described as a scourage, a national calamity, a crisis situation and there have been calls for declaring heroin as Enemy No. 1. However, when all this is compared with the actual projects on t e ground for the control and containment of the problem, the scene fails to present matching efforts.

There is a long tradition of opium and cannabis use in our country. In fact, before the enforcement of the Prohibition Order, opium was freely available through Government-licensed shops and it was mostly used by labourers and other working classes. Its use was not very widspread and the main factor responsible for containing the abuse of opium and cannabis was the attitude of the society which never accepted the use of these drugs in spite of such a long association and labelled the users as "afeemchees", "charsees" and "bhangees".

The gravity of the situation is due to the fact that the problem has crept into our youth and despite measures to check its spread, it is spreading very rapidly. The young drug abuser often claims that society as a whole is too much preoccupied with materialistic values to take notice of the value of the individual. Many feel frustrated and disillusioned with what they regard as the false and hypocritical values of their leaders. The young drug addict actually hates himself and the world for not being able to change the set up that he finds unacceptable. One wonders why there is so much hate, misery and confusion in a world which is essentially lovely, beautiful and enjoyable. Perhaps, because our life has lost its direction and our values have lost their meaning. So, perhaps the solution of the drug problem lies in a basic change in the values of our society, a society which a concerned more with man than material, a society which offers is way of life and not just a standard of living, society where people are valued for themselvrs and not for their money or status. In the rapidly changing society of today, which is becoming more and more impersonal and more and more materialistic, and where emphasis has shifted to acquiring money and becoming overnight rich by whatever means available, young people are bound to feel lost. There is need for young people to be supported in thinking through and working out an important and meaningful identity and their roles in the moderm society and meaning relationship to life and life's Creator without which the attempts to cope with the drug problem are bound to fail. It is not only useless but illogical to blame the drug abuser and to expect him to give up his only means of escape and enjoyment without providing him with a way of life which is more constructive and more satisfying and more meaningful, a way of life which gives meaning to existence and helps to solve the jigsaw puzzle of this universe and one's place in it no matter how small.

MANAGEMENT of a drug dependent starts with identification of a drug addict. At times it becomes extremely difficult to point out a drung addict and many a time even close family members are unaware of the fact for months and years. Some suspicion is aroused by the changed behaviour of an addict. He may start spending lot of money, remaining away from home for long periods and giving various lame excuses to justify his absence, may start neglecting his personal hygiene and show fall of academic performance. He may have problems with his colleagues at work or conflicts with his employer. His mood may become irritable and he may start losing temper on trivial issues and ultimately may be involved in some unlawful activity like stealing, etc. A change of friends' company may also point towards it. Occasionally, he may confess himself being a drug addict or may be caught red handed using some illicit drugs.

The drug dependent must be approached without prejudice and the psychiatrist should have a kind, supportive towards him. A humanitarian, active and vigorous treatment approach should be adhered to from the very beginning. No single treatment regimen is effective and multi-disciplinary approach is the most appropriate after a detailed psychological assessment and diagnosis which requires careful evaluation of his addiction pattern, the drugs used, the amount used, duration of addition, the route of administration of the drug and careful assessment of the personality. The various treatment approaches are as follows.

It is the treatment of the acute phase of the abstinence syndrome. The usual methods of detoxification are :

1. Sudden withdrawal of the drug, with no active support during the abstinence syndrome. This is referred to as the "Cold Turkey" method and is usually not recommended.

2. The addictive drug is stopped and 'substituted' by other drugs, which decrease the severity of abstinence. A long-acting drug such as Methadone or Phenobarbitone is substituted in case of heroin or barbiturate dependence respectively. The long-acting drug is then gradually tapered off, and is likely to lead to a less severe withdrawal as compared to the original drug. Methadone is not used in Pakistan because of its addictive potential.

Phenothiazines (Largactil, etc.) and Butyrophenones (Haloperidol) are also used as substitute drugs. Presently, clonidine has been succssfully used in the opiate withdrawal substitution therapy. In some centres, opium tablets are used during the abstinence syndrome.

3. The drugs are gradually withdrawn and symptomatic treatement is given during this period. Gradual reduction is the preferred form of treatment in Barbiturate and Benzo-

diazopine dependence. This method is used for drug dependents in whom the substitute therapy is contra-indicated.

During the detoxification phase, the drug dependent is symptomatically treated for aches and pains by analgesics, diarrhoea by antidiarrhoeals and symptoms such as lacrimation, rhinorrhea by antihistamines. Care is also taken to correct the fluid balance and treat any associated medical complications. If there is an underlying psychiatric disorder, it is treated accordingly.

Drug dependents are alienated members of the society; they have escaped from reality, situations and sought refuge in drugs. A lot of motivation is needed to give up drug dependence. Supportive psychotherapy in which reassurance is given and motivation enhanced is extremely important in management. Drug dependence usually has its roots in strained family relationships and faulty communications. Family therapy is usually employed to improve communication among family members. Group therapies are important for amelioration of the problems of drug addicts both during hospitalisation and in the crucial follow-up period.

Follow-up, after-care and rehabilitation are the most important aspects of treatment to prevent relapse. Rehabilitation into a responsible and proper role in society so that the drug dependent develops meaning in his life is the key to successful maintenance of abstinence from drugs. Rehabilitation of a drug dependent is not only helping the person to free himself from peer group pressure but also helps him to restore his education, find a suitable occupation and re-establish his social status. In a successful rehabilitation programme, regular follow-up is carried out, motivation is continuously enhanced and family support is established. In some countries therapeutic communities are successfully used in the rehabilitation of drug addicts.

GOVERNMENT and world organisations are spending a lot of money in an attempt to control the problem of drug abuse and drug dependence and on the rehabilitation of drug addicts. The age-old maxim, "Prevention is better than cure," holds as good here as anywhere else. The family, as an institution, has a more profound role to play than the State or any other organisation parents can help their children by creating a warm and friendly atmosphere at home. They can help their children in staying away from drugs by developing effective means of communication and by being open and honest with them. Parents can help their children by spending more time with them and by strengthening moral and spiritual values not by preaching or moralising but by presenting a model of behaviour. Youngsters should also be told that drug taking is only a form of escapism and anyone who takes drugs is simply incapable of coming to grips with the realities of life. Drugs are indeed a very poor substitute for real living. To prevent drug dependence, it is important to provide alternative means of recreation. There should be broad-based youth development programmes and vocational and skill training programmes. From an early age, creativeness should be encouraged, so that youngsters can find happiness in self-expression and not be frustrated by the boredom and commercialised entertainment offered by the box called television. Children and teenagers will not accept the word of their parents and teachers as gospel truth unless there exists open communication between the two. It is important for parents to be able to tune into the wavelength at which their children might be functioning at various stages of their development and to try to understand their feelings and needs. Only then is a bond of trust and respect established and the youngesters are then receptive to the guidance and advice of their parents and teachers. Proper religious background and a well-defined value system helps children and young adults to see their way through life more clearly and thus prevent them from falling prey to artificial anchors.[4]

MQM Chief Altaf Hussain on November 19, 1990 warned the district administration and police against any delay to root out narcotic dens and the peddlers in the city (Karachi) otherwise he said he "will have to talk to Jam Saliq to get them removed."

He said narcotics were being openly sold in every nook and cerner of the city with complete impunity and the younger generation was being destroyed.

He was speaking at a "national unity" function organised by the MQM Hyderabad Zone at Latifabad. He made it clear that the MQM leadership will not come to the rescue of any narcotic dealer or addict or any one else involved in any criminal activity."

The MQM Chief unequivocally declared that any MQM worker found involved in criminal activities or extortion of any kind will be "thrown out" of the organisation. Altaf said that the message of the MQM had not only been heard loud and clear in Islamabad and all the provinces of Pakistan but its revolutionary programme had been universally acknowledged.

Amidst thunderous applause, he told the crowd that foreign media had described the MQM as the only party which represented the poor class.

He said, the political commentators had expressed the opinion that not the Mohajirs alone but all the oppressed people of Pakistan had pinned their hopes on the MQM for a better tomorrow.

He said a new dawn will emerge on the horizon of Pakistan when the "Muttehida Qaumi Movement" is launched in all the provinces of the country. He said, the MQM will not rest till the representatives of the poor and lower middle class reached the legislative assemblies.

He, however, cautioned his followers that these objectives could not be achieved without perserverance, hard work, discipline and sincerity of purpose.

Paying glowing tributes to the martyrs of pucca Qilla, Qasba Colony, Shah Faisal Colony, Ajmer Nagri and those of

Sept 30 and Oct 31, 1990 Altaf said that the victory of the Haq Parast candidates owned to the sacrifices of the persons and those who had lost their limbs, including women and children in the MQM struggle.

In an emotional voice, the MQM Chief said, "I have nothing to offer for your sacrifices for I have neither gold nor silver but my gratitude." I salute you from the core of my heart", he said.

He said : "I refuse to accept the maximum that blood is thicker than water for as far as I am concerned my companions who have suffered with me are dearer to me than my blood relations."

He exhorted the people to get their names registered with the census staff as otherwise half of the population of Hyderabad may go unrepresented in the assemblies.

Earlier, when the MQM Chief came on the stage, he was given a standing ovation and quite a few people were injured in the scramble. The "national unity" function was attended by thousands belonging to various nationalities including women, children.

It is reported that one out of every 42 registered cars is stolen. The theft is at its peak in December every year. In 1990 there was seven per cent increase in theft of cars in the first six months in urban areas; five per cent increase in the suburban areas. About 40 per cent of thefts take place in largest ten cities and suburbs. The theft has an impact on 4 million people every year. The US crime department has neither enough resources nor personnel to tackle this problem. It has more pressing tasks i.e. prevent drug traffic. The champion of human rights over the world is faced with a large dose of drug abuse in its own population. It may make a lot of noise about drug trafficking but its equanimity towards narcotics and gun smuggling in Afghanistan. Pakistan and across the border of India is part of continual winter fare.

Nearer home, it has to be more serious about the problem. It is bound to come in conflict with Latin America. It may continue to play a global role—playing up the values of pluralism and interdependence. It equally needs to look inwards into its economic vitals. These latter concerns may prevent global role. If Soviet Union is becoming a European power, will the US countenance to be an American one with less of a hegemon that the logic of interdependence and the call to improve quality of human life at home may imply.[5]

Along with a class of army top brass and big businessmen Pakistan has now another class of brokers (*dalals*) who have come up in the race thriving on trade which includes contraband heroin and other goods, business. This element caters to the needs of luxurious goods of the neoelite and Jahangirdars who control vast land holdings in Pakistan's agrarian sector. It is this class which is now wanting to turn Karachi in a free hold on public affairs in league with ruling clique of army generals.[6]

A good many Afghan refugees are presumed to be active in the heroin trafficking. Pakistan has been turned into a base of international espionage. The common man seems to be fed up with this inter-national conflict and is eager that the peace returns to their frontiers; the so-called Mujahideens go back to theit homes and the Geneva accords are implemented in letter and spirit without further delay.[7]

Drug barons and criminals have pumped crores of rupees into the election funds of their nominees in North-West Frontier province. Known as a smugglers' paradise, the Frontier province has over the years become an important link for the International drug syndicates and Afghan rebels engaged in the opium-for guns trade. A kingpin arrested earlier this year made stunning disclosures about the nexius between the drug lords, pliticians and army officials. He alleged that serving Army and Air Force officers were acting as "carriers" of heroin and charas.

With four days to go for polling, conflicting signals are still coming from the electorate making it difficult to decipher poll trends, says a local journalist. There are 150 contestants for 26 National Assembly seats in the province. To give a fillip to the faction-ridden Pakistan People's Party in the province, Benazir Bhutto has agreed to contest from a Peshawar constituency. The other seat to be fought by Benazir Bhutto is from Larkana, her home town in Sindh.

Bhutto had won a major palitical battle when the Peshawar High Court on September 26 ordered restoration of the dissolved provincial Assembly and re-instatement of the PPP-ld Aftab Ahmed Khan Sherpao Government. But the Supreme Court stayed the High Court-order. The case will now come up only after the elections. The Sindh and Lahore High Courts have upheld President Ghulam Ishaq Khan's decision to dissolve the National Assembly and sack Benazir Bhutto's Government. Benazir Bhutto is pitted against the Awami National Party leader, Ghulam Ahmed Bilaur, who was defeated by a margin of 8,711 votes in the last elections Sherpao is contesting from another Peshawar seat.

The veteran ANP leader, Khan Abdul Wali Khan, is all set to retain his seat from Charsadda. He had defeated the IJI rival by 28,640 votes in the 1988 elections. He faces Jamaat-ul-Ulema-i-Islam (Fazlur group) nominee, Maulana Hassan Jon, who is backed by the PDA. A keen contest is on the cards in Abbottabad where the IJI condidate Gohar Ayub Khan, son of late Field Marshal Ayub Khan, takes on Umer Asghar Khan, son of the Tehrik-i-Istiqlal Chief, Air Marshal (Retd) Asghar Khan, who is fighting on the PDA platform. Making a last-minute change in Mardan, the IJI has replaced Lt-Gen (Retd) Fazle Haq by the caretaker NWFP Chief Minister, Mir Afzal Khan. Talking to reporters in Peshawar on Thursday, Ms Bhutto alleged that a cell had been set up at President's House in Islamabad with plans afoot to rig the polls. Bhutto claimed she has information that the results of the elections would not be declared without prior clearance from President Ishaq Khan. She said she did not rule out her arrest before elections. Addressing an election rally at the Younas Stadium in Mardan, she lambasted the President for acting like a "dictator". His days in office are numbered, she told cheering crowds chanting "Jiye Bhutto". For the PDA, the electoral understanding between the IJI and the ANP has been a big blow. The two groups have decided to field consensus candidates with the sole purpose of defeating Benazir Bhutto's alliance.

But the presence of JUI (Fazlur group) in the contest is likely to affect the IJI-ANP combine. Most of the constituencies will now have multi-cornered contests. A large number of independents and smaller parties are also in the fray. "If elected, they will pitch in for the highest bidder from either said," says an analyst.

In his election speeches, Khan Abdul Wali Khan hits out at the Bhutto family charging it with wrecking Pakistan's sovereignty. Their U.S. connexious have been thoroughly exposed with Begum Nusrat Bhutto lobbying in Washington for suspension of the U.S. aid to Pakistan till the elections, he says. In Manshera, following stiff resistance by the IJI caretaker provincial Minister. Salauddin Saeed, the former Premier, Mohammad Khan Junejo, was forced to withdraw his nomination papers. Saeed, who had won the seat in the last elections by a margin of 6,293 votes, will have a tough fight from Syed Qasim Ali Shah (Ind) and others.

Two old rivals, PPP's Iftikhan Hussein Gilani and IJI's Maulana Naimatullah, are once again pitted against each other in Kohat. The IJI nominee had won by more than 11,000 votes in the last elections.

In Chitral, Begum Nusrat Bhutto had defeated her IJI rival by more than 9,000 votes in the 1988 elections and the seat was retained in a by-election. This time the PPP has awarded the ticket to a local PPP leader, Payar Ali Allana.

One of the most prestigious contests will be witnessed in the D.I. Khan constituency where the JUI (F) Chief, Maulana Fazlur Rehman, take on a strong PPP aspirant, Fazal Karim Khan. Of the 25 seats for which elections were held in 1988, the PPP and the IJI won eight each, three went to JUI (F) one to JUI (Darkhwasti group), two to ANP and three to Independents.

Forces are out in Pakistan to nip its nascent democracy in the bud. A people's government is obviously not good for the health of the drugs smuggling mafia which has ruled the roost during the eleven years of Gen Zia-ul-Haq's martial law in the name of Islam. The mafia was well guarded because the press was shackled and could not tell the truth if it hurt the perpetrators of crimes against the nation. The scenario has changed for the better despite the limitations on the popular government of Prime Minister Benazir. She has restored the right to assembly of the students and the working class and the freedom of the press. The atmosphere of fear no more exists. But the legacies of the dictatorial rule are there. The political forces in Pakistan are clearly polarised between to distinct groups. One, the Pakistan People's Party (PPP) the Mohajir Quami Movement (MQM), the Awami National Party (ANP) and the Baluchistan National Alliance (BNA) along with a large majority of the people of Pakistan in all the four provinces are on the side of Benazir. On the other side of the fence are the Islamic Jamhoori Ittehad (IJI), President Ghulam Ishaq Khan, Chief of Army Staff Gen Mirza Beg, the Inter-Services Intelligence (ISI), the drug smuggling mafia and the United States, represented in Pakistan by its Ambassador for Rober Oakley. The revel Afghan groups nurtured by Gen-Zia for more than a decade are the second line of defence for this group.

The Jamiatul Ulemia Islam of Maulana Fazlur Rehman is on the fence. It supports the progressive and democratic policies of PPP but opposes Benazir, a woman as the head of Government. The IJI President and Punjab Chief Minister

Nawaz Sharif, a powerful industrialist, is projected by the ISI-CIA-Mafia group as a champion of Islam and heir apparent of Gen Zia. As one will put it: Nawaz Sharif has emerged as the Chief orphan of Gen Zia. The Jammat Islami, though a minor component of the IJI, is the dominant force in the combine and lays down the policies of the group.[8]

The other important person in this group is Gen (retired) Fazle Haq who was the Governor of NWFP till Gen. Zia found it expedient to throw him out. He is said to have been a king-pin of narcotics smuggling in his province. His relations with Gen. Zia were not very good but it was said that the latter was mortally afraid of him and therefore allowed him to continue as the Governor. Pakistani and Western Press has often accused Gen. Faz.e Haq's father-in-law of owing 22 heroin factories in NWFP. When Fazle Haq was removed as Governor of NWFP, and Nawab Hoti succeeded him, Fazle Haq allegedly manipulated things to frame-up Hoti's son in narcotics smuggling case. The poor boy was caught in New York and Hoti had to resign in ignominy. After Junejo was dismissed as Prime Minister in May 1988, Fazle Haq emerged as the Chief Minister of his fieldom (NWFP). He continued in this position till he was defeated in all the four provincial and one national assembly constituencies from where he had contested the November, 1988 elections. Before the polls, he had tauntingly said : "Running the affairs of a country was not for chokris". "Now he is busy trying to dislodge the PPP. ANP Government led by Aftab Ahmed Sherpao in NWFP. Narcotic Mafia is all powerful in Pakistan. It earns three billion dollars annually in black money and runs a parallel economy in the country. "You will not get a currency note of less than a hundred rupees on the other side of Attock Bridge, "a Pakistani leader had told this writer once). (Attock Bridge marks the boundary separating Punjab and NWFP). The heroin suness was so flourishing that people had become very wealthy. With the advent of the popular government in Pakistan, it is no more easy to run the heroin factories and smuggle narcotics abroad. The number of narcotic addicts has risen alarmingly to nearly two million in the country. Benazir has often said that she would save the future generations of Pakistan from this evil. Benazir's Government is determined to put an end to the evil of heroin and has decided to destroy the poppy crops in the frontier areas by a real spray but the drug mafia has threatened to shoot down the spray aircraft. The poppy cultivators have acquired surface-to-air misiles, so generously supplied by the US Secret Service CIA to the Afghan Mujahideen, to shoot down these spray aircraft. These cultivators have also dug trenches and are fully prepared to fight the Government if it tries to curb heroin production and smuggling. The United States no doubt makes all the noise about curbing narcotics but in case of Pakistan, it just does not bother how the mafia works there. It has found drug trafficking an easy way to keep its supporters happy and do its bidding. Gen Zia himself posed as a God-fearing Muslim and one should not speak ill of the dead. But during one of his sojourns to the United States to address the United Nations as the representative of the Muslim Ummah, New York police found large quantities of heroin in his gift packages meant for some of the worked celebrities at the UN. These packages were transported in a plane no other than the one in which Gen Zia travelled. Norwegian Police caught hold of one Raza Qureshi, said to be an adopted son of Gen. Zia, for narcotics smuggling. It was said he confessed he had links with high officials, including Mr Hamid Gul, Chief of Pakistan's Inter-Services Intelligence (S) which put together the Islamic Jamhoori Ittehad of Nawaz Sharif to defeat Benazir's PPP in November polls. The Bank of Credit and Cooperation International, run with Arab Money and managed by Pakistani banker Agha Hasan Abdi and Pakistani personnel was recently indicated by American authorities for involvement in cocaine smuggling. Agha Hasan Abdi was a great friend of Gen. Zia and provided fund for running Pakistan Government during the lean pre-budget months when the General was in financial straits. These are the groups and vested interests who want to ban the press freedom in Pakistan and are after the blood of Prime Minister

Benazir Bhuttoo. They are propping in Nawaz Sharif to fight Benazir., Nawaz Sharif has allegedly misappropriated Rs. 400 crores of public money and, to hide his own misdeeds, he is reported to have engaged a private American firm, Robinson Lake Kerer, for lobbying for him in the United States. Lake is the former Director of President George Bush's election campaign. The other partners of the firm are former Secretaries Richard Lugard and D Munian. Huge payments are paid to the firm for doing bolstering the IJI against the PPP.[9]

A bountiful poppy harvest is expected to hit a new high in Pakistan's northern frontier. The poppy harvest stretches beyond the fields, the opium reaching clandestine laboratories, and eventually hitting the streets of New York of Amsterdam and the habits of heroin addicts all over the world. Local authorities report that Pakistan has emerged as a major opium producer, at least in the 1985-86 session with a favourable weather. Not long ago, farmers planted about 5,000 acres to poppy, the plant which produces opium that is processed into heroin. This is 2,000 acres more than last year's plantations. And this, despite the country's earlier successes—however limited—is curbing poppy growing. As one American official puts it, enforcement "has slackened off as Pakistan shifts from martial law to a civilan government. The problem is much closer to the home. Until five years ago, heroin addiction was considered a rare phenomenon in Pakistan. Today, the per capita rate of heroin addiction is higher than that of the USA. Based on "extremely spongy data", authorities estimate the number of heroin addicts in Pakistan at around 400,000.

In the past, Pakistan was criticised by Western countries for not batting even an eyelid over the fact that it was the largest producer of poppy and heroin. Identified as the "most significant heroin threat" to Western Europe and the USA, Pakistan succumbed to international pressure by proclaiming a total ban on poppy growing in the poppy-growing belt in the

North. Traditionally, poor peasants in the North have grown poppy for centuries. Nobody until recently bothered with them, and the opium extracted from the flowers got absorbed by the locals without much ado. They never hit the headlines nor did their paltry poppy fields appear as veritable gold mines. Life was pretty much uneventful as far as they were concerned. And then the Afghan refugees, fleeing the Soviet invasion of their country, started pouring into Pakistan. And along came their home-made laboratories to convert opium into heroin. Soon much of the sleepy towns and hamlets have changed. A run for war opium led to increased prices which, in turn, led to the cultivation of additional acreage. Finally, the favourable weather for the last couple of years produced bumper poppy crops.

What irks most Western governments is that the heroin is destined—through an intricate and illicit international network—for the narcotic habits of American and Western European addicts. Recently, the son of the Governor of the Frontier Province, a paradise for poppy growers, was convicted on charges of drug smuggling in New York.[10]

Observers point out that Pakistan's sporadic drives against drug dealers or the efforts of Customs to foil smuggling attempts cannot be taken seriously until operators who hold important government positions are taken to task. Observers say it is these operators, and not the small fry, that are actively engaged in the illicit trade. A Bill for an effective law against poppy cultivation is soon to be present before Parliament. The Bill covers the trafficing, illicit trade and chemical processing of poppy. But some politicians have also encouraged their constituency to sow poppy. Reliable observers say that mostly illiterate farmers are unaware of the ramifications of heroin extracted from opium and are taken in by shrewd politicians who also have vested interests in poppy cultivation. Law enforcers are also in a quandary. They do not know whether to enforce the ban in the current sowing season. The police are desparately waiting for a

Federal Government policy statement on the sensitive issue. A belated statement could mean trouble as enforcing a ban on poppy growing is difficult and hazardous. Last March, poppy growers of Gadoon-Amazal clashed with the police who were trying to destroy the village's only source of income. Lives were lost, sending shock waves across the country and creating a storm in Parliament. "This is our land and we will grow whatever we like on it", says a Pakhtoon leader egging farmers to defy the poppy ban.

And why not when they reap what they sow? One acre of poppy crops yields as much as 10 kilos of opium. A kilo of opium, when processed into high-grade heroin, fatches as much as Rs. 10 million in the under-world market. In 1976, Pakistan attempted to launch a development project with the aid of the UN Found for Drug Abuse Control. The aim was to lure poppy growers into planting other cash crops. Swat, considered the most beautiful valley in the country, saw hundreds of acres of land developed for cultivation, livestock, poultry and fruit orchards. The best irrigation and drinking water schemes were provided. Soon, the people of Swat learned to earn a living other than poppy growing. And in 1983, the valley was declared a poppy-free zone by the United Nations. A similar programme of crop substitution was started in other parts of the North.[11]

References

1. Ghulab Nabi Khayal, Zia-ul-Haq—The Survivo, *Illustrated Weekly, of India*, 26 July, 1987.
2. I.A.K. Tareen, Drug Abuse, *Nation*, 16 November, 1990.
3. *Ibid.*
4. *Ibid.*

5. Rakesh Gupta, After the Cold War, *Patriot*, 20 December 1990.
6. Mr. Jam Saki's views, *Clarity*, 2 April, 1989.
7. Raghuraj Gupta, Pakistan Panorama-IV, *Pioneer*, 27 May, 1989.
8. Syed Ziaullah Pakistan, *Madhya Pradesh Chronicle*, 22 April 1989.
9. *Ibid*.
10. Zeenat Hassan, It's bloom time for Pak proppy, *Pioneer*, 28 June 1987.
11. *Ibid*.

14

In Search of Economic Aid and Debt Payments

Foreign economic and military aid is an important part of foreign policy process. The aid-giver and receiving countries are supposed to maintain close contacts as it is must for monitoring the progress and other aspects of foreign aid. No country in the world is self-sufficient and dependence on one another for the basic needs, is the need of the hour. This give and take process helps only in strengthening the foreign trade and clearing the foreign loans. The foreign economic aid comes into picture when it is needed for the building of basic infrastructure for the execution of a country economic policy. For building ports, acquiring and manufacturing ships and transport network, modern equipment to handle the cargo, the money has a definite role to play. There is a little need to examine the already established fact that the aid-given country has some stakes in the region where she is pumping money and feels satisfied when the aid-receiver gives due recognition to its foreign policy objectives. Otherwise, the political leadership of that country won't be able to survive for a long time and the public opinion which has always a role to play, would compel her to stop provining economic and military aid. The domestic and international milieu, are the two determinants whose impact on a country's external policy is recognized by the scholars. Both are unstable determinants and from time to time there are lot of fluctuations in their setting.[1]

The aid suspension preceded Pakistan's national elections in November 1990. The perceived affront to Pakistan's nuclear sovereignty became an election issue. The Islamic Democratic Alliance (IDA) which won the elections, charged Benazir Bhutto's Pakistan People's Party with colluding with the US in the sabotage of military and economic aid to Pakistan. (While military aid is linked to the bomb, economic aid for 1991 was made on the condition of holding free and fair elections). Last year, Pakistan gave the US a proforma, a private assurance, that it was not engaged in a bomb programme. But around April or May 1990, the US began entertaining doubts about Pakistan's assurance. Even if the US is willing to settle for a publie assurance by Pakistan, no government will be able too give one. Any government which abandons the pursuit in todays Pakistan will fall. It is not surprising therefore that Munir Ahmed Khan, Chairman of the Atomic Energy Commission said a few days ago that Pakistan 'would not foresake its nuclear development programme under pressure from the United States', and Gen Mirza Afzal Beg has spoken of its as a deterrent to an Indian bomb. This raises the old issue of India's nuclear options. India had not felt threatened when China acquired a nuclear bomb with its first explosion in 1964. Like China and Pakistan, India is not a signatory to the nuclear non-proliferation treaty. India'a objection to the treaty is that it discriminates against the have-nots because it limits horizontal profliferation but does not touch vertical proliferation.[2]

Prime Minister Nawaz Sharif said that his government was determined to fight unemployment, inflation and injustice and not to accept aid with strings.

Speaking as the guest of honour at a meeting held at the Alhamra Art Centre in Lahore on November 9, 1990 to celebrate the 113 the birthday of poet philosopher Muhammad Iqbal, the Prime Minister said that he was fully aware of the fact that his government would have to go if it could not tackle the problem of unemployment inflation and injustice.

He said that his government had to do what had not been done during the past 43 years. He could not say that the problems would be solved overnight orin a few months or years, but he wanted to assure the nation that atleast a beginning would be solved overnight or in a few months or years, but he wanted to assure the nation that at least a beginning would be made in the right direction and that the people would not be disappointed.

Nawaz Sharif said that his intensions were good and he wanted to undertake the task before him with full determination to complete it. How would like the people to pray for his unsuccess in his mission. He said he liked to be straightforward and believed in neat and clean politics. He knew that many of his predecessors had fallen in the trap of sycophants and ousted. He, therefore, did not want to fall a prey to flattery.

He said a heavy responsibility had fallen on his shoulders after becoming the Prime Minister and sometimes he trembled when he thought about the problems and difficulties lying ahead of him and the expectations the people had from his government. He said he was determined to serve the nation rising above his personal interests.

The Prime Minister said he did not believe in leading the people up the garden path. He would like to be straightforward with them. He said he appreciated Allama Iqbal because his poetry was full of good advice. Those reading Iqbal could not go astray. He said that in Iqbal's words he had started his flight and would not accept the food which hampers this flight.

He said he believed in Allah Almighty and knew that it was He who provided 'rizq' (food) to all. Man did not give 'rizq' to anyone. He said he would like to have communion with the Allah Almighty in accordance with the thoughts of Iqbal. He would make sincere efforts to serve the nation and the country. People should pray for his success in his mission.

Nawaz Sharif said the country was facing serious internal and external problems. It was burried under the heavy burden of foreign debt. Now when he thought of the Chief Ministership of Punjab, he envied Ghulam Haider Wyne who had taken his place in the Province. There was an enormous difference between the responsibilities of a Chief Minister and the Prime Minister. He could not reach his destination without the good wishes and prayers of the people for his success.

Referring to the Kashmir and Afghanistan issues, the Prime Minister said that a pleasant change in the form of weakness in a neighbouring country (India) was in the offing. Referring to allegations of rigging the elections levelled by the Opposition, he said the polling system was foolproof and those clamouring about rigging were in fact deceiving themselves. He said the Opposition should accept the reality of its defeat. He said the elections had been rigged only once in the history of Pakistan (1977) and the people had seen the results of the rigging later on.

He said he wanted to seek cooperation of both his opponents and his supporters in the larger interest of Pakistan. There would be no citicisation of the opponents, but those who had looted the nation would not be sparee under any circumstances. He said he would like to frame a law under which the sitting government could be subjected to accountability while it was still in power. The accountability of the past rulers would also continue side by side.

The Prime Minister said the Iqbal Day meeting was the first public function he was attending after the assumption of his office and he felt greatly honoured on being invited to it. Referring to the circle of sycophants around the rulers (Prof. Pareshan Khattak talked about it) he said he did not know weather the learned professor wanted to break it or widen it. He said nobody should expect that he would fall a prey to flattery.

Justice (Retd.) Javed Iqbal, son of Muhammad Iqbal, said that the motive behind the creation of Pakistan was the creation of a new Muslim society, because the Muslims were allowed to observe their religious rituals even during the British rule in India and were governed by their personal law. The nations continued talking about the ideas of Quaid-i-Azam and Allama Iqbal for a few years after the independence, but failed to create the Muslim society which was the objective of the creation of Pakistan.

He said the Muslim society could not be created in Pakistan due to dictatorial practices of the rulers. "Mulla-hism" and "peerimureedi". A Muslim society could not be created without giving a positive shape to these three negative forces. Only the scholars conversant with the problems and "Sufis" having staunch belief could strengthen democracy.

Dr. Javed Iqbal said the recent general elections had exposed the hollowness of the attrative slogans of the sympathies with the poor raised by the feudal lords. People had reposed their confidence in the leadership of industria-lists and businessmen. If this class succeeded in solving the problems like unemployment it would be its best achievement.

He said the nation was groaning under the heavy burden

of foreign loans. Even the new generations would have to repay these loans. There was lack of national integration and people had started hating each other instead of coming closer. More than half the history of the country was the history of dictatorship and the lion's share in the national budget was being spent on defence. The priorities would have to be re-defined for the creation of a Muslim society in Pakistan. Pakistan did not need the politicians for solving its problems, it required political sages.

Punjab Chief Minister Ghulam Haider Wyne, said the people of Pakistan in general and the people of Punjab in particular had repeated the history of 1946 in the recent general elections. It was now the high time for turning the Pakistan idea given by Allama Muhammad Iqbal into a reality.

He said that India claimed to be a secular state but had failed to provide security to the Muslims, who were the largest minority in the country, despite its tall claims. The world conscience was asleep over Babri Masjid issue and the blood of innocent Muslims was being spilled in Kashmir. He called for teaching the Pakistan Ideology in the educational institutions and called for positive proposals in this regard for implementation.

Maulana Kausar Niazi, a former Federal Minister and Senator, said that Allama Iqbal had been born at a time when the Khan Bahadurs and feudal lords in Punjab used to consider the chains of slavery as ornaments and the 'mashaikh' were exploiting the religion. Iqbal adopted poetry as a medium for spreading his message and gave immortal similies and sayings to it.

He said that Allama Iqbal was a great Quranic thinker and played a significant role in organising the Muslims under the leadership of Quaid-i-Azam Muhammad Ali Jinnah. His birthday was in fact the birthday of a new world which was being celebrated in an atmosphere of rejoicing over the victory of the democratic aspirations.

He said it was for the first time that Punjab had been selected for the leadership of the nation. But those at the helm of affairs should not forget that the word "dar" (hanging) was part of the word "iqtidar" (power).

He said the time had come for translating the centuries old dream of the nation for the enforcement of an Islamic system in the country into a reality. He said the task should be undertaken in the light of the philosophy of Allama Muhammad Iqbal which was opposed to amassing wealth beyond ones requirements and wanted the people to rise above sectarianism for enforcement of the Islamic system of Justice. He said the evils of provincialism and linguistic and ethnic differences would end with the ushering in of the Islamic system.

Dr. Israr Ahmed, a prominent religious scholar and thinker, said it was for the third time in the history of Pakistan that the nation had got a golden chance for the enforcement is Istamic values. He said the victory of Islamic Jamhoori Ittehad in the recent general elections was surprising even for itself and was no less than a miracle.

He said the nation had got the first chance for the enforcement of Islam in Pakistan at the time of independence, but it could not be availed due to the sudden demise of the Quaid-i-Azam and great influx of the refugees from India. The second chance came after the success of the Nizami-i-Mustafa Movement in 1977, but even this could not be availed. He said the IJI's landslide victory in the recent general elections was the third chance given to the nation for the enforcement of Islam in the country. The nation might not get another chance for the purpose even if this one was not availed promptly.

He said the main hurdle in the enforcement of Islam

was the contradictory concepts of the Islamic system. The religious scholar thought of Islamic system as belief, worship and a system of punishments. The concept of socio-economic justice did not exist in the concept of Islamic system given by the religious scholars. The highly educated Muslims did not agree with the concept of the Islamic system given by the religious scholars.

Dr. Israr Ahmed said the Quaid-i-Azam and Iqbal did not agree with the idea of a government of the religious scholars and considered it against the dictates of Shariat. The Quaid-i-Azam himself used the word "Islamic Socialism" and Iqbal described Islam as Marxism plus Allah. He said the religious scholars had now closed the door of 'Ijtihad' and attached more importance to the sayings of Imam Abuhanifa's disciplines to the words of the Imam.

He said the religious scholars did not have a way with the civil and military bureaucracy, but they had constant rapport with the people whom they met five times daily at the time of the payers. They could be used for motivating the people for the enforcement of an Islamic system in the country.

He said that Allama Iqbal stood at the meeting point of the modernism and orthodoxy. His thinking was very progressive on the one hand but he hated the Western civilization the most and loved the religion on the other hand. He favoured an 'Ijtihad' having based on fundamentalism. Iqbal was also against feudalism.

Dr. Israr referred to a recent interview in which Prime Minister Nawaz Sharif had refused to be described as a fundamentalist and said that one should feel proud of being one. He said the Muslims should also take the description "Islamic Socialism" back from the atheists and materialists. He said that Iqbal did not speak about the Scandenavian Socialism in his works, he talked about a socialism that could take the 'Ummah' back to the 'Khilafat-i-Reshida'.

He said that Islam did not want imposition of Zakat only on the bank deposits. This had only brought discredit to the Zakat which if enforced in letter and spirit could dispense with the need for imposition of other taxes. He said the interest should be abolished totally. The interest on defence loans was nothing but treason. He said that feudalism should be abolished totally and a land commission comprising the religious scholars and experts should be formed for suggesting ways and means for the purpose. He said that absentee landlordism was 'Haram'.

Dr. Israr said that religious scholars had not been able to speak against the feudalism and capitalism because they were subservient to the capitalists and fuedal lords. He said the Pakistan Muslim League government now enjoyed absolute majority in the assemblies. It was high time for it to enforce Islam in walks of life. The nation might not get another chance for the purpose even if this opportunity was not availed by the PML. He hailed the nomination of Justice Tanzeelur Rehman on the Federal Shariat Court and called for lift restricitions on the Court in respect of examining certain laws so that it might play its role in enforcement of Islam in the country.

Professor Pareshan Khattak said that Allama Iqbal was a poet with great foresight. His eyes could foresee what was going to happen 60 to 70 years ahead of his time. He said that Iqbal had not spoken about linguistic, ethnic and sectarian differences while giving the idea of Pakistan. He criticised monarchy, democracy and socialism and favoured the Islamic system. He said that Islam had not been enforced in Pakistan because every ruler considered himself as an emperor and every leadership supported by the people finally betrayed their confidence.

The Asian Development Bank on November 7, 1990 approved a $ 150 million concessional loan to Pakistan along with three technical assistance grants totalling $ 1.042 million.

The interest-free loan will support the country's agricultural credit programme, in which five nationalised commercial banks are also involved. The ADB loan will be relent by Islamabad to the Agricultural Development Bank of Pakistan (ADBP).

The loan has a term of 35 years including a 10 year grace at one per cent per annum service charge, the Manila-based bank said in a statement.

The technical assistance grants will be used to help implement an improved soil tillage technology programme, improving ADBO's legal services, and to help implement a resource mobilisation plan.

The bank said the loan will help Pakistan increase rural income, sustain high rates of agricultural growth, diversify crops and promote export-oriented agricultural products.

The loan, the 40th loan to Pakistan's agricultural sector, will directly benefit over 1,00,000 rural families expected to use the money to buy tractors and other farm equipment.

Trickish and wicked manoeuvring has become a universal trend and policies of all the countries particularly with the superpowers. They preach and advocate rule of law and respect for humanity but they do not actually believe in it. This is evident from the policies adopted by the Americans. They rendered moral and financial support to Iraq during the Gulf war with Iran but condemned her occupation of another Muslim State in the same region. They helped Muslims against Russia in Afghanistan but at the same time render unconditional and ultimited assistance and support to Israel against the wishes of the entire Muslim World. India also advocates democracy and respect for the sovereginty of all nations but does not feel ashamed to enter the forces in Sri Lanka. They do not feel ashamed after having prepared and procured atomic weapons to resist Pakistan's peaceful nuclear programme. Unfortunately this attitude has penetrated deep in our life as well. In schools, children do not get knowledge but they are prepared to pass examinations and obtain certificates. Teachers instead inculcating knowledge stress on students to memorise some selected topics without having any concept. In our politics, we advocate and talk about democracy but we actually do not believe in it. We condemn horse trading so far as it goes against us but never feel ashamed to manoeuvre it in our favour. There are hundreds of examples in which the opionion of the poor public is effected through biased information provided on TV and other medias. The American Aid was a burning issue during election 90 campaign and people were told Ghaas khha leyn gey (we will eat grass) but we will not accept conditional Aid. People in general are already eating ghaas (grass) the benefit of Aid is always enjoyed by the high ups.

The politicians manoeuvre power by raising slogans of improving the conditions of the poor, providing them cheap justice and not justice. The poor are unfortunately poor in all respects and they do not understand that if their conditions are improved, what slogan would be left without politicians to remain in politics. Where would they bring millions of people for their hours long processions bringing everything to stand still.[3]

With Pakistan's international creditors awaiting repayment foreign reserves tumbling and massive price hikes unavoidable former Prime Minister Benazir Bhutto, may have found the silver lining behind her stunning defeat in the October 1990 elections.

The Opposition benches appear to be the safest seats in parliament for any politician now.

Reeling from skyrocketing oil prices, short-term borrowing and rapidly depleting foreign reserves. Pakistan put out a billion-dollar cry for help.

"There's no way we can cover the losses ourselves", said the Finance Minister, Sartaz Aziz.

Dollar one billion we can make up on our own. But we need help with another billion dollars, Aziz said.

Japan was the first to respond offering a $ 500 million assistance package announced in mid-November 1990 in several Urdu language daily newspapers.

Food security for the entire population has been a goal for the World Food Programme (WFP) since it commenced operations in Pakistan in 1968. Assistance to Pakistan since its inception to the end of 1989 amounted to US $ 883 million, WFP assistance in Pakistan concentrates on four major sectors i.e. Emergency Operations for Afghan refugees, Forestry and Watershed Management. Rural Development and Health and Nutrition.

Nearly 500,000 mt of food is being delivered to Pakistan each year for Afghan refugee operation. The refugee population which exceeds three million, lives in about 340 refugee camps of which 69 per cent are in NWFP, 26 per cent in Balochistan and 5 per cent in Punjab. Total value of WFP assistance to Afghan operations so far is about US $ 598 million.

WFP's assistance in the areas of Watershed Management and environmental control in this country has been and will continue to be very effective and helpful. The process of environmental degradation & ecological deterioration in terms of soil erosion, situation of dams and water courses and flash flooding is a common feature all over the mountainous areas of Pakistan. The principal causes for this ecological deterioration are pressure of population and livestock on natural resources. Population pressures in such areas and the daily struggle of the rural poor to obtain the basic necessities of life are taking a tremendous depends. In this process vital watersheds, such as those in the north-west frontier province are stripped, exposing the soil to erosion and increasing the risk and volume of floods.

The World Food Programme (WFP) ever conscious of the need to arrest environmental degradation as a pre-requisite physical resource environmental resource conservation has been very active in the field of watershed management in Pakistan since 1972. Between 1972 and 1989, through ten WEFP supported projects (7 completed and 3 ongoing) some 550,000 acres of denuded lands have been brought under forest cover and have been protected from further erosion and destruction. For these projects the value of WFP contribution (in food aid) is about US $ 50 million. The return on investment, however, must be a multiple of this figure.

The watershed management activities supported by WFP have mainly been carried out on private lands and have achieved excellent results. The implementation of these projects in the food deficit areas has provided food rations for the needy labourers and has helped in creating employment opportunities for the unemployed people. The success of WFP watershed management projects has encouraged other bilateral donors and as a result USAID, and the Netherlands Governments have been contributing added financial support to some of these projects. EEC is the latest to join WFP in its Forestry Programme. Apart from providing food aid, WFP has been instrumental in bringing technical expertise from various UN organisations to assist the government in the design and formulation of these projects.

An interesting feature of these projects is the increasing participation of the community. By its very nature Food aid is targeted to labour intensive projects and such projects as Watershed Management and Rural Development are people centred. Consequently we find increasing demands for short-term income generating activities within these projects. As a result of this demand arrangements have been made by WFP to obtain from Donors Rootstocks of valuab'e varieties of fruit trees for villagers to grow in their home gardens. This has now become an integral part of all Watershed Management/Forestry Projects of WFP.

Currently in addition to the Afghan refugee operation, six other projects (3 watershed management, 2 rural development one nutrition and health) are operational in the country. Their brief descriptions are given below.

Since 1980 WFP has been actively involved in the support of an increasing number of Afghan refugees who have been registered and accommodated by GOP in refugee camps in NWFP, Balochistan and Punjab and whose careload has now reached approximately 3.3 million individuals.

So far more than four million tonns of different food commodities donated by the International community and from its own resources have been handled by WFP for this operation.

The main objectives of the Project are to stabilize the ecology in parts of the catchment area of the Mangla and Tarbela dams in order to preserve the natural fertility of the land, prevent damage to infrastructure and in particular, reduce the rate of soil erosion and siltation of the reservoirs and distribution systems. The creation of additional seasonal employment and the promotion of improved agricultural practices are important sub objectives. In order to accomplish these objectives, labour-intensive works are being undertaken in the related fields involving 16.9 million mandays of work. The cost of this project of WFP is $ 19.2 million over seven years and nine months. A daily food ration with a value of about Rs. 15 is paid to the workers.

The objective of the project in Dir and Swat which costs WFP $ 4.6 million is to reduce soil erosion, increase the production of timber and fuel wood and generate short and long term employment during the 3 years of project duration.

Some five million mandays will be utilized for afforestation of 40,000 acres of land, soil conservation and range management activities.

The Netherland Govt. is contributing US $ 4.2 million for cash wages and purchase of nursery materials.

Workers are paid a family ration valued at about Rs. 15.00 and a cash payment of Rs. 12.50 per day.

The pilot project construction of Rural Roads in Kashmir with a total WFP input of $ 680,000 aims to construct 127 km of new roads and to improve 38.4 km of old roads in all five districts of AJK over three years period.

The project will employ about 1000 workers for 200 days per year during the projects period. Workers receive a family ration, valued at about Rs. 15.00 and a cash payment of Rs. 10.00 from AJK Government.

The project watershed Management in North East basis objectives are the reduction of soil erosion specially for the protection of the Mangla reservoir from heavy sedimentation, production of timber and fuel wood, generation of short, and long term employment and improvement of eaviron-ment with a total cost to WFP of $ 3.24 million over three years.

Apart from the WFP daily food ration valued at about Rs. 15.00 the workers are getting a daily cash wage of Rs. 12.00 from AJK Government.

The objectives of the project are to provide road access to remote villages, improve agriculture and land use by means of labour intensive irrigation and flood control earthworks, improve living conditions (especially for the benefit of women and children), provide out of season local employment for underemployed rural poor, check exodus to urban centres and improve the economic and nutritional status of the families of the poorest segments in the food deficit areas.

WFP input of $ 18.9 million over a period of five years is to accomplish 15.25 million mandays of work under this project.

Supplementary feeding of pre-school children, pregnant women and nursing mothers.

This project aims at providing supplementary feeding for upto 200 beneficiaries (pregnant/nursing mothers and pre-school children) at each of the 1500 pre-selected health centres throughout the country, over a period of five years and nine months. The total cost of the project to WFP is $ 32.9 million.

Specificially the objectives are to :

Reduce the high incidence of protein-calorie malnutrition among beneficiaries; and

Encourage malnourished beneficiaries to attend primary health and family welfare centres and take part in health and nutrition education classes.

The nationwide project besides being of great benefit to the underprivileged mothers and children acts as springboard for other UN agencies especially UNICEF to launch their programmes. The much herladed success in immunizing small children had a big contribution from this project.

A new phase of the project has just been approved by the CFA for a 30 months period involving WFP's food input of about 27 million dollars. These projects are : Primary School Feeding, Rural Development Works in AJK.

The Asian Development Bank (ADB) said on December 20, 1990 that it had approved a 215 million dollar loan and two technical assistance grants totalling 1.2 million dollars to a power project in Pakistan.

The project is intended to improve the reliability of power supply in Pakistan through a Water and Power Development Authority (WAPDA) programme to improve transmission and distribution, the ADB said in a statement.

The Manila-based bank said it made one grant totalling 788,000 dollars for the government to review the WAPDA's structure.

Another 415,000 dollar grant would be used to help the organisation formulate a modern management information system, it said.

The ADB also said it had granted 480,000 dollars for a marine resource evaluation and planning project fasibility project in Indonesia.

The study is intended to formulate detailed specifications for the project, which is aimed at developing Indonesia's marine resources, the bank said.

The grant will be financed by the ADB's Japan special fund.

The bank also approved a 1.83 million dollar equity investment in a private capital investment firm in India, the bank said. The investment in the Twentieth Century Venture Capital Corp. Ltd (TCVC) is intended to help develop India's private sector, the ADB said.

TCVC will provide risk capital and related investment and management services to projects being set up by new entrepreneurs or for new technologies, it said.

A bill of about $ 280 million which includes import payments and loan amortisation is due for payment during the November 1990.

At the moment the government has a little less than $ 100 million in the kitty. There is also the $ 75 million of deposits acquired from the BCCI (50 million) and Habib Bank (25 million) for window dressing not for use.

In order to get out of this tight corner, the government is looking around for short term loans from the commercial markets at the rate of 1.5 per cent over LIBOR.

Mennwhile it has been learnt that the US has also cut off the $ 80 million or so of the food assistance under PL 480 because of now issuance of Presidential Certificate under the Pressler Amendment.

This means while on the one hand Pakistan will have to mobilise cash resources for the import of part of its wheat and edible oil requirements on the other it would cause a short-fall in the budgetary resources to the extent of the amount that would have accrued the government from the sales of those commodities in the open market.

The US had allowed Pakistan to use the proceeds from the local sales of wheat and edible oil imported under the PL 480 programme to balance its budget.

In one way the curtailment of the inflow of PL 480 assistance is good for the country as the soyabean oil imported under this scheme usually cost Pakistan is daily because even the vegetables ghee manufactured from cheap palm oil has to be sold to the consumers at high prices.

And also because re-export of anything having even a trace of items imported under PL 480 is banned, most of the exportable surplus ghee manufactured in Pakistan used to be smuggled to neighbouring countries. Now the country can earn badly needed foreign exchange by exporting this exportable surpluses legitimately.

But then the savings and earnings from this one measure would not be anything more than about $ 100 millian maximum. And to this if another $ 100 million of savings is added from linking the import of tea with exports from Pakistan to the tea exporting countries then the total reduction in the annual balance of payments position would amount to nothing more than $ 200 million which would still leave a gap of billion dollars to be bridge annualy in the short term.

The country does not have any foreign assets by selling which Pakistan could meet its balance of payments position obligations in the short term as the government is trying to do with regard to budgetary deficit by proposing to sell all the public sector units including commercial banks within this year.

This is a one shot measure and the government should know that even if it succeeded in unburdening the government of its liabilities through auctions, it would still need to improve its tax collection system and reform the existing banking laws to enable the legal economy to generate enough resources to meet the budgetary gap in the longer run.

Pakistan does not have even this one shot measure to see it through its immediate foreign payments obligations. There appears to be no way out but to go out with a begging bowel or default.

The new government seems to have decided to believe its election propaganda that Pakistan can fend for itself without foreign assistance.

The presidential speech to the inaugural session of the parliament which is supposed to reflect the policies of the new government oozes with this confidence.

And talk to any civil or military brass these days in Islamabad they seem to be in a sort of trance they give the impression that they have decided to cut off all aid links.

For the first time in their careers these top managers of

Pakistan seem to have awakened to the fact that foreign assistance has strings attached to it.

And also probably for the first time in their careers these very important governmental personages feel that self-respect is more important and self-reliance was more necessary than foreign assistance.

None of these people have ever done anything but manage Pakistan's economy by borrowing. They do not know any other way of running the country's economy and managing Pakistan's national security needs. That is why this sudden awakening and the shouts of eureka?

What is the new government upto. If it does not want any foreign assistance, nothing better than that. The nation would go along with it even if it meant further tightening of the belt. But if this rhetoric is meant for the galleries and the truth is what the President requested the Japanese for (aid of $ 500 million), then what the government is doing is highly irresponsible.

There is only one way out of the foreign assistance trap and that is by refusing to repay loan and meet import obligations and following it up with curtailing imports by at least about 50 per cent.

But does the government know what would happen to the local export oriented industry if the imports were curtailed by 50 per cent?

And even the sector which is looking after the consumer and industrial needs of the local population would suffer because most of the local industry is largely dependent on imports.

The decision not to import those machines which could be fabricated inside Pakistan is commendable but most of such machines come under aid in any case and if imports of these items are banned then the exporting countries could gang up and say okay we will not import textiles from you.

There are many ramifications to such a radical policy. The government should not be carried away by its enthusiasm and take course that would prove to be counter productive in the long run.

There is nothing better than reducing dependence on foreign assistance. But this should be done gradually and in a manner that would not unnecessarily cause the world to turn hostile towards Pakistan.

Pakistan on November 8, 1990 called for solving the developing countries debt problem through "concerted" global action that would allow them to produce the manufacture to their full potential, reports APP's special correspondent.

"Reduced interest rates, roll back of protectionist measures enhanced cooperation in technology transfer, stabilisation of commodity prices, are some of the essential elements for creating a growth oriented environment on a global scale", Ambassador Jamsheed Marker told the General Assembly's Economic Committee.

"Global measures need to be agreed upon and unforced expeditiously in a coordinated manner," he said.

Speaking in a debate on the external debt crisis, the Pakistan Ambassador said the developing countries were not unmindful of their responsibilities to contribute to an effective solution of the problem. But he said, the adjustment could not be undertaken beyond a point without serious social and political disruption.

In many countries, Marker said, adjustment had already

been synonymous with punishment. "It would be unwise to push the developing countries beyond realistic parameters in pursuing the adjustment process."

The Pakistan Ambassador said the report of Bettino Craxi, the U.N. Secretary General's Personal Representative on debt, presented a comprehensive approach to debt relief, encompassing the application of new forms of debt reduction for low-income countries, among there recommendations.

Marker said he expected that those proposals would be given serious consideration by the creditor governments, the commercial banks and the multilateral financial institutions.

The Craxi report, he said, had also recognised the needs of the low income countries whose debt was largely official, advocating the need for enhancing the degree of concessionality of their debt. He strongly supported Craxi's appeal that the industrialised countries should reach the level of 0.7 per cent of their Gross Domestic Product (GDP) as Official Development Assistance (ODA) to the developing countries.

The onset of the Gulf crisis had added a new dimension to the debate on the debt crisis, the Pakistan Ambassador said. It was imparative that oil-dependent countries were provided timely assistance and meaningful debt relief to forestall major econmic dislocation.

"A durable solution of the debt problem will remain elusive without a marked improvement into he overall external environment which continues to adversely affect the developing countries", Marker said.

The Pakistani Prime Minister Nawaz Sharif's visit to the United Arab Emirates from November 24, 1990 immediately after the conclusion of the SAARC summit at Male is part of the hectic efforts being made to persuade traditional donors to enhance the quantum of assistance. The country faces serious economic difficulties compounded by the Gulf crisis and the abrupt suspension of United States' civil and military aid.

President, Ghulam Ishaq Khan has sought and received assurance of assistance from Japan and Germany and the issue is understood to have figured in Shari's talks with King Fahd of Saudi Arabia and the Emir of Kuwait, prior to the SAARC meet.

The German Chancellor, Mr. Helmut Kohl, in a letter to Ishaq Khan has expressed his Government's willingness to consider commodity assistance over and above the 25 million Deutsche Mark aid recently made available to ease Pakistan's balance of payment problem.

A German delegation which is to visit Pakistan towards the end of the month to discuss details of a bilateral programme of development cooperation, will also discuss further assistance.

Ishaq Khan who had pressed Pakistan's case for assistance during his visit to Japan to attend the coronation of Emperor Akihito had, described the Japanese response as positive.

He had suggested to the Japanese that part of the $600 million aid in the pipeline be converted into quickly disbursing commodity assistance and that Japan increase imports from Pakistan to redress partially the adverse annual trade deficit of $400 to 500 millions.

Pakistan's immediate balance of payments problem arising out of the Gulf crisis, was put by Ishaq Khan at $ 2.5 million at the present price of imported oil. Another problem which has been pinpointed of *The Dawn* newspaper is lack of foreign exchange to meet a bill of about $ 280 millions for import payments and loan amortisation, due for payment this month.

According to the newspaper, the Government has less than $ 100 millions in the kitty and is looking for short-term loans from the commercial markets. These pressures are coming at a time when Pakistan has to buy wheat and soya-bean from the world market.

Recently the Government raised the domestic prices of oil by 40 per cent to meet part of the International Monetary Fund conditionalities to qualify for $240 million loan. West Asian countrise have usually been generous towards Pakistan, but faced with a major crisis in their own region the sheikh-doms have not reacted with the accustomed alacrity. Pakistan's reserves are believed to be sufficient for only four days worth of imports.

Initiatives towards Japan and Germany are being looked at from the point of bringing long-term as well as short-term benefits.

Much of these new concerns and exploratory attempts have been triggered by the abrupt suspension of U.S. aid the realisation that it is unlikely to be restored in the short-term and the consequent genesis of a desire for self-reliance at the higher levels of Pakistan's policy making apparatus.

The flow of U.S. military and civil aid to Pakistan was cut off when the U.S. President, Mr. George Bush, failed to certify that Pakistan did not possess a nuclear device as required under the Pressler Amendment on October 1, 1990.

Pakistan's efforts to get the aid restored have received a setback with Robert Qakley, U.S. Ambassador in Islamabad, having pointed out that his Government does not accept Islamabad's definition of a nuclear device and that Pakistan would be disqualified from receiving assistance even if it possessed only the components of and not necessarily a whole, nuclear device. Oakley, in a letter published in *The Nation* also pointed out that it was only the Congress which was authorised to extend the period for certification under the Pressler Amendment and that they had refused to do so.

Oakley has broadly hinted that Pakistan should reconsider the scale of outlays on defence. Defence allocation has been kept under tight wraps, but diplomatic sources maintain that besides foreign assistance, defence eats up over 40 per cent of the budget. Cutting down on expenditure in defence has generally been considered anathema here, but with the present perception that the threat from India has receded (at least till next summer) possibilities might be weighed.

The Bush Administration has halted the flow of US military aid and suspended deliveries of military equipment to Pakistan since October 1, 1990, the day US fiscal year 1991 began.

However, economic assistance from previous year funds that is already obligated (legally committed to be spent through contracts and other commitments) will continue to flow at least until early 1991.

Us food aid likewise will continue to Pakistan until current funds run out.

The situation has arisen in view of President Bush's inability to make necessary certification to Congress that Pakistan does not possess nuclear weapons—a precondition for the supply of US aid to Islamabad.

The question of certification is constantly under review, according to the US State Department.

At stake for Pakistan is the future of a six-year four billion US dollars commitment of US military and economic aid made by the Reagan administration in 1986 which has three more years to run.

The commitment, following upon an earlier six-year programme involving some 3.2 billion dollars in US aid, had made Pakistan the third largest recipient of US aid after Israel and Egypt.

The current development is but the latest episode in a struggle between Congress and the executive over the problem of reconciling US foreign and nuclear non-proliferation policy interests in South Asia.

In this situation, the options available to the Bush administration and Congress are a few; these include; providing aid under the required certification, taking no action thereby terminating US aid. Continuing aid under a walver to the certification requirement and legislatively structuring a new 'firebreak' that would provide for the restoration of aid if Pakistan takes acceptable steps of freeze its nuclear weapons programme.

It is doubtful that President Bush can make an annual required certification that Pakistan does not possess a nuclear explosive device.

Though analysts tend to see nuclear proliferation in South Asia as part of a linked chain involving China which tested is first bomb in 1965—India, which tested its 'peaceful nuclear explosion' in 1974 and Pakistan which has yet to test a device so far as is known open sources but is considered capable of doing so.

The linkage arises from long-term rivalries that have resulted in four conflicts to date. India-China in 1962 and Pakistan-India in 1947-48, 1965 and 1971-72.

For China, US policy has been constrained by China's recognised inclusion in the nuclear 'club' and the existence of other even more pressing issues in US China relations, such as China's past role as a strategic counterweight to the Soviet Union and the Taiwan question.

As for India, US influence has always been limited by India's size and its unwillingness to put itself under any obligation to support US foreign and nuclear non-proliferation policy objectives.

The patriotic rhetoric of self-reliance and independence emanating from the political and military leaders of Pakistan will have to be tested against the hard economic realities of the world. If American aid is broken off on the nuclear issue, Japan will find it difficult to be a major aid giver to Pakistan because the Japanese are even more sensitive than American about proliferation. Here enter the Islamic factor. Will the oil-rich Islamic governments adopt Pakistan for economic help and arms transfers thereby replacing the United States and Japan? The calculation of the Pakistani army that by making Pakistan a "frontine state in the Gulf, Islamabad would be able to stay in an affectionate corner of the American bosom has failed to work Washington does not need Pakistan in the Gulf as much as the Pakistanis thought it would. In any case, the Americans are not prepared to pay the price of continuing to wink at Pakistan's nuclear programme. War preparations have been taxing the economies of Saudi Arabia Kuwait and the United Arab Emirates (UAE) heavily, they are under pressure to share more of the massive costs of the huge American arms build-up. A war in Gulf will devastate the economies of the oil-rich countries of Arabia as it will mean near economic doom for all countries in South Asia. The political-military ruling elite in Pakistan is unable at this time to make a reliable assessment of the turn of events in the Persian Gulf. They will have to wait for a decisive question—war or peace in the Gulf? Which may not emerge before the spring of 1991. Up till now, the ruling elite in Pakistan is not in the least willing to turn to India and South Asia as real partners of the country's future in the post cold war world. They will not until other choices are exhausted. India has to wait until Pakistan changes its mind. And employ its diplomacy with vigour and a sense of purpose to bring Pakistan into South Asia. For this India has to work with the United States, China, Iran, UAE and even Saudi Arabia. And India must take sweet to the people of Pakistan even to its government without relenting from what it needs to do to cope with the difficult situation in Kashmir.[4]

If India follows a cessation of US military aid to Pakistan with an announcement that it would exercise the nuclear option, it will be a noholds-barred situation. The US would find justification for restoring military aid, and Pakistan would openly go about building nuclear weapons. More than India, it is the US which is on the horns of a dilema now. The Bush administration cannot resume military assistance on the basis of a private assurance by Pakistan because that would not convince India. Such an assurance last year did not impress even the US. George Bush had suggested to the Pakistan President, Ghulam Ishaq Khan, in October 1990 that aid could be resumed if nuclear facilities were opened to international inspection. But this smacks of discrimination, because US military aid to Israel was stopped up in November without any such demand. Here, Pakistan equates India with Israel. But the US cannot demand international inspection of Indian facilities because India does not want military aid. How the Bush administration will resolve the issue of aid to Pakistan will have a bearing on India's nuclear options.[5]

References

1. S.S. Bindra, Daterminant's of Pakistan's Foreign Policy, New Delhi, 1988, p. 326.
2. Mohan Ram, The Great Nuclear Hoax, *The Independent*, 14 December, 1990.
3. Naseer Ahmad, Manoeuvres, *The Nation*, 17 November, 1990.
4. Bhabani Sen Gupta, Coming Talks in Islamabad, *National Herald*, 14 December, 1990.
5 Mohan Ram, The Nuclear Hoax, *The Independent*, 14 December, 1990.

15

Balance of Payments

Prime Minister Nawaz Sharif has started his career in a determined manner. He has acknoledged that the country is facing serious internal and external dangers and has to pay foreign debts of abount 14 billion. All governments of the post 43 years failed to solve the problems of unemployment, inflation and injustice despite their tall promises but the new government is serious and intends taking steps to solve these problems. At least it is making a beginning in the right direction. Nawaz Sharif believes in neat and clean approach and administration. He will not fall into the trap of sycophants-the common brand of flatterers who surround and adulate the highups for their selfish ends. He wants everybody, like himself to earn rizq-halal. As the IJI celebrated its unprecedented victory in a humble way, the Prime Minister called upon everybody to make a solemn pledge to weed out corruption sifarish (recommendations) and injustice, Merit will be the sole criterion in all departments of the new government while self-reliance the pillar of all future policies. He made it clear that no extension in service would be granted and that re-employment of superannuated persons would not be sanctioned. This would be evident to the public in a couple of months. Similarly the policy of plots quotas and permits will be forsaken. The poor would continue getting shelter and justice without any discrimination. He is keen to eradicate unemployment and banish proverty. He intends denationlising banks, insurance corporations and industries. Industrialisation in urban and rural areas will be accorded priority. He is in fact resolved to usher in an industrial revolution. According to the Prime Minister everybody would be encouraged to set up industry. Islamic principles and laws would be promulgated so that the nation could fulfil the objectives for which Pakistan—a Muslim homeland was created.

The Prime Minister faces an extremely difficult situation —inflation, expanding debts, fall in exports and foreign exchange remittances in the wake of the Gulf crisis. The United States, under a lame plea, suspended civil and military aid amounting to about $600 million. The move was initially calculated to support Banazir and her party in the elections and since they have been dicisively defeated, the US now seeks shelter behind foreign publicised propaganda of Pakistan exploding a nuclear device. India and Israel play a mischievous role in propagating this myth.[1]

President Ghulam Ishaq Khan, in his address to the joint session of Parliament on November 8, 1990 stated that Pakistan did not want US aid to impinge on its independence and it would not compromise on principles and national honour.

"We may be poor but we highly cherish our national honour and dignity." He called upon America to face facts squarely and it is hoped that the US will climb down considering the Gulf crisis and the strategic position that Pakistan occupies, standing as a sentinel on the gateway to the oil-rich Persian Gulf, situated on the cross-roads of Central Asia, Western Asia ann South Asia. Pakistan is vital to the defence of South Asia and America is fully cognisant of this.

It therefore appears to be a question of time before aid is restored, to the mutual benefit of parties. This is not the first time that aid has been withheld, thanks to Stephen Solarz, Monyhan (former Ambassador of India) and that ilk.

Prime Minister Nawaz Sharif has voiced identical sentiments and besides referred to the Kashmir and Afghanistan questions which are close to Pakistan's heart and call for a settlement on a fair and equitable basis, taking the will of the people into consideration.

The US must play a constructive role worthy of a superpower which spearheads the movement of protecting fundamental human rights the world over. Nawaz Sharif is seeking co-operation from both his opponents and supporters in the larger interest of the country. He wants to set up a broad-based government. There will be no victimisation of the opponents, but those who have plundered the government treasury and emptied banks, would not be spared under any circumstances. Simultaneous, accountability of those who wielded power during the past 20 months and those who are now in power will continue without let-up. The nation always desired enforcement of Islamic laws of justice which the new government has taken upon itself as its foremost duty.

The task before Nawaz Sharif is tremendous and formidable. He is not going to shirk his responsibilities. The IJI's election manifesto itself is a big challenge to the Prime Minister and his government. The new government's survival depends on the fulfilment of promises made by it the electorate. The new leaders have inherited a debris of socio-economic-political problem of a complex nature and varying intensity. They are determined to go ahead with new measures and may even go in for agaricultural tax which is being defied by vested interest. The new measures may have to be seriously weighed and implemented to raise funds to overcome multifarious crises. The feudals are yet very powerful and will put up stout resistance to agaricultural tax, but a decision has to be taken on merit. With an increase in prices of diesel and fertilizers, the average agriculturist's lot too is unenviable. *Vaderas* (Landlord) who live luxuriously, must be made to contribute to the exchequer to relieve general misery. The small farmers and petty landlords deserve relief. Nawaz Sharif's family has built up a huge industrial empire through hard work, astute planning and honesty of purpose. Let Sharif apply that system and urge to other nation-building departments. He has associated the industrialists with his policies and promised stability especially in Sindh where Jam Sadiq Ali, with the cooperation of MQM's Altaf Hussain, has undertaken to set matters right within three months or so. The Sindh cabinet has decided to give top priority to the law and order situation and supremacy of the rule of law. The government is committed to a policy of deregulation and denationalisation and would adopt a concrete programme to implement this policy. Six committees to prepare concrete proposals have been set up and the country is about to embark on the road to peace, progress and prosperity.[2]

During this decade, workers' remittances increased at a phenomenal rate-from a modest level of only Rs. 231.8 million in 1970-71 to over Rs. 17 billion by the end. And even this was an under-estimation since 10-15 per cent of the remittances which came through non-banking channels were unaccounted for. These remittances were major source of foreign exchange carnings, and on an average they accounted for about 39 per cent of the total foreign exchange earning. This dramatic rise provided timely support to the balance of trade, but even this trend was not enough to close the growing trade gap.

During the seventies the rapid rise in external borrowings led to an almost three-fold increase in the net outstanding debt from US $ 2959 million in 1969-70 to US $ 8658 million in 1979-80. The rapid rise in debt service payments which constituted 18.8 per cent of the total foreign exchange earnings in 1979-80, and reduced net transfers below gross disbursement by almost 45 per cent. However, this adverse trend was to some extent, offset by a steady, through transitory rise in the share of grants in the total aid committed.[4]

Pakistan's dependence on foreign trade has been due to a lack of diversification in the resource base. Over the years, the dependence on trade has not been altered. During the seventies, too, the degree of dependence on trade (as measured by the aggregate of imports and exports expressed as a percentage of the GNP) underwhat substantial fluctuations around a more or less horizontal secular trend. Except in 1973-74, the terms of trade during the seventies shifted to the country's disadvantage because the rise in the international prices of Pakistan's exports was much slower than in the prices of its imports. In the early seventies when the US Government compelled by unavoidable circumstances devalued the dollar, it conferred some temporary benefits on Pakistan in so far as its terms of trade with the rest of the world somewhat improved. Pakistan's exports did not grow during the seventies at a very satisfactory rate. Except in a few years 1976-77 to 1979-80, it suffered from domestic stagnation, various structural defects and adverse international competition. Traditional exports, mainly primary commodities, dominated Pakistan's trade. Their high commodity and geographical concentration were responsible for large fluctations in aggregate export earnings. For most of the years during the decade, increases in international prices were responsible for the growth in export earnings. The only exceptions were rice and cotton cloth exports which grew significantly in real terms as well. However, in the later years of the decade, quantity increase were the major source of growth, while prices remained more or less constant. Pakistan's economy, which grew at a relatively faster rate among those in South Asia, especially during the previous five years, suffered a setback in 1983-84 due to failure of crops. In 1983, earnings from the export of most commodities were higher, but earnings from the export of cotton yarn and thread, carpets and rugs, stood fish and fish preparations failed to recover. Export earnings have suffered mainly on account of cotton. Total export earnings for 1983 showed as 28 per cent improvement over 1982. Although data for the first quarter of 1984 showed a 4.1 per cent rise in export values, with continued difficulties in cotton.[5]

In the recent past. Pakistan's manufacturing sector has emerged in the economy most dynamic segment and has shown high growth rate considerably above those of total GDP. According to data publishd by the Ministry of Information, the real growth rate of Manufacturing Value Added (MVA) surged up from 19.9 per cent in 1976-77 to 9.9 per cent in 1977-78. After having peaked at 13.2 per cent in 1981-82, it declined again to 8.9 per cent in 1982-83 and finally to 7.7 per cent in 1983-84 which was considered high by international standards.[6]

The main driving force behind Pakistan's geographical export diversification starting in the early seventies has been the increasing role of the Gulf countries (comprising Abu Dhabi, Baharain, Dubai, Kuwait, Oman, Qatar and Saudi Arabia) in general and of Saudi Arabs and United Arab Emirates in particular as rapidly growing markets for Pakistan's exported goods. In 1982-83, the Gulf countries share in Pakistan's total exports (imports) increased to 22 per cent (29 per cent) with Saudi Arabia alone accounting for 9 per cent of all exports. Although rice has been the most important single item in value terms, also 40 per cent of machinery exports have been directed to this region.[7]

The importance of the Gulf States to Pakistan lies not only in its area but also in its geographical proximity to Pakistan. It is easier for Pakistan to export its products which otherwise entail high transport cost and deterioration during tranist, Pakistan has been aking strenuous efforts to enter into the Gulf States' market and get a firm hold there. For this purpose special selling missions are sent, single country exhibitions are organized and display and commercial centres are opened for projecting and promoting Pakistan's export to Gulf region.[8]

The Iran-Iraq war has added a new dimension as far as Pakistan attitude towards the Gulf is concerned. So far Zia regime has successfully pursued tight rope diplomacy maintaining equidistance from both Tehran and Baghdad. Pakistan has been called upon to take a definitive stand because of its enmeshment in the US strategic aims in the area on the one hand and the influential domestic pressure from Pro-Iranian Shia groups and anti-American public opinion not to antagonise Iran with which it has a 400 Km. long land border on the other. The stakes are very high for the Zia-Junejo regime, for displeasing the Americans might deprive it of a massive economic and military aid package and further cause a possible rupture in a highly profitable relationship with the Arab oil rich countries and at the other end antagonizing the Iranian regime might result externally in the opening of a third front of confrontation on the Baluchistan border after the Afghan and the traditional Indian fronts.[9]

Penetration in the Gulf market is by no means easy as selling in the Gulf states differs in several ways from other major markets due to vast and varied range of requirements and tough competition in quality and prices offered with practically no import and exchange restrictions. Pakistan with large labour force and varied experience in agriculture and industry has been asisting these states in their economic development. A number of joint ventures have been set up. Pakistani agencies may promote technology and expertise for development programme of the Gulf states.[10]

Zinger has rightly said that "Pakistan economic relations to the rest of the world have been characterized by high trade and balance of payment deficit, growing indebtedness, and the uniquitous problem of debt servicing despite a three-fold increase of the export earnings since the late 1960s (measured in US $ credit mechandise), almost two billion US $ of the remittances each year and repeated debt rescheduling."[11]

At present Pakistan is maintaining trade relations with over 180 countries, having high trade G.D.P. ratio ranging from 25 to 30 per cent and Pakistan is greatly susceptible to developments in international trade. Primary commodities like rice and cotton continue to be the main items to exports sharing 209 per cent of total exports in 1986-8ˉ. On the imports front raw materials for the Pakistani industry and capital goods are maintaining a dominant position. During the fiscal year 1986-87, Pakistan's imports were estimated to be $ 5.2 billion as compared to $ 5.6 billion in 1985-86. There was marginal increase in Pakistan total exports from $ 30 billion in 1985-86 to 3.6 in 1986-87. Efforts are being made to increase the level of exports to $ 4.2 billion in 1988-89 and $ 5.5 billion in 1989-90. In future some restrictions on imports have been planned.[12]

The economic policy planners of Pakistan are taking a number of steps to strengthen the trading of Pakistan. The new policy has made significant departure from the past and contained several initiatives and innovations. First, the entire policy was one compact measure instead of two separate ones-import policy and export policy. Major emphasis was on exports and import policy, apart from meeting some requirements of consumption and development, is now supposed mostly to push up exports. Second, the new Trade Policy goes beyond the realm of visible trade and an effort has been made to divert national resources, particularly home remittances from home consumption to investment. Third, an attempt has already been made to effect an accelerated growth of the economy through the Trade Policy. Innovations include linkage between tax concessions with value added contents of exports, liberal import of no less than 136 banned items, duty and quota adjustments in the export of cotton yarn and pressure on developing countries to remove all restrictions on imports of textiles and clothing from Pakistan, otherwise it would be forced to restrict of machinery from those countries. Last, export-import balance would be attempted by each country. In this connection six countries, Japan, the US, the UK, West Germany, Kuwait and Malaysia have been selected with whom 90 per cent of the country's import-export gap is concentrated.[13]

Since independence, political development outside Pakistan are having close relations with Pakistan's economic and social development. Her strained and unfriendly relations with her two immediate neighbours, India and Afghanistan, "stemming from territorial claims and altogether jeopardizing the country's survival, may explain the fact that foreign policy played a major role over economic policy that Pakistan sought the support of first the US, later of Iran, China and the Arab states and that no fundamental economic and social reforms were taken."[14]

The cherished goal of achieving a major breakthrough in the field of exports by Pakistan still remains a dream. We have not been able to come even close to the desired target in exports simply because the country lacks the manufacturing base which could serve as a pringboard to launch it into a higher orbit of exports and enable Pakistan to join the comity of major industrialised exporting nations. It is not that there has been a dearth of export incentives. The single most important factor is the inadequacy of the exportable surpluses particularly of the high value added products. Export drive relying primarily on the export of commodities and semifinished items can at best produce modest success, which has been the case over the last few years. The export target of $ 5.5 billion for the fiscal 1989-90 envisaged in the three year trade policy was revised downwards to $ 5 billion and the final figure arrived at was $ 4.9 billion. Barring the remarkable growth of about 21% in 1987-88, exports rose by less than 5% in 1988-89 and only 6% in 1989-90. The continued failure to reach planned export targets is despite the massive devaluation of the Rupee since its delinking from the Dollar and the introduction of the so-called managed float in January, 1982. It is thus important to evaluate whether our policy of managed devaluation has had the desired result of increased exports. In classical economic theory—if all other things remain constant—devaluation should increase exports and decrease imports. But in practice other things don't remain constant. Competitors adopt measures to protect their share of the international market while importers impose quotas, counter-availing duties, etc. to protect their local industry. Since delinking the Rupee has lost on the average about 160% of its value against major world currencies which translates into an average yearly depreciation of about 18%. This means that we had to export at least 18% more each year just to compensate for the loss in the Rupee value while factually the exports have risen to US $ 4.9 billion in 1989-90 from $ 2.70 billion in 1982-83—an increase of less than 100%. The most important reason for this sorry state of export growth is the sad ffact that our economy has not been and is even now not capable of producing exportable surplus to the extent of 18% per annum. Thus, substantial increase in export earnings cannot be achieved merely through devaluation. Moreover, a substantial portion of the increase in exports can simply be attributed to inflation during the past decade. The average annual inflation of 10 to 15% leads one to reach this conclusion.[15]

It is time that a scientific study be conducted to analys and assess the relative merits and demerits of devaluation and its impact on the overall economy including its socio-economic cost to the ordinary Pakistani.

Introduction of several fiscal and other incentives in the export regiment has not had the desired impact in boosting the country's exports almost half of which comprise of primary commodities and semi-processed goods. The dependence on Rice and Cotton for exports is still critical although Textile Made-ups. Leather Goods and Carpets have emerged as substantial foreign exchange earners. To overcome this malady and to achieve the cherished break-through in exports we must rapidly build a vast network of export-oriented industries based on indigenous raw materials and latest technology to substantially widen the export base.

The concept of export-led economic and industrial growth has been in vogue for some years now without considering the crucial truth that significant growth in exports cannot be achieved without first having the exportable surplus of manufactured items. Thus, the concept of growth led exports needs all the emphasis that it commands. Let us first endeavour to erect the industrial infrastructure and the manufacturing base predominantly in the export sector. Greater exports will follow as a natural corollary because meaningful industrial growth will lead to substantially higher value of exports. A good recent example of this phenomenon is the cotton textile sector where increased investment in the spinning, weaving and garments manufacturing activities is leading to an increase in the export of cotton manufactured items which is more than offsetting the loss in foreign exchange earnings due to decrease in the export of raw cotton. The projected decline in the export of raw cotton for 1990-91 is $25 M. while the projected increase in cotton manufactures is $351 M. It is thus inevitable that we should quickly build export oriented industries.

The Trade Policy 1990-91 incorporated fundamental structural changes and included special incentives for setting-up export oriented industries production of value added items and promotion of export services. Of special mention is the application of the concept of EPZ to individual manufacturing units to reduce the cost of investment in export industries by providing exemption of import duty, sales tax and surcharge on imported machinery and spares if a minimum 70% of the output is exported. Also praisworthy was the Government's decision to place on priority the promotion of export of services which is an area where not only potential for growth is enormous but where Pakistan can compete with developed nations on equal terms[16].

Income Tax exemption of 75% on income derived from export of services, issuance of insurance guarantees in foreign currencies for bids and performance bonds and availability of concessionary export refinance for bid bonds are steps that have gone long way in taping this rich resource of foreign exchange earnings. Surely these measures, over the long run, will help increase our export earnings and will generate self-reliance and economic prosperity. The Commerce Ministry deserves full credit for staying the course set in the last Trade Policy and for progressing further on the road to glory in the export trade.

I hasten to point out that the spinning sector of the textile industry was left outside the scope of the Open Bond Scheme whereas I strongly feel that the spinning industry should be included in the Scheme because additional spinning capacity is still needed to convert the entire raw cotton production, which is rargeted for 1990-91 at over 9 million bales, into value added yarn and madeeups. It is the declared policy of the Government to productively utilise all available raw material resources. Export of low value raw materials in any case has to be discouraged. As long as there is one surplus bale of cotton available for export there is justification of the more spindle. Abolition of export duty on yarn manufactured by open end spinning units has provided them the direly needed financial relief and will also help increase the export of yarn. Additional excise duty of Rs. 2 per kg. levied on the production of yarn in the Federal Budget 1990-91 was also removed totally for the open end mills and 50% for conventional units. I wonder why the conventional spinning units were ignored with regard to both these concessions thus putting them at a distinct disadvantage vis-a-vis the open end units. To restore parity and induce healthy competition it is advisable that the export duty as well as the additional excise of Rs. 1/kg, on the yarn produced by conventional spinning units be immediately removed. Formulation of Trade Policy on long term basis facilitates sound planning and instils stability and confidence as the process of industrial development and capturing of foreign markets can literally take years to yield meaningful results. If the Government shows necessary patience and keeps introducing bold initiatives in the future Trade Policies in consultation with trade and industry, there is no reason why in the next 5/10 years Pakistan should not become a model export country—the envy of their developing nations. I propose a measure which if adopted will provide a tremendous boost to the growth of export industries. At present the required debt/equity ratio for setting up new industries by existing industrialists is 60 : 40 and the bridge finance is counted as debt. This means a minimum investment of 40% equity is a major provision of 40% equity is a major handicap towards rapid industrialisation. Debt/equity ratio for all industries-should be reduced to 70 : 30 and bridge finance provided by financial institutions should be counted as equity.[17]

For export oriented industries i.e. industrial units exporting at least 70% of their production, the requirement of debt/equity ratio should be further reduced to 80 : 20 with bridge fiance considered as equity. This measure will effectively reduce the time frame required for generating sufficient equity and putting up/ a new unit, thus leading to speedy industrialisation in the export sector. Before concluding I want to highlight a few problems in the export sector which the Government should hasten to redress. The problem of exports of hand knotted woolen carpets, surgical instruments and sports goods, etc. against unsecured credit is growing with each passing day as increasing numbers of exporters are selling on D A. basis to enhance their turnover. Unsecured credit inevitably leads to delays in remittances by the importers as well as bad debts. Undountedly tens of crores of Rupees worth of foreign remittances are held up abroad for months and years altogether and the exporters lose millions of rupees each year due to bad debts. Pakistan is poor country and cannot afford this continued heavy loss. In case the world economy continues to weaken, it will further render a large portion of the unsecured export credit proceeds in jeopardy. Government statistics reflecting a very low bad debt percentage do not present the true picture as most exporters out of fear of harassment by the FIA and scared of losing their white capital, arrange remittances themselves by Hundi, Government should ban exports on D.A. basis and should allow it only aginst L/C Bank Guarantee or D/P.

Without announcement in the Federal Budget or the Trade Policy for the fiscal year 1990-91 the Government has quitely increased interest rate on export refinance to 7 percent.

This increase will directly effect the cost of production of the exporting units and will not be passed on to the importers. Government apprehension that the export refinance facility will be misused is not correct because no exporter can afford to pay heavy penalty of 23-27% imposed by the SBP in case of non-shipment/non-performance. It is therefore, strongly suggested to reduce the rate of interest on export re-finance to 3%. This would be a substantial cost reduction and would make our export products competitive in the international market.[18]

Exporters all over Pakistan particularly in cities other than Karachi and Lahore are facing serious liquidity problems due to inordinate delays in realisation of foreign remittances against exports. Almost 90% of the export invoices are Dollar/sterling denominated and the remittances reach ex-potters via New York/London-Karachi. Nationalised Commercial Banks offices in New York/London and Karachi are big bottlenecks where remittances are stuck up sometimes for weeks causing undue hardships to the exporters who are not compensated for the delay. It is proposed that once the payment is received in New York or London office of the NCB, it should be credited to the exporters account within 3 working days of the said receipt. It case of delay beyond 3 days Banks should pay profit at the normal rate to the exporters for the delay period.[19]

During the 1980s. Pakistan's trade performance showed some improvement, with the trade deficit having declined to the lowest in the decade at $2.2 billion in 1986-87, on account of a decline in imports by 3.2 per eent and a rise in exports by 19 per cent. However, the trade dificit widened in some years and during 1983-86 it ranged between $3-3.5 billion. In the fiscal years 1988-89 there was a deterioration as the trade deficit rose to $2.61 billion from $2.56 billion in 1987-88. This was because of a much slower growth in exports at 5.3 per cent compared to a rate of 24.7 per cent registered in the preceding year. Imports had risen by 4.13 per cent to $7.2 billion. This emerges from a recent analysis by the National Bank of Pakistan. In the last five years, barring 1988-89 when the growth of exports slowed, the remaining years have witnessed a substantial rise in export earnings. Slower growth in 1988-89 was attributable to reduced exports of rice, cotton fabrics and leather, and also lower export prices of cotton, cotton yarn and thread cotton fabrics, carpets and rugs, fish and fish preparation textile clothing and accessories and synthetic-textiles. Production of rice had fallen, so had its per hectare yield because of adverse weather conditions. The cotton crop also suffered due to heavy rains and floods in the latter part of the season which caused some damage to the crop. Despite a rise in the area under cotton cultivation, its per hectare yield declined. The IMF in a recent report has said that Pakistan's export base was narrow with two primary commodities (raw cotton and rice) accounting for about one fourth of total exports, and cotton-based manufactures, for more than one third. The remaining export commodities are divided between other traditional exports, leather, fish and fish preparations, carpets and some non-traditional exports including leather manufactures, surgical instruments and fruits and vegetables.[20]

Another factor responsible for slower growth in export earnings were the recurring disturbances, particularly in Karachi, which affected both production and movement of commodities. Closure of industrial units due to the imposition of curfew in many parts of the city, with labour not being able to reach the factories, had adverse effects on production and exports. Manufacturing sector grew by only 3.1 per cent in 1988-89 with large scale industry recording an increase of only 1.2 per cent. Estimates for July-December 1989 have shown that exports rose to Rs. 44.81 million or by 17.2 per cent over the corresponding period of 1988, when exports totalled Rs. 37,953 million. Imports have risen by 18.5 per cent to Rs. 69,237 million from Rs. 58,445 million in July December 1988. The trade deficit has widened to Rs. 24,756 million from Rs. 20,492 million in the same period last year. The main foreign exchange earners which showed a substantial improvement during this period were rice, cotton yearn, cotton fabrics, leather, readymade garments and bedwear. These commodities contributed 53.4 per cent to export earnings during July-December 1989, against 47.2 per cent in the corresponding months of 1988-89. The increase in export earnings during July-December 1989 was mainly on account of a substantial rise in earnings from export of cotton yearn which fetched Rs. 7,247 million as against Rs. 4, 987 million in July-December 1988. In the same period, earnings from the export of bedwear rose by 44.8 per cent from Rs. 1,492 million to Rs. 2,160 million, cotton fabrics by 32.4 per cent from Rs. 4,214 million to Rs. 5,581 million, leather by 29.0 per cent from Rs. 2.074 million to Rs. 2,676 million and rice by 17 per cent from Rs. 2,119 million to Rs. 2,481 million.

A major foreign exchange earner, raw cotton suffered a marked drop in earnings to Rs. 1,621 million in the first six months of 1989-90 from Rs. 5,675 million in the corresponding half of 1988-89. Earnings from carpets are rugs fell by 18.2 per cent from Rs. 1,965 million to Rs. 1,607 million as quantities exported declined. Tarpaulin and canvas goods exports moves down to Rs. 246 million from Rs. 359 million.[21]

The total value of world trade in merchandise in 1988

was estimated at $2880000 million of which approximately $7,30,000 million was attributable to growth after 1983.

From 1983 to 1988, the volume of world trade in merchandise grew 34 per cent, or an average of 6.1 per cent a year—up from a sluggish annual pace of 2.8 per cent from 1973 to 1983, but in line with growth rates of 6.1 per cent from 1953 to 1963 and 8.9 per cent from 1963 and 8.9 per cent from 1963 to 1973, according to figures compiled by the General Agreement on Tariffs and Trade (GATT), which adjusts the value of world trade in dollars to take account of both inflation and currency fluctuations.

Far from slowing down or going into reverse, world trade has thus returned to the pattern of robust expansion during most of the period after World War II.

This expansion in world trade is running far ahead of growth in the world economy generally. Since the 1982 recession, world output has been growing at an annual rate of around 3.75 per cent, trade volumes have been expanding half again as quickly.

This fact signifies two important trends. First, it suggests that the trade boom—with its resulting increases in competition, sepecialisation and economies of scale is leading the world-wise economic expansion.

Second, it means that the international compenent of world economic activity is growing. In other words, markets are truly becoming global in scope.

The United States, meanwhile, is purportedly vulnerable in this new era because of its continued and anachronistic attachment to free trade. The fear is that by maintaining open markets while the rest of world hides behind protectionist barriers, the United States is committing the economic equivalent of unilateral disarmament.

If America is to survive as a great power, it must learn to play by new rules. In other words, industrial policy at home and "managed trade" (that is, import and export quotas) broad.

Pakistan's greatest trade trade deficits are at present with USA (Rs. 11 billion), Kuwait (Rs. 10.5 billion) and Japan (Rs. 8.33 billion) which constitute almost 60 per cent of the total trade deficit.

This has been stated in the latest report published about Pakistan balance of payments (BOP) prepared by a group of economists.

According to the report, the imports are gradually pulling away from export surpluses. In 1972-83 we had a modest plus account of Rs. 155 million (8,551 million exports and Rs. 8,398 imports), the report states.

Therefore, the reverse trend started in 1973-74 while imports exceeded exports by 3.32 billion.

The report further stated that in 1977-78 the deficit became Rs. 14.84 billion, 1978-89 Rs. 23.52 billion, 1980-81 Rs. 24.26 billion, 1981-82 Rs. 33.21 billion, 1982-83 Rs. 33.71 billion, in 1983-84 Rs. 34.10 billion, 1984-85 Rs. 51.00 billion, 1985-86 Rs. 41.35 billion, 1986-87 Rs. 29.08 billion, 1987-88 Rs. 34.10 billion and 1988-89 Rs. 45.66 billion.

According to the report, 15 out of 21 nations of the Arab League including Egypt, we had a net deficit of Rs. 12.30 billion 1988-89 almost 25 per cent of the total trade imbalance. With ECO (originally RCD) countries (Iran and Turkey), the deficit is approximately Rs. 3 billion, (6 per cent of the total trade) with other Muslim countries of Asia and Africa except for Thailand and Indonesia, we have modest surplus of Rs. 0.95 billion.

With the Council of Mutual Economic Association our

deficit is Rs. 0.378 billion, whereas we have export surpluses in SAARC amounting to Rs. 1.25 billion. With ASEAN countries our deficit is Rs. 3.60 billion. We have virtually no trade with South and Central America.

While with European countries (Malta and Yugoslavia) a surplus of Rs. 0.70 billion. With the other Asian countries such as China, Hongkong etc. we have a net surplus of Rs. 1.40 billion, with African countries we have a net deficit of Rs. 1.70 billion.

Countries like Saudi Arabia with which our trade deficit is Rs. 3.42 billion. United Kingdom Rs. 2.4 billon, West Germany Rs. 4.19 billion, France Rs. 2 billion, Holland Rs. 1.1 billion, Malaysia Rs. 4.5 billion, China Rs. 2.3 billion and Kenya Rs. 0.90 million constitute about 40 per cent of the total trade deficit.

Prime Minister Nawas Sharif, on November 13. 1990 called upon the industrialists and the business community to assist the nation in moving towards the objective of greater self-reliance by paying their taxes fully and by increasing exports.

He invited the industrialists and entrepreneurs to join hands with his government in usherinp in a new era of development and industrialisation in Pakistag.

He was addressing leading industrialists from all over the country in Islamabad, on November 13.

Explaining the strategy for strengthening and streamlining the institutional framework for industrialisation, the Prime Minister said the new government would like to start a new partnership with private sector to promote common objectives to replace the present relationship based on lack of confidence and distrust.

He also pointed out that the major problem of the

country was unemployment which could only be tackled through rapid industrialisation in the country. The Prime Minister said his government was considering special incentives for rural industrialisation and agro-based industries.

The Prime Minister said the strong political mandate which the people of Pakistan had given to the new government will have a positive impact on the lives of the people only if it leads to a sharp acceleration in development activities.

The Prime Minister said the government was fully committed to a policy of deregulation and denationalisation in the economy. His government was thinking to adopt soon a concrete programme to implement this policy.

The Prime Minister announced that the cell created by the PPP government in the Prime Minister's Secretariat to sanction investments and loans had been abolished with immediate effect. The banks and the DFLs had been instructed to sanction loans purely on merit, based on economic considerations and without any political consideration or influence from any quarter.

He extended his assurance that the law and order situation in Sindd would be improved on priority basis and he would himself monitor the situation. He also drew attention to the positive statement made by the Chief Minister of Sindh on the subject.

The Prime Minister announced that industries based totally on locally available raw material will not require government sanction irrespective of cost. The Prime Minister emphasised the importance of looking after the education and health needs of industrial workers and their families by the industrialists.

The Prime Minister announced the establishment of six committees to prepare concrete proposals for new policies and their implementation in different priority areas within the next 6-8 weeks. These are : 1, committee on self-reliance, 2. committee on tax reforms, 3. committee on exchange and payment reforms, 4. committee on export promotion, 5. committee on de-regulation and dis-investment, 6. committee on industrial policy.

He invited the industrialists and businessmen to propose their representatives on these committees.

Earlier, in his welcome address the Minister for Industries, Shujaat Hussain, highlighted the main objectives of convening the meeting and said the newly elected government wanted to fully consult the representatives of trade and industry in formulating the government's polieies and strategies. The Prime Minister had also invited the concerned federal ministers and federal secretaries so that new policies can be formulated in coherent and concerted manner.

The industrialists thanked the Prime Minister for convening this meeting in the very first week of assuming the high office and pledged full support of the business community in carrying out the challenging task spelled out by the Prime Minister. The representatives of the various chambers and associations made many specific suggestions on overall economic policies, industrial policy, fiscal policy and export policy.

References

1. Bashir Ahmed, Need for an Industrial Revolution. *Pakistan Times*, 22 November 1990.
2. *Ibid.*
3. S.S. Bindra : *Determinants of Pakistan's Foreign Policy*, New Delhi, 1988.
4. S.N.H. Naqvi and K. Sarmad. *Pakistan's Economy Through the Seventies*. Islamabad, 1985; pp. 98-103.

5. S.S. Bindra, *Op. Cit.*, p. 113.
6. Industrial Development Review Series. *Pakistan*, New York, 1985; p. 12.
7. *Ibid.* p. 21.
8. M. Naseeruddin. Gulf countries : Natural Market for Pakistan. *Pakistan and Gulf Economist* 3(8) Feb-Mar 1984; p. 29.
9. John Kaniyalli. Pak Problems in the Gulf *The Tribune* 22, September, 1987.
10. M. Naseeruddin. Gulf countries. *op. cit.* pp. 30.
11. W.P. Zingel Some Economic and Social Problems of Pakistan in the 1980s. In *Pakistan in the 80s*. Lahore, 1985, pp. 496.
12. I. Haridari Pakistan Trade Policy, 1987-1990. *Tribune Times* 21 September 1987.
13. *Ibid.*
14. W.P. Zingel. *op. cit.* pp. 502-3 Quoted in S.S. Bindra *op. cit*; p. 116.
15. S.I. Ahmed, Priority to Exports. *Pakistan Times*, 11 November 1990.
16. *Ibid.*
17. *Ibid.*
18. *Ibid.*
19. *Ibid.*
20. K.S. Ramachandran, Pakistan *Financial Express*, 16 July 1990.
21. *Ibid.*

16

Foreign Aid and Financial Benefits

Developments in Pakistan in quick succession since May 1988 dissolution of the National Assembly, dismissal of the civilian Junejo government, the announcement by Gen. Zia-ul-Haq of general elections for November 16 on a non-party basis, his subsequent death in a plane crash, the immediate "constitutional changeover" to an interim civilian set-up headed by Ghulam Ishaq Khan, the eventual elections and the 2nd December 1988 swearing in the Pakistan People's Party's (PPP) Benazir Bhutto as the Prime Minister of the country and currently taking over of the Prime Minister's office by Nawaz Sharif, on November 6, 1990—all these convulsions in the body politic of Pakistan have brought the country into sharp international focus.

The newly elected government of Nawaz Sharif has assumed office at a time when Pakistan's economy faces a near collapse with the loss of US economic aid and the Saudi Arabia refusing to accord Islamabad any significant role in the Gulf.

Pakistan has not been included in the list of countries most affected by the Gulf crisis and after the US congressional aid embargo because of Islamabad's nuclear programme, there is no sign of anyone coming up with $2 billion the new government needs immediately to avert the collapse.

Pakistan hopes that the Gulf crisis could become a bonanza, like the Soviet intervention in Afghanistan proved to be a decade ago, now appears unlikely to be fulfilled.

The recent talks between Pakistan and Saudi Arabia on sending Pakistani armoured division to the Gulf have broken down following the Saudi's refusal to provide the tanks needed for the force.

The news comes as a heavy blow to Pakistan's military establishment, which hoped to gain greater regional clout and financial benefits from the Gulf crisis.

Pakistan, which has all its armoured tied up because of tension within the country, had offered to provide all the man-power for an armoured division to defend Saudi Arabia as long as the Saudis were prepared to supply the tanks. Hopes that Pakistan could also provide extra maintenance for western units already in Saudi Arabia have also been dashed.

Pakistan has so far sent just 2,000 of a promised 5,000 infantry troops to Saudi Arabia. These soldiers were sent without any heavy equipment, and the Saudis have said they are not interested in the remaining 3,000.

Pakistan's powerful military has been banking on the Gulf crisis to stave off a looming economic crisis due to the huge rise in the cost of oil and recent cut-off of US aid because of Islamabad's nuclear weapons programme.

In recent times Arab leaders have made it clear that they will not welcome non-Arab Muslim states playing any leading role.

The upswing in the world market in 1988 brought about a

greater demand for raw materials, and also some manufactured goods produced in developing countries. As a result, these nations foreign trade sprang up, Soviet experts of the USSR Academy of Sciences Institute of the World Economy and International Relations noted in their review of the economic situation in the Third World. They stated at the same time that since oil prices fell and were not compensated for by greater oil exports, the exports and, to a certain extent, the imports of the OPEC countries dived.

The year 1989 saw an invigorated investment activity in the Third World, mostly due to a greater activity by certain Japanese corporations in some South-East-Asian and Mid-Eastern countries. However, this influx of capital mostly went to a limited group of nations, those with a more favourable economic and political situation, while the nations which were in the greatest need of development aid because of their extreme poverty got little or nothing.

Developing countries foreign debt problem is as acute as ever. According to OECD statistics, the influx of finance into these states in 1988 was just half of the 1981 figure in real terms, while the payments under the debt-repayment programmes grew by 60 per cent over that period.

The heavy burden of foreign debt has impeded major Third World nations economic development. But as a result of the upswing in foreign trade the gap payments and the receipts from the exports of goods and services exports of goods and services narrowed in 1989, and, according to forecast, is going to narrow further still this year.

Some scholar also noted the fact that a specific group has emerged within the Third World (including the new industrialized nations and ASEAN countries) which maintains a relative economic stability through its flexible and extensive integration into the international division of labour, while a majority of developing countries have seen a decline in their economic growth rate and have been gradually ousted from the international exchange in goods and services.

Over half the investment in Pakistan's state economic development programmes comes from abroad. That has pushed up the nation's foreign debt, which stands at over 15,000,000,000 dollars today (amounting to over 30 per cent of GNP). The debt-service payments have equalled 26 per cent of the annual receipts from exports.

Pakistan's economic growth has also been held back by its immense military expenditure, which grew by 360 per cent in the 1977-88 period, currently amounting to nearly 40 per cent in the 1977-88 period, currently amounting to nearly 40 per cent of its national budget. As a result, Pakistan has been plagued by its budget deficit, and trade and payments deficit.

In expert opinion there may be a certain growth in the flow of foreign capital to developing countries, particularly through loans granted by banks and inter-national financial institutions. At the same time, it will hardly relieve the situation because interest rates continue to grow.

The current trends in economic development give some hope, however, that this year certain measures will be taken to settle the foreign debt problem.[1]

Foreign aid is an important aspect of developing economies of developing countries. It is must for the poor countries and is for those countries which are relatively having sound economic capability, it is a tool in their hands by which they exploit the peoples living in the developing countrics by directly or indirectly interfering in the internal and external matters. So much so the aid givers are to be pleased at any cost and in return they look after the economic needs and sometimes, even invest million in establishing a particular type of political system in a region or country. Over the

Net Transfer of Resources

outstanding external debt

U.S. dollars in million

Year	*Gross disbursement*	*Net transfer*	*Net transfer as percentage of gross disbursement*	*External debt outstanding (disbursed)*
1978	856	482	56	7189
1981	861	186	22	8765
1983	1122	322	29	9312
1984	1021	129	13	9469
1985	1107	148	13	9732

Source: Pakistan Economic Survey 1985-86.

years the unnecessary interference in the internal affairs of aid receiving countries is becoming a permanent feature of the recent political culture.

There is no second opinion that they have definitly a big role to play in the foreign policy process by directly or indirectly giving directions hints to the political elites of these countries. They dump outdated and discarded machinery in the form of technical assistance and provide outdated technical know how with great publicity. The multinational companies are encouraged to expand their activities in these areas and political leaders are usually advised to follow a particular type of economic, industrial, import and export policies. Their impact on the political, social and economic conditions of a country is usually clearly visible.

The concept of foreign aid is not very old. The international environment after the end of the Second World War was more or less responsible for the growth of the politics of foreign aid. The US took the lead in this direction when it provided economic assistance to the certain European countries which had been completely destoryed by the Second World War. Since then, there is continuous flow of economic assistance to the less eveloped industrialized and economically sound countries, dominated by of course, the US.[3]

There was a feeling particularly in a section of the intellectuals in the US that foreign aid has done some good after all. They felt that West Europeans, Asians and Africans criticise the American way of life but it has made inroads into these continents and countries. American presence is being felt in economic, political, military and cultural fields all over the world. The cultural exchange programmes have particularly helped in promoting understanding of different cultures.[4]

Foreign aid is a historical necessity. That economic development is a pre-requisite modernization. Modernization in its turn means Westernization of sorts, specially heavy industrialisation and it requires imports of equipments and technical knowhow for which foreign exchange is needed. Hence, the need for foreign aid.[5] John D. Montgomery strongly felt that "international politic lie at the heart of foreign aid.[6]

The economy of Pakistan when it attained independence was in poor shape. The problem of foreign exchange was acute and to meet this problem, reduction in the import of consumer goods was suggested. Raw materials which were needed by Pakistan urgently could not be arranged because of the shortage of foreign exchange which resulted in idle capacity. Private investment, respecially in industry was also restricted, although in absolute amounts by the import of capital goods and materials for their production continued to increase.

Because of defective and inexperienced import/export policy machinery was imported to establish new capacity in some industries while existing capacity was laying idle because imported raw material was in very short supply. Furthermore, Pakistan in the 1980s is facing the problem of balance of payments. It is believed that to set the Pakistan cconomy in right direction, efforts should be made for the increase in agricultural production and imports for domestic consumption should be cut drastically. The flow of foreign resources in fact saved the Pakistan economic infrastructure. Otherwise it would have collapsed because of the emergence of declining trends in foreign export earnings and ever increasing demand for imports and with exchange reserved used up. No multi-national company was keen to invest in Pakistan because there was no internal market and readily exploitable raw materials which is must to attract foreign private investment. In the early 1960s, Pakistan's foreign exchange position improved as a result of rising agriculture productions, exports of cotton, rice and other agricultural products increased. Foreign exchange earnings rose on an average 7.5 per cent per year and Pakistan's experience thus ran counter to yet another widely held view that underdeveloped countries not endowed with valuable mineral resources connot rise export earnings significantly by their own policies.[7]

Some political factors also encouraged the Government of Pakistan to seek economic assistance. In the mid-fifties, Pakistan lost all hopes of the peaceful or negotiated solution of the Kashmir problem. She needed money to build the industry which is in backbone of a country's military set up. Without strong industrial base it is unthinkable to build the industry which is a backbone of a country's military set up. Without strong industrial base it is unthinkable to build military capability and she started looking towards the US and her allies. No doubt, to strengthen relations with the US seemed to be the main plank of Pakistan's foreign policy as is evident from the thinking of Liaquat Ali Khan, the first Prime Minister of Pakistan. An eminent Pakistani scholar while analysing the foreign policy of first Prime Minister has pointed out that: "Mr. Liaquat Ali Khan was not a doctrinaire politician. He was a realist, whose aim was to raise the living standards of the poorly stricken masses of his people. This could only be done through large scale economic development, for which there was neither capital nor plant nor technical skill in Pakistan. These could only come from the West. So that he was actually dependent upon the West for the vital economic needs of the country.... There was great enthusiasm in Pakistan for Mr. Liaquat Ali Khan's projected visit to Russia. He had to postpone-in effect to abandom it and instead go to the US, only on account of priorities.[8] Pakistan Government was not happy with the USSR attitude towards the Kashmir issue. The latter consistently abstained and even its representative not even once participated in the debate.[9]

Plenty of economic aid was provided by the US to Pakistan for its economic growth and development. US aid to Pakistan can be divided into two periods i.e. pre-Consortium and the Consortium period.[10] In the pre-Consortium period i.e. up to 31 December 1961, $1,728.95 millions were allocated to Pakistan by different countries, the UN and its specialised Agencies and the Ford Foundation. Of this overall economic aid to Pakistan, the US alone allocated $1,523.83 millions, of which 1,213.46 millions were utilized by Pakistan.[11]

In the Consortium period, Fy 1962 through FY (FY means U.S. Fiscal year) 1965[12] $1,818.7 miltion was pledged in foreign aid to Pakistan through the Pakistan Consortium. The US share of the Consortium pledges amounted to $925.0 million, 50.9 per cent of the total. The American aid share of the total foreign aid to Pakistan from both the Consortium and non-consortium sources during the Consortium period was 46.4 per cent, a considerable decrease from the pre-consortium period, when the US share of total foreign economic aid to Pakistan was approximately 88 per cent.[13]

The US aid, being a by product of international political scene, increased from a mere $ 12 million to FY 1945 to $ 67 million in FY 1955, immediately after Pakistan joined the military pacts formally-and continued to increase in the years to come and reached to FY 1963 and FY 1964 with $ 380 million and $ 377 millions respectively. The aim of US economic and to Pakistan was not to build Pakistan's economic capability but because of political considerations. The situation in the Indian Sub-continent changed to a great extent when during the Sino-Indian War of 1962, Pakistan openly sided with China and condemned India for attacking over Chinese territory. The US did not want Pakistan to be on Indias's side but at least was in favour of Pakistan's neutrality in the crisis.[14]

As a nation Pakistan has always been happy to live beyond its means. Its equanimity is shaken only when it faces an economic squeeze and the prospect of a cut off of foreign aid. When that happens the ruling classes climb the house tops and start proclaiming the virtues of austerity and self-reliance. It is worthwhile, however, not to take these tear-jerking performances too seriously, for austerity in Pakistan is a very selective concept not applicable to the ruling elites.

But why, you might ask, should this always be the case? Why must only the poor be expected to tighten their belts while the rich are allowed to get away with cosmetic gestures (such as one dish parties) which the purveyors of the official truth then hail as being revolutionary in character? The poor in this country, who form the bulk of the population, have barely enough to live on. Most of the things that are normally counted part of a reasonable standard of living are beyond their reach. Preaching to them about the virtues of austerity is, consequently, little better than pouring salt into the wounds of their eternal poverty.

Why do the ruling classes take such a dim view of the intelligence of the masses? Our elites know everything there is to know about corruption. They do not pay their taxes, they think nothing of filching public funds whenever they can and they use what means they can to make money. And, yet, whenever, there is an economic crisis, such as there is at present, while prating about the good that comes from standing on one's own feet they try every trick available to them to pass the burden of any sacrifice that has to be borne on to the shoulders of the common man. Who will be hit the most by the rise in petrol prices and all the inflation that will be generated as a result? The common man of course, but to hear high government functionaries it would sound as if they and the class to which they belong were on the verge of making historic sacrifices. Nothing of course could be further from the truth. The extent of their sacrifice is defined by the Prime Ministerial dictum that at the gatherings of the good and the great no more than one dish should henceforth be served.[15]

But is it not pertinent to ask whether it is the menus of the rich that need to be curbed in this country or the unequal distribution of wealth which enables them to indulge in the kind of lavish consumption that would put the later Romans to shame? Roman decadence often had something artistic and epicurean about it. Pakistani decadence has nothing to distinguish it except perhaps the inordinate vulgarity which accompanies it.

Why, for a change, should not the rich also carry some of the burden of development? All these increases in the prices of petrol and gas and electricity come under the head of indirect taxation which, by its very definition, comes down heavily on the poor while sparing the rich. Why not in this season of American-induced angst (because America has suspended its aid) go in for a bit of direct taxation that should ease some of the pressure on the destitude classes and be aimed instead at the pocket books of the rich? Conspicuous consumption cannot be ended by passing, in the style of the Crars, ukases against it. Economic ills need economic remedies. The quantum of conspicuous consumption can accordingly be affected only if luxury goods are priced out of the market. But the fact that they are not can readily be seen by the amount of money the lesiure classes spend on luxury goods and amount they pour into real estate.

What takes the cake is that the very people who sound the most unctuous about austerity are themselves the worst offenders in this regard. The great preachers of the austerity brigade are the various functionaries of government ; civil servants, parliamentarians, Cabinet Ministers, etc. What is so austere about their lifestyles? In fact Islamabad itself is at odds with the rest of the country. Its chief purpose seems to be to provide an environment to the governing elite that is at a convenient distance from the noise aad dust of the rest of Pakistan. Talking about austerity from within its glided towers is in itself a contradiction in terms. But let this pass.

There was a time when the Generals of the Pakistan army used to live what by today's standards would be a pretty spartan life. But no longer. The decadence that has swept through the rest of society has affected them as well. The lower ranks of the army men still pride themselves on their professionalism. But the higher echelons are full of chocolate soldiers as given to a life as splendour as anyone outside the army. Even so, the inequalities of life one can take in one's stride. After all one of the things history teaches us is that the gap between the rich and the poor can never be bridged (except in a utopia of which we have no foreknowledge.) It is the self-righteous hypocrisy accompanying life's inequalities and injustices which is more difficult to take.

The trouble, however, is that the majority of Pakistanis are at present disfranchised. They have no representation in the power structure, no say in the councils of government. All the political parties in Parliament, be it the IJI or the PPP, speak for the prosperous classes of society-not for the village artisan (or the kammi as we still call him), the peasant, the industrial worker or the small shopkeeper. (Some of the religious parties, represent sections of the petit bourgeosie but these parties are essentially obscurantist in nature; the MQM speaks for the lower and lower middle class Muhajirs but it remains par excellence an ethic organisation appealing to the sensibilities of the Muhajir community only).

Whether Marxism is a relevant factor any more in the politics of today is another matter. The more pertinent point is to see whether the Pakistâni political spectrum is adequately represented from ene end to the other. But if you look at it the dismaying reality is that whereas the right end of it is adequately represented and indeed over-represented, the left part of it has no voice at all. The PPP has abdicated its historic function as the mouthpiece of the poor and the deprived classes. As for the traditional leftist parties, they never amounted to much at the best of times. There is accordingly little point in looking to them for any sustenance at this critical juncture.

But the question is, should this late Reganite revolution be allowed to sweep over Pakistan unchecked? It would not be a good thing if it is. Even when Reaganism in America and the Thatcherism is Britan were at their productive best, they were responsible for inflicting a good deal of misery upon the poorer sections of American and British society. While the rich get richer, the poor got poorer. Must this be allowed to happen in Pakistan? Milan Nawaz Sharif's Government can represent only the country's commercial interests. It would be too much to expect that it should be the nation's conscience as well. That task has to be undertaken by someone else.

An alternative to the rightwing government of Nawaz Sharif has to be created. And given Pakistani reality it can only be created from amongst the so-called progressive elements of the Pakistani society that are still reeling from the shock of the PPP's defeat in the recent elections. Can anyone perform this task? It is difficult but not wholly impossible. Provided there is a leader, a platform and a clear message it can be done. The depressing truth, however, is that all three pre-requisites, for the moment, seem nowhere in sight.[16]

Pakistan is currently beset with a number of crises and it is certainly heartening to hear President Ghulam Ishaq Khan talking boldy and emphatically to US and asking it to keep its blood money. The President has directly tied US aid to sovereignty and has called upon the people of Pakistan to tighten belt and be prepared for sacrifices. Since the President's call is matched by a mass-mandated Prime Minister Nawaz Sharif, Pakistan's economic and foreign policy perceptions appear clearer and more promising.

The general mood and response in the country is so upbeat that even the vanquished PPP leadership is also joining the national chorus of 'keep the peanuts' 'Yankee go home', a beat they failed to discern and demonstrate during the hustings. The President's call is not an empty rhetoric, nor is he playing to the gallery. It is a frontal replay of solid strength he secretely gave to General Zia during 1979 when the aid was cut off and then the US crawled back to us during 1981, flying the Afghan Mujahideen flag.

Among the aid-receiving countries, Pakistan has been a model for disciplined money management, if not for economic development though we were touted to be one in the early 60s. The current debt watermark of around 21 billion dollars appears frightening, but when seen against the debt power of heavyweights like Brazil, Turkey, Mexico and some other Asian tigers, we present a humble picture, especially if population is taken as one of the vital criteria of ability of to repay.

Egypt's debt is 50 billion dollars for a 50 miliion population. Korea's is in the same league. Turkey too has a heavy borrowing. The Turkish lira which in 1980 had a parity of 1 : 50 is now 1 : 600 lira, a 32 times devaluation. However, Pak rupees vis-a-vis dollar has moved from Rs. 10 to Rs. 24 in an 18-years period, which speaks volumes of our monetary management by Ghulam Ishaq Khan and others.[17]

Pakistan despite the trauma of 1971, has continued to service its debts with singular regularity and has even been repaying the debts dating back to pre-1971 Pakistan. We received no write-offs, no reparations from India for her act of aggression against us and to cap it all, received no aid from friends between 1971-75. On the other hand the US wrote off 30,000 billion dollars in debt owned to it by India, thereby saving the Indian economy from virtual collapse. The Indians exploited the 'debt bomb' and got away with an unspecified moratorium, which gave tremendous relief to their economy. More recently, Egypt has been given write-off of US 7.00 billion dollars and probably more has been agreed to under the table. Why Pakistan must not be given an instant and real relief, despite its excellent track record, boggles one's mind. The current compounded crisis, in its economic and security dimensions, is nothing else but for and by the US and its rule the world Israel megalomania.

Whilst restructuring our economic blue prints may require some time, immediate bolstering can come from three sources, in order of priority they are : belt tightening debt moratorium of 5 years and from export of nuclear technology.

— Belt tightening could yeild at least Rs. 20 billion and certainly reduce internal debts if expertly planned and honestly executed. Demostrations of simplicity and Islamic life-style must also flow, in real earnestness, from top to the lower echelons of society.

— Debt moratorium can save 2.00 billion dollars and ward off the imminent crisis, whilst off the allowing us to shop around in a currently depressed arms bazar to keep upto date our defence system, which in any case, is not entirely US dependent, as is innocently perceived to be. This will also rescue our economic policy from being tailored by the IMF, which for helt cash transfer of 200.00 million dollars imposed disastrous import-inflation prescriptions on us.

Increased internal nuclear facilities-export of nuclear technology. The break-through achieved in nuclear technology, especially in the 'reversal route' has given Pakistan a tremendous twin advantage; 200/300 megawatt plants can be built partly-exclusively in Pakistan and could go a long way in reducing the power gap whilst the debate on Kalabagh etc. goes on. Moreover, technological perfection, has brought home possibilities of the Pakistan being able to export nuclear power-plants as well as defence-oriented units at around half the price of the current contenders in the nuclear market. Some insides view this factor to be the most galling one, for the US to swallow and hence her unprecedented pressure on Pakistan.

Nuclear technology exports could yield as much as 2.00-3.00 billion dollars per year with the added advantage of receiving the full added payment upfront; which a nbmber of countries are prepared to do. Moreover, the policy of privatisation of economy now seen in the light of a massively mandated federal government and the stable harmonious centre-province relations all around, lends more credibility than that of the past two years, when economic privatisation policy was cancelled due to a number of factors. By all accounts and assessments, despite the clouds of disaster lingering on the region and on Pakistan, an economic turn around is not viewed as too optimistic, especially in view of the fact, that the two principal stewards of government, President Ghulam Ishaq Khan and Prime Minister Nawaz Sharif are both basically economics-oriented with good track records of resource management capability and more than anything else, have, little reason to have a stand off relationship which bedevilled Pakistan during the Zia-Junejo-Ishaq-Bhutto years at tremendous cost to our strength and democracy. Ghulam Ishaq Khan—Nawas Sharif cordial relationship can bring in 1 to 2 billion dollars foreign investments from Pakistanis abroad as well as some Arabs looking for safe investments.[18]

While all the afore-mentioned scenarios and possibilities appear credible and achievable, we must not allow our sovereignty to be compromised nor permit any interference in our internal affairs. Let's pause for a moment and ask why is US still entangled in our efforts on the Norcotics control? We know its 'production', 'cycling'. It is nature's atom bomb, gifted to us for putting it to good use and we can also earn foreign exchange from its sale proceeds. The US teams and advisors on norcotics should better pack-up and if they have any fears, they must exercise better control on their borders and on their people. Our sufferings and sacrifices should not be for some body else's comforts and conveniences.

Doomsday analysts say that in our battle for 'sovereign survival', the 'heroin option' should not be discounted and we must go to the length of seeking refuge in the region of religious edict, that, when faced with death, even carrion is permitted to be eaten. If the US, to protect its interests, can have 5 million Muslims slaughtered in the Iraq-Iran war, Afghan Jehad, Palestinian occupation, and now brings the region into the vortex of an infernic war, why cannot we officially export heroin, as a mediciane, to other countries. It could yield us over 10,000 billion dollar a year. After all heroin option was exercised by the CIA to fund and fight its 'dirty wars' in Nicaragua when Congress cut off its purse strings. We would only be done it in an open and purely business-like manner to earn much needed foreign exchange for our defence needs and other development projects.

Let us judiciously, wisely and courageously employ the 'debt, nuclear, heroin bomb' options to advantage. Turning strength of to weakness and weakness to strength depends on intent and capability. But first the US must reduce its presence in Pakistan. The 1200 odd hangerson and the Justice Council Cell and over 300 drug enforcement agency operators need rest and recreation. This would also stop them from going around hunting politicians and making them to create problems for the new government.[19]

Quantity of raw cotton exported fell substantially during July-December 1989 to a mere 52,603 tonnes from 288,000 tonnes in the corresponding half of 1988. Production of cotton has been affected due to rains which has caused some damage to the crop and it is estimated that output for the year may be lower than the target of 9 million bales yet for the year is likely to be between 1.5 to 2 million bales.

The import bill during July-December 1989 is estimated at Rs. 69,237 million as against Rs. 58,445 million during the corresponding period of last year. Growth in imports at 18.5 per cent was a little more than the growth of exports at 17.2 per cent. During the first six months of the current fiscal year, major increases were recorded in the import of petroleum crude and products, chemicals and wheat. The import bill of petroleum rose by nearly 80 per cent to Rs. 12,095 million from Rs. 6,734 million in July-December 1988. The quantity imported rose by 22.2 per cent. Its unit value has risen to 2,958 per tonne from Rs. 2,014 per tonne in the corresponding period of last year, due to a rise in the price of a barrel of oil. The import bill of wheat more than doubled to Rs. 4,367 million from Rs. 2,009 million, while for chemicals it rose by 14.7 per cent from Rs. 9,989 million to Rs. 11,454 million in July-December 1989. The import bill has gone up due to continuing depreciation of the Pak rupee from Rs. 18.50 to one US dollar in July-December 1988 to Rs. 21.24 to one US dollar in July-December 1989.[20]

Foreign aid flows have grown through the years. Though these have helped sustain the pace of growth in the economy, the rising external debt has put mounting pressures on the economy. Debt service payments have risen from £ 959 million in 1984-85 to the £ 1,237 million in 1988-89. A major chunk of the aid disbursed goes in servicing the debt obligations. For instance, in 1986-87 of £ 1,398 million disbursed, net inflow was only £ 175.1 million or 13 pér cent of the total. Net transfer had, however, risen to nearly 53 per cent in 1988-1989. Total external debt as on June 30, 1989 was put at £ 14 billion or nearly 33 per cent of the GNP. Foreign asisstance is now available with a shorttened maturity period and at higher interest charges, the analysis by the National Bank of Pakistan says.[21]

Despite the standard of living having been continually dragged down by years of economic mismanagement, Pakistan's new government of Nawaz Sharif is now promising a robust future for the country's aid-addicted economy.

"Where is the collapse?" Finance Minister Sartaj Aziz shot back when questioned about the dark comments abroad that suspension of U.S. assistance and all fallout of the gulf crisis get spelded disaster for the muslim country's economy groaning under a foreign debt burden of £ 16.5 billions. "Our industry is doing better than last year. Agriculture is in fine shape. The inflation is settling down to 11. We have not defaulted even a cent in on-time repayment of foreign loans. So where is the collapse," he said in Islamabad on December 31, 1990.

Aziz confirmed that the country's foreign exchange reserve went below 100 million dollars in the two months following Iraqi occupation of Kuwait, and that inflation rose to 12.5 per cent.

A 25 per cent increase in exports and seven per cent rise in remittances by Pakistanis elsewhere have boosted the reserves to around 200 million dollars.

Islamabad hopes the International Monetary Fund and the World Bank will come to the rescue by March 1991, in the mean-time it has arranged about 150 million dollars in short-term commercial loans from two gulf-based Islamic banks and two Western banks.

There is however, little prospect of Washington resuming its much-needed aid to Pakistan as the Muslim country has rejected the condition of opening its secret nuclear facilities for inspection.

'We are effectively borrowing to pay back past debts,' Aziz said, relecting the popular argument that Pakistan does not need foreign aid.

But Benazir Bhutto, who was dismissed as Prime Minister in August 1990 and who now leads the parliamentary opposition, thinks differently.

'I believe very third world country needs aid. And Pakistan needs it more than any other, because we have such terrible problems with the budget,' she said.

References

1. Hussian Musadeq, Economic Gap, *Pakistan Times*, 13 November, 1990.
2. S S. Bindra, *Determinants of Pakistan's Foreign Policy*, New Delhi, 1988, p. 116.
3. M. Ayoob, U.S. Economic Aid to Pakistan, 1954-65, *India Quarterly* April-June 1967, p. 127.
4. K.N. Sharma, Foreign Aid and, Foreign Policy, *Ibid*, July-Sept. 1967, p. 271.
5. *Ibid*, p. 268.
6. S.S. Bindra, *Op–cit*, p. 117.
7. G.F. Papanek, *Pakistan's Development*, Mass, 1967, pp. 17-18.
8. *Pakistan Horizon*, Dec. 1951, p. 184.
9. *Ibid*, p. 186.

10. The Pakistan Consortium (Aid to Pakistan club) was organised in 1960 under the aegis of the World Bank.
11. M. Ayub, *Op. cit*, p. 131
12. F.Y. Stands for U.S. Fiscal Year.
13. M. Ayoob, *Op. cit*, p. 131
14. S.S Bindra *Op. cit*, p. 119.
15. Ayaz Amir, One-Dish Economic Plan, *Dawn*, 19 November 1990.
16. *Ibid*.
17. S.A.I. Tirmazi, Economic Options for Pakistan, *The Muslim*, 21 November 1990.
18. *Ibid*.
19. *Ibid*.
20. K.S. Ramachandra, Pakitan, *Finance Express*, 16 July 1990.
21. *Ibid*.

17

Manpower

Harlan Claveland and Mochtar Lubis in their new book "The Future of Development" say that the cheap and uneducated labour which once produced most of the goods in Third World countries, giving, them an edge in competing for world markets, is no longer effective. Technological innovations have destroyed that edge and today labour costs comprise a very small fraction of production costs. The fact that most developing countries do not recognise this basic change in economics bodes ill for them, they warn.

Of course, an industrial revolution presages a real revolution within the bureaucracy, particularly in the taxation departments. Instead of remaining controllers of the economy they have to become promoters of the economy and engines of the industrial revolution. Nawaz Sharif does not want a slow moving or obstructive bureaucracy in this supersonic age. But changing a slow moving and largely corrupt bureaucracy, and particularly its taxation departments, will be an overwhelming task.

An industrial revolution should have its right mix of heavy, large-scale, medium and small industries. The last two categories have to be promoted assiduously to solve the unemployment problem early as they employ more workers.

But we should not expect an industrial revolution to solve all our problems, even our economic problems. To achieve a real industrial revolution we need to have social and cultural revolution as well and a change in our work ethics. And religion should not be allowed to be used as road-block to economic progress. Are we really prepared for such extensive and radical changes?

As for the condition that Prime Minister Nawaz Sharif wishes to place on industrialists for availing this concession, that they should look after the educational and health needs of their workers, it may be in order to refresh his memory in respect of a few things that he, being an industrialist, should know. Almost 40 per cent of industrial labour in the large-scale sector consists of contract labour. And, contracted workers are not the 'employees' of the manufacturing unit at which they are working. The legal distinction is critical because contract workers are employees of the 'contractor' who has a 'legal' contract (although there may be no legal contract, as in many cases there is no contractor except in the books of the company) with the mill owner. These workers not being his employees, the government will not be able to enforce any employee related conditions on him. And it would be unthinkable for any government, in particular an IJI one, to legislate against contract labour. This writer along with some trade unions has, for some years, been pleading with the government to agree to a much simpler proposition of asking the factory owners to merely issue a certificate that the person had been working at his manufacturing factory. We are realists and know that the system of contract labour is here to stay. Our reason for placing this request was merely to get some documentation to prove that the worker concerned was an earning member of the family, so that his dependents could apply for different payments made by the government, in particular dues under the government insurance scheme, on the death of a bread-earner. We failed to even get agreement to such a basic concession, which, by no means, threatened the existence of a well-entrenched system of contract labour. It is, therefore, difficult to believe that the Prime Minister's conditions for the tax holiday incentive can, in fact, be implemented.[1]

An industrial revolution has to be backed by a rapid agricultural expansion. Food production, and not cereals alone, has to expand with the increasing population. The supply of vegetables, dairy products, meat, chicken and fish has to expand a great deal to produce more productive workers and a healthier people. Cotton production may have to reach a target of 15 million bales and sugar production, too, has to rise to meet the rising need. Per acre yield in agriculture has to increase rapidly to make our agricultural products more competitive abroad and the quality of many products has to improve to get higher prices abroad. Employer-employee relations in the industry have to improve vastly. The adversary relationship has to give ways to co-operative relationship for any kind of industrial revolution. Otherwise the employers will opt for less and less labour intensive technology or prefer industries which employ a small number of workers. What Pakistan needs is not cheap labour but more productive labour which will produce quality products.

About the industrial sector, the Prime Minister said, in Islamabad, on November 7, 1990 that his government intended to lay foundations of an industrial revolution. "The corner stone of this policy will be that each factory, firstly, gives the peasants who produces the raw material and the labourers their due remuneration."

He said, the investors would be duly encouraged. "The foremost gift for them is, freedom. Henceforth, no restrictions would continue on setting up of new industries. The cumbersome bureaucratic hurdles and processes are being done away with. The necessary infrastructure requirements will be made available—a crach programme about, which will be announced and implemented shortly. Industries are not established through formulation of policies alone, they entail certain basic requirements. The industries are not set up without bare facilities of roads, water, electricity, telephone, air linkage and raw material—my government will do everything possible to extend these basic civic amenities, so as to expedite pace of industrialisation," he added.

The repeated announcements about denationalisation, whieh are being made to attract foreign capital and to allay the fears of the new investors, created great apprehension in the minds of the employees of the public sector industries. The fear of unemployment loomed large and they felt the gains of their struggle slipping from their hands. In order to meet this challenge, the employees of various public sector industries held meetings to consider ways and means to defeat this policy of the government. A mammoth procession was taken out which started from the Nasir Bagh (Goal Bagh) carrying huge banners condemning the policy of the government and red flags flying over their heads. The procession ended near the "Masjid's Shuhada", where the representatives of various organisations made forceful speeches, vowing to continue the struggle, till their demands are met and threatened the powers that be, that they would resort to "Wheel Jam Strike", if any further step to denationalise the public sector industries is taken. Nevertheless, the government is firm on its policy and has already published a plan to transfer the shares of Muslim Commercial Bank. Bank employees have started agitation against this step and some of them have gone on fast upto death. On December 12, 1990 the Government had called a Kisan Conference in Islamabad to consider the recommendations for improving the conditions of the peasantry. On the same day, for the first time in the history of Pakistan, a unique action took place in Kasur District, where the peasantry is known for its hard work and innovative methods of cultivation, The peasants, armed with lathis and "Tambas", encircled the City of Kasur and did not allow anybody to go out of the City or to enter it. Those who tried to break the siege were forcibly stopped. The small police contingent stood impotently watching this unprecedented action. The peasants demanded the slashing of increased prices of fertilisers, insecticides, diesel, electricity and spare parts of tractors etc. and they accused the district administration of corruption and inefficiency. After hectic efforts, they were persuaded to lift the siege of the city. Within two months of the formation of the new government, these sporadic and scattered actions of the various segments of society are a pointer to the future struggles of the downtrodden and the working people of Pakistan.[2]

Of course, an industrial revolution cannot take off without a full concord with labour. So a tri-partite meeting was convened in December 1990—after the reports of the six committees was made available. But previous tripartite meetings of representatives of government, employers and employees have not been a success for nearly 12 years with the workers opposing the right of employers to hire and fire on which they insist. Indisputably industrial peace is a vital pre-requisite for an industrial revolution and for solving the major unemployment problems.

What Nawaz Sharif has enunciated are the principles, Details will be known only after the six committees submit their reports and the banks come up with their positions. But the future of the industrial revolution will really depend on the kind of roles industrialists and entrepreneurs are ready to play, keeping in mind the welfare of industrial manpower.

The Federal Minister for Labour, Manpower and Overseas Pakistanis, Ejaz-ul-Haq, has said that there would be total overhaul of his Ministry as he was not fully satisfied with its present working.

He said in Faisalabad, on November 16, 1990 that he

was holding two grand sessions on November 18-19, 1990 in his Ministry when the present performance of the Ministry would be put to detailed security and the weak points and difficulties would be removed and recommendations for the future course of action would be chalked out.

He said, he was fully aware of the difficulties of the overseas Pakistanis, particularly, hundreds of families stranded at the border of Turkey who were neither allowed to go back by the Iraqi government nor being allowed to go forward by the Turkish government. The problem, he said needed immediate attention and he was planning a visit to Gulf state to sort out the difficulties of the overseas Pakistanis.

Talking about rehabilitation of Pakistanis who have returned from Kuwait and Iraq. Mr. Ejaz-ul-Haq said that their problems needed to be attended with more diligence and sympathy and conceded that full payment of compensation was not being made by the government.

Regarding the future plans, he said that a comprehensive programme would be chalked out to acquire optimum utilisation of manpower export strategy by exporting ouly the relevant and requisite skilled manpower to Middle East as well as continental countries. There would not be haphazard emigration of unskilled workers and 'Dubai chalo syndrome' (go to Dubai movement) would not be repeated.

The Federal Minister for Education, Syed Falkhar Imam, has said that the new government would follow an education policy which would enable the country te meet the future challenges of human resource development. He said that expansion of scientific and technical education would be given special attention to have trained manpower for the rapid industrial development in the country. It need hardly be pointed out here that human resource development is one of the most neglected sectors of our economy. Manpower training is a pre-requisite for rapid industrialisation in the country and it is the only solid asset on which the industrial future of the country can be built. The country need trained manpower to run its industrial units efficiently and keep the wheels of production moving. There is in the country an acute shortage of technical training institutes. It is a measure of the stepmotherly treatment meted out to this vital sector by the education planners in successive administrations that there are in 25 districts of Punjab eight boards of intermediate and secondary education but only one board of technical education catering to the needs of 20 polytechnic institutes, 130 commerce colleges and commercial institutes and 98 vocational institutes for women with a total enrolment of 58,000 students.[3]

A solid industrial base in the first requirement for a country which wishes to make tangible economic progress as today's world is a world of science and technology. As promised by Prime Minister Mian Nawaz Sharif in his inaugural address to the nation, sizeable expansion in the industrial base in the country is very much on the cards. In order to meet the long-term needs of an expanded industrial infrastructure and to gradually banish unemployment from the country, it is imperative that the curricula at the secondary level are entirely restructured to shift the current emphasis on liberal arts education to technical education throughout the country. Institutes geared to offering "crash programmes" for training of students in different technical trades should also be established. The private sector entrepreneurs can be associated in this venture because such institutes will eventually meet the needs of industrial concerns. There does not appear to be any reason why the private sector should not extend a helping hand if suitable inducements are offered by the authorities concerned. If properly planned and wisely handled, such a basic shift in curricular orientation, backed by commensurate increases in budgetary allocations, can go a long way to strengthening the industrial base and reducing unemployment in the country. It will also help the nation prepare itself to meet the challenges of the 21st century.[4]

Prime Minister Nawaz Sharif said in Islamabad, on November 7, 1990 that money and administrative power could never substitute for the qualities of advancement, leadership and creativity. "In these domains, brain alone has a say", he maintained.

"My government will remain committed to giving a rightful place to intellect and knowledge," he declared, and added, befitting measures in this respect would be initiated.

He said, a conducive atmosphere, opportunities and a free hand would be extended to the workers. "Our endeavour shall remain that no creative and constructive idea cropping up in the minds for national welfare and uplift is wasted or drained out, "Nawaz Sharif asserted.

Current economic context is depressing; especially the unemployment and lack of even educational (or vocational training) opportunities for the youth. This is as true for Old as it is for New Sindhis. To talk of only one and forget the other, in the context of a single economy, will be wrong. Everybody deserves a better economic deal. The government that there is has the responsibility to do what it can. But its financial limitations are also known. In the current phase, without massive private initiative and effort, the outlook for it is bleak. One does not favour feverish private economic activity to alleviate popular misery merely for the sake of Jam Sadiq Ali or the government he heads. It is for the sake of suffering people, no matter who may be the ministers. Here one would make an earnest appeal again to Altaf Husain. He enjoys such a great deal of personal popularity, and so many advantages. Let him start a movement for greater educational and economic opportunities and improvement for the people—at least of lower and lower-middle classes' youth. There are many number of unemployed but well-educated scientists and educationists and competent engineers, doctors and what have you. Altaf Husain's ability to collect donations is also proven. Let him help establish a series of autonomous polytechnics in the first instance, in the Jamia Millia style or the 1920s—only on a larger and wider scale to include education and training of all kinds. These institutions should be open to all and only small or nominal fees should be charged. The training can usefully range from simple welders, electricians, plumbers, etc. to highly specialised engineers and medical specialists. Next question to arise will be : where will they all get employment ? No matter really. But given vital skills and scarce knowledge or worthwhile learning, new avenues would constantly open. For the rest, the same leadership can promote a series of producers cooperatives or even factories. If these institutions—educational, training or employment creating ones—ideally as large as the demand and if they admit or employ all who need knowledge or skills or want jobs. it will be the surest road to true integration.[5]

References

1. Shahid Kardar. Buying Prosperity, *The Nation*, 16 November, 1990.
2. Sardar Shaukat Ali : Troubled Times for Nawaz Sharif. *Patriot*, 31 December, 1990.
3. *Pakistan Times*, 14 November, 1990.
4. *Ibid.*
5. M.B. Naqvi, Ethnic Breach. *Dawn*, 19 November, 1990.

18

Road to Recovery

Everybody in Pakistan is talking about the economic crunch. Most people have felt the sharp edge of the crisis because, after the increase in petroleum prices, the charge for just mending a tyre puncture has done up from Rs. 5 to Rs. 7. The housewife has also not been spared because the maid sevant threatens to quit if her pay is not raised.

Although Pakistanis have a long history of living dangerously from moment to moment and are accustomed to endlessly debating one crisis or another without trying to resolve it, their present anxiety has a touch despair never seen before.

The reaction to the grim economic situation takes two forms. One, after years of profigacy and economic masmanagement, anyone bound by traditional concepts cannot do a quick salvage job. Two, it is too early to judge the new government's plans or its capability to achieve a quick economic revival.

However, it goes to the credit of the Nawaz Sharif government that it has tried to overcome the heavy strain on its financial resources caused by the Gulf crisis and suspension of US and IMF aid. The government has also deferred unveiling of its policies till later this month because the six committees set up to study the situation and propose reforms have still to submit their reports.

Although the Gulf problem and aid cut-off may have aggravated the situation, the economic crisis has been visible for years. Further, the areas of inquiry assigned to new committees, industrialisation, employment generation, export promotion, deregulation, taxation, and self-reliance, have been studied by experts many times over.

The present crisis has its roots in history. Pakistan's early rulers had little aptitude for modern economic management. The accountants who shaped its economic policies were quite happy to balance the budgets so long as primary exports (jute and cotton) yielded enough foreign exchange to meet the needs of the administration.

Easy availability of foreign aid and advice, from early fifties onward, kept the leaders from any need to think for themselves. They also became indifferent to suggestion on land reform, human resource development and creation of an essential infrastructure.

During the Ayub period, the green revolution and state-aided industrial expansion facilitated transfer of agricultural profits to industry's "robberbarons". Bhutto distributed the profits to the manufacturing and banking sectors to curb mass discounted and hoped that the enlarged public sector would provide funds for further industrialisation and public welfare. This did not happen.[1]

Ehe economy ran into difficulties because the public sector did not work efficiently and the private sector was paralysed. The situation was partly saved by improved aid flows (from Muslim states) and a substantial increase in remittances from expiratitates.

General Zia began by vowing to disband the public sector and promising a more dynamic role for the private sector. He could not achieve any of these objectives. Heavy loans were contracted and squandered and trouble began with aid-donours and the IMF. The situation became so bad that in 1981 the government was forced to accept IMF conditions based on guarantees of a fairly high rate of growth that it could not easily sustain and measures to increase resources and cut wasteful expenditure that it did not have the political strength to implement.

Till 1988 no serious attempt was made to arrest the drift towards what the World Bank described as "bankruptcy". It was assumed that remittances consituted a never-ending bonanza and it did not matter if the money coming in was spent on real estate. Luxuries and ostentatious living. Availability of big loans was justified as proof of the economy's soundness.

It did not matter if these loans were consumed by the non-productive sector. Foriegn creditors and auditors were palmed off with promises that their advice would be accepted once the domestic emergency was over. They relented because Pakistan, or more so the Zia regime, was needed to prosecute the western policy on Afghanistan.

The good time the General and his backroom boys were having made them oblivious of the imbalances growing in the national economy. The IMF and World Bank kept asking for a radical restructuring of the economy and kept receiving the answer, patently false, that the necessary restructuring had been done.

The IMF had asked Pakistan to slash non-development expenditure, reduce fiscal deficit to no more than 5.5 per cent of GDP, generate additional resources by broadening the taxation base and raise the charges for service land utilities. In October 1988, the IMF compelled the government to sign a three year bond of fiscal discipline which left the government with little room to maneouvre. Compliance with IMF conditions was again deferred till after the elections.

The PPP believed it could not change the policies of the previous regime and it did not also seem to have tried. It accepted the need to reduce non-development expenditure but with little success and ended up by spending 20 per cent more on defence.

Denationalisation was set as an important objective but again with minimal success. Ten per cent of the national airline's shares were sold to the public but that was hardly considered as privatisation. A decision was taken to privatise the nationalised commercial banks, beginning with Muslim Commercial Bank, but could not be implemented in the face of resistance by employees. The most notable initiative was the approval of projects in the energy sector.

Ffforts were made to satisfy the IMF by raising power and gas tariffs and transport fares. Oil prices were also increased. The government did not tax the farmers or the traders. An obligation to impose a general sales tax only resulted in more confusion and the early exercise to reduce the fiscal deficit was a failure.

The Nawaz Sharif government has taken over at a time when the IMF is not prepared to accept its word. One of its representatives hovers around the Ministry of Finance to check the validity of the statements made by the country's leaders. Another IMF expert is believed to be examining the country's internal debt, though it is doubtful whether this falls within IMF's sphere of concern. The announcements made by Prime Minister Nawas Sharif do not indicate any new economic initative that would be of significance.[a]

In his first address to the nation on November 7, 1990, the Prime Minister promised a tax holiday and speedy denationalisation. A week later he told industrialists that the procedure for sanctioning new units was being liberalised further and that projects costing more than 1000 million rupees (no upper limit was mentioned) would not require sanction.

References have been made to further reducing the list of specified sectors from seven to two. Steps to boost exports have also been announced.

These statements do not indicate any substantial change over the Bhutto government's policies.

There may, however, be some differences on the level of priority to be given to various sectors. The crucial question is whether Nawaz Sharif will be able to overcome the constraint that prevented governments over the past decade from achieving policy goals.

The economy cannot be made sound unless the administraiion expenditure is drastically reduced and the country learns to live within its means.

Significantly, nobody is talking about the defence burden. While economists agree that a sizable reduction in defence spending is a essential for Pakistan's economic revival, no parliamentary party dares to talk about it.

The Benazir Bhutto government not only failed to reduce the defence budget, but could not also check unbudgeted expenditure shown under defence but which did not qualify as such. It is extremely unlikely that Nawaz Sharif will be able to achieve a break-through in this direction.

The taxation is an equally difficult field since Sharif does not believe in taxing industry and trade.

Barely two months after assuming power, Pakistan's Islami Jamhoori Ittehad (IJI) Government faces the worst economic crisis of the decade brought on by the Gulf crisis, but whose repercussions could plague the country's economy long after the Kuwait-Iraq conflict is over.

The price hike, also caused by the Gulf situation, has already resulted into two nation-wide strikes which paralysed the entire country. The new Government faced its first crisis when it enforced the Islamic law of retribution and compensation in early November. The Law requires a driver who may kill a person by negligent driving to pay Rs. 175,000 in compensation to the relatives of the deceased.

The drivers, who have refused to accept the law, saying the Government should demand compensation from the vehicle owners, went on an indefinite strike from November 7, 1990. The Government made the drivers end their strike by promising to appoint a religious committee to review the law.

The Government, however, soon plunged into another crisis when it announced 41.5 per cent hike in the oil price on November 14, 1990. This was the 26th raise in oil price since 1963 and biggest in the country's history.

The unprecedented price hike not only annoyed the people but also the oil dealers who demanded a raise in their commissions as well. The dealers stopped oil supply for almost a week and the Government finally had to raise the commissions.

The rise in oil price, urged by the International Monetary Fund in September 1990 as a condition for disbursing their—£500 million grant, now threatens to escalate prices of all essential commodities across the board. Protracted delay in the US aid suspended in the September has also worsened the situation.

According to Pakistani economist, Dr. Akmal Hussain, Pakistan needs money urgently to buy wheat, soyabean and tea from the world market because of an acute shortage of these commodities.

However, the Nawaz Sharif Government started its prooccedings with a bold face when the Prime Minister promised in his first address to the nation that he would begin a new era of industrialisation." He later announced a more liberal industrial policy aimed at a reducing Government control over industries and an attractive tax holiday to encourage investment in the industrial sector.

Pakistani economists believe that announcing tax holidays may not encourage investment as it would lead to a severe shortage of energy, trained manpower, infrastructure and foreign exchange.

The newly elected Government of Nawaz Sharif has assumed office at a time when Pakistan economy faces a near collapse with the loss of US economic aid and the Saudi Arabia refusing to accord Islamabad any significant role in the Gulf.

Pakistan has not been included in the list of countries most affected by the Gulf crisis and after ther US congressional aid embargo because of Islamabad's nuclear programme, there is no sign of anyone coming up with the £2 billion the new government needs immediately to avert the collapse.

Pakistani hopes that the Gulf crisis could become a bonanza, like the Soviet intervention in Afghanistan proved to be a decade ago, now appears unlikely to be fulfilled.

The recent talks between Pakistan and Saudi Arabia on sending Pakistani armoured division to the Gulf have broken down following the Saudi's refusal to provide the tanks needed for the force.

The news comes as a heavy blow to Pakistan's military

establishment, which hoped to gain greater regional clout and finencial benefits from the Gulf crisis.

Pakistan, which has all its armoured tied up because of tension within the country, had offered to provide all the manpower for an armoured division to defend Saudi Arabia as long as the Saudis were prepared to supply the tanks, hopes that Pakistan could also provide extra maintenance crew for western units already in Saudi Arabia have also been dashed.

Pakistan has so far sent just 2,000 of a promised 5,000 infantry troops to Saudi Arabia. These soldiers were sent without any heavy equipment and the Saudis have said they are not interested in the remaining 3,000.

Pakistan's powerful military has been banking on the Gulf crisis to stave off a looming economic crisis due to the huge rise in the cost of oil and last month's cut-off of US aid because of Islamabad's nuclear weapons programme.

In recent weeks Arab leaders such as President Hosni Mubarak of Egypt have made it clear that they envisage a Pan-Arab force to maintain security in the Gulf and will not welcome non-Arab Muslim states playing any leading role. Egypt and Syria have already sent thousands of troops and heavy armour to defend Saudi Arabia.

Pakistan has launched a diplomatic offensive within the Organisation of the Islamic Conference (OIC) to arrange an OIC force for the defence of the Gulf, but these moves have been rejected by most Araab leaders and the United States.

Some Pakistan officials suspect the Americans, whose relations with Pakistan are strained, influenced the Saudi decision.

Pakistan's GDP growth rate is estimated to have

improved from 4.8 per cent last year to 5.2 per cent in 1989-90 in real terms.

According to the Economic Survey for 1989-90 issued by the Government of Pakistan, the GNP has been estimated at Rs. 8,190 billion which is 9.6 per cent higher than last year. In real terms, the GNP growth rate is placed at 5 per cent.

GDP growth of 5.2 per cent was contributed by sectoral growth rates of 4.0 per cent and 7.9 per cent in agriculture and manufacturing respectively. The agricultural growth of 4 per cent is on top of high growth rate of 7.1 per cent experienced last year. Implicit in this growth is the estimated production of wheat at 15 million tonnes, cotton at 8.6 million bales and sugarcane at 36. 2 million tonnes.

Particularly encouraging is the improvement in large scale manufactuturing subsector which is estimated to grow by 77 per cent as against 2.4 per cent last year. The small-scale manufacturing sub-sector maintains its conventional growth of 8.4 per cent.

The consolidated sectoral growth indicates that commodity producing sector rose by 5.5 per cent and services sector by 4.8 per cent maintaining their relative share at 52.48 almost at the same as witnessed last year.

Within the services sector, the growth in trade declined from 5.3 to 4.9 per cent, contrasted with transport/communications, showing rise to 4.7 per cent from last year's 0.6 per cent.

Total investment outlay for 1989-90 is estimated at Rs. 157.7 billion, 16 per cent higher than last year. About 78 per cent of the total investment was financed through national savings, and 22 per cent through external resources. In 1988-89, the share of external resources was 28 per cent.

By the end of March 1990, total monetary expansion amounted to Rs. 21.1 billion or 7.5 per cent as against the target of Rs. 30.4 billion. This is in line with the quarterly phasing of monetary expansion.

The consolidated budget for 1989-90 envisaged 11.3 per cent increased in government revenues. This was meant to bring down the budget deficit from the level of 7.3 per cent of GDP last year to 6.3 per cent in the current year. This scenario was based on the one hand on the projection of additional resources worth Rs. 15 billion through various tax and non-tax resources and adjustments in the administered prices of fertiliser, gas, POL products and power tariff and, on the other, allowing only 4.4 per cent expenditure growth implying a reduction in real terms of over three per cent.

In absolute terms, the overall deficit was envisaged at Rs. 56 billion, to be financed to the extent of 39 per cent from external resources and 53 per cent from domestic non-bank borrowing and 8 per cent from the banking system.

The balance of payments situation, for the first time in many years, underwent reverse gear through 6.1 per cent increase in exports and notable accent on value-added exports and of cotton yarn, textiles etc. This was despite decline in exports of raw cotton and rice.

At the same time, import growth was restricted to 2.7 per cent despite rise in POL prices and further trade liberalisation. Home remittances, too, are estimated to rise from dollars 1.90 billion in 1988-89 to dollars 1.98 billion in 1989-1990.

Some analysts who claim to be "realists" feel that Nawaz Sharif has just placed a crown of thorns on his head. The serious economic crunch, that the country is faced with, due to the economic cost to the country of the Gulf crisis combined with possible US aid cut off and compounded by IMF's insistence on an immediate price hike of 40 per cent in gasoline prices, would make it difficult to balance the country's finances.

To announce at the same time that poverty alleviation, putting a curb on inflation and increasing employment would have priority in the policies of the new government may sound somewhat rash.

The government is seemingly poised between the devil and the deep sea. The cassandras claim that the Prime Minister may have rushed in where angels fear to tread.[3]

Finance Minister, Sartaj Aziz, may have added to the unease when he said on 4th November that oil price increase was necessary to avoid a loss of Rs. 400 million on oil imports each day. This translates into Rs. 120 billion a year or 5.5 billion dollars a year (of 300 days), which is a very high figure.

Sometimes earlier, he had talked of a loss of £ 600 million out of a total loss of £ 1100 million due to oil price increase from £ 17 to £ 25 per barrel. On that computation even if the oil prices were to remain at £ 40 a barrel for a whole year the total loss due to oil price increase would be no more than £ 1.7 billion.

In case of a war in the Gulf when the oil prices are expected to jump to £ 65 a barrel the loss to Pakistan would be £ 3.6 billion on an annualised basis. However prices have declined to £ 32 a barrel lately and barrind outbreak a war may remain around £ 30 a barrel till such time the uncertainty remains while the most influential parties, expecting USA and UK, are in search of a political solution. On that basis the annual loss to Pakistan should be about £ 975 million only. And to that £ 300 million as loss of remmittances from Kuwait and another £ 100 million for return and rehabilitation of 85,000 Pakistani expatriates from Kuwait, the total loss should be somewhat less than £ 1.5 billion.[4]

For this loss we can look to the fund collected under the ageis of the Gulf Crisis Coordination Council set up by President Bush on 25th September, 1990. A sum of over £ 22 billion had reportedly been collected in this fund : £ 6 billion from Saudi Arabia, £ 4 billion from Japan, £ 2 billion from Germany, and from others including Kuwait government in exile. In any case we should persue this line of approach. The IMF has insistent on oil price hike which is very likely to come soon. That should release £ 240 million held back from the four year stand-by and structural adjustment loans. That should ease the foreign exchange situation somewhat.

It is the US aid with about £ 300 to £ 400 million of economic assistance received by us on grant basis from year to year which has become doubtful thanks to the particularly harsh and invidious operation of special provisions attached by the stalwarts of India-Jewish lobby to aid to Pakistan. If it is stopped then we may not be able to undertake many new projects because out of a total annual aid package only about 20 per cent is left over after debt servicing. But we still have about £ 10 billion in the pipeline and most of the projects on the ground or those in advanced stage of implementation need not suffer.

There is also a silver lining in that the World Bank and IMF, cognisant of our difficulties (we are counted among the 10 most seriously affected countries by the Gulf Crisis), have decided to undertake debt rescheduling in our case. Since Egypt had had £ 8 billion US debt and £ 2.8 billion French debt written off recently we deserve at least a reasonable debt rescheduling.

Let the cassandras scratch their heads but the situation does not seem to be getting out of hand.

So far as internal finances are concerned it would be difficult both to increase oil prices, which would have a spiralling effect on all goods and services, and simultaneously to protest the poor and the needy as the Prime Minister has offered.[5]

If the inflationary impact of oil price increase results in subsidy for the poor for some foodstuffs especially atta, dal, onions, and coking oil we will be faced with IMF conditionalities about reducing budget deficits and existing subsidies. What from the help to the poor and the needy should take needs much deliberation?

At present, we do not even know for sure what is the classification of people in the society. Nor are we sure about the rate of inflation thanks to the misrepresentation of the figure of inflation by the government.

According to the sensitive price index released on 5th November there was a rise of 25 points from 186 to 211 in it during one year i.e. from 15th November, 1989 to 31st October, 1990. For all economists that is the rate of inflation for one year. The government talks only of year to year increase in the rate of inflation, which would work out only to 13.4 per cent. But year after year increase in rate of inflation is merely a tool of demand management. It does not reflect the erosion in the value of money experienced by the common man. How can such sharp price increase which seriously hurt the poor can be compensated? This world would need much deliberation.

Nawaz Sharif has shown great enterprise and foresight in declaring that he would rely on industrialisation, especially development of agro-based industry, to create more employment and production. For this reason all controls on industry are to be lifted. The President during his address to the opening session of the new Parliament elaborated on this plank of the new government policy. He said that barring defence related industries and heavy chemical all other sectors would be opened for the private entrepreneurs. Since the Prime Minister has also declared that all further industrialisation would be tax-free and foreign assistance would be without restriction one finds that the whole climate of production would undergo a change for the better.

With more jobs and better availability of goods the lot of the common man should improve. It may take time. But hope sustains and nourishes and when one sees a brighter future emerging one ceases to grumble.

That leads us to the question of financing the new revolutionary industrial policy. I would recommend that having withdrawal taxation from industry the classification of black money also should undergo a metamorphosis. All those who may have black money should be encouraged to invest freely in industry. They may, however, be asked. This freeing of our private sector with its latent dynamism from the shackles of bureaucracy would indeed usher in a new revolution.

Moreover, finances should be released through denationalisation and privatisation. At least a sum of Rs. 70 to 80 billion is presently tied up in inefficient industries which have become sinecures for political favourites and assorted hanger-son. A plan to transfer all such industries to the public and workers can be quickly prepared and may be implemented in the next 2 to 3 years if not earlier.[6]

A popularly-elected government in times of economic recession is virtually caught between the devil and the deep sea. On the one hand, it is forced by circumstances to adopt harsh economic measures which hurt the people and make their lives more difficult and, on the other, it has to constantly watch out for adverse popular reaction and will-nilly give concessions that would placate them. In case the scene of action is a Third World country and the economy has been held to ransom by international aid-giving agencies which is the general rule, the government has zero options unless it has the will and the capacity to mobilise the entire people for a gigantic rescue operation. The newly-elected government in Islamabad is confronted with a text-book scenario. The inevitable rise in oil prices, whether an offshot of Gulf crisis or a dikrat of IMF conditionalities, is bound to trigger off a price-hike over more menacing for the common man than it has been officially projected. And if stalemate on the suspension of US aid is not resolved in good time, the prospects for the economy would be good gloomier than even before.

The government has, no doubt, decided to take some steps aimed at giving relief to the consumer, nonetheless the surging rate of inflation can hardly be checked by piecemeal measures. The next logical development in a situation like the one emerging in the country would be an all-round clamour for wage raise and the industrial sector will be an all-round clamour for wage raise and the industrial sector will be most vulnerable to unrest. At a time when the government is contemplating large scale denationalisation to ensure higher growth rate, a measure which in the short-term is likely to increase unemployment, mass discontentment will thwart the chances of economic rejuvenation. Unfortunately, things have been happening too fast for the new government and it hardly had time to think of long-term policies. Nevertheless, sensing the gravity of the situation and the magnitude of the task ahead, the people at the helm of affairs have been talking about self-reliance. Rhetoric apart, if safeguarding national honour has any place in our scheme of things, the nation will sooner than later have to learn to cut its clothes according to the cloth. The path of self-reliance, however, entails colossal sacrifices and the tightening of belts will have to be shared by all and sundry, including the ones who have traditionally been considered more equal than others.[7]

A key structural weakness of Pakistan's economy is the low rate of domestic savings in proportion to the GDP. From 7.8 per cent of the GDP in 1977-79, it came down to 5.6 per cent during the next eight years, touching a low of 3.6 per cent in 1984-85, to pick up remarkably to 6.2 per cent in 1985 86. The federal budget for 1987-88 reported a further improvement to 9.4 per cent.

However, in addition to the concept of domestic savings in proportion to the GDP, there is also the concept of national savings as a proportion of the Gross National Product (GNP). The basic difference between the two concepts is that the computation of national savings includes thc whole of expatriate remittances. But calculations of the rate of domestic savings excludes these remittances. Such computation of national savings is basically incorrect.

The Pakistan Institute of Development Economics (PIDC) found some five year ago that 63 per cent of expatriate remittances. But calculations of the rate of domestic savings excludes these remittances. Such computation of national savings is basically incorrect.

Even with this doubtful methodology, Pakistan's savings rate is low,—the lowest amongst the developing countries as the accompanying chart proves.

Domestic savings as a proportion of GDP—1984

	percentage
Pakistan	4.2
Jndia	22.00
Sri Lanka	20.00
Kenya	20.00
Burma	17.00
Nepal	10.00
Bangladesh	4.00

An Asian Development Bank study in 1985 found the Pakistan's level of domestic savings was low because the rate of interest provided by the financial institutions was negative in relation to inflationary pressures. This incorrect because the Defence Savings Certificate fields 32 per cent and the Khas Deposit Certificates 15 per cent—which is appreciably higher than the inflation rate of 3.5 per cent while even saving's deposits in banks fetch 7 per cent to 7.5 per cent interest.

So the low level of savings in Pakistan is not so much economic as cultural. It flows from the social attitude of the people to the long-term interest of the economy.

Unless the current level of savings as stepped up significantly in the near future, a third of the investment needed would have to be through external borrowing, pushing the outstanding debt liability beyond reasonable limits.

Pakistan is already regarded a heavily indebted country with its total outstanding debt liability of $ 10.20 billion in 1985-86 which accounted for 30.08 per cent of its GNP. This rose to $ 11.7 billion by December 1986. Pakistan's debt servicing liabilities neutralised 34.50 per cent of its total export earnings in 1985-86 and 12 per cent of its total foreign exchange earnings. Some improvement is claimed in the total export earnings in 1986-87 but a fall in remittances from abroad might well push up the proportion of debt servicing liability in 1986-87.

Prescriptions suggested for raising the savings rate include discouragement of non-essential, conspicuous consumption and the promotion of the banking habit.

Pakistan's economy is likely to grow slower in the mid-term at below 5 per cent rate a year, internal and external economic imbalances, declining remittances slower increase in exports and restrictions imposed on the economy by the IMF and World Bank sponsored stabilisation programme are blamed for the slow down.

The impact of the Gulf crisis had further compounded the difficulties necessitating additional budget for imports rehabilitation of more than 100,00 Pakistanis returning form Kuwait.

While the sheer force of circumstances has pushed economic issues to the top of the newly-installed Pakistan Government's agenda, some difficulties are likely to be encountered in maintaining the political stability necessary for the fulfilment of these tasks.

On the economic front the Government has to tackle immediately the resource crunch and also achieve the long term objective of self-reliance so that the country is not subjected to periodic resource constraints and consequently political pressure would be from donors.

The most question however is whether the Federal Government would have the breathing space before simmering tensions in the provinces once again boil out of control.

In Punjab and the North West Frontier Province where the party ruling at the Centre, the Islami Jamhoori Ittehad (IJI) is in power on its own and in coalition with the Awami National Party respectively, the problems are of a relatively minor nature having more to do with disafection among elements within the IJI fold.

The other two provinces, where again IJI-led Governments are in power, the issues to be addressed are of a more serious nature. Swift and effective measures would have to be taken if the unresolved ethnic conflict in Sind is not once again to reach the levels witnessed before the ouster of Benazir Bhutto's Government.

Baluchistan threatens to reassume its mantle of a problem province. Here the Federal Government has to cope with the sullen bitterness of a former ally who has latched on to the demand for greater provincial autonomy as the medium through which he will express his resentment. Former Chief

Minister, Nawab Mohammed Akbar Khan Bugti apparently feels betrayed since its ally in the anti-PPP front before and during the elections. The IJI, did not fully back his bid for chief ministership.

Nawab Bugti's Jamhoori Watan Party (JWP) failed to obtain a majority on its own at the hustings and he could only have formed the Government if the IJI as a whole had supported him. Despite pressure from the central IJI leadership, a section of the provincial party led by Taj Mohammed Jamali joined with other parties, including former opponents the PPP (now in its new form as the Peoples Democratic Alliance) to form the Government.

Nawab Bugti who clearly feels that the IJI leadership was not tough enough on its provincial wing has not countenanced the IJI's argument that his inability to secure a majority was the primary factor which aborted his bid to form the Government.

As part of his efforts to apply pressures through the autonomy issue, Nawab Bugti, who was one of the four pillars of Baluch nationalism in bygone days has revealed a secret agreement he had struck with the IJI at the time they sponsored a no-confidence motion against the former PPP Government. Under the agreement the IJI had conceded Baluch demands for greater autonomy, enhanced development assistance and enlarged employment opportunities.

The IJI, especially Cabinet Minister, Shujaat Hussain who currently holds the Interior portfolio as an additional charge and who is the only IJI signatory to the agreement at present in power, has admitted the fact of the agreement and promised its due fulfilment.

But the JWP which regards the autonomy issue as a means to apply pressure, would at every stage seek to upstage the IJI's central leadership and Chief Minister Jamali who would have to move slowly in implementing the contentious proposals for autonomy. Jamali's position has been made more untenable due to the fact that his coalition Government consists of disparate elements bound together more out of hatred for Nawab Bugti than respect for the Chief Minister's personality.

The cabinet has representatives from the IJI, mainly the Muslim League, Pakistan National Party (PNP) and the PDA. Though the Baluch National Movement (BNM) and the Pakhtunkwa Milli Awami Party (PMAP) had supported Jamali's bid for the chief ministership they have not chosen to join the Government while the Jamaat Ulema-i-Islam led by Maulana Fazlur Rehaman is likely to be inducted soon.

Inherent contradictions between the centre-right IJI and the centre-left PNP, PMAP and BNM can become accentuated in the future if Pakhtun and Baluch ethnic interests pull in different directions.

The Baluchistan issue, in the forefront now, could be overtaken in the days to come if Sind Chief Minister Jam Sadiq Ali fails to deliver on his promise of ensuring peace within three months.

While the spate of dacoities and kidnappings continue unabated in rural Sind there has not so far been the recrudesence of ethnic strife which threatened to tear the province apart in the earlier months of the year.

But there is no guarantee that there will not be a virulent revival of Sindi nationalism focussed on the point that the Government in their province is in the hands of outsiders, meaning the Mohajir Quami Movement, and that the clutch of Sindi feudal lords who have been contributed by the Jam to the coalition are merely the MQM's agents.

Sindi nationalist parties are already speaking out against

the coalition and their activities could get a boost and take a dangerous turn if the only party with a base in the interior of the province, the PPP implicitly throws its weight behind them. Such covert support would be forthcoming if the PPP continues to believe that the Provincial Government is following a repressive policy towards them and more so if some action were to be taken against Ms. Bhutto.

The Army which views the situation in Sind with great concern, and which had asked for special powers from the former PPP Covernment, would be looking to the Jam to sort out matters expeditiously.

The Chief Minister is reputed to be gifted with considerable acumen and if he failed to match up to the demands, the Army might have to step in, a development which could well worsen the situation.

Jam Sadiq Ali's difficulties would be considerably more if the conflicts within the Sind IJI, slowly surfacing now, become sharper. Ghulam Mustafa Jatoi and Mohammad Khan Junejo, both former Prime Ministers and veteran Sindi politicians have expressed resentment at the fact of a Punjabi becoming the Prime Minister and misgivings about a situation in Sind.

Besides these two stalwarts Jam Sadiq Ali might also have to confront the ripples let loose by the MQM's attempts to convert itself into the "Muttahida" (United) Quami Movement. In its yet to be assumed from the MQM would seek to project itself as the party of the "downtrodden" and not merely as that of the Urdu-speaking immigrants from India.

Its appeal in particular would be directed towards the rural labouring classes, the "Har is" with a view to roping them into a common front against Sindi feudals. Such attempts are hardly likely to be appreciated by the feudals who have backed Jam Sadiq Ali.

The problems in Punjab and the frontier are minor when compared with those in Sind and Baluchistan. In the frontier the Muslim League's close ties with the Awami National Party (ANP) have annoyed the Leagues partner in the IJI, the Jamaat Islami.

The Jamaat which feels it has not been given its due has gone against the rest of the IJI by putting up a candidate against the ANP in the elections to the Senate which are to take place soon.

In the Centre as well, the Jamaat which desired the foreign affairs and information portfolios has begun a campaign against some of the appointments made, especially that of Sahabzada Yaqub Khan. All in all the IJI's leadership has enough worries on the political front to make its task in the economic field that much harder.

Now that Nawaz Sharif has taken oath as the Prime Minister we must wait, with crossed fingers, for the ultimate outcome. Most have a feeling that he will prove to be the one Pakistan has been longing for, even those strongly opposed to him are reconsidering their opposition.

He is the only leader who has been urging quick and inexpensive justice, the basic requirement of any developing country. This is one of the most effective ways people can fight for their rights and expose the wrongs. Justice in Pakistan at the moment is not in the most ideal form, a simple case can take the better part of a year, if not more and therefore people are almost invariably compelled to conclude that the courtroom is best avoided, and that taking law into their own hands is the only alternative.

He does not come from a feudal background and being

a successful businessman himself he can understand the economic factors which cause disturbances in the market, the price-hike will have a considerable Impact on him too. A business-minded leader is what Pakistan needs in this period of economic changes taking place so rapidly. He stresses the importance of saving and that wastage, of whatever it may be, is to be regarded no less than a criminal offence.

It is somewhat safe to say that if bats well, then not only is he the Man-of-the match but could be easily nominated for the Man-of-the-match but could be easily nominated for the Man-of-the-series award.[8]

References

1. *The Business & Political Observer*, 4 December, 1990, p. 7.
2. *Ibid.*
3. M. Hasan, Economic Miracle, *Dawn*, 17 November, 1990.
4. *Ibid.*
5. *Ibid.*
6. *Ibid.*
7. *The Nation*, 17 November, 1990.
8. Mohammed Ali, Tasks Ahead, *The Nation*, (Lahore), 16, November, 1990.

19

Overcoming Hardships—Financial Reforms

Prime Minister Nawaz Sharif has said that his government would not accept foreign aid with strings. Pakistan, like many other developing countries, has been relying on foreign assistance to supplement national savings for financing development. In order to bridge the resource gap it started foreign borrowings as early as the 1950s. Pakistan has been receiving aid from three main sources : consortium, non-consortium and Islamic countries. The consortium is the single largest source which provides 82 per cent of the total gross inflow. The remaining 18 per cent, including 4 per cent relief assistance for Afghan refugees, is shared both by the non-consortium and Islamic countries. By the end of June, 1990 the total external indebtedness of Pakistan stood at 21.56 billion dollars, out of which the disbursed amount was 14.18 billion dollars.

A marked shift in foreign aid composition has taken place from grant and grant assistance to loans repayable in foreign currency with increasingly strict terms and conditions. The share of grant and grant-like assistance in total commitments was 80 per cent in the First Plan which has declined to only 18 per cent in 1988-89 and is estimated to go down to only 15 per cent in 1989-90. Continued reliance on external borrowings has led to enhanced debt servicing liability thereby reducing the net transfer of capital. In 1989-90 it is estimated that the net transfer would be only 39 per cent of the gross disbursement. This is due to misuse of past borrowings, forcing us to into additional loans just to service the old loans. It reflects the extent of economic mismanagement indulged in by the past regimes. Now if we want to maintain our economic independence as a respectable nation we should endeavour to get out of the debt trap by reducing our reliance on foreign assistance. As borrowers cannot be choosers, we should make an all-out effort to achieve the goal of self-reliance. This demands not only structural changes in our economy to increase the volume of revenue, but to practise austerity at all levels. Exports should be maximised and imports reduced considerably. This is the only way to avoid resort to foreign aid.[1]

On November 1, 1990 an instalment of $ 300 million was due for repayment to the IMF. But Pakistan had only $ 150 million in foreign exchange reserve on October 31. The instalment could not be paid. The Pakistan-aid consortium meeting for pledging aid to Pakistan was due to be held in mid-November. This has not been held so far. The IMF standby credit of $ 244 million was withheld because Pakistan failed to observe the condition that it must cut its budget deficit to 6.5 per cent of the GDP. The IMF told the caretaker government that the Fund's estimates showed the deficit to be 8 per cent of previously committed aid is in the pipeline. But if the government defaults in repayment of due debt instalments, the pipeline could be turned off immediately. There is a real danger of this happening because repayments due this year are $ 1.5 billion which Pakistan is in no position to pay unless it receives fresh foreign assistance of $ 2 billion. The country is in such a tight debt trap that it has to repay Rs. 90 out of every Rs. 100 loan it receives in foreign aid. The IMF has intimated that it would give further balance of payments support to Pakistan only if the country agreed to put up its petroleum prices by 41 per cent and of fertilizers, wheat, and some other goods by 10 to 20 per cent. The new government has raised petroleum prices by 41.5 per cent which has caused a great deal of public resentment. An IMF team is currently in Islamabad discussing the resumption of assistance to the country. The new government of Nawaz Sharif is finding it extremely difficult to meet all the conditions the IMF has laid down.[2]

The good news from Pakistan is that the minimum wages of workers have been fixed at Rs. 3,000 a month and the salaries of Government servants have peen enhanced. The bad news is that the prices of petroleum and its products have been raised by 41 per cent. And, on the political front too, all is not well.

New Prime Minister Nawaz Sharif had complained that the predecessor (Government of Benazir Bhutto) had "looted" the coffers of the country. However, he is still carrying on the administration under the budget passed by the National Assembly under the leadership of Benazir Bhutto. The question is : if the previous Government had "looted" the treasury, how is Nawaz Sharif going to pay the enhanced salaries to the Government servants? In a commentary on the economic situation of the country, *Radio Pakistan* said the return on a massive number of expatriates from the Gulf countries had adversely affected the economy and the suspension of economic and military aid from the United States had worsened the situation. It quoted the Prime Minister as saying that his Government had decided not to bow before any pressure (obviously of the United States and the World Bank) from abroad in the interests of the country and had adopted the policy of "self-reliance". Very brave words, indeed. But his finance Minister Sartaj Aziz, a representative of the military bosses had a different story to tell the same day. He said the Gulf crisis and the suspension of US aid had not seriously affected the country's economy. He too said that Pakistan would not barter its "Khudmukhtari" (automony) to get US air. "Autonomy" and not "freedom" of Pakistan, where United States is concerned.[3]

Giving details of the situation, the Finance Minister said that the 573 million dollar economic and military aid has been suspended because President Bush had not certified that Pakistan did not possess nuclear weapons. About 85,000 expatriates working in Kuwait had come back of the trade, with Iraq had been suspended under the embargo imposed by the UN Security Council, he added. These two factors he said, had depleted the country's income by 1.5 billion dollars. The Gulf crisis had increased the import bill of petroleum and petroleum products by 100 million dollars a month and the foreign exchange reserves had depleted to a bare 200 million dollars, the Finance Minister said and expressed the hope that these reserves would touch the 450 million dollar mark the next two months if 250 million dollars worth of loans could be obtained. The radio commentary said Pakistan was getting 500 million dollars in aid from the Western countries and was paying 1.7 billion dollars in debt servicing. It is estimated that the debt serving charges come to about 30 per cent, which is very high by any standards. Meanwhile, Radio Pakistan also said a committee of the Security Council has recommended that 18 countries, worst hit by the Gulf crisis and trade embargo on Iraq, should be given aid and Pakistan has had asked for a loan of two billion dollars. Pakistan's external debt was 17.2 billion in 1987, and the inflation rate in Pakistan has gone up 15 per cent now. Despite the brave words of Prime Minister Nawaz Sharif that his Government would not cow down to pressure from abroad, it is obvious that Pakistan is trying to fall in line with the conditionalities of the IMF World Bank. A Pakistani executive vice-president for operations of the World Bank, Moeen Qureshi wrote in an Islamabad magazine on December 21 last that Pakistan should shift economic and social management away from the state to the private sector. Otherwise, he warned, Pakistan would be in a deep economic crisis because its exports had lagged, the balance of payments was severely strained and the Gulf crisis had aggravated the economic problems. Within a week, Finance Minister Sartaj Aziz announced the Government's intentention to abolish exchange controls and slash tariffs on imports as part of a radical economic reform programme, which he described as a "calculated risk". This liberalization and privatization policy might help Pakistan get some loans from the World Bank. This also shows that Sharif's Government has buckled down under pressure from the International Monetary Fund (IMF). *Radio Pakistan* quoted Sharif as saying that the purpose of the "denationalization" of Government-owned banks and other corporations was to provide employment to the unemployed and that it was not intended to dole out favours to any particular section of the people. He said the nationalisation policy had adversely affected the country's economy and had taken it back by at least two decades. But the employees of the six state-owned banks and three trading corporations are opposing the privatization move. Earlier in 1990, too, they had prevented the Benazir Government from privatizing the Muslim Commercial Bank (MCB) and they are up in arms once again to prevent denationalization.

Other press reports say that the "De-regulation Committee" recently formed by the Nawaz Sharif government had recommended the immediate dismantling of the Trading Corporation of Pakistan (TCP), Cotton Export Corporation of Pakistan (RCEP) and the Rice Export Corporation of Pakistan (RECP). The TCP was formed in 1967 (during Gen Ayub Khan's dictatorship) while the other two corporations were set up by executed Prime Minister Zulfikar Ali Bhutto, a socialist, who wanted to regulate the export trade of the country and bring thn profits earned in the international markets to the doorsteps of Pakisan, eliminating the middle man. But now Nawaz Sharif wants the middlemen to rule the roost by dismantling the corporations. The ruse was clevery manipulated. One of the charges against former Prime Minister Benazir Bhutto in the nine references now being heard in various special courts in Karachi and Lahore, is that her government had sold accumulated stocks of cotton at a lower price resulting in a loss to the country. Nawaz Sharif is not cutting the nose to spite the face by dismantling the corporations themselves. And he is not doing this as a free agent. He is doing it under pressure from the World Bank. So much for his brave words that he was not going to bow down before the pressures from abroad.[4]

Coming to the claim that denationalization was intended to provide employment to the unemployed, the logic itself is perverted, if not ridiculous. Denationalization means that the shares which the government now holds would be sold to the public. Benazir's government had at least promised that the shares of the institutions to be denationalized would be sold to their employees. No such precautions would be taken by the Sharif government. Private parties would be allowed to buy the shares. The transfer of shares from the government to the private parties does not generate employment opportunities. Under these circumstances, the only conclusion one can draw is that either Nawaz Sharif does not know what he is talking about or he is deliberately trying to fool his own people. In the political field, the Shariat Bill is again not news. It has been introduced in the Senate, the Upper House of Pakistan Parliament, by a private member. The Islami Jamhoori Ittehad (IJI) came to power on a promise of Islamizing the country. One of the charges against Benazir's government was that it had failed to do that. In fact, when the Senate had passed the Shariat Bill in early 1990. Benazir was quoted as having said that Islamic punishments were inhuman. Some ulemas (Muslim religious scholars) even went to the court seeking her disqualification on that count and others said she was a "Kafir" (infidel). She had said at the time that she would go to the National Assembly Lower House of Parliament with a comprehensive Shariat Bill. The current Islamization campaign is now in its 13th year. It started when the USA decided to do away with Zulfikar Ali Bhutto in 1977. The anti-Bhutto conglomerate, the Pakistan National Alliance (PNA) started a campaign against the alleged rigging of March 1977 elections, but when it found that adequate popular support was not forthcoming, it switched over to the demand for "Nizam-e-Mustafa".

When this religious demand created the requisite quantum of frezy among the people, Gen Ziaul Haq, who claimed to be the "Soldier of Islam", stepped in to overthrow Bhutto. He did not think of Islamizing till Bhutto was executed. His Islamic punishments Ordinance made Islam a laughing stock of the world.

Gen Zia's next instalment of Islamization came when he decided to discredit, disgrace and dismiss his hand-picket Prime Minister Mohammad Khan Junejo in 1988. A couple of weeks after the dismissal, he issued the Shariat Ordinance which lapsed after his death in August that year because the National Assembly, which had to ratify it, was not in existence.

Gen Zia's successor in office, President Ghulam Ishaq Khan, re-issued the Shariat Ordinance with some amendments a little before the 1988 elections which swept Benazir Bhutto to power. This National Assembly too did not ratify the Shariat Ordinance issued by Ishaq Khan. Efforts were made to dislodge Benazir Bhutto through various means, including a no-trust move. They, however, proved to be abortive.

Finally, the Senate which had an overwhelming IJI majority and a nominal Pakistan People's Party (PPP) presence, was persuaded by the establishment to pass the Shariat Bill. The Bill as passed by the Senate had to come before the National Assembly in its session beginning on August eight, 1990. But President Ghulam Ishaq Khan dissolved the Assembly on August 6, 1990 and dismissed Benazir government. One of the charges against Banazir was that her government had failed to take Islamization measures. To show his own zeal for Islamization, Ishaq issued the Qisas and Diyat (flood money for loss of life) Ordinance (Q & D Ordinance). It came into force on October 3, the birthday or the holiday Prophet of Islam (Eid-e-Milad-un-Nabi). This Ordinance replaces the relevant provisions of the Indian Penal Code (IPC), compiled by Lord Macaulay in 1860. (The IPC was adopted by Pakistan in 1947 as Pakistan Penal Code).[5]

Pakistan's pro-IJI Urdu daily *Nawa-I-Waqt* quoted experts of the caretaker Government of Ghulam Mustafa Jatoi as saying that the decision to bring the country's penal laws within the parameters of Islamic jurisprudence was taken on July 5, 1989. The paper does not say who took the decision but blames the Benazir Government for not enforcing it on March 22, 1990, according to schedule. The paper, however, quoted the Federal Shariat Court as directing the caretaker Government of Jatoi to immediately take measures to expedite the enforcement of Islamic laws. Exactly a week after dismissing Benazir, President Ishaq Khan issued the Q & D Ordinance on August 14. Another Ordinance was issued on September 5, 1990, while the election process was on, to fix the date of endorsement of the Q & D Ordinance on October 3. However, it is interesting to note that the Federal Shariat Court had come to the conclusion as early as in 1980 that Macaulay's IPC, which, as stated earlier, Pakistan had adopted as its own penal code in 1947, was violative of the Islamic tenets. But the Federal Government of Gen Mohammad Zia-ul-Haq, "the soldier of Islam", went in appeal against the Shariat Court's judgement. Now again the Senate has taken up the Shariat Bill. Was it because the right wing of religious leaders in the Senate were in too much of a hurry to Islamize Pakistan? Or was it because the Islami Jamhoori Ittehad combine in the National Assembly had cold-shouldered the Shariat Bill? Why did the Sharif Government not come up with its own Shariat Bill in the National Assembly in pursuance of its own election manifesto? There are no clear cut answers to the question. But, it is said that the Sharif Government would come up with its own bill later on. Keen observers of the 13-year history of Islamization in Pakistan say that the Islamization hullabaloo is a non-issue. Every Muslim submits himself to the Shariat laws. Even in Pakistan there is no intention or indication that the non Muslims would be subjected to the Islamic laws. All this is an exercise in futility, observers say. The vested interests, namely, the military bosses, the civil bureaucracy, the feudals and now the industrialists, have always exploited the name of Islam for their own ends. The observers point out to a custom in Pakistani Punjab under which women are denied their Quranic share in the landed property of a deceased head of household. They ask why landed property is not partitioned in accordance with the Quaranic injunctions. Why are women denied their share by the Islamization zealots? Under the Q & D Ordinance, the relatives of each of the persons who die in road accidents are to be paid Rs. 1,75,000 as blood money. The drivers and the owners of vehicles protested against this. The minister clarified that the money could be paid by insurance companies. Islam ordains the payment of blood money by the murderer as a deterrent punishment. The legal representative of the deceased could even demand that the killer be put to death. This is to deter the killer from taking a human life, intentionally or unintentionally. But if an insurance company were to pay the blood money the element of deterrence would be eliminated from the penal fine. This goes to show that the Pakistani rulers are trying to somehow show that they are keen about implementing the Islamic formalities and give no importance to the substance of Islamic laws. As for the Shariat Bill now before the Senate, former Prime Minister Benazir Bhutto has said that it would divide the people on sectarian grounds. This is because the four schools of Sunni Fiqh (jurisprudence) is different from the Fiqh-e-Jafaria, followed by the Shias. The Shias form about 30 per cent of the Pakistani population and they would oppose it. Besides, the Sunnies are demanding that Pakistan should be declared a Sunni state and that the Shias in Pakistan should be subjected to all those disabilities suffered by Sunnies in Iran. The followers of the four schools of Sunni Fiqh and the Whabis are bitterly opposed to each other. It is, therefore, feared that the enforcement of the Shariat Bill would open a pandora's box.[6]

Pakistan's business community has welcomed in early December 1990 government announcement that at least one state-owned bank, the Muslim Commercial Bank, and half the telecommunications business it to be privatised. Pakistani and foreign banks will also be allowed to open new commercial banks.

But promises of financial reform appeared hazy, and even the government's supporters among the business community suggested it was moving too cautiously. Critics say the new government of Prime Minister Nawaz Sharif appears to lack a coherent plant for rehabilitating an economy stumbling towards one of its severest crisis. On taking office, Nawaz Sharif, one of the country's top industrialist, announced his prescription for the economy : rapid, large-scale industrialisation. But he has not specified how this is to be financed. The private sector does not have any foreign reserves for buying foreign capital goods; these must be provided by the government under the regime of rigid foreign-exchange controls, which are to remain in place. In reducing unproductive expenditure, the Prime Minister has laid off about 30,000 civil servants recruited under the previous government and has imposed a three month moratorium on recruitment. A committee has been appointed to find ways to end dependence upon foreign loans. But to some economists, this is just tinkering around the margins while the country continues to live beyond its means on expensive short-term credit from foreign banks, with the rice crop used as collateral. The government's blithe assurances that the worst is over are not believed. To be fair, the Gulf crisis has further knocked the stuffing out an economy that was such in the first place. In September, Islamabad submitted an aid-memoire to its Paris Club of aid donors in which it estimated that the loss of Kuwait as an export market, the soaring cost of oil and the drop in home remittance would increase the current-account deficit by US $ 849 million to US $ 2.18 million for the fiscal year ending June 1991.[7] The economic crisis comes at a time of estrangement from Washington, the country's principal aid donor. The US Congress cannot approve annual aid without the US President certifying that a country neither possesses, nor is developing nuclear weapons. This year, the President has not issued such a certificate for Pakistan.

As a result, US military supplies to Pakistan have been halted, as has military and economic assistance totalling US $ 600 million. Additionally, some congressional leaders and aides have stated that Pakistan will have to choose between US aid and continuance of its nuclear programme.

Pakistani officials assert that there is no immediate aid crisis since about US $ 10 billion pledged by various donors is in the pipeline and could be halted only if Pakistan defaulted on repayment of interests and loans. It has not defaulted and is unlikely to do so in the immediate future. Other members of a World Bank aid consortium are currently releasing pledged loans worth an aggregate of US $ 3.2 billion. Islamabad's real fear is that a consortium meeting scheduled for April 1991, donors will take their lead from Washington and from a critical IMF and World Bank. Both agencies are unhappy with Pakistan's management of its economy, particularly the size of the military budget, which accounts for 39.1 per cent of total expenditure. Debt servicing, the biggest single drain on the ex-chequer, seaks up for 42.3 per cent of revenues. Until 1985, Pakistan's annual debt liability did not exceed US $ 500 million; it is expected to be about US $ 3.2 billion during current fiscal year, largely due to military purchases abroad on deferred payment. Not a single development project in Pakistan is financed domestically. Called in to help in 1988, the IMF agreed to extend a standby loan and a special-adjustment facility in three annual instalments upto 1991. Two tranches for the current fiscal year totalling US $ 244 million have yet to be released. An IMF technical team arrived in Islamabad on 30 November to assess Pakistan's economic progress. The IMF is impatient with Pakistan for its failure to observe the basic conditions of its loan, especially the stipulated reduction of the fiscal deficit to 6.4 per cent of GDP in fiscal year 1989 and 5 per in fiscal year

1990. Nor is it convinced that domestic credit expansion has been sufficiently curtailed.[8]

As part of the effort to overcome the shortage in domestic resources the government is to raise Rs. 12 billion (US $ 550 million) by widening the tax base. For electoral reasons, rises in the retail cost of petroleum products were delayed until after the 24 October polls. The knock-on effects of a belated 41.5 per cent rise in oil products and 40 per cent on fertilisers have yet to be quantified.

References

1. *Pakistan Times*, 13 November, 1990.
2. B.M. Bhatia, Pakistan, *The Hindustan Times*, 26 December, 1990.
3. Syed Ziaullah, Nawaz Sharif Buckles under IMF Pressure, *Link*, 6 January, 1991.
4. *Ibid.*
5. *Ibid.*
6. *Ibid.*
7. *Far Eastern Economic Review*, 13 December, 1990.
8. *Ibid.*

20

Business—Bureaucracy Nexus

Nawaz Sharif's ascendancy in Pakistan's politics has been generally viewed by observers as the emergence of a strongman from the heartland who has, for a variety of reasons, acquired sufficient clout to be able to override the claims of leaders from peripheral areas. Though he is the third Punjabi Prime Minister in the history of the country, the other two preceding him probably would not have stood the test of popular verdict if elections had been the order of the day. It may not, thus, be incorrect to describe him as the first authentic leader from Punjab since independence. And his elevation to the high office has for the first time accorded legitimacy to Punjab's leading role in the power-structure, hitherto articulated through the civil-military bureaucratic complex. Popular mandate, however, is not the only trait that distinguishes Mian Nawaz Sharif from other Punjabi strongmen at the helm of affairs prior to him, such as, Ghulam Mohammad (Governor General, 1951-56) and General Ziaul Haq (President 1977-88).[1]

Nawaz Sharif has reached the top via provincial politics, at one stage projecting himself as the spokesman of 'Punjab' and 'Punjab rights' and thus deviating from the plank of 'strong Centre' traditionally adopted by politicians from Punjab. Though his stance was basically a compulsion of the circumstances in which he was placed as a provincial Chief Minister in defiance of the Centre, he has, as a policy, opted for seeking alliances with 'regionalist' parties from smaller provinces, hitherto seen as 'anti-national' in the Punjabi heartland. To an extent the PPP was itself to blame for alienating potential allies and the ANP, the MQM and the JWP were amenable to joining hands with the IJI, nonetheless, the successful wooing of parties known for their anti-Punjabi bias has been a singular achievement for a Punjabi politican. And Nawaz Shrif's two-fold strategy of winning support in his own province as 'son of the soil vs outsider' and seeking allies in other pravinces as co-sharers of power has been the mainstay of his bid for power. It was in line with his scheme of things that he did not yield to the Jama'at-e-Islami pressure to dump the ANP and the MQM after having won a comfortable majority.

Nawaz Sharif's rise to power has also been interpreted by some Marxist-oriented intellectuals as a political manifestation of the growing economic power of the bourgeoisie and a prelude to its triumph over the feudals. There is no denying the fact that the new Prime Minister does not belong to the country's traditional ruling class and his urban background and business interests make him think and behave differently from a politician reared in the classical feudal tradition. The recent elections have also brought to the force the power money has assumed in the country's politics and how it is threatening to overtake conventional factors like 'the family, biradari, feudal authority, etc., as the crucial variable for political success. That the phenomenon is not entirely to the liking of the gentlemen of the landed aristocracy was vividly brought home by Pir Pagara's cynical remark that "we cannot have a businessman as Prime Minister."

Nonetheless it does not seem to have caused an alarm in the feudal ranks since sharing power with the representative, of big business is not a new experience for them. While the landlords has won elections and dominated the Assemblies, the bureaucracy which was not only the most constant component of the power structure but had also wielded immense influence in decision-making was the patron saint of the business class and largely instrumental for whatever industrial development took place in the country. The Ayub era was the golden period of capital formation, which under the stewardship of civil-military bureaucracy witnessed the emergence of 22 families and its fall-out on national politics. The Zia years though not successful in giving the business class the sense of security it needed to enhance the rate of investment. were basically a follow-up of the Ayub era and the establishment was by no means an organ of feudal power.[2]

The business-bureaucracy (civil and military) nexus has been a fait occompli and the feudals have learnt to live with it since the coalition did not theaten their economic interests. There is enough evidence to suggest that the business class had always felt more at home under authoritarian regimes and its interest articulation was facilitated by the absence of feudal dominated Assemblies. However, Nawaz Sharif success story as a popular leader signifies the growing self-assurance of the entrepreneurial class and their readiness to accept the challenge of open competitive politics, albeit it does not imply that the feudals have been, as a class, displaced from their position politiacl eminence. The new Assemblies are still packed with famous surnames of the rural gentry cutting across party and regional divisions. And though they may have taken a back seat by accepting a nouveaurich as Prime Minister, they are yet strong enough to forestall any change that hurts them economically or disturbs the status quo in rural society. Regardless of what Altaf Hussian may have to say about taking agricultural income instead of raising the oil prices, the prospects of the IJI government accepting his advice and adopting an explicitly anti-feudal policy perspective is as remote as it has always been.

The economic decision-making process in Pakistan

has been much under the influence of Pakistan's history. "including the legacies of the traditional societies of the region and of the Muslim strand of the South Asian policy, are modern intellectual and religious movements, growing numbers of urban workers in non-traditional jobs, rising industrialists and other elements". They all have different aims and fears and the process of policy-making rivals around them.[3] The Government of Pakistan has failed to check their growing demands and the ways and means they adopted to achieve their objectives.

The interests of varying power and influence bring pressure to bear upon the governmental institutions which formulate the economic strategy of Pakistan. They include ministries and agencies of the central administration and the executive office of the head of State. Various national representative assemblies have had a range of roles from "rubber stamp" to moderately meaningful. Domestic economic policies and foreign economic policies including export policy reflect at any one time the divergent skills and strength of interest groups.[4]

In planning her development the policy of Pakistan was based upon since its emergence on prcatical needs than upon any theoretical formulations, i.e. capitalism or socialism. She happily received foreign economic assistance and technical knowhow. She cannot see any theoretical rigid demarcation line between the public and private sectors of national development.[5]

The political behaviour of Pakistan over the years is another aspect which has a direct impact on the decision-makers of economic policy. The stability of a particular political set up and its continuity is needed for the overall development of economy. A number of ups and downs are visible as far as the political behaviour of Pakistan is concerned. The following are the main features of its political behaviour which from the very beginning served as one of the determinant of Pakistan's economic and foreign policy.[6] They are:

1. "The State of Pakistan was created more through subjective mediation of the colonialists than through objective realization of the masses.

2. The 'Vice-regal disdain' of the founding father of Pakistan who was also the first administrative head is clearly reflected in his frequent dismissals of provincial chief ministers and ministers.

3. Rash bureaucratic behaviour of subsequent Governor-Generals who not only dissolves the Constituent Assembly but the Central Cabinet twice (Nazimuddin and Suhrawardy) not to speak of the irresponsible conduct of the elected ministers.

4. While a much awainted opportunity for civilian politics was presented by the 1956 Constitution, the party floated by the last Governor-General Mirza chose to distabilize both the coalition governments of which it was a partner, till it become the dominant partner in the third and the last civilian government which was overthrown by Ayub. It is characteristic reflection of ongoing statist authoritarianism that the Prime Minister, Feroz Khan Noon openly declared his government as 'one of landlords and not of city dwellers'.

5. Military directly captured state power in 1958 but before that it was no less influential. Ever since Nazimuddin's dimissal from the Centre (1953), the army was always taken into consideration on important Civilian matters, this process culminating in the induction of two army officers (Ayub and Mirza) who not only (recommended) dissolution of the Constituent Assembly but came to form the ministry immediately thereafter.

6. Above all, there were seven Prime Ministers who changed power during the first decade of civilian statist rule, the last there during the last two years of constitutional operation. Political opposition to the ruling Muslim League was declared a treason.... From Liaquat's PRODA through Ayub's EBDO to Zia's Disqualification Tribunals is a continuous chain of authoritarian links which never permitted any political opposition to emerge in any form whatsoever."[7]

The economy of Pakistan so far is not fully developed and the Government from time to time initiated a number of measures to strengthen it. In 1972, Z.A. Bhutto Government nationalized the industry in the hope of giving a new direction to the Pakistatn economic set up. But later on it was realized that to implement the decision was very difficult and the Government was compelled to change the policy. Both public and private sectors are in existence in Pakistan. The financial policy planners are more or less flexible in their attitude as is evident from the existence of large number of multinationals hopefully enjoying the patronage of the Pakistan Government.

The shape of Pakistan's economy is determined by agriculture which has been adopted by the number of people living in the rural areas. More than half of the labour force is associated with the agriculture. Wheat, rice, sugar cane and cotton are the main crops.

Pakistan is having large range of minerals, but this sector, is not fully developed in Pakistan. Almost fifty per cent export earnings are from rice and cotton. Growth in G.N.P. averaged 7.4 per cent annually from 1977-78 to 1979-80, compared with an average annual growth rate of 3.4 per cent in 1971-77. During 1979 movement towards an "Islamic Economy" was announced.[8]

At the time of partition, there were very few organized

industries in Pakistan. The Government of Pakistan paid from the very beginning active attention to industrialization and every effort was made to strengthen the country's industrial base, To provide basic amenities and facilities to the industrialists in Pakistan was the basic aim of the Government. But because of unforeseen reasons and shyness of the private enterprise and technological difficulties, the process of development was not quite up to the mark in the beginning. In the first three years very few units were commissioned. Even up to 1952, the pace of industrialization was extremely low. But after that considerable growth in industrialization was registered when the Government of Pakistan established the Pakistan Industrial Development Corporation and initiated improvements in basic facilities and liberal tax concessions.

Of the total 14,569 industrial establishments in the British India in 1947, only 1,406 industrial units were situated in the area allotted to Pakistan. The lack of manufacturing capacity was highlighted by the fact that while the population in areas forming Pakistan was about 20 per cent of undivided India, the manufacturing capacity (1,406 units) located in Pakistan was barely ten per cent. Another major factor which made the situation more worse was that Pakistan lacked all sorts of industrial credit facilities; technical and technological institutions and research laboratories. The Government of Pakistan was naturally worried and in order to achieve a reasonable measure of economic security, framed a new industrial policy. According to the new policy, the Government was entitled to own and operate exclusively the following industries :

1. Manufacture of arms and ammunition for war.
2. Generation of hydro-electric power.
3. Manufacture of railway wagons, telephones, telegraphs and wireless apparatus.[9]

In Pakistan, transnational corporations (TNCs) have the

Table 1

Index of Industrial Production

Year	*Mining*	*Manufacturing*	*Industrial Production, Mining and Manufacturing*
1950	66.7	27.7	39.5
1951	72.4	46.6	48.2
1952	89.1	58.6	60.5
1953	99.5	76.3	77.7
1954	100.0	100.0	100.0
1955	105.9	126.9	125.6
1956	123.3	143.9	142.6
1957	128.6	152.4	150.9
1958	146.3	162.4	161.4
1959	151.9	181.9	180.1
1960	178.9	192.4	191.6
1961	193.8	203.1	202.5
(Jan. to March)			
1961	198.2	204.9	204.5
(Jan. to June)			

Sourecs : *Pakistan Basic Facts*, 1961.

red carpet rolled out for them. So much so in the last four years that they can hope to take away as profits what they have invested as capital. The total fixed assets of the TNCs in the manufacturing sector in 1981-82 was Rs. 3,683 million while the capital employed was Rs. 3,962 million. But the repatriations during this period exceeded total investments.

In Pakistan, the total TNCs share in the manufacturing sector is about 22 per cent and their share in the GNP is 3.6 per cent. Direct foreign investment has not risen significantly since 1981-82. But repatriation has been rising gradually, by 38 per cent between 1981-82 to 1984-85 in value terms from $84.84 million to $117.45 million. Remittance of profit rose from $8.92 million to $18.83 million, royalties from 1.74 million to $2.09 million and technical fees from $48.49 million to 49.79 million.

However, these figures could be misleading because the TNCs have managed to show profits to be lower than what they are. This is done through massive transfer pricing and heavy expenses on their executives. Further, TNCs have been invited to operate even in areas where they are not needed and without a guarantee of transfer of technology.

It is not really unexpected that the controversial People's Work Programme launched by the Benazir Bhutto government has been discontinued since August 1990. Given the fact that from the start the general impression was that the PWP was essentially designed to boost the political image of the then ruling party, it was almost inevitable that it would be scrapped with the ouster of its sponsors from power. And so it was. But this by means justifies the arbitrary decision of the caretakers. For irrespective of the criticism of its management and implementation' the PWP had some merits as well. It had a basic-need orientation, with its emphasis on the provision of potable water, health care, primary education and a communication network. Some of the projects undertaken were of definite value to the people of the areas where these were located. Since they were concentrated mainly in the rural areas which are the most disadvantaged and poverty-stricken, the PWP did promise a degree of betterment where none existed.

The problem with the scheme was that it had a basic structural weakness in terms of its abministration. The people's Patty MNAs, MPAs and activists were to administer it. This obviously made it a convenient political tool in the hands of the ruling party. With the programme so politicised, it became intensely controversial. The two provinces, where the PPP was not in power, namely, Punjab and Balochistan, reacted strongly and resisted the PWP tooth and nail. So much so that instances of projects being attacked and dismantled a'so reported. But this does not mean that the entire programme was ill conceived and worthless, although a more judicious pattern for its planning and implementation could have been envisaged.

It would make better sense if the government were to reorganise the structure of the PWP so that it is planned and implemented by the local bodies. It is axiomatic that a development process can only be meaningful if it is par icipatory as well. This means that the people for whom a project is meant should be involved in its planning and implementation at every stage. This is possible if the development programme is carried out at the grassroots level through elected local bodies. Mercifully, the government has decided not to discontinue the on-going schemes. Each of these will be scrutinised and it will be decided on the merit of each case whether it should be completed or not. The same criterion should have been applied to all the projects that had been planned. The fact of the matter is that the resources are so limited and the claimants so many that those who control the purse strings want to use development funds to benefit their own constituents. This is not a sound approach. The government should take a non-partisan view of development planning. Economic rather than political yardsticks should determine official priorities, Junejo's five-point programme and Nawaz Sharif's Tamir-i-Watan programme sought political dividends for their initiators in addition to economic benefits for the people. Hence the five-point programme met the same fate as the PWP when Junejo was dismissed, If the age of democracy has really dawned in Pakistan, we should be prepared for periodic changes of governments. If every new government makes it a practice to dismantle the economic and development processes initiated by its predecessor. there would be no continuity of progress and the country and its people would be the ultimate losers. Good sense demands a clear break with this unhealthy tradition.[10]

Prime Minister, Nawaz Sharif is unlikely to face many problems from the opposition. This is in contrast to the turbulent state of affairs which the erstwhile regime had to face in Pakistan. As compared to the 1988-90 period, when the PPP headed the federal government, the provincial administrations were run by the opposition parties except in Sindh. In the present scenario, in contrast, the IJI represents all the provincial governmants. Under the present dispensation, there is hardly likely to be any oppprtunity of confrontation between the federal government and the provincial government.

In the Pakistani context, the President and the armed forces constitute the real centres of power. There is good rapport between the present Prime Minister and the armed forces Chief General Mirza Aslam Beg, President Ghulam Ishaq Khan, who represents the bureaucracy, he too enjoys good rapport with Prime Minister Nawaz Sharif.

The opposition's capacity to create problems for the ruling IJI is limited. As it has been decimated everywhere, the PPP already stands isolated with the exception of perhaps Sindh province. Though the PPP has emerged close to an absolute majority in Karchi it wouldn't form a government. as others were unwilling to cooperate with it.

The IJI government is primarily haunted by the economic issues, since Pakistan is likely to lose foreign remittances to the tune of 4.80 million dollars—which is 6.2 per cent of the GDP—in 1990 from Iraq and 300 million dollars from

Kuwait. All this is bound to generate the seeds of inflation in Pakistan's economy. This apart, Pakistan is also among the Third World countries which are not only hurt by higher oil prices, but also loss suffer the loss of remittances from citizens settled in Kuwait.

Another domestic problem that stares the Government in the face is the problem of Sindh. The Government has to address itself to this challenge. Moreover, the accountability court cases started by the caretaker regime, now need to be settled. It is unlikely that the Nawaz Sharif regime will allow the law to take its own course, without being accused of witchhunting.

The present government in Pakistan is likely to continue for a five-year term. Since the IJI and its allies dominate the national as well as the provincial assemblies, there is no stopping them to get their man elected as the President of Pakistan, after the term of the present President is over in 1993, and that of the army chief in 1991.[11]

References

1. Khalid Mahmud. The New Man in Islamabad. *Nation*, 22 November 1990.
2. *Ibid*.
3. J. Adaims and S. Iqbai *Exp.rts, Politics and Economic Development Pakistan, 1970-82*. Colorado, 1983; p, 65.
4. *Ibid* pp 65-66.
5. L.F.R Williams. *The State of Pakistan*. London, 1966; p. 161.
6. S.S Bindra. *Determinants of Pakistan's Foreign Policy*, New Delhi, 1988; p. 82.
7. Panday Nayak. Political Economy of the State of Pakistan. In *Pakistan*. New Delhi, 1984; pp. 62-63.
8. S.S. Bindra, *op. cit*.
9. *Ibid*.
10. *Dawn*, 17 November 1990.
11. John Kaniyalil. Economic Pressure—the Main Issue. *National Herald*, 25 November 1990.

21

Towards Islamic Economy

Nawaz Sharif in his inaugural address as Prime Minister of Pakistan declared to give more attention to the health of the economy. His perception is that without a strong economy, based on the principle of self-reliance, one can't imagine to have a stable political system. His declared strategy is to infuse into the economy, massive doses of industrial investment, geographically spread all over Pakistan. This is supposed to accelerate the process of restructuring the economy, so as to attain a rational sectoral balance. The process is also expected to generate large employment opportunities and earning of foreign exchange by export of value added goods. The main vehicle in this exercise is expected to be private sector.

Within a week of this pronouncement, he initiated moves, aimed at implementation of his programme. Invitations were sent to all the industrialists of the country, on behalf of the Prime Minister, to reach Islamabad. At 10 a.m. on November 13, 1990 the "P" Block Auditorium of Planning Commission was filled with the representatives of the business community.

The Prime Minister sat at the driving seat and set the

ball rolling, after the recitation of the Holy Quran. He was very precise and to the point. He said that he wants to rely more on the domestic resources, physical and human, in the process of economic development. He repeated his advice to the nation, to stop thinking what this country has given but to concentrate more on what the nation has done for Pakistan.

He announced that the special cell in the Prime Minister Secretariat, to monitor the lending activities of nationalized commercial banks and development financial institutions, has been disbanded. Now the banks have been asked to govern their affairs, according to the merit of the cases. Any deviation from this rule will not be tolerated in future. Steps will also be initiated to increase the participation of the private sector in the ownership of the existing financial institutions. There will be no bar on the opening of the new comercial banks in the private sector. The new healthy competition, he said would raise the efficiency in this sector.

He said that there exists no ambiguity between the roles of private sector and public sector. Their roles are complementary rather than competitive. The public sector is required io provide a conducive milieu, in which the private sector can play its role of cementing the foundations of the economy. The public sector should use its energies in the establishment of law and order and the provision of the infrastructural facilities. This specialisation of the economic function of the public and private sectors is expected to give optimal results.[1]

Talking about taxation system of the country, he said that presently the system is such that it provides an incentive to concealment and corruption. On the one hand this attitude is adversely affecting the moral fibre of the society and on the other hand, it hinders the provision of financial resources to the government ex-chequer. The government is forced to either borrow at home or abroad, or to print more notes.

This strategy has brought us to a stage, where the debt servicing has become the number one item in our revenue budget, pushing defence expenditure to a second position. This is the negation of the principle of self-reliance and all efforts will be made to curb it. The first step in this direction will be to reframe the taxation system in such a way what in future the tax assessees should pay according to their real ability to pay and these payments should reach the government teasury without any leakage. Additionally the taxation proposals will not only aim at revnue generation alone but would also be designed to give maximum boost to the economic activity of the country.

He was very clear about the directions of the new industrial strategy. His idea was that there should be no restrictions in the way of industrial investment. No sanction be required the establishment of industries, of any size and type anywhere in the country. No question will be asked about the source of funds. He reiterated that the constitutional guarantee with respect to take over, will be strictly adhered to. The whole system of sanction and follow up will be deregularised. Labour policy will be formulated to meet the demands of justice and equity. In order to rationalise the geographical distribution of industrial investment, rural areas and agro based industries will be provided more lucrative incentives. Every effort will be made to induce foreign investment. The government role will be restricted only to provide assistance to the entrepreneurs, irrespective of their political affiliation.

He announced that Committees will be constituted to work on Tax reforms, self-reliance, deregulation and disinvestment, exchange and payment reform, export promotion and on commercial banks. The Prime Minister asked the representatives to volunteer themselvee, to work on such committees. These committees were supposed to give their opinion by the end of current month, after which the action plan is expected to become operative.[2]

ECONOMISTS in the colonial times generally paid little attention to discover how poverty itself caused continued poverty. Besides, there is a structural difference between the Third World and the industrially advanced society. The determinants that are used in the advanced economies as ingredients of a model will perhaps be found useless in the context of a developing economy where sever nutritional problems have their own consequences on labour productivity. It is ridiculous to assume that increased savings by the poverty-stricken masses of the developing world will increase the possibilty of development or at least create conditions for it.

The mehodological approach to the problems of the developing economies that persist today, is directed at development which has many dimensions of incongruity. So a section of the Third World economists have revolted against the classical ideas of development stemming from the West. Besides, it was felt that studies on certain pressing issues-such as health, education, housing, black money, etc., would be supportive to finding the solutions to developmental problems.[3]

Right from the beginning, development was understood as simply growth. This resulted in presenting statistical information of aggregate gross product or income. Social reforms to minimise inequality have not been popular ideas among those working on development models. In other words, economists, for some reason or the other, were not much interested in studying other social experiences to draw support from them. However, lately issues like distribution of wealth and income have been recognised as necessary ingredients for development. Following this, the antagonism between growth and expanding inequality among the developing peoples has made its own impact.

Experiences indicate that there is a strong need in the developing economies for various reforms to evolve indigenous growth strategies for which transfer of technology may be recommended though one has of be extremely cautious on this score.[4] One must recognise the fact that mere sale of machines is not transfer of technology. Through the import of machines with the label of transfer of technology, powerful pressure groups have been in sight in the developing world whose bonafides have been questioned at least in some quarters of the world.[5] In the colonial times there was a built-in mechanism that almost automatically led a metropolitian power to ally itself with the privileged groups in a colony and often to create such new groups. The practice still persists in some form or the other. It only proves that despite the freedom that the former colonies enjoy today, certain economic interests have not been transformed in the light of the changed political experiences. Notwithstanding the strong concern about the problems of development, there has surprisingly not been much academic interest to analyse the roots and functioning of corruption which is a significant factor of the slow growth in most of the developing economies. One of the failures of contemporary economics has been its reluctance to be assertive on ethical questions. Especially, micro-economics, the bias of the market economy forces, has reduced itself to mere firm economics with a clear motive to maximise corporate profit to which ethical questions have very little access. One must recognise that no realistic and honest deliberation on development through international cooperation is likely to be purposeful unless a strong nationalistic political economy evolves after the experiences to the colonial period. This is a hard task and it does require various alternative ideas and even rejection of certain values that have dominantly and persistently inherited a good number of colonial ethics.[6]

The old rich-poor polarity in a typical Third World country is yet another subject on which much will be heard in the coming weeks and months. Pakistan has been many popular movements caused by economic discontent. The coming months are sure to see a surge in prices while unemployment is deepening as well as spreading. In which the events will move remains to be seen. That discontent is sure to increase is certain and the way Mr. Nawaz Sharif is delaying increasing prices even after the IMF has been forced to cut off disbursement of agreed credit shows how worried Nawaz Sharif is.[7]

Economically Pakistan's condition is becoming increasingly vulnerable. Its industrial production is decreasing rapidly although in the agricultural sector, some progress has been recorded of late. Even in the technological sphere, the country continues to be dependent on the West. Its scientific personnel is severely handicapped and in the absence of adequate infrastructural support, the progress of all sectors of the economy is being affected.

Notwithstanding this dark scenario, there is a glimmer of hope. Demographically by 1995 a majority of Pakistan's population (of 110 million) will be below the age of 40. This younger segment of the polity, unencumbered by the unhappy legacy of the past, will, in all probability, forge closer political and social links with neighbouring countries. It is this section of the population which has come to realise that war and conflict as instruments of national policy, can be self-defeating.

The middle-class in Pakistani society is also capable of understanding and appreciating such contemporary realities. They are prone to introducing advanced methods of industrial management and economic planning in their country.

In fact going by present standards, Pakistan can well become a mini Germany of the Indian sub-cotinent in purely economic terms.

With its industrial base capable of expanding three times and the farming sector once modernised showing similar potential, Pakistan is in a position of becoming the bread basket of West-Asia. Even now, there is no grinding poverty in the country, the like of which is visible in several parts of

India. If only the two countries can liberate themselves from past prejudices and hatred, a new era of social and economic development could be drawn over the sub-continent.[8]

Nawaz Sharif has been elected Prime Minister at a particularly difficult economic period, aggravated and complicated by the Gulf crisis. The journey to be-coming the executive head of the government may have been a political obstacle course, but the incumbent PM has now to apply his entrepreneurial background and experience in taking Pakistan out of our present economic doldrums.

On November 13, 1990 Nawaz Sharif addressed the crisis of confidence prevailing in the business community by calling a selected doyen of industrialists and traders to Islamabad where he laid out his economic action plan and invited discussion. This hardened lot of businessmen had heard such rhetoric about privatisation, denationalisation and tax holidays before. Coming from a fellow businessman this time, it somehow seemed credible, and the Karachi Stock Exchange duly registered confidence. The businessmen left with a general feeling about the elusive light at the end of the tunnel and their skepticism molified.

The partition of Pakistan in 1971 (and the destruction of the complementary economy theory) gave a hard shock to the economy, while indiscriminate nationalisation thereafter deepened the trauma. A combination of factors saved Pakistan from total economic collapse, not the least being the Middle East boom which helped in creating a parallel black economy. The aberrations of the last two decades of the bureaucracy's commercial/industrial inexperience and incompetence were forced multiplied by rampant corruption, rendering most of our medium and heavy industries bankrupt. Our salvation lies in bold economic initiatives that will free, or unshackle, the economy while hoping and working for another great and selective employment boom in the Middle East, particularly Saudi Arabia, where up to one million or so jobs could be available as Yemenis and Palestinians depart. An increase in the number of our troops in Saudi Arabia to pre-1985 levels, may be even doubling that, will hope in defraying part of our burgeoning but necessary budgetary outlay for defence services.

Nawaz Sharif must act immediately on his pronounce ments, freeing the economy from bureaucratic shackles in a phase manner by denationalising the taken over industries, privatising industries in the public sector, and denationalising the commercial banks. A large segment of public sector blue and white collar workers will be reluctant to give up the virtual sinecures that they enjoy presently and ex-change that for the highly competitive field of private business and industry where employment is obligated against performance and profitability (with overheads slashed to ensure that). Resistance among this lot may foil expected governmental moves. The bureaucracy will not be averse to encouraging this to retain their commercial fiefdom.

The Benazir government had a credibility problem when their rhetoric did not translate into deeds. The apprehensions of the business community at the beginning of the PPP regime were groundless, however the hopes raised by Ms Benazir's Thatcherite pronouncements remained far from realisation. In all fairness, she was hobbled to an extent by extenuating circumstances. As time passed, frustration set in among the business community, the climate was further complicated by widespread chicancery and cronyism. Given the political track record in Pakistan, one may be forgiven for being skeptical, but Nawaz Sharif must be given a fair chance to implement the promises made.[9]

Tacking widespread unemployment must be given the highest priority, Job opportunities can be created if the economy is allowed to run without any fetters. To encourage private foreign investment, the Board of Investment (BOI), should go on better. Operating on the concept of the Export

Processing Zone (EPZ), Free Industrial Trade Zone (FITZ) should be established for a specified number of industries situated throughout the country deep in the rural areas, particularly in the interior of Sindh and along Pakistan's coastline. Depending upon availability, the price of industrial plots of landsold to foreign and local investors must include charges for roads, water, sewerage, telephone, telex electricity, gas connections, etc. To prevent land speculation, bank guarantees should be taken from the investors for establishing their enterprise within an acceptable time frame. The land should be handed over within four weeks of payment, all the requisite facilities ready to be plugged in.

Nawaz Sharif has declared the entire country a tax free area for private foreign investment, this tax heaven status should be extended to selected domestic investment. Complete freedom enjoins, psychologically, the abolishing of individual income tax and materially, a general tax holiday for selected new industries. To give protection to industries against imports, whether capital goods, usables or consumer items a formula must be devised balancing monopoly control by competitive price structuring by supply-demand market forces. Incentive difference must be instituted between capital goods and consumer items, not so much as to discourage a consumer oriented society but to encourage establishment of medium and heavy industries. These measures must give further incentives to high-teach industries.

New Public sector projects or the re-habilitation of old projects constituting the socio-economic infrastructure of the nation, like roads and highways, bridges and flyovers, telecommunication projects, railway sector, medical and others in the services sector, etc. Other than the balancing and modernisation of our deteriorating public infrastrucre, investment in this sector means that many jobs will be created, at least temporarily. Resources may be mobilised locally for the most part rather than in foreign exchange with a judicious selection of public sector projects spread over the length and breadth of the country. The Indus Highway is already under implementation. Another which comes to mind is a possible modern Coastal Highway with a parallel rail track.[10]

All this costs money but by the eligination of the Federal tax burden on the individual (by abolishing individual income tax) and mobilisation of domestic resources, much needed projects may be implemented to bolster the economy. Costs of construction material, cement and steel particularly, should be kept down by increasing production, encouraging people to invest money in new units of housing. Construction creates its own solid economic cycle. Properly husbanded it can lead to an economic boom in contrast to the present world economic situation.

Without the mobilisation of domestic resourc s, in layman's languag without the availability of cash, there can be no question of economic emancipation. The investment companies fraud (twice in the last decade) showed that the masses invested (and wanted to invest) their hardearned money in companies offering highly lucrative returns. An artificial economic boom was created to an extent rooted in the parallel black economy that is now a fundamental part of our economic life as a nation. Mainly because of (as still mysterious) bureucratic inaction, fraudulent investment companies proliferated. Given proper regulations for investment (banks) companies, the State Bank of Pakistan could have exercised judicious control and positive punitive action could have deterred these fraudulent companies from resorting to widespread fraud and chicanery. There is an anomaly about corrective action even now, though during ex-PM Junejo's time a start was made to bring in duly regulated investment banks as well as punishing the recalcitrants.

The fradulent investment companies have shown that the domestic mobilisation of resources is possible. The establishment and functioning of investment banks will mobilise domestic resources for setting up industries and development of the services sector, while providing the "financial services" that are necessary for a dynamic increase in the economic potential of the nation. The Nationalised Commercial Banks (NCBs) have an aversion to risk and have stayed away from term lending and project financial, thereby restricting the investment horizon. This is to an extent has been taken up by the Development Finance Institutions, (DFIs) like BEL, PICIC, IDBP, NDFC, etc., including "services" like underwriting, equity investment and consultancy services.

Foreign banks have not played any significant role despite windfall profits due to various considerations but leasing companies and moderabas have been a major source of providing long-term finance. In effect they have been the leading edge of the potential for financial dynamism. Investment banks can carry out "commercial activities" like (1) Issuing short/long terms Certificates nf Deposit and Investment (COI) (2) trading in commercial paper and listed securities, whether equity or nonequity instruments, (3) underwriting, (4) floating and managing Open-ended and Closed-ended Mutual Funds, (5) issue Negotiables and Debt Instruments to clients, (6) providing guarantees for loans and other obligations. The "financial services" can include (1) acting as a broker or as a manager of pension fund or provident fund, (2) assisting clients in fund raising through public issues, etc., (3) assisting in raising equity through venture capital, just to mention a few of an exhaustive list. The advantages of investment banks over retail banks is that (1) they are allowed to invest in high yielding tax-exempt government securities, (2) higher profits are anticipated by them without increasing their capital base and (3) higher post-tax return on equity if government perserveres with the expected low tax bracket.

At this time, the sanctioned investment companies are not really functioning due to various lacunaes in the governing regulations. Unless the controls are relaxed they will not function as they should, for the capital base required will be missing from our efforts to generate the economy.

Judicious but immediate deregulation of the financial sector is the need of the hour to ensure mobilisation of the resources required for economic emancipation of the nation.[11]

Prime Minister Nawaz Sharif in his first broadcast to the nation committed himself to alleviating the economic misery of the masses and revamping the national economy. The Prime Minister has also promised to produce his detailed future plan for the uplift of the peasants and labour soon. While the economy will bear an additional burden of two billion dollars (Rs. 40 billion) due to the Gulf crisis, the people will be protected from the new wave of general price-hike. Increases in the prices of atta, ghee, cereals, pulses and cotton cloth would be checked. Civic amenities would be expanded. Katchi abadis throughout the country would be given proprietary rights and a Development Authority would be set up for them. He has called upon the experts, whose services would be utilised for the benefit of the poor people, to recommend how the affluent classes can be taxed to meet the budgetary deficits-the main cause of inflation. The new government's thrust will be towards ushering in an *Islamic economic system* in the country.

Pakistan's economy has suffered less from paucity of resources in the past and more from poverty of planning and management. This has resulted in the heavy burden of external debts. The Prime Minister has decided to adopt the course of self-reliance because this is the course of self-respect. He has asked the people to practise austerity to achieve this goal. The example set at the top should go a long way in inculcating the spirit of simplicity among all sections of the society. Non-development expenditure by the government should be cut down to the minimum to release the resources for achieving an economic breakthrough. Industrialisation in Pakistan has had a chequered history. The ad-hoc industrial policies of the previous governments has kept the country industrially backward. It is for the first time that the Prime Minister has removed all roadblocks in the way of bringing about an industrial revolution in Pakistan. The whole couutry will be declared a tax-holiday zone. Bureaucratic bottlenecks will be eliminated. A crash programme for developing and strengthening the necessary infrastructure will be announced. The Prime Minister has proclaimed his economic charter to the people. Its implementation would usher in the long awaited era of progress and prosperity in the country.[12]

Pakistan's new trade policy, announced on June 25, 1990 contains "structural changes" aimed at ensuring greater exports and better import framework for the promotion of overhall trade.

The policy for the new year (1990-91) has fixed an export target of 5,494 million dollars on FOB basis, higher by 15 per cent over the preceding year.

The imports are estimated at 6.9 billion dollars, almost equal to the estimated import bill of the preceding year.

Ninety items have been made freely importable and the number of items on the restricted list has been reduced from 52 to 11 to ensure cheaper availability of imported raw materials.

The new policy is aimed at liberalising imports and creating a climate of competition between the industry and foreign suppliers.

The government wants to gear import policy in a direction where the agricultural and industrial needs for raw material and machinery are fully met and items required by the common man are made easily available.

A separate corporation for the administration of export credit guarantee scheme will also be set up with an initial capital of 25 crore rupees.

At present exports worth 120 crore rupees were covered by the scheme, but with the new corporation this coverage will increase to exports valuing 500 crore rupees.

Seventy per cent of the income derived from the export of services will be exempted from income tax and the existing 100 per cent exemption in case of export of concsultancy services will continue.

Leading insurance companies have been allowed to issue insurance policies in foreign currencies for the protection of bid bond and performance bond.

Travel agents and tour operators have been allowed to utilise five per cent of their foreign exchange earnings for opening offices abroad for marketing purposes.

A new scheme has been evolved to increase investments in the export-oriented industries. Under this scheme, export-oriented industries will be eligible for exemption from duty and surcharges on the import of their machinery, and with regard to duty and surcharges such units will be treated at par with those in the Export Processing Zone.

Pakistan's budget for 1990-91 denotes a singnificant effort to mobilise new resources with the minimum possible burden on the common man while reflecting the compulsions of the critical geo-political situation in the region.

Out of the total current expenditure of Rs. 167.1 billion for the year, Rs. 76.7 billion or 45 per cent has had to be set aside for debt servicing.

The revenue receipts are estimated at Rs. 175.4 billion in to the budget. After deducting the provincial share of Rs. 34.2 million in taxes, the Current Account Deficit will be Rs. 20.5 billion.

The income from capital receipts has been estimated at Rs. 25.6 billion, and self-financing of autonomous bodies at

Rs. 6.5 billion. An amount of Rs. 41 billion is expected to accrue from foreign aid.

Thus, after taking into account non-obligatory grants to provinces to the tune of Rs. 5.4 billlon and estimates of development axpenditure amounting to Rs. 63 billion, there emerged a deficit of Rs. 15.7 billion.

However, the budget provides a number of relief measures in taxes etc., and readjustments in the existing taxes for mobilisation of additional resources which are estimated to raise the resource gap to Rs. 19.41 billion. But additional resources mobilisation measures will envisage the increase in revenues to the tune of Rs. 14.11 billion, leaving a net deficit of Rs. 5.2 billion.

In the current year, the external receipts had stood at Rs. 38.4 billion and bank borrowing at Rs. 5 billion.

The projections for the current year in respect of banks borrowing and external aid signify lesser dependence on these instruments of deficit financing.

For the 1990-91, third year of Pakistan's Seventh FiveYear Plan, the net size of Annual Development Programme after adjustment of expected operational shortfall has been fixed at Rs. 63 billion.

The new budget envisages to reintroduce the self-assessment scheme, while doing away with the anomally which arose from the previous government's measure of exempting those firms showing less than an income of Rs. 1 lakh from submitting any details of income and from scrutiny. This measure benefited mainly the tax evaders and proved detrimental to those who declared their income as above Rs. 1 lakh.

The budget also terminates the system of income tax panels, thus doing away with one irritant vis-a-vis the commerce and industry. To encourage voluntary compliance by the tax-payers, it has been decided to issue national tax cards to prominent tax payers.

Another significant measure proposed in the new budget is the abolition of many exemptions on direct taxes such as those allowed to companies providing agro services and hiring out farm machinery, and cooperative societies engaged in financal transactions.

The new taxation proposals also include increase in taxes on luxury goods as well as concessions aimed to stimulate local production.

The budget provides relief in import and excise duty for several items including domestic appliances, leather and newsprint.

The private educational institutions will be given special incentives including grant of depreciation allowances, besides allowing them facility to take loans from the commercial banks.

PAKISTAN intends to abolish exchange controls and slash tariffs on imports as part of a radical economic reform programme, Finance Minister Sartaj Aziz said.

Within three to four months there will be a major liberalisation of exchange controls provided the nations foreign exchange reserves are at an adequate level, he said in Islamabad on December 26, 1990.

"We are going to, reduce gradually and ultimately abolish ex-change controls", said Aziz. He described the plan as a "calculated risk".

The uncertainty created by the Gulf crisis could eventually benefit Pakistan as middle east capital looked for a more secure home, the Minister said. "Don't forget that after problems in Lebanon there were people looking for a place to put their money", added Aziz.

Currently Pakistan has tough restrictions on transfer of funds in and out of the country. Pakistan's highly protective tariff system would be dismantled over the next two years with the average tariff rate cut to 30 per cent from 75 per cent currently. The plans are part of an ambitious drive to reform the economy. The new conservative government of Prime Minister Nawaz Sharif, which was elected at the end of October, 1990 has announced a major privatisation programme and a package of tax and duty incentives to promote industry.

If Pakistan could make its economy more outward looking then annual economic growth rates of 9 to 10 per cent would not be beyond it.

The Pakistani government is desperately trying to promote exports through incentives and is seeking emergency economic aid to increase its foreign exchange reserves and replace lost revenue.

The revenue gap had been partially closed by a 25 per cent rise in export earnings in the first five months of the fiscal year ending June 30, 1991 from the year-earlier period. He did not disclose the precise figures. In June the government of former Prime Minister Benazir Bhutto set an export target of $5.5 billion for 1990-91 against $4.8 billion in 1989-90.

Meanwhile in Karachi the staff at most of Pakistan's major banks went on strike for two hours on Wednesday to protest against the privatisation of the state-owned Muslim Commercial Bank (MCB), Union leaders said.

The stoppage stretched beyond two hours in some cities and effectively closed many banks, which are open to the public for four hours daily.

The strike was in defiance of an injunction for Pakistan's top labour court declaring it illegal.

Pakistan's six biggest commercial banks are state-owned and wednesday's industrial action affected five of them. The banking unions have long opposed privatisation and prevented the government of former prime minister Benazir Bhutto from selling shares in MCB early 1990.

An adverse international aid environment and diverse domestia problems notwithstanding, Pakistan has embarked on a major programme for the reformation of its economy, the Federal Minister for Finance and Economic Affairs Sartaj Aziz, said in Islamabad, on January 10, 1991.

He was delivering the inaugural address at the seventh general meeting of the Pakistan Society of Development Economists in Islamabad.[13]

While the broad thrusts of thc new economic programme have been spelt out at various fora by Aziz and others, what was significant about Tuesday's speech was the note of alarm regardtng Pakistan's economic situation. International aid is at a premium now and the Gulf crisis has not onlp pushed up domestic oil prices but has also threatened the flow of remittances from Pakistani workers abroad. Recession in the developed world has adversely affected Pakistan's exports at a time when the costs of imports continue to rise. The cumulative effects of these developments could be gauged from the fact that the country's growth rate of six per cent per annum over the last decade was largely sustained by external borrowings.

On the domestic front resources could not be mobilised. The tax base remains extremely restricted and direct taxes make up only a very small share of the total tax collection. There is a lull in investment activity.

The situation is daunting but believing that adversity brings out the best in the country, the Government has evolved a bold strategy, Mr. Aziz said, (Several commentators have noted that many features of the new economic policy have been tried before). Keeping in mind the circumstances, the growth rate of the economy could be increased. The Minister said it will take Pakistan 50 years to reach the level of a medium developed country with the present growth rate of two per cent. The population growth has to be curbed.

The answer to the problem is a dynamic industrial policy coupled with a bold rural development programme. Sartaj Aziz said a strong rural orientation has been built into the new industrial policy with the emphasis on building infrastructure and providing employment opportunities in the villages. Pointing out that the cost of providing a job in the rural areas is just one-fourth of the cost in the urban centres, he said that the Government's role should be one of improving health, education, communication and other facilities in the villages. This will be a more profitable role than running industries and ex-porting rice or cotton.

A programme to denationalise public enterprises and throw open sectors till now reserved for the public sector has been launched. Deregulation of the economy will lead to a more meaningful use of resources while a reduction of tariffs will correct the distortion in prices. Macro economic imbalances will be corrected basically through an abandonment of the policy of "big government". Aziz pointed out that billions of rupees had been swallowed up by public enterprises.

As the first step in the policy of denationalisation, 26 per cent of the shares of the Muslim Commercial Bank (nationalised in the 1970s) has been transferred to a private consortium of textile and leather tycoons called the "National Group". Effective managerial control of the bank will come into the hands of this organisation by June this year when the

Government wlll disinvest a further 25 per cent share holding. Ultimately the Government will retain only one of the five banks now in its hands.

The share certificates were transferred by Prime Minister, Nawaz Sharif, at a brief ceremony here on Wednesday. Each of the 12 business houses which make up the Group will invest equally in the purchase price of Rs. 838.8 millions.

Nawaz Sharif said the transfer is the symbolic beginning of the process of denationalisation and a fulfilment of the promises made before and after the elections by his party. Private housing finanance corporations and banks and investment in roads and telecommunications will soon be allowed.

At the same time, Aziz assured labourers that their interests will not be jeopardised. The 12,000 plus work force currently with the MCB is not to be retrenched for one year. Adverse revision of their terms of employment will not be permitted either.

References

1. Sajjad Haider Economy, *The Nation*, 16 November, 1990.
2. *Ibid.*
3. Frantz Fanon, *The wretched oj the Earth*, Pengnin, 1977. See also. Pranab K. Banerjee, Crucial aspects of North-South Relations. *Mainstream* Anaual 1990.
4. See G E. Skoroue (ed.), *Science, Technology and Economic Growth in Developing Countries*, Oxford, Pergamon, 1978.
5. See H. Stephen and Douglas A. Hellinger, *Employment and Multinationals*, New York, Kennikat Press, 1976.

6. Pranab K. Banerjee, *op. cit.*
7. *Indian Express*, 15 November 1990.
8. N.M. Khilani, Pakistan. *Pioneer*, 11 December, 1990.
9. Ikram Sehgal. Challenging the Issues. *Nation*, 20 November, 1990.
10. *Ibid.*
11. *Ibid.*
12. *Pakistan Times*, 9 Nov., 1990.

22

Freedom of Press

Recently, when President Gulam Ishaq Khan re-issued the Registration of Printing Presses and Publications Ordinance, pressmen in Pakistan realised with pleasure that they had been living for over two years without the dreat of the 'Black Press Law'. Even more welcome was the realisation that there were brief periods during the preceding 14 months or so when the country's press functioned without any special regulatory press law. For a quarter of a century, from 1963 to 1988, newspaper editors and working journalists were engaged in a bitter struggle to get the press and publications ordinance of 1963 repealed. The ordinance was promulgated by General Ayub Khan about a year after he had changed his martial law regime into one-men non-military rule, and it marked the beginning of wider plans to control activities and though process in processes in the field of literature, performing and fine arts, and journalism. Based on the 19th century enactment of the colonial period, titled Registration of Book Act, this ordinance incorporated the emergency press laws enforced by the British Indian government, especially the Act of 1930, and made harsh curbs on the press, part of a regular, permanent law: Country wide agitation by journalists, editors and proprietors forced the Ayub regime to make some changes in the law and the procedure for appeal against executive's actions was made less unreasonable than before. During the mass movement for democratic revival in the late sixties the regime yielded some more ground and agreed to a moratorium on the ordinance's application. But that was all the success newspapermen could achieve in their struggle against the draconian legislation. It remained on the statue book and the moratorium pledge was soon forgotten. Repeal of the ordinance was high on the list of promises Z.A. Bhutto made during his agitation against President Ayub Khan and the election campaign on 1970, but the commitment was never honoured. Instead the ordinance continued to be used to deny declarations to people wanting to bring out new publications, to suppress newspapers and to punish publishers for dissent. Although General Zia issued special martial law regulations to curb the press, which had borrowed heavily from the Press and Publications Ordinance, he let the Ordinance stand as a second line of defence against a free press which he detested as much as he deprecated democracy. In May 1988 the Federal Shariat Court, the religious court created by General Zia, ruled several provisions of the Press Ordinance to be contrary to Islamic junctions and declared unless the ordinance was amended to meet the court's objections it would lapse after the expirty of three months. Faced with the prospects of the press becoming free of restraints placed by the ordinance, the Zia regime issued a new law called Registration of Printing Presses and Publications Ordinance of 1988, and the 1963 law was repealed.[1]

Amazingly, the Press Ordinance of 1988 was among the ordinances that the Benazir Bhutto government never brought to the National Assembly. Thus, the ordinance was re-issued in January 1989, May 1989, November 1989, April 1990 and again in November 1990. That may well be a record in the history of law-making in the subcontinent because it is doubtful if any other ordinance has led to be re-issued so many times. Of course, the punitive provisions of the ordinance were never invoked by the Bhutto government. The ordinance deprives the government of the power to deny the right to publish by witholding authentication of declaration. It also reduces the executive's power to kill a newspaper by denying its application for change of printing press. Still, it retains several features of the repressive laws of the past, such as some restrictions on the reporting of court proceedings and happenings in the Parliament that do not form part of proceedings. There is a long list of do nots for newspaper publishers and editors and violations can invite forfeiture of publications. In some cases such action can be taken first and the victim asked to offer explanation and defence after. The ordinance was never wholly approved by newspaper editors and working journalists. The Council of Newspaper Editors suggested several amendments early in 1989 and even worked out proposals to enforce a code of ethics and set up a press court of honour to enable the government to drop the punitive clauses of the ordinance. These proposals were not heard of during the later half of the Bhutto rule, presumably because the press was freer than ever and the existence of curbs in law that were not in operation did not cause anxiety. Hence, so far as working journalists are concerned (except those belonging to pro-establishment unions), there is no need to suggest changes in the oft-revived press ordinance; it has to be scrapped in toto. Indeed, leaders of journalists' unions have stopped taking notice of the ordinance when it is re issued, except for a cursory look at the text to see if any change has been made in the 1988 draft. In a sense the soundness of the journalists' viewpoint has been proved. As can be seen from the dates on which the press ordinance was issued during 1989-90, there were gaps between its expiry and reenactment, signifying periods when no press law was in force. Neither the press nor the government seem to have been handicapped by the withdrawal of the press law. There is nothing to suggest that the experiment would not work over longer periods, except for the reluctance a government may feel about giving up some coercive powers it has enjoyed for decades.[2] However, it remains to be seen whether the new government will take the press ordinance as lightly as its predecessor. Most probably the ordinance will be elevated to the status of an Act adopted by Parliament. It may not be long before editors and journalists have a reason to recall the adage that no society should be complascent about unjust laws only because they are dormant; so long as they remain on the statue books they are likely to be used.

The President's promulgation of the Registration of Printing Press and Publication Ordinance (RPPO) albeit for reasons largely technical, in advance of the next session of the National Assembly is nevertheless as good an occasion as any to examine the issue of Press freedom in our context. It is appropriate to do so not least because a new government has just taken over. It is faced with many challenges and in the months to come its mettle will certainly be put to the test. Unfortunately, in such circumstances freedom to the Press has usually been among the first casualties in the past. Successive regimes, almost without exception, have persisted in the illusion that keeping unpleasant facts from their own people will somehow render their task easier and perhaps, their stay in power permanent. While there is no doubt that the present Ordinance is not the draconian law that the repealed Press and Publication Ordinance (PPO) 1963 was, the question still remain as to why a special law is needed to "regulate matters relating to publications and printing presses". After all with regard to all the serious offences envisaged in the RPPO such as incitement to violence, libel, sedition, etc. there is already a plethora of laws on the statue books applying to all citizens including obviously, those involved in printing and publication Clearly, the Press—much as any other sector of society or state—cannot be allowed to run riot. But additional laws are not necessarily the best means of ensuring this objective. As in some other countries a self-regulatory machanism could well suffice. The Press, it should be clear by now, is not the enemy. Nor are those in the profession any less patrioric or responsible then the rest. To seek to manipulate their functioning in any manner through additional laws or indeed with the help of less obvious, but often equally effective, means such as the practice of press advise or the use of government advertisements eventually serves neither the cause of a particular government nor, in fact, the national interest. We hope then that when the Ordinance is presented before the National Assembly—barring the unlikely even of this its being done away with altogether—suitable amendments will be made drawing from the best traditions of Press freedom critical to a functioning democracy.[3]

Pakistan on November 11, 1990 called for a balanced inter-flow of information to strengthen international peace and understanding.

"The world of information is characterised by lopsidedness Pakistani delegate H.R. Gardezi told the General Assembly's Special Political Committee.

Speaking in a debate on questions relating to information, he said he changed world situation had not the desired effect in the field of information and that steps were required to correct the prevailing imbalances.

Gardezi said the developed western countries, which had enormous resources, monopolised the uni-directional flow of information through their technologically advanced wire services, and media networks, along with financial and professional leverage.

At the same time, he said, the rest of the world was plagued by colonial exploitation, strife and paucity of resources. The budget and infrastructure of a single western news agency was greater than all those in the developing world, where the population represented more than 80 per cent of the human race.

A new world information order must, therefore, include a transfer of technology from the developed to the developing countries, the Pakistani delegate said. "A sharing of professional expertise will facilitate a two-way channel of communications to promote harmony and understanding between diverse cultures and societies."

Presentations of distorted realities and falsehoods about a society were sometimes motivated by prejudices, but in most cases were due to a lack of socio-cultural information about other societies, Gardezi said. "A vast majority of the world today goes unheard", he said, adding that the existing lopsided situation deprived the world of useful contributions those people could make.

Pakistan, he said, was committed to the freedom of information and expression. He said the new popularly-elected Government of Prime Minister Nawaz Sharif had lifted the state of emergency and restored fundamental rights and freedoms. "Our Prime Minister had shown his determination to further strengthen free Press in Pakistan", Gardezi said.

The Standing Committee of the Council of Pakistan Newspaper Editors (CPE) at its meeting in Lahore, on November 12, 1990 under the chairmanship of its President Arif Nizami has urged in a unanimous resolution all political parties and elements in the country to reiterate their commitment to Press freedom.

The meeting rejected all forms of pressures and threats to newspapers and pressmen and urged the governments at the Federal and Provincial levels and also all politicians that they must support the CPNE in its effort to ensure the freedom of Press in the service of democracy and the ideological foundation of Pakistan.

The meeting opined that a positive attitude towards the Press must follow in the wake of the induction of an elected government at the Federal level and the Provincial levels in

Pakistan and supported a continuing dialogue with the government to secure this objective.

A CPNE Press release issued here said that the meeting expressed satisfaction over the announcement by the Prime Minister, Nawaz Sharif, that his government would stand by its manifesto on Press freedom and encouragement to the Private sector.

The President of the CPNE Arif Nizami, informed members that he had invited Prime Minister Nawaz Sharif to a reception by the CPNE at which all issues relating to the Press including the viewpoint of the CPNE on these issues would be taken up. He hoped that the reception date would be finalised soon and all members of the CPNE would be invited to this important meeting with the Prime Minister by the CPNE Secretariat.

He said that matters relating to Press freedom, de-regulation and decentralisation of government controlled advertising, further reduction of duties levied on new-print as also an overall better deal for the Press would be discussed at this expected reception-meeting with Prime Minister. Members opined that all these issues were of an urgent nature and looked forward to this important meeting at an early date.

The meeting deliberated at length on the subject of Government-Press relations and strongly felt that continued government control and centralisation of advertising ran counter to the commitment of Press freedom by the government. Under the new government at the federal level and at all the provincial levels, there must now emerge a media policy that protects and furthers the commitment to Press freedom in actual practice. The meeting hoped that the new government at the federal level led by Prime Minister Nawaz Sharif would give the lead in this matter.

The meeting discussed further improvements in the RPPPO and directly that the office-bearers of the CPNE, constituting the committee, should pursue this matter. It also made a fervent appeal to the newly-elected members of the National Assembly to adopt at the earliest the RPPPO as an Act of the Parliament. It noted that the RPPPO, which had continued to be an Ordinance and the previous National Assembly did not find time to adopt it as an Act of Parliament. It pointed out to the MNAs of the new National Assembly that all the political parties taking part in the elections had pledged to uphold Press freedom, therefore, it should not be difficult for the National Assembly to adopt the RPPPO as an Act of Parliament at its very next business sitting.

The meeting heard complaints from member publications on threats of violence by political parties and elements in the recent past and strongly felt that these threats must now cease and it should be the effort of all governments and political organisations to strengthen the base of democracy in Pakistan and allow it to function effectively in the service of the nation, a task in which the Press has to play a crucial role.

The meeting declared in its unanimous resolution on the subject of Press freedom that any threat or pressure exercised on any CPNE member amounts to threat and pressure on the organisation itself. It said that it shall uphold the right of dissent and Press freedom, in keeping with the CPNE Press code of ethics, for each and every member. The meeting said that it would welcome the addition of newspapers published by any political party, because that was part of Press freedom. However, every political party in the country must allow newspapers in the country the exercise of editorial freedom in keeping with the CPNE Press code of ethics. In the same resolution, the meeting also rejected adhocism in the media policy and called for a new order that fully met the requirements of the objective of a free and responsible Press in Pakistan.

The meeting regretted that the issuance of airport entry passes for the Press had remained an unresolved issue and deplored this delay. It accepted the offer from Senator Syed Fasieh Iqbal, Chairman of the concerned standing committee of the Senate, who is member of CPNE standing committee also, to take up the matter with the concerned ministries at the earliest and resolve it amicably, to the satisfaction of the CPNE.

The meeting also considered a communication on the subject of PIA travel concession to journalists from their professional work. It noted that at this stage of economic constraints which newspapers suffered from and the growing requirements of field coverage any reduction or revision of the PIA fare concession for journalists would only create difficulties and hamper the Press in the performance of its duties properly. It, therefore, advised PIA as also the Federal Government to ensure that the facility continues and is enlarged to include all members of the CPNE.

The meeting deliberated on the subject of equal treatment to the national news agencies in their growth by the Federal Government and endorsed a memorandum submitted by the UPP, Pakistan's oldest private sector news agency, that a reasonable media policy on a long term basis be implemented and the UPP must also be given full encouragement in its development by the government. The meeting directed the President of the CPNE Arif Nizami, to take up this issue urgently with the Prime Minister, the Minister for Information and also present it at the reception for Prime Minister.

The meeting in a unanimous resolution condemned the sacrilege of the Babri Mosque, It also condemned in strong terms the continued reign of terror let loose against the newspapermen in Occupied Kashmir and the ban imposed on newspapers in the Occupied Kashmir Valley. It called upon the Pakistan Government to bring this matter to the notice of the United Nations and all the members of the UN including its political committee for urgent action.

The meeting offered 'fateha' for the late editor Mr. Shifaat of Maghribi Pakistan and Syed Abdullah Shah, uncle of CPNE member Syed Siddiq Shah. The meeting also accepted a suggestion for holding sessions of t' e standing committee at Faisalabad and Hyderabad Sindh. The meeting also considered applications for fresh membership and in a secret ballot approved membership for the Trade Chroncile of Karachi by two-third majority votes in favour.

The members of the CPNE standing committee attended a dinner hosted by Chief Editor Nawa-i-Waqt and Nation, Majid Nizami, which was attended among others by former adviser on Press to President Ghulam Ishaq Khan, R.A. Suleri. On the occasion Mr. H.B. Khokher, who is President of the Third World Newspapers Editors Conference, presented. Majid Nazami with a golden pen on behalf of his organisation in recognition of the 'pioneering services rendered by Majid Nizami in upholding the cause of Press freedom in Pakistan and in fighting for it fearlessly and courageously even at a time when almost all others in the profession yielded to pressures and threats. He also urged CPNE members on the occasion to adhere to objective analysis of news events and hoped that the Press in Pakistan would gain strength in the days to come under the banner of the CPNE.

The man in the grey Pathan suit leans forward to propound his theory on English newspapers as opposed to the Urudu and Hindi ones. "English is a linear language; it's sequential, with logical thought flow. Urudu and Hindi, on the other hand, are not linear. In Pakistan, you can't be with an English paper if you're not liberal." The editor of the Peshawar and Lahore-based newspaper, *The Frontier Post* has been frequently been called "controversial" sometimes even "firebrand". Editing the Lahore edition *The Frontier Post* under martial law hasn't been a bed of roses for Khalid Ahmed. With an academic background, besides a short stint, in the foreign service, Ahmed adopted journalism as his raison d'etre in 1978 when there were hardly any privately owned newspapers in Pakistan.[4]

He started with The Pakistan Times, and then moved to The Nation as a joint editor. It was a time when the Constitution was, as he puts it, obsessively progressing towards an ideological state with less and less tolerance to dissent. "However, the outer world did penetrate. Books from outside were never burnt. An ideological state has great drawbacks—intellectual dissent is not allowed. But Pakistan itself never became a totally ideological state." In 1986, when the Emergency was lifted, the emphasis was still on Urudu newspapers as opposed to the English ones. The Peshawar-based, The Frontier Post, owned, by Rahmat Shah Afridia, a 'Tribal from the North-West Frontier Province (NWFP), was considered a "rebellious" newspaper. In 1988, Ahmed joined the Lahore edition of the growing paper as editor, and was immediately noticed, thanks to his viewpoints.[5]

Reproduction of comments published on Pakistan affairs in the foreign English language press has become a commonplace in Pakistan publications, specially the Urudu newspapers. Increasing coverage is being given to foreign writings. Sometimes, foreign journalists and writers' comments run contrary to Pakistan's national interests. It seems that Pakistani media has made it a sign of progressiveness to public all kinds of reports published by the foreign magazines and newspapers. Generally, translations are published without proper editing but the English versions are reproduced unabridged. Most of these reports thus published by the Urudu press malign Pakistan and those Pakistanis who do not subscribe to the liberal social ideas prevailing in the Western countries. Certainly, the American, British, German, French or any other foreign magazine and newspapers writers see events from their own national point of view which, in most cases, undermine Pakistan's interests. These foreign commentators when giving opinion of foreign affairs, specially on events in the Muslim world, fail to liberate themselves from the age-old prejudices which are deep-roorted in the mind and soul of the Western intelligentsia. They may be liberal in their outlook vis-a-vis their own affairs but the moment they write about the Muslims, their liberalism disappears, subdued by their hatred of Islam. For them, every believer in Islam is a "fundamentalist" a term which may be applicable to Christian societies where church and state are two separate entities, but it has no meaning for Islam wherein Din circumscribes all aspects of human life, politics and affairs of the state included. Pakistani politicians and journalists have been overwhelmed by the Western media to the extent that they too have started using the terms fundamentalists" and "fundamentalism" without giving serious thought to its implications. They seem to be obsessed with inferiority complex, and to overcome this complex, they seek refuge in getting certificates of liberal outlook from Western media by reproducing their ideas, analyses and commentaries on Pakisian affairs.[6]

Has any American, British, French, German or Japanese magazine or newspaper ever reprinted material written by Pakistani journalists and writers on foreign affairs and initially published in the Pakistan press? Articles written by Pakistani journalists on American or British subjects and published in the Pakistan press are of no interest to the media in those countries and they do not care to apprise their readers of our views on their affairs. The Pakistani writers' viewpoints are not native. They carry weight, they view things in proper perspective and derive conclusions according to our own interests. Their analyses of happenings in foreign lands is also based on logic and reasoning. But since they do not conform to the interests of other countries, the foreign press does not bother to circulate these comments to their readers. They do not give any importance to our point of view.

Therefore, the reproduction of our experts' commentaries does not rise. On the contrary, we are so impressed by the western media that we give excessive importance to foreign opinions on our domestic affairs. What BBC says, what the German VOA broadcasts and what Duetsche Welle comments on events in Pakisran are carried by all newspapers very faithfully. Generally, their comments do not support Pakistan's position on a given subject. Still, our print media selects and circulates these stories among its readers. Why can't we ignore them? Why should we give undue publicity to foreign opinions on our internal affairs? We have to tackle our affairs from our own national point of view. The foreign commentators and journalists should not be given extraordinary preference in these matters. Their views should be taken with a pinch of salt. After all, they are not part and parcel of the Pakistani society, and, therefore, cannot feel and think as we feel and think about our affairs. So why should our press give importance to foreign opinions and views on our domestic matters? The overemphasis on publishing the foreign point of view on Pakistan affairs has made the readers, and also the so called intelligentsia, including politicians and political workers, partial to liberal attitudes towards social issues and problems of Pakistani society. They now see our problems through the prism of foreign comments, ignoring our own views on a given subject. When recently, a political figure of Pakistan expressed the view that religion is the private affair of the individual and it should have no bearing on the affairs of the state, the foreign press supported this view in chorus and their commentaries were prominently displayed in our newspapers. When reproducing foreign comments on this vital subject, no one gave serious thought to the implications of such a statement. Separation of religion from state affairs is not an appreciable concept in our society. The very foundation of this country was laid on the two-nation theory which implies cohesion between religion and politics. Hindus and Muslims are two nations because of religion. If we negate this theory and make religion a private affairs or the individual then we demolish the very foundation of

Pakistan. Many commentaries by American and British writers published in their press on this subject were freely reproduced, specially in the Urudu press. Similarly, foreign writers 'commentaries on Hadood,' Diyat and Qassas have been reproduced without proper editing. The non-Muslim writers views on these typical Islamic issues cannot be favourable and, therefore, should not be considered worthy of publising them among the Muslim masses. Our newspapers, specially the Urudu press, publish many stories and comments on the evils of western society. How many of these have even been picked up by Western media and published in its columns? They do not give a damn about our opinion on social affairs. It is we, the liberal Pakistanis, who donate our newspapers, valuable space for giving air to Western madia's views on our affiars with which they should have no concern.

During the October 1990 elections, the foreign journalists made all sorts of absurd comments on the possible results. They played up the candidates of their choice. They supported a particular political party which stands for values and systems held in high esteem in Western civilisation but despised in Muslim society. You support the opening of bars and dance halls and the whole Western media will support you with one voice. You allow the display of human bodies and the Western media will hail you as "civilised people." You encourage free mixing of sexes and they will portray you as people of "modern age." Any group or party opposing these liberal acts are branded "fundamentalists", backward and remnant of the dark ages. If you want support from Western media you must follow their norms of social conduct. If you adopt their social behaviour and attitudes then you are closer to their heart as Israel is closer to them. The West wants Pakistan to follow the same way and adopt their system in political, legal, and social spheres. Forces in Pakistan upholding the Western values are, therefore, closer to the Western heart. All the analyses, all the commentaries done by Western media revolve around one objective. By reproducing their political columns and write-ups on social affairs of Pakistan, we unconsciously support their cause and inadvertently undermine our own national objectives. The media will do service to Pakistan if it refrains from patronising foreign press comments on Pakistan affairs. Pakistani affairs should be looked from Pakistan's own perspective. We do not need foreign media to guide the people of Pakistan on their national affairs.[7]

References

1. I.A. Rehman, Freedom from Press Law, *The Business and Political Observer*, 5, December, 1990.
2. *Ibid.*
3. *The Muslim*, 16 November, 1990.
4. Prabha Jagannathan Talks to Pakistani Journalist Khalid Ahmed, *Sunday Observer*, 9 December, 1990.
5. *Ibid.*
6. Khalid Latif, Western Media on Pakistan Affairs, *Pakistan Times*, 12, November, 1990.
7. *Ibid.*